Shannon's Gift

Shannon's Gift

A Story of Love, Loss, and Recovery

Nate Bennett

with Echo Garrett

BOOKLOGIX®
Alpharetta, GA

While containing some medical information, this book is not intended as a substitute for the medical advice of physicians. The reader should consult a physician regularly in any matters relating to his/her health, particularly with respect to any symptoms or illness that may require diagnosis or medical attention. Some names and identifying details have been changed to protect the privacy of individuals. The author has tried to recreate events, locations, and conversations from his memories of them. In some instances, in order to maintain their anonymity, the author has changed the names of individuals and places. He may also have changed some identifying characteristics and details such as physical attributes, occupations, and places of residence.

Copyright © 2014 by Nate Bennett

ISBN: 978-1-61005-479-9
Library of Congress Control Number: 2014939280

10 9 8 7 6 5 4 3 2   0 4 2 4 1 4

Printed in the United States of America

♾ This paper meets the requirements of ANSI/NISO Z39.48-1992 (Permanence of Paper)

For Shannon.

You are unforgettable.

Contents

Preface

In September of 2011—just about a month after our twenty-sixth wedding anniversary—I lost Shannon. We had just become empty nesters; weeks earlier we dropped our youngest son off at the University of Colorado. Shannon had waited until our son was settled to schedule routine shoulder surgery. Post operation, the doctor came out to tell me the procedure was a success, and he sent me to get the car. In those next few moments, Shannon collapsed and never regained consciousness. Shannon died, and I went from being half of a couple, anticipating the joy of time and travel with an amazing partner, to a person struggling to find a way back into the light.

Anyone who knew Shannon will testify that she was one of the kindest, sweetest souls ever put on earth. I was extraordinarily lucky to have her in my life. We met at college in 1981. Though I wasn't paying adequate attention the first time I met her, I thankfully had a second chance. I thought she was beautiful right away, and I learned how compassionate, patient, and strong she was over the next 28 years. I couldn't have had a better partner. As you read our story, you will get to know her, and I bet you will miss her, too.

After she passed away, I looked for stories that might help me understand my pain. I wanted to know what to do to stop hurting. I wanted to know what to do so I could be there for the other people who were hurting with me—especially our sons. I was in a place that was completely unacceptable; I had to find a way out. What I found didn't help cut through my haze of grief. None of it came close to describing how hopeless I was. None of it pointed me to the set of concrete steps towards the recovery I desperately wanted.

Since I couldn't find enough of the right stuff to read, I started to write. During Shannon's hospitalization, a friend started a website we could use to keep everyone informed of what we naïvely hoped would be progress. I took over the effort on September 13. I have no doubt that the writing—and the responses from friends—is the primary reason I can sit here today as a mostly functioning adult. My blog and support from the online community that assembled around it kept me from feeling quite so alone. They were invaluable in my effort to work through my grief and to find my way to love again.

What is collected here are my blog entries, as well as some of the responses from friends and strangers alike. My hope is that this book will help people out there who have lost a soul mate feel less alone and eventually more hopeful. Or maybe it will help someone understand what a friend or family member who has lost someone is feeling.

Shannon gave me many gifts over the years. I choose to think that she gave me this opportunity to try and help others by sharing my grief and my efforts to get better. If I can manage that opportunity, she will have given a gift to those struggling with mitochondrial disease, the condition that hastened her death. She will have given a gift to people struggling with loss, as well as to people who care about friends or family who are trying to get up from what I promise is a terrible blow. And, finally, Shannon was brutally honest regarding her challenges and her likely prognosis due to her struggles with mitochondrial disease. Her unselfishness in repeatedly and unequivocally expressing what she expected of me should she predecease me is a gift that has made it possible for me to not simply survive losing her, but to find love again.

Nate Bennett
Marietta, Georgia
March 2014

Fall

September 9

On Fri, Sep 9, 2011 at 4:40 p.m., Nate Bennett wrote:

Class,

I am sure some of you have heard, but I wanted to let you know that I will not be able to attend class this weekend. My wife collapsed after waking up from a shoulder surgery. She has been in a coma since, and we are hopeful that there will be some positive signs this weekend.

Arrangements are being made to make sure things move forward in a way that minimizes disruption to your studies. I know you will all do your part to help make sure it all goes well.

You all don't know Shannon, but trust me that I "married up." She is a great person who, after suffering 26 years of being married to me, does not deserve this. Please keep her in your thoughts.

I appreciate the notes I have received—and I promise I will reply to all of them—but it may be a while before I can do it.

Good luck this weekend!

September 10

From: Nathan Bennett
Date: Sat, 10 Sep 2011 13:32:33-0400
To: <jshoffne>
Subject: Shannon Bennett

Dr. Shoffner,

I am so thankful to hear from you (through friends) on a weekend. I will pass your name and number on to the neurologist treating my wife, Shannon. His name is Keith Sanders. Another doctor is watching the case over the weekend. When we last spoke with Dr. Sanders, he recommended we see where things are on Monday—which I imagine will mean updated tests. It would be great if conversation with you could be part of the Monday activities.

I am not entirely clear, but for as long as my wife has been dealing with her mitochondrial condition, your name has been used a lot. She may have seen you or consulted with you previously—perhaps many years ago during her pregnancy. In any case, I know that if she were able to make a call to someone who could help her now, it would be you. Every time she sees a doctor about a procedure that requires anesthesia, she brings them a copy of the work you did some time back on the topic.

Long story short, Shannon went in for an outpatient shoulder procedure on Wednesday. She regained consciousness; they sent me to bring the car around, and in the interim, she had a "cardiac event" and had to be revived. She has not regained consciousness. We are at St. Joseph's now. Tests have ruled out the most obvious reasons someone would crash like she did. MRI negative, CAT scan negative, EKG indicates some heart issues that the cardiologist wants explored if she recovers, but no evidence of why she had that trouble on Wednesday. EEG shows basically confusion in the cerebrum. (Please forgive misspellings and misused words!) We are encouraged that multiple people have seen what we

2

consider "more than twitches" in responses today. She got big eyes and big smiles upon seeing two people today; she made a relieved face and cried a little bit when she heard her parents had made it to town. This is progress over yesterday.

I have attached the records we requested from the surgical center that might be useful to you. While I am interested in understanding "why" she is in this position, my main concern is that someone who really understands mitochondrial disorders has a chance to be heard on issues like how to treat, how long to wait watchfully, and so on. I have no reason to believe Dr. Sanders is on an improper course—but if there is any nuance that your experience would provide that could help him, it would be so greatly appreciated.

I love my wife dearly, and I need her back. I know how much she thinks of you and your work. I would be so honored and appreciative of anything you can offer that would help me be sure something that might help her in her special circumstance isn't overlooked.

Thank you so much for your consideration.

September 11

On September 11, friends created a blog to keep everyone informed about what was happening to Shannon. I took over on September 13.

Sunday, The First Four Days   9:27 p.m.

After Shannon was stabilized at the outpatient surgery center where she had her shoulder operation, she arrived at St. Joseph's ICU late Wednesday afternoon (9/7). Everyone was hopeful she had experienced some difficulty with the anesthesia and would wake from her sleep.

3

Unfortunately, that was not the case. Over the first 24 hours, Shannon underwent a battery of tests on her brain, heart, and other vital organs. The results of these tests indicate an injury to her brain consistent with oxygen deprivation. There is no conclusive evidence that she suffered a heart attack or stroke, but her brain activity is not functioning sufficiently to enable her to control speech, body movement, etc.

Over the first four days since the event, Shannon's condition has remained fairly constant. She remains in ICU, in a coma supported by a ventilator. She seems to be resting peacefully. She does not move her limbs or speak. She has occasionally opened her eyes, smiled, frowned, and cried. We continue to provide stimulus and engagement to assist with Shannon's recovery. She is listening to her favorite music, books she is familiar with, and stories from the old days. Most importantly, Nate is extending to her your well wishes and prayers. Injuries of this nature take their own course. We all remain hopeful and determined that Shannon will soon awaken and recover.

As many of you know, Shannon lives with mitochondrial myopathy, a disease that among other things, saps energy from her cells. Nate has engaged Dr. John Shoffner, a renowned expert in neuroscience and mitochondrial disease. Dr. Shoffner will be providing consult to Dr. Sanders, the lead neurologist on Shannon's case at St. Joseph's. We are looking forward to his input beginning.

Shannon is resting quietly as she has done for most of the day. Her mom, dad, and sister were able to visit and spend time with her. Nate and the family continue to improve the connection with her by playing music and reading from her library (romance novels). Nate has now mastered passive PT and is working her legs, arms, and shoulder.

Shannon remains unconscious and, for the most part, unresponsive to stimuli. Her movements so far have been limited to twitches and jerks with an occasional opening of her eyes and a change of facial expression. Thankfully, she does not seem to be in pain. The family, friends, and nursing staff around her continue to love on her and provide support.

Your continued prayers, well wishes, and positive energy offer strength to Shannon, Nate, Spencer, Reid, and Lyal and Joyce. We remain hopeful and determined that Shannon will respond and recover.

Keep the faith. Pray for Shannon.

September 12

7:07 p.m.

It's a beautiful 85 degrees and sunny in Atlanta. The morning started off with coffee and the neurologist. He summed up the information from the weekend's reports, noting no significant change but also shared that today would be a busy day. The neurologist welcomed the opportunity to talk with Dr. Shoffner, a mitochondrial disease expert, to better understand his perspectives on the influence Shannon's mitochondrial myopathy may be playing.

In late morning, Shannon had an EEG to compare to the one taken last Thursday. This afternoon it was off for another MRI. We continue to await the results of the EEG, but we did receive some news on the latest MRI. The area of Shannon's brain that is damaged is the thalamus. The damage was characterized as involving a few points on the thalamus but not as something massive. On another front, upon consultation with Dr. Shoffner, Dr. Sanders shared that it's a possibility that a folic acid issue could potentially explain Shannon's current state. People with mitochondrial myopathy have challenges processing folic acid, and if those levels are too low during a stressful situation (like her surgery), it could cause a person to experience issues similar to what Shannon experienced Wednesday.

Tomorrow morning Shannon's folic acid levels will be tested, and if low, she will be treated for that condition. Dr. Shoffner said "it would not be

5

unusual" for someone in Shannon's condition—once folic acid levels are corrected—to show marked improvement.

So as the day closes, we are anticipating tomorrow's test and really hoping for a lack of folic acid in her spinal fluid. It is really encouraging to have a strategy that may provide some better insight into how Shannon got here and hopefully a path to bring her forward. No one is offering any guarantees, but we are in a more optimistic place than we were earlier today.

For now, Shannon continues to rest comfortably. Nate will be staying with her overnight tonight and hopes that perhaps all she needs is a chance to settle in with him to watch the Patriots on Monday Night Football.

Thanks for keeping the faith and for your prayers for Shannon and her boys. The people at St. Joseph's continue to take amazing care of her.

September 13

6:27 p.m.

The day began with anticipation of testing Shannon for cerebral folate deficiency (CFD) based on the strategy decided upon Monday afternoon. Shannon's test was scheduled for 8 a.m., but a couple of delays from the hospital pushed things back until after lunch. Around 2 p.m. the doctors began the spinal tap procedure. Just before 4 p.m. Shannon had done her job and was resting comfortably back in her room, as the sample was whisked away to a nearby lab.

Although the results of the test are forthcoming, late this afternoon Shannon's doctors began treating her for CFD. CFD is more and more frequently being recognized as a cause for neurological dysfunction. Hopefully in time, Shannon will confirm that by positively responding.

So as the shadows began to stretch on Monday afternoon, the folate is flowing and today ends with what hopefully will be one step forward. Nate, the boys, and Shannon's family continue to be strong and supportive, doing everything they can do for her. Perhaps tomorrow will bring some additional insight and more steps forward.

Keep the faith and pray for Shannon and her family.

September 13

Tuesday, 11:04 p.m.

Friends,

I want to thank you all for stopping by and sharing your memories and best wishes.

If there has ever been someone with a "better half" it is me. For more than 26 years, no matter what crazy stuff happened during my day, the one thing I knew with certainty is the day would end with Shannon telling me that she loved me. I am really hopeful that I'll get to hear her say that again this weekend. I also know that I couldn't have found a better partner with whom to raise our kids. She isn't done with them yet, and they would even admit to being ready for some mom-like hassling.

Thanks for your every kindness. I've been sharing your posts with Shannon tonight. I know they bring me comfort, and I hope that somehow she is able to feel the love and support. And most of all I hope that we have some encouraging news to share with all of you tomorrow.

September 14

I had some time at the house today and came across this picture—one of my favorites. I took it in 1985 at the Louisa May Alcott house in Concord just a few months before we were married.

Several weeks ago we bought tickets to go see one of Shannon's favorite performers, Robert Randolph, at the Georgia Theater tonight. He'll take the stage around 10 p.m., and I will be playing this link for her in her room instead (http://www.youtube.com/watch?v=tenPRs-MUXA). It won't be music to everyone's liking, but I assure you that the only person who has a bigger smile on their face when Robert Randolph is playing slide guitar (especially starting around minute 5) than Randolph himself is Shannon. If you like, you can listen with us from wherever you are. If she can be smiling, I promise you she will be then.

> 9:54 p.m.

Things are wrapping up here on Wednesday—we are getting ready for Robert Randolph.

Tiny steps, but good steps. A good friend came to visit Shannon tonight, and she got by far the biggest smile. Something about taking Shannon for a big bowl of Pho. Shannon was able to stay with us smiling and making good eye contact for 8–10 seconds. So far, Shannon is excited by the visits of other men and the mentions of ethnic food.

We are just going to not overthink this too much, chalk the day up as a win, and hope for a good day tomorrow. Thanks so much once more for the positive thoughts!

September 15

> 11:08 p.m.

I just can't tell you all how much it helps to take a break a few times each day and get some virtual hugs from so many people who have been such neat parts of our lives—so thank you very much for your posts.

As Shannon was headed off to surgery last week, I remember that I almost passed on the chance to give her a kiss. After all, this was routine, and I would see her in 90 minutes. I am so glad I didn't listen to that voice in my head and that I gave her that kiss. Please make sure you do the same for someone special to you today and every day.

September 16

	6:57 p.m.

Friends,

Today we continued to work with Shannon's physicians to understand her prognosis and best path forward. As has always been true with Shannon, every medical situation is complex and full of equivocal information.

Shannon's sister is taking hospital duty tonight, and I am thankful for the chance to sit with my boys and some friends and relax.

We received some great care packages and what has to be the world's largest bouquet of flowers. Thank you all so much for the continued well wishes—they make a great difference in each of our days.

September 17

	4:14 p.m.

For the past ten days, the medical staff and Shannon's family have been looking for signs that Shannon was improving. Unfortunately Shannon has not improved beyond the condition that brought her to St. Joseph's last week. Earlier today Nate met with Dr. Sanders to review Shannon's situation. After reevaluating the results of the many diagnostic tests, her clinical evaluations, and a consultation from a second neurologist last evening, Nate has decided it is time to honor Shannon's advance directive and withdraw life support. Nate, Reid, and Spencer are together with her.

Please continue to pray that Shannon will be at peace.

> ### 6:36 p.m.

As you learned earlier today, the medical team and I determined this morning that it was time to let Shannon's advance directive take over in regard to her decisions about ongoing medical care. Since that time, Spencer and Reid had a good chance to visit Shannon—we shared lots of memories of Mom and actually had some good laughs about days gone by.

Shannon and I are alone and together now; she is comfortable, and in a way I am, too.

I am overwhelmed by the support you all have offered us these past 10 days. At this point, I can only read about three posts before I get overwhelmed, but I do read and truly appreciate every single one of them—eventually! Thank you so much for the support—I had no idea how much it would help.

GUESTBOOK

9:20 p.m.

Nate,

Our family has been praying for Shannon all week, and we are truly saddened to hear the latest news. Even though we did not know Shannon personally, it seems by reading all of the posts, that she had a sweet spirit that has touched so many lives in so many ways. Her love for her family and friends will never leave those that were lucky enough to have her in their lives. With the

> bit of peace that you are feeling tonight in your heart, is already Shannon's spirit assuring you that things will be all right and she will make sure of that.
>
> You, your boys, families, and friends were very lucky to have God share such a "sweet spirit" with you. Those people are rare, and we all wish we had more of them in our lives.
>
> LM and family

September 18

2:23 p.m.

Friends,

It's been almost 24 hours since Shannon's wishes regarding end of life care were put in place. Last night, I was glad that our friends and Spencer and Reid had a good gathering at our house. Spencer cooked, everyone ate, and I am told there are some leftovers for me.

Shannon and I spent last night together in a quiet hospital room. I am pretty sure we now hold the record for longest sustained hand-holding session. The two of us have always been comfortable just being together in the same place—so together and quiet was really very nice.

Since Shannon is no longer receiving critical care, she has been moved off of the ICU. We are going to TERRIBLY miss the wonderful team down there that has looked after her so well for so long.

Plans going forward are very much in flux. I am working to balance time with Shannon with time with the boys during this waiting period.

I am sorry I have run out of ways to thank you for your support. You all are amazing—you've helped me remember great things I had forgotten about the old days, you've provided lots of comfort—and you have found so many nice ways to say what I have always known about Shannon.

6:51 p.m.

Friends,

At about 5:30 this afternoon, Shannon calmly passed away. She took a big bet on me all those years ago when I, as a semi-starving graduate student with few prospects, asked her to marry me. I am so glad she was up for the ride.

There is no doubt that she gave me the two best presents I ever got in Spencer and Reid, there is no doubt that she gave me 1,000s of wonderful memories, and there is no doubt that she made me a better person than I could have been without her in my life. Her support and her friendship have been a constant that I know I will struggle to do without.

GUESTBOOK

Prof. Bennett,

I'm so sorry to hear that Shannon passed away today. I've been waiting eagerly for your posts each night in hopes of positive news, and I'm so sad for you and your sons. I am sure you find comfort having them with you now. Tonight at about 6:30, I was driving back from taking a walk along the Chattahoochee River with the kids, and my wife pointed out a big spot of rainbow peeking through the clouds over downtown Atlanta. It made me think of your wife, and I said a prayer for her and your family. I then saw the latest post once we got home.

Thank you so much for sharing your journey with us these couple of weeks. I hope you take as much time as you need before coming back to school, but once you're ready, we all will look forward to seeing you again.

TA

September 19

8:00 a.m.

As we get ready for something that is happening about 40 years too soon, I wanted to share one last appreciation of Shannon with you all.

Many of you know that Shannon loved live music. One of her favorite performers to go see was Jamie Cullum. Last night I was driving her car home from a get-together, and she had left his CD in the car. One of the songs, "Photograph," is about a guy reflecting back on his life. It has a line something like, "When I look back at my ordinary life, I see so much magic though I missed it at the time."

One of Shannon's gifts to me was she made sure I always saw the magic at the time—I didn't miss it as it happened.

Friends,

We are thankful for every one of you who has thought of us these past weeks—and particularly for those of you today at the service for Shannon. I appreciated every hug, every kind word, and every story. I only wish I could have spent more time with each of you who made such an effort to be with us.

The boys and I were so comforted by the service. Shannon would have been pleased (but also embarrassed by all the fuss). As many of you know (or figured out), our family has known Father Michael since he was a little kid who we couldn't keep from just hanging out around our house. He was one of the boys' first babysitters, and Shannon and I are so proud of how he has grown up. His family is like family to us, and they have been so important to us for many years. I am appreciative of his comfort and guidance over the past few weeks— and I thank the people from his parish in Louisiana for letting us kidnap him during our time of need.

Tomorrow Reid and I head back out to Boulder to see about "replanting" him at school. He has already made good friends there, his teachers seem willing to work with him, and I think he will be glad to return to his big adventure. I attached a picture of Reid and Shannon from a couple of weeks ago when we moved him out for freshman year. As you can see, she was a proud mom.

On Sep 22, 2011 at 10:56 p.m., "Michael Alello" wrote:

Thanks for the update, I wish it was better, but I'm not surprised. I figured today was going to be a tough one. You are making the right decision with Reid, but I'm glad to know he has some options if things don't work out. Once he gets into a groove, it will get a little easier.

Remember, that's the most time Spencer and Reid have spent together in a long time. It was good for both of them and will help in the future. Hell, I was missing all of you today. Two weeks together in a real crappy situation tends to strengthen relationships.

I'll polish my notes from Shannon's mass and send it to you in the next few days. Call if you need anything.

September 23

10:16 p.m.

Today was a day spent helping Reid understand his options here at school. The people we have spoken to have been great. Reid actually has lots of options: He can stay with a reduced load, he can stay with an even further reduced load, or he can decide as late as December 9th to say "never mind" and withdraw without grades for the semester. All of this is less academic progress than he would have hoped, but it protects him from an academic mess. He can also have as many as three semesters to sit out, and the school will hold his spot.

It seems to have helped Reid to know he has options. We had a long talk about sunk costs, escalation of commitment, and the importance that he realizes he is not in a tough man competition. He understands hard work is expected, but not being miserable. So we will see where it goes from here. He also spent some time biking with friends and other "normal" kid stuff.

In the meantime, Spencer is holding down the fort in Marietta. He reports all is well, and he and I have a dinner date for Sunday. Tomorrow is the first time in over 26 years I will return home from a trip without Shannon to greet me, anxious to hear about how it went. That will be uncomfortable. So I am glad to have classes Monday to look forward to.

September 24

11:09 p.m.

I was going to take a break today, but today's events reminded me of a few things I wanted to share before I forget.

First, if you don't have an advance medical directive, please, please, please get one done. It is hard for me to imagine being in a more miserable situation than the last weeks have provided—but it could have been worse. I took tremendous comfort and relief in knowing I was doing what Shannon wanted. It helps those who are helping you do a better job at it, too. And I am learning it helps in the weeks that follow, too.

Second, going to a concert without Shannon is like eating a French fry with no salt. I went by Chastain tonight (we had bought tickets long ago to Elvis Costello) and just stayed for a couple of songs and a beer to toast Shannon and to remember all the shows we saw there. I can't remember them all, but I remember the first: Jethro Tull, probably the summer of 1987. It poured rain, and we had a blast. Anyway, feels like I said good-bye to the venue in a nice way.

Finally, on the Chastain note...one of the most surprisingly good shows we saw there was Seal. Maybe last year or the year before. Shannon was a big fan—I became one after seeing the show. Those of you who know us well know Shannon and I have pretty different takes on many things—including the afterlife. So just in case Shannon is right, I'd share with her the sentiment in this lyric from Seal's song "Prayer for the Dying," that the space between us now is simply time.

Among the many phone messages when I returned from dropping Reid back at school were eight from Shannon's mother—each a bit more hostile than the previous. Here is one, and my e-mail response follows:

> *You know my name and you know my phone number and if I had known what you were going to do with my daughter after her death I guarantee you would have never, ever married her. And then you were too god damn lazy to tell me you were going to have her cremated. We were right there—we loved her—we had a place she could have been buried, but no, you had to be Mr. Cockylocks. You son of a bitch.*

From: Nathan Bennett
Date: Sat, 24 Sep 2011 22:16:58-0400
To:
Cc: Subject: Updates

L&J,

What a time of grief for all of us. I am focusing very hard on trying to take care of Shannon's children who you can imagine are, like each of us, struggling to understand what happened and how to move forward.

I just returned from Colorado where I spent three days trying to help Reid see if he could feel hopeful about resuming studies this semester.

Upon my return, there were about 8 increasingly hostile phone messages from J, who is clearly very upset about Shannon's wishes to be cremated. On various calls, J insulted me for making the decision (which wasn't mine), for not telling her Shannon's wishes (not really something that mattered last week), for not returning her call promptly (I couldn't, because I was caring for her grandchild in Colorado and had no idea she had called), for not respecting her wishes for Shannon's remains, and so on.

On Monday or Tuesday (schedule permitting) I will send you a PDF file of Shannon's advance directive, which makes it completely clear that it was her wish to be cremated. I will also provide you with the attorney's contact information. I respectfully request J direct any concerns about the advance directive to him.

I will not be answering any calls from your phone number until I feel some effort at respectful discussion is likely. I will not be returning any messages that are left until the same conclusion is logical. If the calls continue I will simply change the number and not share the new one with you. Please don't call—we have caller ID, and I will not be picking up. Please don't leave messages—I will simply delete them.

I don't deserve her abuse on any day, and I will not tolerate it under these circumstances. I am struggling on my own to cope with losing my partner for life. I am using every single piece of energy I have to try and protect and support your grandchildren. I will not allow a single bit of my energy to be consumed in an effort to deal with J's hostility. As much as I understand her frustration, it is simply not fair for her to dump it on me.

I wish J was not making it this way, but she is. To protect me and my children requires that I ask you to leave us alone unless you can be loving, supportive, understanding, and compassionate. J is not the only one suffering—and my family is not here to take her punches.

Today was my first day back at work. I haven't been that nervous in front of a class—and I faced three today—in a very, very long time. Thankfully, Tech puts pretty great people in the seats for me. We talked about motivation at work (ironic topic 1 for the day), change management (ironic topic 2 for the day), and had some laughs. It was great to have some moments that were both real and normal. Those have been too few.

For my evening class, I gave an exam...students said it was "great to have me back." Expressing happiness at seeing a professor who is there to give a hand-cramping exam is kindness above and beyond the call.

I finished class and was packing up to rush home—then I realized that there really wasn't any reason to rush. So I figured I would pound out this update in my office.

As I shared with a friend today, the big waves of sadness are easy to see coming and to ride out—they suck—but not as bad as the many, many little stabs. When I was with Reid in Boulder last week I was killing time in a shop, and three times I picked up something little to get Shannon. Then I remember. Those REALLY suck. That's like the "no need to rush home" tonight thing. I hate that so much. I'd love to have a reason to rush home.

Haven't heard from Spencer today, but last night we had an amazing dinner at HD1—the latest Richard Blais concept. It is great to go out to eat with a chef who is friends with the chef—the only decision I had to make was when to stop eating. Spencer is very busy getting ready for an event this weekend working for Richard Blais at one of the

September 26

8:03 p.m.

corporate hospitality tents at Road Atlanta, and then he is off with him to New York for another event the first part of next week.

I talked for a bit with Reid tonight. The weekend had a lot of down time, and I think that was hard for him. But he reports today was much better—cleaned his room, hit the gym, went to class, met with teachers about plans for getting caught up and so forth. Hearing that his day was better really brightened mine. One day at a time.

Shannon would be (and was) so proud of them.

September 28

9:39 a.m.

Today is one week since we said good-bye to Shannon. It's been a terrible week in so many ways. I try to focus on what I have—which is a lot by any measure. But it is too hard to ignore what I lost—which is also a lot by any measure.

Tomorrow I get to see Reid out in Boulder for a couple of days—very excited about that. Last night, Spencer came over and fixed a great steak dinner for the two of us. He has learned so much about food— impressive all the flair he so easily adds to make a basic dinner really excellent.

I am not sure exactly who is following these rants, but I know from the site counter that someone is! I wanted to let you know that I worry about making you feel awkward about whether or not to call, whether or not to engage in conversation. It is easy to see at work, for example, that an elevator ride with me could be uncomfortable—because our elevators are so slow and because the situation is so bad. I understand how hard it is to know what to say to someone in my situation because

I have been in your position as my friends and colleagues have tried to cope with tragedy.

So I guess what I am saying is that you know what I am dealing with—and I know that you know—so let's stipulate that and try to make it less awkward. If you call and I don't want to talk, I won't pick up the phone—no foul. E-mails are always great—I love e-mail. I can read them as often as I like and answer them when I find the words.

Thanks so much for caring. This is a dark time, but it would be so much darker without you.

GUESTBOOK

6:57 p.m.

Dear Nate,

As a cancer survivor, I know exactly what you mean—there's this awkwardness because people just don't know what to say. When all I wanted was normalcy—talk about what you've been doing—what's important and joyful in your life. It always felt good to laugh—to share some in their happiness of something good that has happened to them—to receive a hug. Here's an e-mail hug from my family and me.

CD

10:10 a.m.

Dr. Bennett,

I've been meaning to drop you a line to wish you and your boys as much peace as is even possible during a time of such great sadness. I've been following your journal updates and am continually amazed at how strong you are. I had a couple of former GA Tech classmates over the night we read about you taking your wife off of life support.

The three of us discussed how such a tragedy could not have happened to someone less deserving.

I hope that you are slowly adapting to your new life. I'm not sure if you are back in the classroom yet, but I do hope that you find your way back there soon. Your zeal for teaching is apparent, and it would be a shame if the current students miss out on all that you have to offer.

You and your family are in my heart and prayers. I do hope that our paths cross again someday and that any future communication comes at a much happier time.

EB

10:32 a.m.

Your posts aren't rants. As long as I've known you, this journey and these posts—your willingness to be open and vulnerable to your friends—has revealed another side of you that has made Jim and me feel even closer to you. I don't sleep well, so long ago adopted a habit of my mother's, who also didn't sleep well: when I wake in the middle of the night, I pray for whomever or whatever comes into my mind. Lately, that's been you and Shannon and your boys. Many people have said to you, there are no words. Well, there are no words. Many have said, our hearts are breaking for you. Well, our hearts are broken for you. I cannot picture you without Shannon, even though your work and her physical challenges meant that we often saw you without her, she was never not with you.

PM

September 29

This is all so weird. Last night I slept okay—even though both the Braves and the Red Sox were eliminated from postseason—on the same night. I guess maybe some life events have given me "perspective" on baseball.

The plane ride here to Colorado was torturous. This is "family weekend," and my wife was supposed to be in the seat next to me. I am staying at the hotel where the landing page picture of Shannon was taken just five weeks ago.

Thankfully, my reward on the end of the flight is time with Reid. We had lunch, and now he and I are sitting in my hotel room. He is studying for his economics test tomorrow. He is taking just 10 hours now, and he says that after the economics test, he will feel pretty much caught up. What a relief. He says there are times each day he really hurts, but it seems to me that he is generally happy here.

For so long, a big part of how I kept score in terms of how I was doing was to see if Shannon was happy. Most days I did pretty well. Now I don't know how to keep score; I don't know how to know how I am doing. That is what I need to figure out next.

Thanks for all the e-mails! I will respond to them as I can. I really appreciate each one. Some of you have asked about what I am doing for myself. I have an appointment with a psychiatrist I know professionally next week. He is in the loop. We've been e-mailing, and he is helping me with medicine. The medicine doesn't feel like it is helping much, but I know it helps some. I have looked in to support groups but honestly everything I find near me seems really cheesy. I am eating okay, not drinking too much, and trying to get as much sunshine as I can.

GUESTBOOK

3:35 p.m.

Hey Nate!

My mom informed me about what happened to Shannon after her shoulder surgery, and I wanted to reach out to you. It was so great to have met you and Shannon in London this past summer; you were both such kind and caring people.

You were also the cutest couple—I could tell you love her very much. One of the details I remember my mom saying was that you read Shannon her favorite book while she was in a coma. Not only did that melt my heart, but that thought stuck with me for a few days.

As a nursing major, I am taking a course on sleep, and my professor recently told us the story of her tragic car accident, where she was in a coma for three weeks. My professor remembered everything people had said in her presence while she was in a coma. Apparently studies and research show that most comatose patients still maintain their sense of hearing. She said that it's definitely possible that Shannon had heard you reading her favorite book. I'm not sure if you knew this, but I immediately wanted to e-mail you once I found out.

I am a big believer in fate and the notion that everything happens for a reason. I'm not sure what the reason is here, but I know that you and Shannon have inspired me to appreciate life and love with all my heart.

KK

4:25 p.m.

Nate;

I had to chuckle at your recent update as I'm one of the ghost hits you see. I also realized I was lulled into forgetting the interaction through this website was one-sided and guilty of not reaching out.

One dynamic I've found ironic regarding tragedies is how often it is that the person who loses the most provides the most comfort to everyone else. Your situation falls into this category and to this I say "Thanks" and "Sorry" from all of us. Thanks for the updates and for sharing your insight while we try to come to grips with Shannon's death.

Thanks especially for all you did over the years to support and spoil Shannon. She was a very special person, and special people deserve to have someone like you.

MR

September 30

GUESTBOOK

6:42 a.m.

Hi, Nate,

I find myself "keeping score" the same way. I don't know exactly what I would do instead. It would be related to my son and daughter, but there probably should be something connected to just me.

Perhaps the only thing for you to do is to acknowledge the time that must pass, with memories of wonderful times, waves of terrible pain, joy with your sons, and just rattling around aimlessly. At some point, the waves lessen, and memories organize themselves. Then, you may make sense of where you are going. I know that it is important for you to keep writing and keep talking about it.

CR

9:29 a.m.

Yesterday was such a perfect example of highs and lows—the tough trip, the time with Reid, a great phone call with Spencer after he put in a good day at work and was back at his hotel to recuperate for the event today. A quiet dinner alone enjoying some football at a sports bar and then just another horrible night—too tired to engage in anything, too upset to fall asleep.

I realize there are two things that I am struggling with simultaneously in terms of losing Shannon. First, there is just coming to understand that I am without my partner. I am alone. That was always a risk—Shannon could have decided she had a better marriage deal elsewhere at any time, right? People get divorced and lose their partners. Somehow this part should not be as hard—it happens to people and they more or less manage. I am not saying that looks easy, either—it's just a larger sample of people who find a way to move forward that I can look to. So that makes me hopeful that even though my future isn't what I wanted it to be, it won't necessarily be bad. I should find some solace in the knowledge that there can be a good tomorrow someday.

The other thing that I am struggling with is her actual death. Should we have done something different? Did I do the right things? Did she hurt? Did I tell her enough that I loved her? Did she know we were all there with her? Were we of any comfort at all? Was she scared? She only got 48 years—did we make the most of them? What about the opportunities we missed? It was so hard—those days in the hospital. Cycles of hope, hope dashed. I get brutal, horrible visions during the day and night that shock me. These questions have no good answers, and I am unsure of how to move on without some. It's hard to find the path forward on this one.

12:55 p.m.

Hi, Nate,

I understand some of your struggles and questions. My beliefs tend to run outside the mainstream. My personal experiences and those of others that I know convince me of certain things that I find reassuring. I believe you made the best decisions that you could. I believe she knew without any doubt that you loved her completely. I believe she cherished that. I believe she knew you, her family, and friends were there with her, and it was wonderfully comforting. I believe she was not afraid of death, but she was devastated at leaving you, Reid, and Spencer. Perhaps the toughest thing in passing on is that that person cannot reach out to answer your questions or quiet your distress. I do not believe there are answers to the WHY that we can ever know. I know that in continuing to move forward, it honors them and gives meaning to their lives.

CR

From: AH
Sent: Friday, September 30, 2011 10:19 a.m.
To: Bennett, Nate
Subject: Hi Nate

Nate,

I just read your last post to CaringBridge and feel so sad for you. I can't imagine the pain you are experiencing.

But I have to tell you, your experience has been the catalyst for many conversations in our house as to "what constitutes life." Reading your earlier posts about those last couple of days with her, how you were holding hands, gave me an incredible sense of peace—that she passed in peace. I firmly believe that you all did the right thing—you respected her wishes. You are only human, thus you will never elude the "what ifs" of the decisions you made. From an outsider's viewpoint, Shannon was always a very happy person—content with her life and her family. I have to think that your presence there at the end did make a positive difference.

Continuing to pray for peace for you and your family,

AH

GUESTBOOK

1:37 p.m.

Nate,

Undoubtedly, you are going through the toughest time of your life right now. I'm no expert in psychology, but I know enough to say I'm glad you're seeing your psychiatrist friend next week. The feelings you're having are NATURAL and NORMAL!

I firmly believe you did what you felt was the right thing for Shannon. You and the boys (more so you) knew very well what Shannon's explicit wishes were regarding end-of-life choices. Could you have left her on the vent for a longer time? Most definitely. Would it have made difference? Probably not. Would Shannon have wanted this? According to her directive, absolutely not. Unfortunately, medicine is not an exact science, and no two people will react the same way in the same situation. And Shannon's situation was extremely different. In medicine, we have to put faith in the one to whom we entrust the care of our loved ones. Her neurologist felt that she would not ever return to the person she was. Was he right or wrong? Who knows? We just have to trust in his knowledge and expertise that he knows what he's doing. I've known some pretty lousy MDs in my day, but not one of them ever want to give up and

29

lose a patient. I don't think he would have told you those things if he felt like Shannon had a fighting chance. How do you get past this feeling of not doing enough and did you do the right thing? That's for the psychiatrist to figure out and guide you.

Did you tell her enough that you loved her? YOU LIVED IT! Believe me when I say she knew how much you loved her. And her love for you was just as much, if not more. I've never seen 2 people so perfectly matched. You both have been a huge influence on us.

Did she hurt? Most likely not. She was sedated enough to stay on the vent, so she wasn't feeling pain. We would have known if she was hurting, and the nurses would have given her something for the pain. Did she know we were there? YES! Hearing is the last of our senses to leave us. I know for a fact that comatose patients hear what we say. So put your mind at ease about that one. I also feel like she knew we were there for her and that was a tremendous comfort to her. As we said before, she would not have liked having all the attention on her, but to know we were there would have been a great comfort to her.

Scared? Probably a little. It's always been my belief that ICU patients know what's going on, even though they can't express themselves. That's why we, as nurses, speak with our patients as if they are going to converse with us. We explain all procedures to them and tell them what's going on—why the tube is in her mouth, why she can't speak, etc.

Did you make the most of her 48 years? I have no doubt that you did. You just have to come to terms with that. And I am confident that with time and help (counseling), you will. There are always missed opportunities. You can't do in 26 years what you can do in 40 or 50. No way around that. Y'all did so much together, and I'm sure Shannon was not disappointed.

I know I have rambled on, Nate, but I want you to know that Shannon loved you above everyone else, and you rarely did anything wrong in her eyes. She told me so many times. This year is going to be a VERY strong challenge for you, but I have complete confidence that you will get through it, and at some point, will get better. This will always be a painful memory, but hopefully, with time, you will be able to get on with life. You have 2 wonderful sons to support you and you them. Y'all make a great team.

We love you and miss Shannon terribly, but our memories of her are what keep me going.

DA

October 1

7:13 a.m.

Wow. Last night I had what passes for a pretty good night's sleep in my book. I would love to think it is a new normal, but I know I just need to be thankful for it and not count on anything particular tonight. Knowing the boys both seem in good places helps. Your advice about trying to keep my mind full with good memories helps, too.

I am killing time in the hotel until heading to the airport for the flight home to Atlanta. I can easily see Shannon here with me. She'd be sharing this bagel and salmon with me, sitting with a cup of tea, and reading some terrible book on her iPad. At the appointed time, she would sigh, close the book, set down the teacup, and say, "I know—time to pack."

I want you all to know how much I appreciate your e-mails. I am finding that reading them helps me find strength and—in a good way, sadness. Answering them is hard...there is something about this website that provides sort of an abstraction that helps me focus. When I try to write individually to one of you, I then have specific memories of whatever you, Shannon, and I shared in our lives, and it makes it hard not to just cry. So if you have written, please know that I truly appreciate the thoughts and that they do help—even if I can't find the proper strength (now anyway) to compose something back.

October 2

10:00 a.m.

Shannon never made a lot of noise, but the house is really quiet without her.

Shannon would be upset this weekend with the arrival of what she considered "cold weather" here in Atlanta.

I am glad that between Boulder and Atlanta I haven't seen a literal cloud in over a week. Sunshine helps.

I am glad that Reid introduced me to bands like STS9 because I need music and right now music without words is better.

I am scared because the person I leaned on for years to get me through times like this is the person who is gone.

I am angry that the ICU doctor (who only knew Shannon as a patient on a chart) required Shannon be moved to a new floor after she was taken off life support. In 11 days on the ICU unit, the nurses and our "team" had become close. The "rule" is that since she wasn't getting critical care, she didn't qualify for the unit anymore. The ICU wasn't even halfway full. Everyone we consulted inside and outside the hospital (we had all sorts of medically trained friends getting her vitals regularly via text messages) knew she wasn't going to live through the afternoon. It was cruel to move all of us to a strange place with strange people for a couple of hours to watch her die. It was an unnecessary bureaucratic act that is inconsistent with the mission of St. Joseph's. I'll get over it, but it makes me really angry.

Some of you have asked about Shannon's condition and the role it may have played. Shannon had mitochondrial disease. She went to great pains to make sure all her physicians knew about it. Whenever she had a procedure that involved anesthesia, she had a packet of articles she brought the doctor. She tried to be sure her condition was always front and center. So did her condition play a role? Could be. Were the doctors unaware? Absolutely not. The cardiologist who examined her in ICU ruled out a heart event as a factor in her collapse, but he did say she was showing signs of heart "issues" and that if she recovered she would need to see a cardiologist for evaluation/etc.

GUESTBOOK

11:03 a.m.

Dear Nate,

You are absolutely right to be angry with the Shannon's transfer to a different hospital bed for her last few hours of life. You should not just get over it. You can help a future family by strategically voicing your mistreatment to the hospital. A cost-saving move like that was cruel. It is the sick way many decisions in healthcare are made today. When you are ready, take a stand.

JI

4:41 p.m.

I am sitting on our back porch enjoying the bird sounds and the last of the sunshine for today. I filled the day with grading exams, errands, and all the thoughts in my head.

Fall

There was a lot of mail to go through from the time I was in Boulder. Irony reigns...in one envelope, the tickets we ordered to go see Trey Anastasio play the Tabernacle in November...in the next envelope, the bill from the hospital.

I also got a book I had ordered—*Widower: When Men Are Left Alone* by Scott Campbell. You know professors—we don't "do" anything— we just read about it. Anyway, the book is not bad. The introduction is pretty dark in terms of statistics about widowers—I am 400% more likely to be in a car crash, apparently, now than I was a couple of weeks ago. But most of the book is interviews with widowers at various stages of "recovery" and who lost their wives through various means. I have only read a couple of the stories. I don't agree with all of what these people are saying, but I can relate to it—with one exception.

The widowers talk about being angry with their wives. Of course there were times I was angry with Shannon when she was alive, but I can't see being angry with her in death. She didn't choose this—she didn't "do this to us"—it happened to her. She was the victim, and we are collateral damage. I am angry she is gone, but I am not angry with her.

In reflecting on what I have written over the weeks, I feel a bit selfish because most of it is me focused on me. Next is me obsessing over Spencer and Reid. But I know there are lots of people who hurt because Shannon is gone. I hope you find comfort in the nice things people have posted on this site and I hope you are healing, too. I look forward to the time I am in a better place to share good stories and to help one another.

Finally, I have been thinking a lot about Shannon. I am sad that she didn't get a chance to tell people good-bye. We used to talk about what is the "best way to die"—in your sleep, with a warning of a time limit to accomplish your "bucket list," and so on—not in a morbid way, but in a "after watching that movie what do you think" way. I honestly can't remember how she answered. But I think she would have liked to say good-bye.

October 3

8:31 a.m.

One of the worst moments of the day is the very first awake moment each morning. That moment is when I get hit with "This isn't a dream—it isn't going to end." After that moment the bed is no longer a comfort; I have to get up. It is dark out, and the house is cold and empty. Dreary. I miss asking Shannon if she slept well, and I miss her asking me the same. I miss her trying to sneak quietly out of the bedroom without waking me and always failing.

I read a little more in the widower book last night. It is all the more clear to me that all this hits people differently. One of the men interviewed was talking about the communications he got from friends after he lost his wife. When someone would write something like, "My wife and I held each other more closely last night because of what you are going through," he became resentful and jealous. I wish you would all hold each other a little bit closer tonight—and Shannon would, too. I won't be resentful, but I will be jealous. And that's okay.

GUESTBOOK

9:13 a.m.

I'm going to say something that I don't want you to think is creepy or something out of *Blair Witch Project*. Although I am religious, I really don't even mean this in a religious sense. Let me just put it this way: when I needed my mother, when I hit the wall, she came to me. Twice. And it helped me know that she had never left and was with me in the best possible way, just a different way. Nate, I firmly know that Shannon is with you. Listen to her, relax your mind, suspend all that rational infrastructure we build to succeed in academics, and just rest yourself. She's there, she will comfort you, and when you are ready—and not before—she will go, and you will be okay. And no, I don't mean you are keeping her from going like in a bad movie, only that she's your love, your partner, and she's there for you now as always.

Hope this doesn't freak you out or confirm what you always suspected about me—that I'm nuts. I had to go through it to know this.

PM

10:30 a.m.

Actually I have been trying to do it the old-fashioned way (on paper) like a good Southern man (not the Lynyrd Skynyrd or Neil Young kind, mind you) but yeah...things get in the way so e-mail will have to suffice as it rarely ever completely does.

Please know that I am thinking of you and your family, and I am so very sorry for your loss (yeah, yeah, you've heard it a bunch, but I really am). I can't imagine what you are going through, but your messages online give me a pretty decent idea, and I know I don't want to go through it. When we think about the natural order of things, we all expect that we as husbands and fathers will go first due to that whole hunter-gatherer, higher stress from meetings, etc. My sister passed away unexpectedly last December (she was the same age as Shannon—48), and I watched my brother-in-law deal with what you are going through with his two children, as well as watching my own parents deal with the loss of a child. I guess in a (closer to) perfect world, parents would never bury children, and husbands would never bury wives. Of course that is pretty damn chauvinistic because it assumes that women are better off burying husbands (although some probably think seriously about starting the process themselves), which can't really be true either.

To stop rambling, let me say that your writings have really hit home, and they have made me appreciate my family and especially my wife even more than I already did before (which was a lot). I never met your wife, but from your writings I am sure I would have really liked her, and I think she would appreciate the gift you are giving to others and me by your own words encouraging us to keep this perspective. Your words today were especially well taken. I will make sure to hold my wife a little tighter tonight.

TH

12:21 p.m.

Nate,

I just wanted to drop you a quick note to let you know we are thinking of you. I am sure my wife has shared this with you, but after reading your notes on CaringBridge, I wanted to drop you a note too.

For starters, I just want to say I think you are coping amazingly well given the situation. I am pretty sure I would go into full crater mode if something happened to to my wife, and I would not be able to write anything but gibberish, which is basically my standard writing mode...I had a bad experience with my 8th grade English teacher that still haunts me and my ability to express myself.

It may come across as a little dorky, but I can remember as early as junior high that my primary life goal was to be married and a husband. Sounds kind of weak...but that is what resounded with me the most. So four years of West Point, Ranger training, Desert Storm...all just time fillers for me. I am still amazed I was able to coast through those events, but I managed.

In my mind I envisioned coming home from work, sharing dinner with my wife, going for walks, then sitting down to snuggle and watch TV together (totally clueless that women would have a genetic disposition against watching ESPN). So as you can imagine, I was quite surprised most married evenings (well, none actually) didn't ever pan out like this. Conversely, she usually dragged home a stack of marketing books to pour over after a long day in the office...and I often caught her reading them under the covers with a flashlight...the "Best of Olgivy."

So my marriage did not match the lame vision of marriage I had in my head, but we certainly learned to "dance" over time, and I can say I am a very happily married husband...and I can connect with your writings on CaringBridge. You were clearly a very happy husband too, and your writings are just another way for you to show your love for Shannon. I am impressed. So thanks for sharing so much in your writings. Thanks for showing so much class during this difficult time. I wish you the best and hope you know you can give us a call if we can help in any way. I hope you keep writing your posts and that they get just a tad easier to write each day.

KK

12:49 p.m.

Hey Nate,

Just know I'm pulling for you each day. I always sensed you were very much a person who likes to be in control, so I know this is even more crazy for you as you seek control in your life when everything's out of control (I'm the same!). This is a cruel lesson in letting go, my friend, but the love will never go. And yes, a pastor first coined the "new normal" for me, and I can say, it takes a long time in coming, but it does come as you find your way in these unchartered waters. You will not sink; you will struggle to the other side—flailing at times, but you will get there. And then, Shannon's love will still be there with you—whatever that new normal is for your life.

AH

October 4

Today was—I suppose I shouldn't be surprised—unlike all the others. Mondays I teach three classes—I was a bit worried how it would go. Last Monday was a struggle, and all I did in the night class was give a test. I was surprised—and thankful—that it went really well. It felt pretty normal. Some of the examples I use in class are from my family life, and I am not sure I can continue those. It's like putting speed bumps deliberately in your own path. But overall, class was good. They laughed some, I laughed some, and they asked great questions.

Upon leaving Tech I was feeling good—better than I have in a month. The closer I got to my house, the more the good feeling went away. By the time I was 10 miles from Tech, I was crying. I guess "driving while crying" accounts for the 400% more likely to be in an accident I told you about the other day. The funny thing is that even though the closer I got, and the worse I felt, I desperately wanted to be home.

When I got home around 10, I was feeling worse than when I left Tech, but I was still in positive territory. I was glad I remembered to leave some lights on when I left for work so that I didn't come home to a dark house. I ate, I watched a little football, I read a bit, and I went to bed.

It didn't take me long to realize that I wasn't going to fall asleep any time soon. I thought about getting up and doing an entry here, but I didn't want to go in my office. I thought about taking an Ambien, but I decided to just go with it. I didn't have anything critical to do first thing in the morning. So I just let my head take over for a few hours. Eventually, it wore itself out.

I woke up this morning in the same bad place I wake up every morning. In the moment last night it was good to feel a little "up." But looking back on it now, I am not sure it matters. Imagine you drive a crappy car. Then imagine you get a chance to borrow a great new car for a night. Then imagine the next morning you are back in your crappy car. What was really the point of borrowing the great car? Your reality is that your car is crappy. All the time in the good car really did was help you see just how crappy your car is. I know that is a little dark and that I should enjoy the rare moments and know they will get more frequent and longer as time moves on and all that...but right now, my car is crap. That's just the way it is.

10:35 p.m.

It was wrong this morning to suggest my life is the "crappy car" because it isn't. I have great parents, great kids, a secure job, a wonderful house, and the only kind of car I ever enjoyed driving. Shannon can't take credit for my parents, but she gets a ton of credit for the rest of it. That said, you know I wasn't really saying my life is a crappy car.

I read more in the *Widower* book last night. One of the things a number of the men talk about is the absence of touch in their lives after they lose their wife. I was thinking about that. It has been nearly a month—hard to believe—since Shannon touched me. It has been two weeks tomorrow since I last touched Shannon...in her casket—an important last touch, but not one to anticipate. I miss walking in the neighborhood holding her hand. Last night when I couldn't sleep I knew that if she had been there she would have reached over and scratched my back until I settled down. I miss her standing on the second step of the staircase so we could look each other in the eye for a hug before I left for work.

As I thought more about it, I realized that every one of my senses misses her—it isn't just touch. Today I wondered if I could remember her voice. I thought about how we had video cameras since the kids were little, but we never really used them. We all wanted to be in the action—no one was willing to be outside the fray to operate the camera. So I don't have recordings of her. I realized that the only sound I have of Shannon is her voice on her cell phone voicemail message. I am going to save that forever—it may cost me 10 bucks a month in perpetuity at AT&T, or I will figure out a way to save it. I miss her voice. I know this will sound pretty morbid, but I think a neat gift for you to think of leaving behind is the sound of your voice. It is easy to do now with technology—read a story your kids loved and save the file with your will for them. Record a message for your spouse about why you fell in love with them and ask your spouse to do the same. Tell your parents a story about what you appreciate about all they did for you. I promise that if something terrible happens to you it will be the best gift you ever gave them.

October 5

GUESTBOOK

6:45 a.m.

Hey,

Read your blog post about missing being touched. I had totally forgotten about that part right after being separated then divorced. You don't realize how little, as an adult, that people other than your spouse/sig. other touch you.

It is surprising how you miss it if you are used to it. If you had little kids at home crawling all over you, you would still get a dose of that, but us older (or childless) adults? Nope!

You will get accustomed to it, and the sooner you can, the better. Else one runs the risk of subconsciously or consciously seeking ill-advised relationships that provide it—this accounts for a lot of the temporary insanity of the newly divorced, I think. May be less of an issue for widows/widowers? I don't know.

My tip to newly divorced friends for dealing with it is to schedule a few massages with a good professional massage therapist. No, it is not a substitute for the kind of touch you are used to, but it will ease the transition for your body a bit. Be prepared to cry a little, though. Something about releasing tensions in your body releases things in your mind. But you're crying a lot anyway, so this probably won't make it any worse.

I am sorry if this is TMI (too much information), or awkward to hear from a work-type colleague. I just wish someone had told me these things when I needed them, so will run the risk of looking weird to share them with you.

IF

9:25 a.m.

So much for the theory that posting at night will help me sleep. Tonight it's Ambien's turn to try.

Shannon and I had a pretty natural division of labor around the house. I grocery shopped, and she did laundry. I cooked, and she cleaned up. It worked. While Shannon was in the hospital, I sort of pushed laundry along in a minimal fashion, but last night it was undeniably time to get serious about it. I spent this morning doing a lot of folding. A good indicator of how weird things are is that when I realized every sock had its mate, it made me sad. Sort of pathetic, but a good indicator of how really stupid little stuff just sneaks up and stabs you and then runs off leaving you off balance. My situation would be better if I had lost a sock?

Listening to Michael Franti sing about waiting for a storm to pass him by. Pretty apt. Shannon and I had a lot of happy moments in 2011. It was special, and we thought a sneak preview of how we would manage as empty nesters. One of the best moments was watching Michael Franti at

Jazz Fest in New Orleans. He just seems like a joyful person, and he gave a joyful performance. It was a sunny day, and we were together.

Took a couple of small steps to "remove" Shannon—I hate that—what I am supposed to call it? I gathered up some of her things that were left out for when she came home and put them in a closet so they don't trip me up with sadness during the day. I am not sure I can really trick myself—something that isn't where it should be is about as much of a reminder as something that is. I guess I will find out.

A month ago, Spencer came over and cooked some amazing chicken soup for Shannon. He put it in little containers and froze it for her so she would have an easy way to make a one-armed lunch during her recovery from the shoulder surgery. I can't eat it—it's Shannon's soup. And I can't throw it out—Spencer made it for his mom. That soup will be in my freezer forever.

GUESTBOOK

10:01 a.m.

Eat the soup, Nate.

PM

10:26 a.m.

I cry every day when I read your posts, but sometimes I laugh, too. Sometimes I do both at the same time—like yesterday with the reference to the "400%" statistic...And today's entry about the soup—the visual of Spencer so thoughtfully making soup for his mom—TEARS!

Shannon would want you to enjoy that soup, maybe one night with Spencer. It would not be Shannon's nature for the soup to become freezer burned and go to waste. She would want you to eat and enjoy, right?

I know everyone is telling you this, but these posts you are writing are so inspiring. It gives me something to think about after reading your journal entry each day. I know it is helping you to write, but it is helping all of us, too. Thank you for sharing your relationship and your family with all of us.

EH

From: Nathan Bennett
Date: Wed, 5 Oct 2011 12:54:03-0400
To: MA
Subject: Your request

Nate,

I reviewed what you and Shannon went through on your last day together with my nurse manager and fellow RNs. Between us, we must have 300 years of combined experience in critical care (yes, we are old). No one could believe that you were transferred off the unit after having made the decision to respect Shannon's wishes and withdraw life support and go to palliative care.

My nurse manager said to write to the CEO of the hospital and cc the department heads of medicine, critical care, and nursing...Of course when you are ready. I am not trying to stir you up. You have legitimate anger. You are searching for right and wrong in a surreal situation that does not respect the usual boundaries. When you feel like it, this letter is a way of vindicating Shannon's existence. So many things were unfair to you and Shannon and the boys in the past 3 weeks. That was wrong.

9:10 p.m.

Shannon and I have been fortunate to have many, many special people in our lives. I wanted to take a minute to specially thank one of them. In 1989, Shannon and I moved to Baton Rouge. Spencer was just about 4 months old. I am not sure how long it was, but it wasn't too long before we got to meet two brothers who lived a couple of houses down the street, David and Michael. They liked stopping by, and we liked having them stop by. They played with Spencer—then when Reid came along, they played with Reid. David would babysit Spencer, and when we came home the entire living room would have been turned into a wrestling/couch diving pit. When we had dinner parties, Michael would help Shannon get the house ready; he'd help us cook and clean up. They were like extra kids that we got to enjoy— but that we could send away whenever we wanted.

Time passes; Michael is a Priest. When Shannon fell in to the coma and was brought to the hospital, one of my first calls was to Michael. I didn't really think I would ever need his help in any way other than to watch the roux for me so it didn't burn or to set the table. I certainly didn't expect to be calling him to "come in to work." I am so thankful that he was able to help our family during that horrible time at the hospital. I thank everyone at his Parish in Louisiana who made it work without him so that we could have him. He was a tremendous comfort—he has learned a lot! He helped me at the hospital, he helped me at the funeral home, and he took care of so much.

Shannon was proud of Michael, as I am. She would be pleased with the service he gave for her.

Thank you, Michael. I am lucky to have you in my life. Shannon just thought the world of you, and I hope you know that.

Below is a copy of the message Michael shared at the church. It was perfect.

Shannon W. Bennett
January 9, 1963–September 18, 2011

Anyone who has children, for that matter, anyone that has ever been around children, knows that they all go through a "why" phase. Last week, I spent some time with my godchild, Brady. He's in that "why" phase now! The conversation went something like this:

*"Okay, Brady, I'm leaving." Why? "Because I need to get back to Atlanta." Why? "Because I need to go visit my friend in the hospital." Why? "Well, she's pretty sick." Why? "I love ya, bug, take care!" Why, Why, Why? While we'd like to think we grow out of the "why" phase, we never outgrow the "why" phase. We are inquisitive people; we feed off of data! Information drives most of our decisions. For centuries, people have been asking THE question, "Why do bad things happen to good people?" While we may never come to consensus on this particular question, we can all agree, Shannon's life here ended way too soon. So, I would like to pose a different "why" question: **"Why was Shannon so important to each of us?"***

We gather here in this holy place to remember and celebrate Shannon's faith, mindful that for her, this isn't an end, rather a new beginning. Our gospel reading today finds Peter with Jesus and some of the other disciples, relaxing and conversing after finishing a meal. Everyone's stomachs are full; they're feeling good and enjoying the evening. Jesus strikes up a conversation with Peter and asks: "Peter, do you love me?"

"Yes, Lord, you know that I love you."
*Jesus said, **"Feed my lambs."***

Again Jesus said, "Do you love me?"
He answered, "Yes, Lord, you know that I love you."
*Jesus said, **"Tend my sheep."***

The third time he said to him, "Peter, do you love me?"
He said, "Lord, you know all things; you know that I love you."
*Jesus said, **"Feed my sheep."***

Sometimes, I think we need to overthink what it means to live the "good life." Jesus reminds us today, His invitation isn't complicated, it doesn't require years of experience or education. Actually, our goal here on earth is real simple: we're invited to accept the invitation...Feed my lambs, Tend my sheep, Feed my sheep.

Shannon fed and tended to each of us, whether through a trip to the cleaners, an afternoon on a blanket at Jazz Fest, or through years of friendship. She was the most gentle, loving, considerate person. She tended to everyone she encountered.

Her selfless nature was evident in the way she lived her life. If you were a guest in her house, you had a choice of every type of pillow on your bed: firm/fluffy or full body/normal. Use a special soap, don't worry, Shannon had multiple options for you to choose from! One time, I joked about chocolates on the pillow, and the next day there was a box of Godiva on the bed. She was always thinking about the other person.

Shannon loved music and concerts; she loved great food and wonderful travels, but above all, she loved her boys, all three of them. Shannon was an amazing wife and mother. When Shannon said "yes" to Nate 26 years ago, she accepted him for who he was and CLEARLY made him a better person! Her greatest gift to Nate was her two boys, Spencer and Reid. All you have to do is look at them, and you can see Shannon. She loved the three of you more than anything, and the only thing that could upset this gentle woman was when someone messed with her boys.

It has been said, "You meet thousands of people and none of them really touch you. Then you meet one person and that person changes your life." **"Why was Shannon so important to each of us?"**

It's because she wasn't just another person rushing onto the next appointment or speeding towards another event. There is a reason why the folks at the cleaners and alteration shop cried when they were told of Shannon's passing. Shannon never ran through the

47

door, dropped her stuff on the counter, and walked out. She took time with everyone she encountered. She was attentive to the person in front of her. She truly changed the lives of those she met because she fed and tended to each of us.

As we thank God for the blessing she was for all of us, we hear God inviting us to accept his invitation to tend and feed as Shannon did. May we be attentive to those that God places in front of us each day; may we never rush past anyone. Shannon truly loved each of us and for that, our lives have been forever changed. May we honor her by responding to God's invitation to feed His sheep.

11:19 p.m.

Nate,

I read each and every journal entry you make on the website, and this gives others and me just an insight of what you are feeling. I know that I'm not the only person who continues to think (and pray for) about you and your boys on a daily basis. Mourning the loss of a loved one is a long process. There is no need to rush it.

I was extremely touched when you wrote about forgetting Shannon's voice and how you listen to her voice mail message. I totally understand what you are saying. In August of 2000, I received the worst news of my life: My father was dead. I had just seen him a week before when Steven and I went to Baton Rouge. I can't even express how awful this was. Thankfully, I had a wonderful relationship with my dad and did not have any regrets. It has been 10 years, and I can say I still miss him terribly, but I have learned to move on and I only have wonderful memories and I don't focus on how his life ended. I miss his voice too. It's kinda weird, but every once in a while, I'll have a dream and he's in it and he will speak. And I promise, it's the same voice. I wake up hating that it was a dream, but thrilled I heard his voice. I believe you never forget.

MHD

October 6

Thanks to Ambien. I am not sure which I appreciate more—a basically full night of sleep or the fact that I didn't spend the hours between 11 p.m. and 2 a.m. waiting for my head to wear itself out.

Tomorrow will be one calendar month since I lost Shannon. She didn't die until the 18th, but she fell into a coma on the 7th. It is going to be a hard day. What's extra hard is having three days a month—the coma, the death, and the service—as anniversaries: 7, 18, and 21. It would be best for my heart to pick one, but my head won't cooperate with that.

Tomorrow I teach in the evening. It's a class I haven't seen since I lost Shannon. I am anxious to be back with them.

Shannon and I had tickets to a show for after class. Ben Harper is playing the Tabernacle. A couple of weeks ago, I went to Chastain Park to use our tickets to Elvis Costello. I sat, had a beer, toasted Shannon, heard a few songs, and left. It was nice in a sad way. I will do the same tomorrow. I'll go, I'll stand in "our spot," listen for a bit, and remember all the great dates we had together there, and try to understand the incomprehensible events of the last month. I stopped buying tickets to shows—but I do think a farewell tour to our favorite venues with the tickets I already have is a good idea. Shannon hated to see tickets go to waste. Over the next few weeks, I'll go see Shawn Mullins at the Variety Playhouse and then Trombone Shorty at Center Stage and finally Rebirth Brass Band at Smith's Olde House and that will complete the cycle. All three of those are going to be hard—Ben Harper was just something to do—the remaining acts are all bands Shannon was really looking forward to seeing. It will be hard to be there alone, but it somehow just seems like a proper part of saying good-bye.

I have more I want to say, but I have been stuck for a bit on how to put it together. Maybe I will find the words later. I am afraid of tomorrow. I know it is just another day without Shannon, but the whole anniversary thing is sort of freaking me out. Is tomorrow really any worse of a challenge than today or yesterday? No. I would rather not know what the dates were when any of this happened. It is enough to know it happened. By one month was I supposed to have accomplished something? Every month am I going to be in a state of horrific suspension between the 7th and the 18th, knowing it's the anniversary of that horrible time in ICU? More questions—some just don't have answers, others I know really aren't worth trying to answer—but I really can't control where my head takes me.

5:19 p.m.

The death of Steve Jobs has made this an interesting day of reflection for me.

I have some wishes for Jobs and his family. I hope he didn't hurt too much. I hope he wasn't scared. I hope he got to say good-bye and had peace. I hope he was happy with what he was leaving behind. I hope his family has friends as true as the ones I have and that they take care of each other.

All the reporting stresses the impact that Jobs had on all of us. My family certainly participated in all Apple has done—between us we have three iPhones (Shannon was the lone Blackberry hold out). We have iPads. Father Michael was bequeathed Shannon's. I hope he figured out how to erase all the trashy novels she liked to read. We have Mac computers. We're shareholders. So in a lot of ways, our lives are different—and better—for these products. No doubt Jobs and his leadership at Apple impacted me.

50

So I have been thinking about Jobs's impact on my life and how that compares to Shannon's—not so much in the size of the impact (no comparison), but in the nature of the impact. Turns out there really isn't a comparison there, either. Apple's products changed how I communicate; Shannon changed what I wanted to say. Apple's products changed how I worked; Shannon changed who I am.

Shannon bet on me early and went all-in. She was warned it was ill-advised. She wasn't afraid. She got me through graduate school. She stuck with me through some hard financial times, she gave me two amazing kids, and she moved from a place she loved so I could be happier in my career. She supported me at every turn. She never doubted me. She always had my back. She was patient with me. She took care of me. She trusted me to take care of her.

Apple will be okay without Steve Jobs. I'd be okay without an iPad. It remains to be seen how I do without Shannon.

That's impact.

October 7

One Month Without Shannon	8:09 a.m.

One month ago, we woke up excited. Shannon had been experiencing increasing shoulder pain for a few months. Physical therapy hadn't worked. She needed surgery. The surgery was straightforward and would alleviate her pain. She didn't want to miss helping Reid to college, and she didn't want to mess up family holidays. She didn't want to make me miss too much work. She really hurt, but she waited for her operation until a time that other people wouldn't be badly impacted. That's Shannon.

September 7th she finally would have the surgery that would make the pain go away. She made all sorts of crazy preparations. We bought a recliner with a controller so she wouldn't need to bother someone for help getting in and out of the chair. She loaded up all the clothes that she could get in without help on a rack in the bathroom so she wouldn't need help to get dressed. She even figured out a crazy way to wedge her hair dryer against a mirror and the wall and to then dance around in front of it to dry her hair. I told her I would take care of her chair. I told her I would help her get dressed. I told her I would dry her hair. She said she didn't want to be a burden on me. I said that's why I am here.

We went to the office. She had the procedure. It was ruled a great success—I was so relieved. Shannon would finally not feel pain. They sent me for the car. We were going home. Then something went terribly wrong. Now Shannon's pain is gone. But this isn't how it was supposed to work.

Shannon, I miss you so much. I miss your company, and I miss the purpose you put in each day.

She would never believe that in a month more than 10,000 times people have reached out to see how she was doing, to check on her family, and to express support and condolences. She didn't think she mattered that much. She was so wrong about that.

When I went to the doctor yesterday he said something that really struck me—something like, "You haven't had a conscious moment in 28 years without Shannon in it." Trying to go from something that was true for so long to a way to manage memories and forge ahead on a new path is hard. I can't think of a single thing I do that won't need to be different because Shannon is gone.

I decided I am going to try to make my brain accept the 7th as the marker of this terrible event. It really is when I lost her—I just didn't realize it yet. I don't want to have three markers. Plus, if I use this one

I can try to convince myself that I have survived a month already. My head is not usually good at tricking itself, but I am going to try.

Thanks to each of you for being among the 10,000. Next to the loss, the worst part of this is feeling alone. You have all helped me not slip into some sort of self-pity. Clearly, I am not alone. You prove it every day. I appreciate it deeply, and Shannon would thank you, too, for looking after her family. If all I had was a journal here in the house I would feel alone. Getting the feelings out helps—but feeling heard is what really defeats feeling lonely. Thank you so much.

11:11 p.m.

Tonight after class I went to the Tabernacle here in Atlanta to toast Shannon at the Ben Harper concert. That part felt good. She loved going there to hear music. To be fair, she loved going anywhere to hear music. According to the souvenir ticket stub book she got me for Christmas, she and I went to hear live music 50 times this year. Upon reflection, that's a bit excessive—but it is what we did. I used to joke that it was a way we could spend 2 or 3 hours together without having to make conversation. The week before her surgery we heard Grace Potter in Charlotte and Maroon Five and Train here in Atlanta. The first concert we went to on a date together was, I am pretty sure, James Taylor at the Audubon Zoo in New Orleans in 1984 or so. Back then, the zoo had a concert series—you brought a picnic and a blanket, they let the elephants and giraffe roam around—it was pretty cool.

The music tonight was okay. What I noticed was that it was the first time I looked at other couples and was jealous. Over the past couple of weeks there have been times that I have seen the proverbial cute little white-haired old couple. Shannon and I always talked about how that would one day be us holding hands and moving slowly along. It won't. Seeing those couples makes me sad, but not jealous. Tonight I felt jealous, and I didn't like it.

On that theme, I am told that one day I will be angry with Shannon for leaving me. I don't believe it. I am told that if I do NOT get angry with Shannon for leaving me that it will be the first case in history where that doesn't happen. I am going for it. I am angry, and I will probably get more angry before this is all over, but I just can't see being angry at her. None of this is her fault. As I have said before, she is the victim here. She was cheated out of the second half of her life. She deserved it. I am angry FOR her, not WITH her. I hope I am right.

I learned today that an old friend—a guy I shared an office with when I was in graduate school and who works with me at Tech—was admitted to the ICU at Grady Hospital here in Atlanta today after suffering what appears to have been a stroke. I talked briefly with his wife. Boy, do I know how she feels. I want to go see her tomorrow and give her a hug and the sort of help so many people gave me, but I am afraid of going to an ICU. I guess I will see tomorrow if I can do it.

Several times a day I get a strong feeling that this is just a test and that if I do enough things right, Shannon will come back. That part of me wants to say, "Shannon, the boys and I are working really hard at this—I think you can come back." It's sad that I want that part of me to go away—but it needs to. Shannon isn't coming back.

When I went to the doctor yesterday he used one metaphor that is helping me. He told me that losing Shannon is like my own personal Hurricane Katrina. I will be able to rebuild, but it won't really quite be the same. Even though some things will look the same, underneath they will be different. Other things won't even look the same. That helps. I have spent lots of time in New Orleans—before and after Katrina. I still think New Orleans is a magical place. So maybe that's a good way to think about it. I just have to rebuild. And I have some time and lots of help. That's a good thought to stop with for now.

October 9

I have a lot of time on my hands and not a lot of motivation. I suspect some of it is medicine and some of it is depression. The medicine makes me resigned to my sadness instead of overwhelmed by it; it doesn't help the sadness go away. I have some deadlines this week, and I suspect that will help me get some things done.

Yesterday I did some straightening up around the house in terms of taking care of Shannon's things. The eyeglasses on her reading table, the shoes by the front door, her nail file on the counter, her jacket on the coat rack—I gathered all those things up and put them away. I found an envelope she had assembled of things to mail Reid—reading her note to him made me cry. She really loved her kids and worked so hard to look after them. One of her projects as Reid was heading to college was to assemble a tool kit for him. Her dad had given her one when she went off so the whole thing had important symbolism to her. She knew he wouldn't need most of the stuff in the dorm, but she was determined to get it ready for him. I found her list on the bulletin board. She still had to find him a Yankee screwdriver, a bigger level, safety glasses (like he'd wear them!), pliers, a Sharpie, wire cutters, and a crow bar. How many moms buy their son a crow bar! The note is in her handwriting—I'll never get a note in her handwriting again. More tears.

I have received so much kindness over the last month. A neighbor came yesterday and put fresh plantings in our front porch flower boxes. I spend a lot of time out there now, and I will enjoy taking care of them and looking at them until the real cold arrives. Shannon and I were having a piece of furniture made for the house. I don't really need the piece, but I am going forward with it because it was something special we worked on together. As I was gathering Shannon's things yesterday, I was thinking about what I wanted to save as memories. The idea of putting memories in a plastic or cardboard box was undignified. So I sent the guys making the furniture for us an e-mail and asked if they could give me an estimate for a memory box—maybe something out of reclaimed wood. Shannon would like that. They are going to make me the box for free.

It is really hard to feel so lucky and so screwed at the same time.

I woke up this morning to the image of Shannon and me at Hausman's Jewelers at the Uptown Square Mall in New Orleans picking out my wedding ring. It cost $300. I don't know what a guy's ring runs now, but I know it was a lot of money at the time. I felt bad as she wrote the check. I would like to think Shannon got a decent return on the investment. I don't know what role the ring is supposed to have in my life now. I don't want to take it off. I know I don't have to. But at some point does it mean I am failing at moving ahead? More questions with "no right answers." More "You'll do what seems right to you at the time." Sorry—not satisfactory. I want answers.

8:19 p.m.

All considered, today was a good day. After writing this morning I was able to focus on getting some work done and that felt good. Plenty more work to do, but it was great to get a start.

It was good to talk with my parents—although we all really are sad and miss Shannon it is starting to become a little easier to find other things to talk about.

Spencer came by with Andre (his dog, Shannon's "grand dog"), and we all watched the Saints game. At half time we went outside and threw a lacrosse ball around. Spencer is a lifesaver. I got a few stories about his work over the past week or so. He is starting to get a little restless.

He refers to himself as "casually employed" with special appearances while he waits for Richard Blais's new restaurant to open in January. He is considering things he could do to fill in some time without getting overcommitted so that he can't enjoy the holidays. He knows that once the restaurant opens, he will be really busy.

I heard a little from Reid by text. Months ago, I bought him tickets to see one of his favorite bands—The Foo Fighters—in Denver tonight. With everything that has happened, he wasn't sure he would be able to find a ride and all that. Gladly, he texted me to let me know he was going to be able to go to the show. I hope he has a good time. I'll worry that he gets home safe. He will be in Atlanta next weekend for a quick visit. Can't wait for that hug. From what I can tell, he is getting more confident about school with each passing day.

Some friends had me over for dinner tonight—some regular conversation about regular stuff. Relaxing.

I just paused and read my post from this morning. If it sounds to you like two entirely different people wrote them, then you know exactly what my head is trying to reconcile. I am both right now. I am scared and angry and very lonely and I hurt like nothing else and I cry too much—and I am thankful and I enjoy friends and I get excited for my kids and I laugh.

October 10

> 8:45 a.m.

The next few days are supposed to be the first rainy days since Shannon's death. The sunshine and the ability to be outdoors has been helpful, and I'll miss that way to recharge a bit. I guess the sun will be back on Wednesday.

Have to say that so far I am not a big fan of living alone. I didn't like it that much when I had a 1-bedroom apartment one summer in college, either. I miss having someone to share a funny part of a book with. I miss company to watch a favorite show. I have taped a lot that I am not sure I want to watch alone. I miss spontaneous company—the "let's go see what looks good at Whole Foods for dinner" or "let's go eat sushi" just when it strikes. I miss cooking for someone, rather than cooking just as a chore.

Shannon was good company. We could enjoy each of us doing our own thing in the same space. And we enjoyed a lot of stuff together. She was always up for trying new places and new things; she was fine to sit by with a book while I worked. We had a good rhythm to our life together, and we were looking forward to playing it on a while. I miss her so much. And I am so glad that I didn't die before her. I wouldn't want her to feel the way I feel or to face what I have to face.

10:45 p.m.

Another strange day. Shannon didn't come back. I drove home thinking about her the whole way. When I got to the mailbox at the end of the driveway, I checked and there was no mail...*Shannon already got it,* I thought. Nope—holiday. I'd been thinking about how she was gone for the entire drive home, but at the moment I found the mailbox empty, my reflexive thought was that she was there waiting for me.

In class, I was looking for something in my bag—one I hadn't used in a while. I unzipped a pocket and found the prescriptions I filled for Shannon the night before her procedure, so we'd have the medicine she needed at home when we got home. It was hard to keep moving as if nothing had happened. At lunch, I went to get a credit card out, and I pulled out Shannon's license. She had given it to me the morning of the surgery to carry for her. It's been in my wallet for a month. Totally forgot about it. Jabs all day long. Hard.

I have been totally surrounded by gentleness for a month or so. The people in my East Cobb bubble all know Shannon is gone—my neighbors, the pharmacist, the bank tellers, the cleaners...everyone I run in to knows, and they are all so gentle to me. At work my colleagues all know, my students all know, and they are all so gentle to me. When I went to the concert to toast Shannon last Friday night, the parking lot attendant wouldn't make change for my $50 bill—all I had. I nearly broke down...didn't he understand what I was going through? I had the hardest time not losing it. He must have seen desperation in my eyes. He gave in and helped me out. It was a weird feeling to not be able to cope with something so normal.

Heard a bit from Reid this p.m....just text messages. He "sounded" good—he said the concert was great, and he was glad he went and that he is officially 6'1"...which seems sort of random to have shared. Not sure why he suddenly has an official height measurement— hopefully not from being in a police line-up from some concert-related incident.

I hope all of you are well. I am lucky to have this way to feel less alone. Shannon left a big hole in my heart for having been such a little person. She was so special to me. Thanks for looking after me while I try to move forward.

October 11

GUESTBOOK

8:10 a.m.

Hey, Nate. After the funeral ends, the rest of us get to go home. Those closest still have so much to maneuver, all the collateral damage to deal with. Negotiating all those otherwise seemingly mundane things that can break your heart in a heartbeat and throw you off balance without warning. Thank you for sharing. So many of us have not had to walk this path yet; you are laying it out.

My heart goes out to Shannon, big time. That girl had so much life left to live; yes, she was kind and loving, thoughtful, peaceful, a gentle soul, curious, brave. So many more lives to touch. Your soul mate. She's received her final deserved reward in Heaven; something to be thankful for, but she received that reward way too soon. I know it's not our place to judge our Maker's timing, but instead I just keep thinking she was robbed.

CS

7:58 p.m.

Today was not a good day. Storms kept me up last night, and I had one glass of wine too many. Today's 7 a.m. conference call came too early. I am really tired. It was a rainy and grey day. I don't like those much under good circumstances.

The good news—had a nice e-mail from Reid—he and his friends had a great time at the concert Sunday, and he has a "minor concussion" from running into the wall of his dorm hallway while playing some sort of game. All in all, it was a positive report.

It's been a long time since I worked in my home office. The weather has been nice, and I have just been grabbing work and taking it to the porch to do where I can enjoy blue sky. Since it was gross I sat at my desk. On my bulletin board are two quotes that I had forgotten about—they had become covered with other stuff. One is a line from Rita Rudner—Shannon and I have loved it for probably 20 years..."I love being married. It is so good to find that one person you want to annoy for the rest of your life."[1] The other one is on a card Shannon gave me. It says: "To the world you may be just one person, but to one person you are the world." I love both of those, but I should have been the one giving that card to her.

I have been thinking today about the difference between wants and needs. Usually it is wise to worry about needs and not get too worked up about wants. But I wonder if love—and all those years—changes wants into needs. I want company—but I need Shannon's company. I want conversation—but I need to hear from her. I can get things I want, but I can't do anything about what I need. It is permanently gone. Bassackwards, like a lot of stuff in my world today.

I also realized today that during all the events of the past month, my best efforts have left some of Shannon's friends out of the loop. They don't know she is gone. I don't know how to handle that.

I am going to New Orleans on Thursday with Spencer to meet a friend for dinner. A bit of an extravagance, but what the heck. Some of my oldest and dearest friends have arranged to plant a tree in Shannon's honor in Audubon Park near Tulane. She loved New Orleans; it's where we met and got married, and it is where we had so, so many great times. The tree will be a good place to go and remember her life and our adventures. On Friday I will get a grand tour and be able to pick the spot for the tree and the memory plaque. I also learned that our neighbors are making a little park area in Shannon's memory here in the neighborhood. It is too sweet. Shannon would be so embarrassed, but I say go for it.

I want to end by trying to find a bright spot—I guess it was good to meet with some colleagues with whom I am editing a book. We got a lot done in a long meeting, and I feel like I was able to be in the moment and make some positive contributions. I got a kind call from

[1] Rita Rudner, Rich Hall, and Margaret Cho, *Best of the Improv, Vol. III* (Port Washington, NY: KOCH Vision, 2002), DVD.

a friend from high school. He had just met Shannon last summer when we were up there on business. He is sad. She was just so damn nice. Losing the bright spot...I have great kids, dear friends, a voice to get my thoughts out of my head, a safe house, great students, and they say a sunny day tomorrow. And, if I don't screw it up, clean sheets on the bed. That's all good. Hug somebody for me.

October 12

> 8:29 p.m.

The roller coaster continues. Today was a little better. I slept pretty well, and the bed stayed made. Shannon would have been proud—hospital corners (sort of) and everything. The weatherman lied about the sun, but it was nice enough to take the Jeep to work. Going topless—the car, not me—feels good. See...sense of humor and everything.

I have started listening to music with words again—mixed blessing. I listen a lot to the '70s station. Most of those songs are connected to memories of high school—pre-Shannon. Seems about every 8th song though is an Earth, Wind & Fire song. Shannon was on a dance team in high school and when EW&F comes on I can see her there in the passenger seat "doing her routine."

On the way home, one of my favorite sappy Motown songs—a one-hit wonder for Freda Payne called "Band of Gold"—came on. In the song, Freda is alone for a different reason than mine, but the lyrics sure connect.

Thankfully, Shannon left me a whole lot more than a band of gold—about 300 pounds split across two boys. They aren't as physically close to me as I would like, but they are as close as they are supposed to be. That said, the chorus about sums up how I feel. It is true that the memory of how much better I would feel right now if she was over there in her chair is hard and not getting easier.

Work was good today. Certainly not calling it a trend—just glad to have one to put in the "that was okay" bucket.

I decided that I need to have some company over to the house. Now the house is always quiet—just me. I need to have time in the house with laughter and food and wine and the ball game and friends. I need to cook for more than me. I want to have lots of dishes to do. I want to shop for more than one person. I want to have leftovers from a FUN night spent with friends, not a sad night I spent alone. The few times people have been over it has been nice—so I need to find a way to do more of that.

Tomorrow—New Orleans. It will be great, and it will be terrible. But I know an oyster po'boy will be involved. I just have to decide which place to get it from...Parasol's or Domilise's?

GUESTBOOK

10:00 p.m.

Dear Nate,

Thank you so much for continuing to write about Shannon. Much of what you write makes me cry, but some of it makes me laugh, especially when you write about her love of music and trashy books. I think she would thoroughly approve of your visiting all of the venues that you two enjoyed together; she may have even been with you at some of them.

I can't tell you how much Shannon meant to me and how much I miss her.

Most days I still expect to see her walking in a little before ten and am always hit by a wave of sadness when that doesn't happen. I miss talking to her.

Shannon always said that Pilates was a 50/50 thing—half social, half exercise. There were some days when she would walk in and tell me that she needed an easy workout because she had a lot to talk about. One day she walked in and suggested skipping Pilates and finding somewhere to do tequila shots. She had been on the phone with her mom that morning!

Shannon was my go-to person for mom advice, restaurant recommendations, math tutor referrals, pretty much just about everything. During the past few weeks, I can't tell you how many times something has happened and my first thought is, I can't wait to tell Shannon about that.

CS

October 14

7:53 a.m.

Sun coming up behind me. Sitting in my room at the Riverside Hilton in New Orleans, looking out at the river and the Bridge, listening to Billie Holliday, and having a cup of coffee. Only one thing missing.

It was a long day yesterday—basically trying to fill time until it was time to come to New Orleans. I got some work done, and I ran some errands. I had to go back to the surgi-center to pick up what I hoped would be final records of Shannon's procedure. They still aren't final, but I did paperwork so I never have to go back there again. They will fax or e-mail me the final, final stuff. It was hard to park in the lot and walk past all the people being wheeled out to their rides home. Anyway, the records should be helpful to the mitochondrial specialist I am seeing next week.

Being in New Orleans without Shannon is about what I expected. It's hard, but the memories are mostly of times past—it doesn't hurt the same way it hurts to look around the house and see where she isn't. Don't get me wrong—she should be sitting over in that bed with her book and a cup of tea. I miss her. It is still hard to talk with Spencer about her—but it is getting easier. He is starting to think ahead about how bad the holidays are going to feel and wondering what we might do to make it less bad. Yesterday when it got really bad, I tried to just keep saying to myself, "Shannon would not want you to be hurt; she would not want you to feel bad." Both are true—in the fleeting moments where I can get myself to believe it, some of the sting comes off.

Shannon's favorite Jamie Cullum song just came on..."Get Your Way"...I am going to listen to it and remember being with her at the concert in London last July...thanks all of you.

6:10 p.m.

We found a beautiful place for Shannon's tree in Audubon Park. If you turn on to Calhoun from St. Charles and go just one block there is a little street called Coralie—it is just one block long. It is easy to park there, and then you walk straight into the park towards the lagoon. Dead ahead there is an area surrounded by about 5 live oaks, and Shannon's Ginkgo tree will go in a naked area right in the middle of them. The playground, Tulane, and St. Charles Avenue are just to the right. You can see lagoon, the kids playing, and the streetcars going by. They showed me a couple of places—this place is literally right across the jogging path from an oak tree under which Shannon and I sat and ate crawfish with my mom on one of her visits back in the day—so it must be the right spot.

As I left the hotel this morning, I felt much better than I had in a while. I realized it was because today I was going to do something for Shannon. I haven't been able to do anything for her in a long time. That felt so good.

The good feeling lasted until the plane ride home. There was a woman sitting across the aisle from me who didn't feel compelled to turn off her iPad—even when the flight attendants asked, she would pretend to turn it off, and then when they were gone, she would go about her reading. It made me really angry—here is this woman who is selfish, and she is going to get to play with her grandchildren. And Shannon— who always put others first—won't. I wanted to break the damn iPad over her head. It made me angry because of the unfairness of all this. I have been a much bigger jerk each year in my life than Shannon was in her entire life, so why am I here? Why is that selfish woman here? And it made me angry because it ruined my "buzz" from doing something that would make Shannon smile. I miss that smile so much, and I miss how good it made me feel to bring it to her face. That smile always made my day.

October 15

9:03 a.m.

Sun is back. On the front porch. It's a little cold, but outside is the place to be. All I see is blue sky. Neighbors are driving by to take kids to soccer and all that. I am not sure what I will do when it is truly too cold to work out here.

It was nice to have Reid's noise in the house last night—but at the same time I had trouble sleeping with the occasional thumping from steps, doors, plumbing, and all that. I have become accustomed to real quiet.

This morning I had that feeling of being punched in the stomach as I woke up. It is a terrible way to wake up. It scares me that I can't make the day; it takes an hour to fade away. Eventually my head wakes up enough to stuff that feeling in a box and to sit on the lid. But I know it is still in there, and it is going to get out and punch me again some other morning.

A friend from work sent me a link to a story written by Marjorie Williams, a writer who died at about Shannon's age from cancer. It is a story about her imagining her kids growing up. I appreciated it. Shannon was proud of her boys. She worried endlessly about them. She really didn't need to. She did good work, and they are going to be okay because of that.

Anyway, that story had a link to another story, etc. I ended up reading something her husband had written about losing her. He says what he mourns is not the reality of his wife, but the idea of her. He goes on to include a quote from C. S. Lewis:

> *Slowly, quietly, like snow-flakes—like the small flakes that come when it is going to snow all night—little flakes of me, my impressions, my selections are settling down on the image of her. The real shape will be quite hidden in the end. The rough, sharp, cleansing tang of her otherness is gone.*[2]

I think those words are true and that the thought is beautifully expressed and that it is so sad that it is going to happen to me, too.

I'd really like Shannon back now.

---

[2] C. S. Lewis, *A Grief Observed* (New York: HarperCollins, 1961), 31–32.

12:04 p.m.

Tonight I plan to make another stop on the "saying good-bye" tour. Trombone Shorty at Center Stage. Shannon was excited about this one. When she was in her coffin I gave her three things to take with her: one of the boys' baby blankets, her ticket to our New Year's Eve date for the Cake concert at the Fox, and the new Trombone Shorty CD she was so excited to get a week or so before her collapse. I will go and drink my half of the PBR we would have split, and then I will split.

I want to start writing more about Shannon and less about me. I am finding me tiresome, frankly. I don't think I am breaking much new ground.

It is hard to try to write about Shannon because when I open that door, things just rush out at me. I need to take some time to organize my thoughts. I need to find a way to do it well.

One pair of images has been battling in my head since the trip to New Orleans. Maybe if I put it down in words it will. The last time I kissed Shannon she was unconscious and I had to work around a ventilator. The first time I kissed Shannon was at the New Orleans Police Department impound lot under the North Claiborne Avenue overpass. It was probably about 4 in the morning, and we were there to pick up someone's car that had been towed—I don't remember whose. But I remember the kiss. Two pretty weird settings for a kiss. But that is how it was. The first kiss was much better. Good-bye kisses aren't much fun.

October 16

When a friend started this site weeks ago, we planned to use it as a way to let people know about Shannon's condition and to share our hopes for positive change. I wish so badly for all of us that the story had ended differently. Now you guys are all stuck as unpaid therapists with a reluctant and grumpy patient. So you will all know, you are all good at that job.

Shannon dying is too big; Shannon missing is too big; trying to figure out what happens next is too big.

Sometimes in my life I worried I was up against more than I could handle, but this makes that all look like kid stuff. To think I lost sleep over a grade in high school. To think I stressed about how a presentation would go. To think I fretted over the politics of the boys' sports. Small, small, small stuff.

Trombone Shorty last night was good—Shannon would have loved it—he has so much energy. We saw a lot of fun shows at Center Stage. We had a sneaky place we could always park that was free and close— but the sidewalk to the venue was old, busted up, and full of trip hazards. That was not easy for Shannon because of her vision. My job was to hold her hand and keep her upright. Last night that would have been a challenge because they are completely redoing the sidewalk. Shannon would have been excited about those repairs and the safer trips to come. I missed holding her hand and her post-concert commentary on the drive home. On the way home, as I worked my way around the High Museum, I missed the turn she always had to remind me was coming up. Made me sad. I miss taking care of her, and I miss her taking care of me.

It bothers me to feel like I am spinning my wheels. I need to find a way to mark progress that is more meaningful than just the passage of time. The lack of progress is a fourth thing that is too big. The challenge is I am not sure what progress even looks like at this point. Would I even recognize it?

I said I wanted to start writing more about Shannon and less about me. So far, that's not going so well! I will tell you that I was always amazed at how natural Shannon was with the boys when they were little. She always knew what they needed. She was always prepared—there was never a time we didn't have what they needed in reach. She was never too tired to get up with them. She always knew when they needed to go to the doctor. She had amazing patience. When Spencer wanted to wear the same shirt to school every day, Shannon had it clean every morning. Whatever the boys wanted to be for Halloween, Shannon made it happen—usually by making it. She made Spencer an amazing Ninja Turtle outfit from chunks of foam. She made Reid a classic Fred Flintstone outfit—complete with club. It was harder for her as they got older—teenage boys are a different story—but she always had their backs. And she still had whatever they needed within reach.

7:09 p.m.

This was as good a weekend as I could hope for. I got to spend some time with Spencer and Reid. They got to spend a lot of time with each other and with friends. I had dinner with friends on Saturday. I heard some great music that night.

I just am back from bringing Reid to the airport and am enjoying the last few minutes of daylight on the back porch. Grill is warming up. I have a nice glass of wine.

All that good fortune acknowledged, it isn't hard to see and feel what is missing. I feel like I have had the flu for weeks—or heartburn. Just not quite right inside. Every day I am surprised that I physically hurt. Not a lot—but it is always there.

Yesterday was a little busy, so I only today got to look at yesterday's mail. I received a letter from Cobb County letting me know that Shannon was no longer eligible to vote because she is dead. I had to laugh. I bet she can still vote in Louisiana.

I also got a really terrible two sentence long condolences "form letter"—signed by a computer—from one of Shannon's doctors…not who treated her during her "event" but one who had been providing ongoing care. I had asked his office for help that I never received during the crises. Then a form letter. Nicely played, Dr. What a jerk.

Fortunately, I also got a perfect care package from someone I had worked with years ago and with whom I had more or less fallen out of touch. It contained a perfect, beautiful note that I have now read about 15 times and some thoughtful treats. Totally solved the jerk-doctor-letter problem. As crappy as all this is, it feels so good to experience a kindness like that—especially from someone I thought was out of reach.

Though it was great to have the boys around, it reminds me that they really are heading off on their own. I can't expect them to spend their time looking after me. They have their own adventures to pursue. I will be happy to watch from the sidelines and to support them. But truthfully my nest is just really, really empty now.

I need to find a way to be okay without Shannon and without the boys.

October 17

It is hard for me to look at this picture of Shannon and Reid. But I am also glad to see it. Of all the pictures I have, it is the one that best captures her spirit and her feelings about her kids. She was such a good wife and mom.

I am sitting and writing and waiting for it to warm up enough to move to the porch. I have a lot to get done today—grant reviews, some editing, and some term papers to grade. A huge pile of crap on the floor of the office upstairs needs attention. I need to get the oil changed on the Jeep. If time permits I want to drive up to North Georgia this afternoon to look at some fall color. I need to get back to a gym routine. There is no way all that will get done, but they say stretch goals are motivating, right?

When Shannon was away from home and the boys were little, we used to have "guy rules" about the house. So for example they didn't have to make their beds. We'd eat in front of the TV. That sort of silly stuff. Most dads do it. When I am by myself at the house now, I find myself taking guy rules to new lows. I get undressed in front of the washing machine and get dressed in front of the dryer. I eat standing at the sink. I do still put the toilet seat down—I guess when that habit breaks I will know I have hit widower bottom.

GUESTBOOK

8:38 a.m.

God bless you, Nate—your "guy rules taken to new lows" made me smile—I can see you standing in front of the washer and then getting dressed in front of the dryer. If I look at the glass as half full, I see that you are functioning pretty well—you're still washing clothes, and you still care that you put on clean clothes. I feel as though I see into your soul—the pain is still so fresh and intense—so many of us wish we could make that ache go away.

Hang in there—and if the writing helps, don't quit until you're ready—many of your friends are here and will just keep on reading. I'd feel a little lost if I didn't hear from you.

CD

3:39 p.m.

Empty days are very, very long. It feels like days since I wrote this morning. Time has been passing in an agonizingly slow way since September 7th. That first night in the hospital was unbelievable. I would close my eyes—and then certain at least an hour had passed—I would open my eyes to see it had only been five minutes. That was the longest night of my life.

It is beautiful today. I was pretty productive. A neighbor gave me a heads up that the color hadn't quite arrived in North Georgia, so I hunkered down here. I did the grant reviews, handled a bunch of administrative detail stuff, got the oil changed, got a flu shot, hit the post office, the drug store, and the grocery store.

Fall

When it was lunchtime, I felt like getting something out, and it took a long time to decide on where. The places I like near my house are all places that Shannon and I frequented. I know if I go alone they will ask about her. I don't want to make more people sad by sharing the news. I hate creating the look that comes over people when they find out—about as much as I loved causing the look that would come over Shannon's face when I came home. So I can understand why some people move after something like this; I can see how some things would be easier. But if I moved then I wouldn't have run in to a friend at the post office and had a chance to visit. I'm not moving—I'll just find some new places to eat.

After lunch, I took on the task of the out-of-control office piles. We just had some built-in bookcases installed, and I hadn't yet moved in to them—hence the piles.

At the bottom of one of the piles was a file folder labeled in Shannon's hand "Marriage Certificate." Sure enough—that's what it was. In addition to the certificate there were the "results" of medical tests that we had to produce to prove we were each free of sexually transmitted diseases. I don't know if they still require that in New Orleans, but they used to. I had completely forgotten about this until I saw the doctors' reports. Shannon just had her OB/GYN fill one out. I didn't have a regular doctor, and so I had to go to an office to get checked out. I was not excited about it. I remember that Shannon came with me. The doctor looked at me, he looked at Shannon, and he pronounced me free of STDs. No exam, no nothing. I was relieved to not have to go through anything "too personal" with the doctor. I guess I didn't look like I led an exciting enough life to catch anything. I paid, according to the receipt, $30 and left with the necessary paperwork.

So that got me thinking about the whole process of getting married. Shannon wanted to be married in the Catholic Church. That was fine with me, but since I am not Catholic and had no plans of becoming Catholic, it presented a little bit of a challenge. As has always been true, friends stepped up to help us out. Long story short, we found

74

Father Buddy Poche in Gretna, Louisiana. What a character. We met him, and he told us he would marry us, but that we had to complete the required pre-marital classes. He told us to show up—I think it was on a Monday night—for the first of the classes. We did. At the end of the first class, he asked us to stay behind after the other couples left. We did. He told us he thought we should come on Wednesdays instead—no explanation. He was the boss, so we came back the next week on Wednesday. There were no cars at the church—we were a little confused. We knocked. He answered the door and let us in. We went to the rectory. He explained that he didn't think the Monday class was going to be that useful for us. He made us drinks, and we shot pool and talked about big questions—religion, morality, love, commitment, and kids. That's what we did for the next several Wednesdays. After a few weeks he said, "Okay—you are ready to get married." And we were. We made it work for 26 years and easily had another 26+ in us. I am so disappointed to have lost them.

Maybe the doctor at the clinic and Father Buddy just knew what we knew—that our getting together was just the right thing and that no one needed to get in the way. I'd like to think that was true—it felt true.

Father Buddy stayed special to us. He came to dinner once on his way through Atlanta when I was in graduate school. We waited for Spencer's baptism until we moved back to Louisiana so he could do it. Spencer dwarfed the other babies—he was probably 7 months old or something. He also baptized Reid—that one was more or less on time. He was a big fan of Shannon's, and we were big fans of his. Just another person who helped us have a charmed life.

Speaking of certificates. I can't get Shannon's death certificate. No doctor will sign it. We all know she is dead. What the hell is the problem? They are supposed to provide it in 72 hours. It's been a month tomorrow. Apparently no doctor wants to be on the record as treating her. That makes you feel good about the profession, doesn't it? That goes on top of the pile of stuff that sucks.

I learned about the Pandora streaming service from my students—it has been on in the house an awful lot. I am finding myself stuck listening to lots of reggae music—which surprises me a bit. I had a sort of passing interest in it in high school—like most upper-middle-class white kids from New England, right? I have an old Jimmy Cliff album that I still occasionally listen to. Reggae music is either about some awful wrong and the lyrics are full of righteous indignation, or it is as upbeat and hopeful as music can be. Both of those work for me right now. I can be angry with them, and I can be hopeful with them.

So anyway, I listened for a long time while I worked today, and it was great. Then the Bill Withers' song "Ain't No Sunshine When She's Gone" came on. Pandora has a button you can hit that says "Don't Play This Song Again for One Month." So that is what I did. Now I have a metric for if I am getting better. Around a month from now that song is going to come on, and I'll see if I can get through it with less Kleenex.

I know the true test of whether or not I am better is when I can listen to Eric Clapton's "Wonderful Tonight" all the way through. That song really makes me hurt for Shannon's company.

Later I was flipping through some CDs to look for something different to listen to, and I came across a gift I had given Shannon. For our 20th anniversary, I made a three-disc set called "Shannon's Married Life." I looked at the Billboard Top 100 list for each year that we had been married—1985 to 2005—and tried to find two or three songs for each year that either (a) we loved or (b) were so bad as to be funny memories or (c) just somehow were a play on being/staying married. Then I went to iTunes and made her CDs.

Here they are—you will remember them:

"The Early Years" – Volume One included...

1985 – Eurythmics "Would I Lie to You"
1985 – Aretha Franklin "Whose Zoomin' Who?"
1988 – INXS "Need You Tonight"
1989 – B52s "Love Shack"
1990 – Morris Day and the Time "Jungle Love"
1990 – MC Hammer "You Can't Touch This"
1991 – Lenny Kravitz "It Ain't Over 'Til it's Over"
1993 – The Proclaimers "I'm Gonna Be (500 Miles)"
1993 – Sting "If I Ever Lose My Faith"

"The Middle Years" – Volume Two included...

1994 – Sheryl Crow "All I Wanna Do is Have Some Fun"
1995 – Blues Traveler "Run Around"
1996 – Seal "Don't Cry"
1997 – Third Eye Blind "Semi-Charmed Life"
1998 – Will Smith "Gettin' Jiggy With It"
1999 – Lenny Kravitz "Fly Away"
2000 – Everclear "Wonderful"
2000 – Third Eye Blind "Never Let You Go"

"The Late Years" – Volume Three included...

2001 – Train "Drops of Jupiter"
2002 – April Lavigne "Complicated"
2003 – Toby Keith & Willie Nelson "Beer for My Horses"
2003 – Train "Calling all the Angels"
2004 – Los Lonely Boys "Heaven"
2004 – Five for Fighting "100 Years"
2005 – Coldplay "Clocks"

Shannon really liked those discs. I didn't realize that when I called disc three "The Late Years" that I would be mostly right.

I know that I am observing the 7th as the "anniversary"—but the fact is tomorrow is one month since Shannon died. Today is one month since we took her off life support. One month ago today I held her hand all night long. Tonight it's just me. I'm okay, and I am going to be better, but missing someone gone is no substitute for loving someone here and surviving is not living.

Now I am done writing for today.

GUESTBOOK

10:07 a.m.

Dear Nate,

Word of Shannon's death just reached me in Minnesota last week. I want to offer my deepest condolences on your loss, Nate.

I went to the CaringBridge site, expecting to read about the circumstances surrounding Shannon's unexpected death—instead I found myself drawn into a love story. A real life, compelling love story that can only be written by someone who is going through the terrible grief and loneliness of losing such a life partner. Of course, I never knew Shannon. I barely know you, for God's sake. But I feel like I know her and you through your writing. I was compelled to read every entry. I remember reading an observation by Fred Rogers (yes, Mr. Rogers was more than a host of a simple kid's show) that went something like this: "That which is most personal is universal." The teacher in you shines through as you write your entries, helping all of us connect with Shannon and your family and the loved ones in our own lives.

The right words of support are hard to come by as you acknowledge in one of your posts, Nate. I'm struck by your alternating between moving on because you should and hanging on because you must. And my prayer for you is that, over time, you will find the way to do both...never letting go of Shannon's presence in your life while continuing on without her by your side—living the life you know she would want for you.

My sincere condolences,
LV

5:19 p.m.

Nate,

Love your Father Buddy story. How did he know (after one group session) that not only were you right for each other, but you two would be the people he wanted to get to know personally? His instincts told him that you two knew what you were doing when you found each other. You and Shannon really were made for each other. That made the last 26 years so fantastic and these last several weeks so incredibly shitty. If there is any good news in what you have been sharing these last few weeks, it is that there are so many people like Father Buddy. What a loss you've been through to learn about all the people who are in your corner, but what a treasure to have so many friends who care about you, Reid, and Spencer!

HI

October 18

4:07 p.m.

I am very angry right now. In part, I am angry because the doctors are still not willing to sign Shannon's death certificate. I learned today that technically since she was moved off the ICU, the doctors there could say she wasn't their patient. And because she died on the cancer floor before a doctor there saw her, she wasn't anyone's patient on that floor, either. So she is just dead. Sympathetic clerical folks tell me that none of the doctors want the liability of signing her death certificate.

Assholes. Sorry for the profanity—they are assholes. Is that why the doctors moved Shannon off the floor to die—so they could dodge liability? Classy again, doc. And while everyone says, "It's a problem, and it happens all the time," there is NO ONE I can talk with to get a resolution. No one can make doctors DO anything. The other reason I am angry is that I came home to this mess from a meeting with the mitochondrial expert who helped me get some insight and comfort about Shannon. That buzz is killed. At least it's mostly a symbolic problem—but if we had assets tied up in Shannon's name, etc., it would be a mess. If ANY of you know a sane, compassionate person with pull at St. Joseph's PLEASE help. I need to move past this.

Okay—turning the page. Got to balance that venom out with something sweet. So here is what I was planning to write before I got pissed off.

Those of you who know Shannon—and those of you who were at her service—understand how much of an impression she made on others because of her "others first" sort of approach to life. So I wanted to share a couple of stories about that.

The first is short. When we lived in Baton Rouge, Shannon used to get up on certain winter mornings and make hot chocolate. It wasn't for me; it wasn't for the boys. It was for the trash men. When she heard the truck coming down the street she would pour two to-go cups of hot chocolate and send me out to give it to the guys who picked up the trash. Who does that? Shannon did.

There hasn't been a service person who wasn't a friend to Shannon—she simply didn't look down on—or overlook—anyone. Our plumber is Shannon's friend...same for the electrician...and the tile guy...and the painters...and the bug man...and the alterations lady...and the pharmacist...and the dry cleaners...and the people running most of the lunch places in East Cobb. I learned that our plumber lost his wife a couple of months before I lost Shannon. He called to check on me. I don't think plumbers do that for customers...unless Shannon was the customer.

When all this happened to her, one of the first and most unexpected condolence cards I got was from the lawn guys...and NOT our lawn guys. The card was from the guys that do the common areas in the neighborhood. She used to bring them water, Cokes, etc. She just took care of people. If someone was hot, she brought that person a drink— it didn't matter if she "owed" it to them or even if she knew them.

The second is a bit longer story. Last summer, we went to see Phish in concert at Verizon Wireless—a large outdoor venue here in Atlanta. About 45 minutes in to the first set, it was clear a huge storm was coming. We hightailed it to the bar where we could be under cover. Soon enough, the storm hit. People flooded in to the bar. A young couple asked if they could share our table—they were soaked to the bone. Shannon was making room for them before the girl even finished asking permission.

Next thing I know, Shannon is whipping out a dry towel from one pocket for the girl. From another pocket came a poncho. The woman said, "It's too late, I am already soaked." Shannon said, "But you are shivering, and the plastic will help keep heat in your body and warm you back up." The girl put the poncho on. So now we are talking, and the girl shares that this is their first date since having a baby two months earlier. Shannon then proceeded to help solve myriad baby challenges. I could see the girl thinking, *I need a pad to write all this stuff down.* The husband's jaw was just slack. I just smiled and enjoyed my beer. Shannon in action! In 20 minutes Shannon gave them about a dozen ideas of how to deal with all sorts of new baby issues. When the storm passed, the couple went back to the concert. We went home. It was wet out there, and Shannon's work was done.

So now I can have a good cry instead of an angry one. Thanks for listening.

Thanks to all of you who offered suggestions on how to handle this challenge. I can't tell you how good it feels to have a team that "has my back."

I sent e-mails to the CEO, CMO, CNO tonight. I guessed at the e-mails and sent BCCs to the usual combinations that most companies now use for e-mail addresses (first initial last name, etc.). No bounce backs as undeliverable, so perhaps something got through. I also called Pastoral Care—they were kind and gentle the entire time we were there. They actually called me back. The guy I spoke to knows the admitting physician personally and says he will talk to the doc tomorrow and he said, "I won't make you a promise I'll get it signed because it isn't something I can promise, and you don't need to experience any more broken promises—but I will at least find out what you need to do because this isn't right." He said he will call me tomorrow. And, thank you, Jennifer—I will call the patients' rights office first thing in the a.m. And, long story short, a pledge brother is an attorney here in town whose firm handles medical malpractice—I've just been talking informally to him, and I have asked for his help in terms of a strategy to get the doctors off the dime. Finally, a friend of a friend knows a board member. At some point if I pull enough levers, I will get the right one. Thank you all so much.

This has sort of worn me out tonight. I do need to share with you what Dr. Shoffner shared with me today, but I am going to wait until I get the summary of our discussion that he said he would write for me. It will be more intelligent with that input.

Heard from Reid today—he texted, "Is it okay if I put some stuff from Target on the credit card?" I think that is code for, "I'm fine, Dad—hope you are okay, too—love you." At least that is how I am hearing it. And I said back, "Of course, no problem." Which means, "I love you, Reid—you're a great kid, and I miss you."

I have so many thoughts in my head right now. The whole death certificate issue just churned up stuff that had settled on the bottom. But I am tired, and I've given you too much to read tonight. I am hopeful that some of what I heard from Dr. Shoffner today will help me find some peace. That has to be the first step.

October 19

You all amaze and help me. Every time I post, I get 2 or 3 e-mails—different people every time—never 0; never 200. Those 2 or 3 e-mails have some element or some message that is perfect. I am not sure how you all manage to be so organized, but you are doing a terrific job of looking out for me.

Last night after my last post I heard from a current and a former student. One has a relative on the leadership team at the hospital; one has a relative on the board. They have reached out to those people for help. I am confident the death certificate issue is going to be resolved soon.

That situation got me thinking—and I felt lucky and angry at the same time. I have this forum—I have lots of people looking out for me. We are all connected—the whole 6 degrees of separation thing. I sent a plea for help, and in 45 minutes I had replies with 6 good ideas and 3 people with an "in" at the hospital who had already taken action on my behalf. I was so angry, and in 45 minutes I felt hope again.

What happens to the 70-year-old man in Acworth, Georgia, who loses his wife? He isn't online; he isn't connected to all the people I am connected to. He needs a death certificate to get his wife's insurance money to pay for the funeral he can't afford, and the doctors are engaged in this sort of crappy, petty behavior? What does he do? This is just really wrong. He isn't going to be able to do something and then in 45 minutes experience hope. This has to be fixed.

I spent a lot of time last night sitting in bed and twisting my wedding ring around on my finger. I take it off and try to see what that feels like. It doesn't feel very good. Shannon took her rings off every night—hand lotion issues, getting rings caught on the sheets issues, etc. When she was hurried in the morning and forgot to put them back on before she went out, she used to say she felt naked—uncomfortable way to feel in public. I used to give her crap for making me look like I was out with someone who wasn't my wife. I suppose the new reality is someday I will have to get used to that.

My ring has only been off my finger for a few hours in 26 years. A couple times Shannon got it cleaned/polished. A couple of times I took it off to do messy work around the house. I lost it twice for a couple of hours each time.

The first time I lost it was about 53 weeks after we got married. One of my best friends was getting married in Pensacola one year and one week after Shannon and I had. The whole crew spent the day Friday drinking beer, playing volleyball, and swimming at the beach. About the time we had to leave to get ready for the rehearsal dinner, I realized my ring was gone. I was pretty sure it had slipped off during volleyball. Everyone got on their hands and knees and crawled around in the sand to try and find it—like that was going to work. It was gone.

A couple of friends volunteered to stay and wait for a guy with a metal detector—they are in the phone book in Pensacola just waiting for a chance like this. There was still beer in the cooler, and they were fine with doing that for me. So I left them there and went to get ready for the dinner.

Shannon had left earlier to have more time to get ready. When I got back to the condo we were staying in, I burst in—sunburned, covered in sweat and sand, with a terrified look on my face. She immediately got very worried and said, "What happened?" I said, "I lost my wedding ring." She said something like, "Oh—good—from way you look, I thought someone was hurt—that something bad had happened." I tried to explain something bad had happened—I lost my ring. She said something like, "The ring isn't important—you are. Go get cleaned up."

About an hour into the rehearsal dinner, my friends showed up with big grins on their faces, walked to my table, and dropped my ring on the table. It was 10 inches deep on the beach. I was so relieved. Of course later that night I realized my line at that point should have been, "Thanks, but you found someone else's ring." I hate it when I miss a good line like that.

Earlier this year, it was my turn. Shannon suddenly realized that the diamond was gone from her ring. All she had was a gold ring and an empty mount. She was crushed—really crushed. I told her that now I could afford to get her a decent ring. It could be her ring for our second half. That isn't what she wanted—she wanted her ring—the ring Father Buddy had blessed at our wedding.

Later that night I was putting a suitcase away—we had just returned from someplace. I was running my hand around the lining to grab up any coins or safety pins or whatever, and I found the diamond. We figure she was stuffing something in the bag and as she pulled her hand out the diamond got caught and came out. It's not a very big diamond—I was a poor graduate student. Remarkable we found it. Shannon was very happy. We got her ring fixed.

What I like about those stories is that for both of us the rings mattered more to the person who wore them than the person who gave them. I suppose the person who gave them understood it was just a cash transaction to get a ring to give. But to the person who got them and wore them every day, they were a very special gift.

So I don't know what I will do with my ring. I know it is up to me, and as I said earlier, I know this is one of those comforting/maddening

Fall

"there is no right answer" issues. Having it on feels like I am lying to myself. Having it off makes me sad. I have to figure out which is the least worse.

5:33 p.m.

I wanted you to know that the patient's rights person from the hospital called to let me know that they are going to start over. The funeral home will bring a new request in the a.m., and she will hand walk it to a doctor to get a signature. The funeral home will have it by the end of business tomorrow.

You all helped me go from feeling powerless to feeling empowered. Thanks for that. I am continually grateful for your ongoing support, wisdom, and compassion. That's not something I take for granted; it's special, and I appreciate it.

8:51 p.m.

I wanted to share with you the results of my visit with Dr. Shoffner, a specialist in mitochondrial disorders. Some of you may remember he tried to help us when Shannon was in her coma. Dr. Shoffner is someone whose work Shannon followed. She attended several conferences where he presented. He is one of a very small number of doctors who have devoted their practice to understanding this very rare disorder.

When he learned of Shannon's passing, he offered to meet with me at some point down the road to offer any insights he could. While he hadn't seen Shannon as a patient, he was pretty familiar with the disorder, and I thought he could offer some context. So I took him up on his offer. He had reviewed Shannon's records, and this is my version of what he had to say.

First, Shannon had what was to her a rather unclear diagnosis—it was somewhere between Kearns-Sayre, mitochondrial myopathy, and opthalmoparesis (all are pretty well described on Wikipedia). Her diagnosis was made around the time we were married. There is no cure for any of these, and there aren't really treatments. For that reason, Shannon didn't really spend much time "managing" her illness. She just lived her life. She had surgery years ago to help with her eyelids/ptosis, but there wasn't much else to be done. Not too much has changed in terms of treatment or cure in that time, but more is understood about the disease. So if she were being seen now, she would probably get a cleaner diagnosis—but not much more in the way of treatment or improved prognosis.

The main issue with mitochondrial disease is that the cells don't function properly. Here is a cut/paste from the UMDF website[3]—I can't explain it better:

> *Mitochondrial diseases result from failures of the mitochondria, specialized compartments present in every cell of the body except red blood cells. Mitochondria are responsible for creating more than 90% of the energy needed by the body to sustain life and support growth. When they fail, less and less energy is generated within the cell. Cell injury and even cell death follow. If this process is repeated throughout the body, whole systems begin to fail, and the life of the person in whom this is happening is severely compromised. The disease primarily affects children, but adult onset is becoming more and more common.*

---

[3] "What is Mitochondrial Disease?," United Mitochondrial Disease Foundation, http://www.umdf.org/site/pp.aspx?c=8qKOJ0MvF7LUG&b=7934627.

Diseases of the mitochondria appear to cause the most damage to cells of the brain, heart, liver, skeletal muscles, kidney and the endocrine and respiratory systems.

Depending on which cells are affected, symptoms may include loss of motor control, muscle weakness and pain, gastro-intestinal disorders and swallowing difficulties, poor growth, cardiac disease, liver disease, diabetes, respiratory complica-tions, seizures, visual/hearing problems, lactic acidosis, devel-opmental delays and susceptibility to infection.

So this is what Shannon lived with. Dr. Shoffner felt that given the fact that the disease—though slow in its progression—had been "with Shannon" for 25+ years, her system was simply acutely compromised. He suspects that her body just couldn't handle the stress connected with the surgery. What was routine for someone else was not routine for her. And he said that the disease is so rare that there aren't decent guidelines about what is risky, who is compromised, and what different protocols might be necessary. Just not enough is known about the disorder. Basically, he said, she was teetering on the brink of Niagara Falls. It wasn't necessarily going to take much to push her over the edge. And she had to have the surgery. She couldn't move her arm and hadn't slept through the night because of pain for months.

Shannon was very, very worried about what would happen in her old age. She was scared of being alone and disabled, and she was mortified that she might present a burden to me or to our kids. Dr. Shoffner allowed as to the fact that her fears were probably not crazy, and that for Shannon 60 or 70 probably were not going to be active decades—and maybe not even the 50s.

So here is how I am going to understand it. For whatever reason, Shannon got a body that was only good for 50 years. I got to be with her for more than half her life—and we did all we could with it. We had all the struggles and joys that people are supposed to have. We had great kids, we traveled, we ate, we drank, we laughed, and we took great care of each other. We lived the vows we made to each other when we got married.

We didn't get to do nearly enough, but truly we had a charmed marriage. She got to live 96% of her "quality" life and she did pretty good at using it well. She didn't have to experience what would have been a living hell for her—a slow deterioration to a place where she couldn't love her life. 96% is an A in anyone's book. I am going to try to keep looking at it that way.

I don't like the cards she got dealt, but you don't get to pick those. She played the hand she was dealt with class and I am so, so glad she picked me to play with her. That said, I am not sure how to play on.

Leaving Tech tonight I felt pretty good. I realized that it was for many reasons. First, as I mentioned earlier, the death certificate issue seems to be resolved. I fired a lot of bullets (with your help), and I am not sure which one(s) hit the target, but the message on my answering machine included the line "and the doctor has now agreed to sign the certificate." I feel like you helped me win a battle for Shannon.

Second, I was able to process what I shared with you about Shannon's condition. It doesn't make me feel any better about her being gone, but it helps me feel better about her life. I hope that makes sense.

Third, I just continue to be so thankful for the human contact you all offer. There were a half a dozen episodes today—I'll just share one...I worked late grading and stopped on the way home at a Mexican place for a quick bite/margarita. As I was getting my meal, a former student came to the table to say hello. I haven't seen or heard from him in months, but I know he knows...he just said, "I wanted to say hi—how about we meet for a beer sometime?" That was so normal and so perfect. I am so thankful he wasn't reluctant to approach me and that he offered something kind. I will look forward to that beer.

Dr. Shoffner asked me what he could do for me. I told him that when I feel stronger I want him to help me find a way to honor Shannon by helping other families struggling with mitochondrial disease. I expect all of you to hold me to that promise. I haven't broken any to Shannon yet, and I don't want to start now.

October 20

9:32 a.m.

Waking up still sucks. It is the most alone part of the day. My body wakes up before my brain really comes around. After about an hour and a cup of coffee, my brain takes over and builds a wall around my heart. But that first hour my heart is in charge, and it really hurts. The brain has its work cut out for it during the day, but it keeps the heart in check most of the time. The kindness I experience all day creates a buzz that helps me find peace. Going to sleep is a mixed bag. Some nights—like last night—it comes easy. Other nights, not so much. The day doesn't help predict the night, and one day doesn't help predict the next—but waking up always sucks.

This morning as I was standing at the sink eating my breakfast, I found myself drawn to one of our favorite wedding gifts. I am going to try to upload a picture of it. It is a painting of a little cottage on a bayou somewhere. The mailbox in front says "Shannon & Nate." It was given to us by Marcella Packard—an artist we befriended years ago in New Orleans. Some of you reading this are Chart House people, and you will no doubt remember the Packards. They had a gallery and an apartment around the corner from the restaurant. She and her husband used to come in at least 3 or 4 nights a week at around 9:30 to sit at the bar.

She would have orange juice, and he would have 1 or 2 glasses of Chablis. I have never been good at guessing ages, but I would imagine then were in their 60s. They were pretty much like grandparents to those of us who worked there. They were so sweet. No matter what they drank, I charged them $1.50, and they left a $1.50 tip. It was always nice to have their company as the evening wound down. They came to our wedding, and they gave us the picture. It has always had a treasured spot in our house.

After Hurricane Katrina, we were at an art fair in Marietta Square. Much to our surprise, one of the exhibitors was the Packards' son. We have some of his work in our house, too. We introduced ourselves and got to talking. He was very distressed because he had been out on the art show tour around the Southeast. His dad had passed away quite some time ago, but Marcella was still alive—or had been until Katrina. She was in the nursing home where so many people died because they were not evacuated. He didn't know if she was dead at the home or if she had gotten out of the home. He didn't have access to the Internet—it was a very confusing time in New Orleans, and it was a mess to try and learn anything. We weren't sure what we could do, but we knew we had to do something.

We left the art show with his contact information and went to work. Shannon and her dad chased things down and found Ms. Packard was alive and at a home somewhere in northwest Louisiana. Shannon brought the news to Larry—the son. He made plans to leave the show to go get his mom. I think this might be the only time Shannon's heroism made the paper—the *Marietta Daily Journal*, no less. I guess Larry told a reporter who was there to cover the fair about Shannon's efforts.

Of course, she was a hero to me every day.

I am glad Larry got to find his mom and that in spite of the Alzheimer's that was taking her away she was okay and didn't lose her life in the hurricane. And I was proud of Shannon—she did a good thing for a friend.

5:24 p.m.

So here is today in a nutshell. I got a call from the records room at Pulmonary and Critical Care of Atlanta to let me know the death certificate had been signed and that the funeral home was on the way to come get it for me. You'd think this was good news.

When I got home from the psychiatrist, I got a call from the funeral home. Yes, they had the death certificate, but it had been completed improperly, which means they have to send it to the Fulton County Medical Examiner for correction and release. This could take up to a month.

The physicians with Pulmonary and Critical Care of Atlanta could not determine whether or not an injury had contributed to Shannon's death; they are supposed to be able to figure that out. They also did not check anything as cause of death—they left it blank. They are not supposed to do that. So the certificate, while signed, is of no use to me.

It is possible that they are just honest and don't know enough about medicine to draw these conclusions. It is possible that they didn't like me complaining about them being a month late on doing their job, and this was a way to dick me around. It is possible that they prefer responsibility for things like this be hung around someone else's neck—namely the Fulton County ME. The funeral home tells me that this practice does stuff like this all the time, but that the surviving family members are always too overwhelmed to put up a fuss. NONE of those explanations are acceptable to me, and NO ONE after me should have to put up with this again. They have pissed off someone with time, resources, and a lot of pent up anger. I will keep you posted. I have another fight to fight for Shannon—that gives me purpose, and whether that is healthy or not, it feels good to have something to do for her.

October 21

> 7:54 a.m.

So this morning there are a bunch of small thoughts I need to get out.

Yesterday was the first day that I remember not getting a sympathy card in the mail. Please understand this is not a complaint...our family got so many cards. I still haven't opened them all. I mention it because it hit me as a sign that the world is moving on and that I need to keep working on moving, too. I don't like "moving on" as it applies to me because I am not interested in leaving Shannon behind. So I need a different term for me. I need to find a way to re-configure Shannon in my world, so we can move on together in a way that works.

I told the doctor yesterday that it was weird to me that I could do something like drive the whole way home thinking about Shannon, and when I got to the house and opened the door, the words, "Hey, I'm home!" would start to come out of my mouth. After 40 minutes of thinking about Shannon being gone, that habit still took over. He told me I should go ahead and say it. So I have been talking to an empty house a bit, and it actually helps. If you feel alone, try talking to your empty house—even the sound of your own voice can help make the silence less depressing. And there is no one there to think you are crazy.

I am very careful not to Facebook-stalk my kids—and they have pretty much blocked me from their content anyway. But Shannon would be so honored to know that both of them have pictures with her as their photo. I am sorry they lost their mom, and I wish I could make their pain go away as easily as I could when they were little. There is no toy I can dangle in front of them to distract them from this, and that hurts as a dad.

Shannon and I used to laugh—back in August after Reid had gone to school—that when we unloaded the dishwasher, it was just coffee cups and wine glasses. We pretty much ate out. So now I actually have more dishes to do than when it was the two of us.

The realization that we were celebrating being empty nesters for only three weeks makes me very sad. That snuck up on me. So that's all for now.

3:23 p.m.

It is a bit cold for the porch, but I refuse to be separated from this bright blue sky. Good day so far. I want to finish the list of little thoughts I started this morning.

I have suffered from psoriatic arthritis for about 10 years. About 6 or 7 years ago, I started taking a new drug—Enbrel. It's a once-a-week injection, and it's magic. If I take it regularly, I have no symptoms. When I first started taking it, the process was complicated. You had to mix the chemical, load the syringe, etc. I remember the first batch came with an instructional DVD. Shannon and I both laughed at the line, "The purpose of this DVD is to explain to you the simple 28-step process for taking Enbrel." What 28-step process is simple? It's easier now—pre-loaded syringes. Anyway, Shannon used to inject me. Then she became convinced she was going to kill me, and I had to learn to do it myself. But I digress. The point is, I haven't given myself a shot since Shannon died. Been distracted. I should be unable to move. Maybe she took that pain with her for me. I don't believe it, but it is a nice thing to think. I know she would have if she could have. She would have done anything for me. It's funny how little you need from someone when you know they would give you anything.

I got an "explanation of benefits" form from the insurance company for Shannon's hospital stay. When the EOB form is 38 pages long, you know something bad happened. Good thing I have all weekend to read it.

Interestingly, the doctors who couldn't sign the death certificate because they claim they didn't treat Shannon have sure billed her for treatment.

And finally—an indicator that I am either clever, warped, or need my meds adjusted...I was thinking yesterday about my "journey"—that's how books, websites, and people all refer to it. And I was thinking about my frustration with the lack of a map for the journey. And that got me to thinking about the Game of Life board game. I am sure most of you played it—you get a little car and a little blue or pink peg to put in as the driver, you spin the wheel, and life happens to you. So I started thinking about inventing the Game of Grief board game. At the end of the board is picture of a beautiful sunrise. Everyone would start in the ICU. You would have to take someone OUT of your little car. Then you would draw a card that said, "With the help of friends, you make it through the memorial service...move three spaces towards the light." Then you would spin a wheel, move ahead, and land on a space that said, "You get a text message from your son...move three more spaces towards the light." On your next move, you might land on, "Your doctor jerks you around on the death certificate...go back 10 spaces away from the light." Or, "You pick up your deceased's toothbrush by mistake...move one step away from the light." Could be a real winner if we can get in on the shelves before the holiday. I am weird.

On other news, I am very happy with calls I got today from the powers that be at St. Joseph's. I am hopeful that they are going to take the steps necessary to fix the bad behavior of this physicians' group. If they do, then all of you who helped me should pat yourself on the back because it will mean families down the road will be better treated. When it all is over I'll share the episode—but for now I know some of you are angry and worried about it and me, and you should know the wheels are in motion to make this right. And the power of the network never ends...one of my students is good friends with the Fulton County Medical Examiner.

It is apparently cold enough out here that the track pad doesn't recognize my fingers—so that is all for now. Getting too hard to navigate around!

GUESTBOOK

4:07 p.m.

I'm sitting here reading in my office and laughing out loud at the Game of Grief board game. Good thing you could shoot a cannon ball down most faculty office hallways here on a Friday afternoon and not hit a soul! This cracks me up and just eases me into the weekend, my friend.

PM

October 22

9:10 a.m.

I was up late last night and I slept fairly well, which means I slept a little late. It is much easier to wake up after the sun has started its rise.

Waking up alone in the dark is no fun right now. I guess the time changes soon and there will be more a.m. light. That will help. But since evenings are generally better, I may just need to try to deliberately shift my schedule a bit. Like I control anything in my world any more.

Last night I was invited to come by a campus bar for the birthday party of one of my MBA students. I said—sure—what time? They said sometime after 9. I thought—wow. I am usually pretty tired by then.

So to try to make it work, I went to see the movie *Moneyball*. It is a pretty good movie. Of course it was Friday night at the movies—date night. Me and about 10 couples. Glad it was in no way at all a romantic movie. When I travel, I go eat alone—I go to movies alone—I go to concerts and sporting events alone. And I can enjoy it. But it was a CHOICE to be alone. And when I got back to my hotel, I was going to tell Shannon about it.

It isn't a choice anymore, and I am not going to get to tell Shannon about it. That pretty much sucks a lot of the fun out of it. But I still have to pass the time somehow. It is like the concerts—I had decided I wasn't going to go anymore. It just wouldn't be fun alone. But I have to do something with my nights. I love live music, and cold beer isn't too bad, either.

On that point, I finished the *Widower* book. A lot of the stories are about guys finding new ways to entertain themselves. It made me sad—what were they doing with their wives? The stuff they didn't enjoy? All the stuff I did with Shannon was stuff I love—she never stopped me from doing anything I wanted to do. She jumped on board and did it with me. There isn't "new stuff" I am now "free to do." I have no interest in jumping out of a plane or painting little lead soldiers or collecting stamps. I want to keep living the life I was living. I just hate doing it alone. Doing different stuff isn't going to make the alone part go away.

When you do everything with someone there is nothing you can do that doesn't make you miss them. And I have also realized that I cannot fold laundry anywhere close to how nicely Shannon could.

Back to the narrative. The movie kept me awake until 9:30, so I stopped by the bar and had a beer with the gang. It was a good thing to do. They really are just good kids, and I can see how much they all want to help. They are fun company, and it was a great way to spend an hour. One of the students was talking about plans for a Thanksgiving dinner for the international students in the program who can't go home but was worried about how the logistics would work. A few years ago, Shannon and I hosted about 20 such students at our house. So I said that if they want to have a dinner on the Sunday before Thanksgiving I would help cook, and we could use my house. Seemed like a well-received idea. So that Sunday I guess I am having between 20 and 150 people over for turkey and "fixins." That should keep me busy. Reid and Spencer will be around, and I know they will help. My students will love the chance to meet them.

A final thought on the *Widower* book...a mixed bag. When I first picked it up, it really helped. I completely understood the feelings they were expressing. After a while—as I better realized my own situation—it was unnecessary—I understood it all too well and no longer needed to understand it was "normal." And it doesn't offer any solutions except to point out that what I learned in my relationship with Shannon was how to love, care for, and be taken care of by someone else. Those skills, they say, are the skills that will help me survive. I suppose that's probably true.

Next on the bookshelf...*When You Are Falling, Dive*. Somehow I think the title gives the ending away.

10:10 a.m.

Don't feel bad, Nate. NOBODY can fold clothes like Shannon. Glad you're getting out some.

CD

11:26 p.m.

Working on staying up late so that maybe I can sleep in a bit in the morning until the sun has started its climb.

Last night late I got a call from the funeral home that they had a death certificate for me. I am not sure exactly what happened to get it done—the woman at the funeral home was not my usual contact. I'll try to get the story on Monday. But somehow, the doctors got the certificate back, altered it a bit, and gave it to the funeral home courier. I was told the courier still did not think it was properly filled out, but he took it to the County and they signed off on it. So on the one hand, I have a certificate. On the other hand, it is mysterious. For the sake of my sanity, I will be asking someone who knows to make sure it is "proper."

Today was okay. I finished grading and then went to Home Depot and bought some pots in which to transplant all the houseplants that I received after Shannon's collapse. And that is what I did. It all turned out pretty good, and the plants are all around the house. Watched some football in the basement and cleaned up—it was a mess from Spencer staying down there during Shannon's hospitalization. Tonight a friend invited me out to go catch a minor league hockey game—that was good, too.

Worst moment: sitting on the porch and I heard in the distance an ambulance. I immediately flashed to the day Spencer had to give me a ride from the surgi-center to the hospital. We had to pull over for the ambulance carrying Shannon. I truly hope that none of you ever have to pull over for the ambulance carrying a loved one. That is a terrible memory I could do without.

Best moment: the drive to the hockey game takes me through the neighborhood we lived in when I was in graduate school at Tech. I drove by the restaurant where Shannon took me out to eat as a treat and to let me know she was pregnant with Spencer. My life was changed forever—and in a wonderful way—at that place that night. That is a memory I hope I never forget—and that I hope never fails to bring a good tear to my eye.

I know you don't read this, Spencer—but I love you so much, and I promise I will be in your corner for as long as I am around. You have given me experiences that my life would be empty without.

October 23

9:59 a.m.

Staying up late in order to wake up with the sun has worked one time in a row—which is about as much of a streak I can muster around anything. I have to teach tomorrow at 8 a.m., so there is no avoiding breaking this one anyway. I get to try again Monday night.

Burst of energy this a.m. The dining room was a mess. I had lots of boxes that needed to go downstairs—stuff that we had started to deal with as Reid was heading off to school. I am not a florist by any means, but Father Michael helped me pick all the roses out of the flowers people sent for Shannon before I headed out to take Reid back. I think

I did the right stuff to dry them, and I put them in a vase today. The chest in our hallway is sort of my Shannon spot. Right above the chest are great pictures of Reid and Spencer that I gave her for our anniversary one year—Spencer in high school and Reid in middle school. Her dried flowers are there—all your cards and e-mails are there—the leather binders (this is easily going to become a two-volume set) are there. All the doctor reports are there. Now her death certificate is there. Out of sight in the cabinet is her purse. It is going to be a long time before I am ready to deal with it.

I felt bad last night because I wrote about how much I love Spencer, and I didn't follow up with Reid! Neither boy is reading, so it doesn't really matter, but still. I remember one night in Baton Rouge Shannon and I were out to dinner at Louisiana Pizza Kitchen on Essen Lane—it's long since closed. It was April or May—I guess I could stop to do the math, but it's not important. Shannon brought up the "What are we going to do for the holidays—what parents are we visiting, etc.?" question. I remember saying, "Why are we worried about this in the spring?" And she said, "It's because the baby I am carrying is due December 25th—so travel probably won't happen." I was stunned. As I think about it, Shannon may have only instigated eating out twice—both times to tell me she was pregnant.

Our neighborhood did a big Christmas thing each year. Houses got prizes for best lights, best mailbox decoration, etc. One category was "best live portrayal"…I was all set to build the manger and find a donkey and straw and some wise men…Shannon could have had Reid, and we would have dominated the category. She laughed—but she wasn't up for it. Maybe the only time she didn't go along with my plans.

So anyway, Reid—I know you aren't reading this—but you are a miracle to me. You make us proud. You are smart and kind and thoughtful and so true to your friends. Just like your mom. I love you.

I was paying bills yesterday. It struck me that when you add it all up, it seems like Shannon's funeral and our wedding cost about the same.

Of course, the wedding was 26 years ago. Stuff like that sticks with me—why do I even need to notice stuff like that? I wish I didn't.

The other weird discovery yesterday was in the *NY Times* obituaries. I haven't been reading the paper very regularly. Shannon leaving has really made my world shrink. What I care about is really pretty local now—my kids, my work, my students, my friends, my family. The sunshine. Music. I have no need for news any more.

There was an obituary for Morris Chafetz. I wouldn't expect any of you to know who he was, but the name caught my eye—from a long time ago. Chafetz was a big deal in evolving the way alcoholism is understood. He was the first director of the National Institute on Alcohol Abuse and Alcoholism (NIAAA). When I was in graduate school, my major professors had grants from NIAAA—so NIAAA had a lot to do with my ability to get my PhD.

Chafetz was 87 years old. He killed himself. His 86-year-old wife had died the day before at an assisted living facility. Don't get this the wrong way and don't send the police to my house—I am not in a crisis—I simply understand what he did. Losing his wife at 87, what was he going to enjoy the next day? What was going to give his life meaning? I am happy for him that he had the strength to do what he wanted to do. I don't blame him one bit. I actually admire his courage.

My situation is much different. I have kids who don't think they need me—other than to cut the occasional check—but I know my work with them is not done yet. I have lots of kids to teach out there somewhere. I have stuff I want to write. I have projects at work that are challenging. My situation is both better and worse than Chafetz's. His work was done, and so he didn't have to find a way to live with the pain of losing his wife. My work isn't done, so I must. That sucks, and that's great.

Again the day does not predict the night. Tonight is very hard. I was hoping I was done remembering the day Shannon collapsed—at least so vividly. But I am not. I thought I was past the "this is a test and Shannon is coming back" mind game, but I am not. I was hoping I would be less angry after getting things squared away last week. I am angry again. How do you work through being lonely, angry, frightened, and despondent at the same time?

I took my ring off yesterday—I figured I would give it a try. One of you smartly suggested keeping it on my key chain. That's what I am doing so far. I like that it is always with me—just not where it is supposed to be. Just like Shannon. Always with me but not where she is supposed to be.

The only callous on my hands is a spot where the ring would rub on the palm of my hand. It's been rubbing that spot a long time. So I guess you could say the only hard work I have done in my adult life has been working on being married.

I hope tomorrow is a better day, but I don't know how I am supposed to miss Shannon less. All I can do is try to be busy so that I forget I miss her. I wish there was something more to try that might work better, but I know there isn't. I also know I have had better days so maybe tomorrow will be one of them. I hope so. At least I will be busy and surrounded by people all day long. That will feel good. It is going to be a busy week, in fact. That's good, too.

GUESTBOOK

10:26 p.m.

Prof. Bennett,

When my dad's father passed away, his wedding ring became one of my father's most prized possessions because it was such a strong reminder to him of the love his mom and dad shared for over 50 years. He wanted a way to keep it with him at all times, so he decided to put it on a chain and wear it around his neck. Now if you knew my dad, you'd know he is ANYTHING but a jewelry kind of guy. The chain is cheap, very thin, and extra long so that it's completely unnoticeable even when he's wearing a shirt with an open collar. He'd been wearing that chain 24-7 for the last 10+ years. He never takes it off.

When I read your post tonight I just wanted to share that with you and offer a suggestion. And maybe it'll reduce the likelihood of you ever losing it.

MT

October 24

GUESTBOOK

7:04 a.m.

The "only hard work" comment is priceless. As I reflect, it is certainly some of the hardest I have ever done also. It strikes me that Shannon is such a part of you, the way you think and do things. You probably teach your students in ways that she shaped. In that sense, she is never away.

CR

3:42 p.m.

Nate: I've been following the string on CB and agree with Chris, wait until you are ready, that moment will come. There is no hurry, this will take time and grace. Based on what you have said, Shannon is still very much top of your mind and heart.

Bet you've seen *Unforgiven* with Eastwood. If you remember even that old hard-core gunfighter invoked his ring and vow to that very attractive working woman who offered him a "free one" despite the fact that his wife had been long dead. My dad still wears his wedding ring three years after Mom's death—he says (and he's 87) there's "no other girl for me" despite the persistence of numerous church women.

All to say a good long-term marriage like the one you had was well earned, Nate; you can mourn and savor that for as long as you need to.

DF

October 25

5:08 p.m.

I had one realization today that I think is helpful. It is important that I explain it carefully so that no one takes offense. So please hang with me on this...I have learned that the question "How are you doing?" is one that I don't really want to answer. People ask it—I completely know that they ask it out of concern. I know that they hope I will say, "I am doing okay" or "I am doing better." But both of those statements are lies. I am not doing okay, and I am not doing better. In fact, most of my day is spent trying to stay busy so that I don't remember how badly I am doing. When I get asked, I stop to think about it, and all the efforts to distract are done.

Another way it strikes me is that it has become sort of an intimate question—to me at this time in my life it isn't the "generic greeting" that it is for everyone else. "How I am doing" has become in some ways very personal (in spite of my writing about it to all of you in this way—but I know you get my point).

So what I am going to do from now on when I come across someone who is struggling with a loss or suffering from a horrible disease is I am going to say something like "It is great to see you!" When people tell me that, it reaffirms that there are people who care about me, and it reminds me I am part of something bigger that matters. It's a declarative sentence that doesn't require me to reply with either something depressing or untrue. Hearing that makes me feel good and maybe it would help this other person I run across. If we end up talking for a while, and if it seems right, then I will ask them how they are doing.

I got a beautiful card today from a friend in Germany—another person who crossed our paths years ago and who I get to have in my life because Shannon was so kind. People stuck to us because of her. The card says..."Wer in den herzen seiner lieben lebt, der ist nich tot, der ist nur fern." It is a quote from Augustinus, and I am told it means: "A person who lives in the heart of its loved ones is not dead, just away." That was a good message to hear today.

9:06 p.m.

The death certificate...I had a call from the CEO at St. Joseph's today— the second time he has called. He is really trying to make things right. In the end, I have an "unusual" death certificate in terms of the way cause of death is explained. Shannon would not be surprised. Her entire life was an unusual medical situation. She never got a clean diagnosis...it was always, "It looks mostly like X, but I have never seen X look quite like you." So that is how she leaves the world, too. I asked the CEO, "So in your opinion, the certificate is odd, but it is kosher?" He said yes, that was a good way to put it.

The people at St. Joseph's continue to be very kind, professional, and helpful. He agreed that the behavior of the physicians' practice was not acceptable, and he promised me it would be fixed and that it would not happen to a family down the road. He told me to keep his direct number and to call him any time. I believe him when he says he is committed to fixing the problem, but I am not done with the critical care practice.

Making some progress around the house. Getting some repairs done. Found a service that does personal concierge stuff and am interviewing someone next week. I have friends here who will help me with some of Shannon's things, but I think some of it will be easier if it is a "business deal" with someone who I am not likely to get in to all sorts of stories with. They will help me clean out the basement, get her art room in some sort of shape where it can be presentable, go through Shannon's files, and all that. They also shop and cook and run errands. We will see what I need and if they seem like a fit.

A friend recommended—with some caution—the movie *Up*. I watched it tonight. It was sort of perfect. It made me hurt, but in sort of a warm way. Not entirely unpleasant—and it was nice to "feel" that rather than just sit through yet another episode of *Law and Order*. I identify with that old man. I have lost my Ellie, and I know she would want me to go off on some new adventures. As I shared with the friend, I so wish Shannon had the chance to give me that message, rather than me just having to accept it was what she would think.

Tonight I ate dinner at a fairly consistent and mediocre Italian place in the neighborhood. As I was leaving in the Jeep, I remembered one of the last times I ate there with Shannon. We were getting in the Jeep to leave just as a family was entering the restaurant—a mom, a dad, and a boy about 5. We were parked right in front, top down and all. As Shannon and I got in the car, I heard the boy say to his dad, "I want a car like that one." And the dad said: "Son, everyone wants a car like that one." I grinned and squeezed Shannon's hand...I wouldn't have bought it without her. I thank her every day I get to drive it instead of the "practical" car I would have bought.

On Sunday I have tickets to see Stephen Stills here in Atlanta. I have not been able to give away the extras. I think my friends are all too young to care about him. Oh well. I am going. The last time I saw him was with Shannon at the old Roxy. It was perhaps one of my favorite concert nights ever.

We went to see Van Morrison at Chastain Park. He is notorious for starting right on time—he plays 90 minutes and is done—no encores. He is an odd duck. Anyway, I knew this was perfect. We saw him, left at 9:20 to beat traffic out of the park, and drove to Buckhead. We got to Stephen Stills during his second song. Two of my favorites live in one night at two different venues with my longtime date. Awesome.

As we were leaving Chastain Park, Shannon took the bottle of wine we hadn't finished and gave it to the couple sitting next to us. Of course she was great friends with them by this point. She said, "Here—we aren't going to finish this—you all enjoy it." The guy said, "Why are you leaving early?" Shannon said, "We are leaving to go see Stephen Stills at the Roxy." The guy said, "Oh my God...you are my heroes!"

We laughed the whole way to the Roxy.

Finally, I want to again say how much you all help. You are familiar with my chicken soup dilemma. Most of you don't see it as a dilemma—you basically told me to eat the damn soup. But one of you had a perfect idea—so I am going to listen to it! I am saving the soup until I get the unavoidable terrible cold this winter. Then I will eat the soup—it will be a last time that Shannon can take care of me. I like that a lot.

October 26

1:40 p.m.

I had what felt like an important realization last night after I turned off the light. I came very close to getting up to write an entry, but I was sure I would remember it this morning. I can't remember it, and that's frustrating. I suppose it will come back at some time. In the meantime, I don't want to lose more thoughts so when I have them—and have a spare minute—I will just post them. So here is what is bouncing around in my head as I pass some time before heading to the airport.

It is a perfect afternoon. 78 degrees, blue sky, and sunshine. Slight warm breeze. From what I can tell, a tabby cat has taken up part-time residence on a front porch chair. I have seen it a few times around the yard but it is very, very shy. I was surprised to find a cushion covered with cat hair. I'd like it to be less shy.

Sometimes little things happen that make me wonder for a split second if the coincidence is too coincidental. Today I turned on the radio here on the porch, and the first song was Paulo Nutini's "New Shoes." I remember the first time I heard it I HAD to play it for Shannon. I bought the CD, and I told her that this was a song she would totally get. She laughed so hard at the song—it was great. For those of you who don't know it, it's a song about a guy who feels off, can't quite get it together for his day, is unhappy with the shoes he picked to go with his outfit, finds a new pair of shoes and suddenly, his day is made right.

Pretty silly but right up Shannon's alley. We saw him in concert shortly after at the Variety Playhouse—our very first show at that venue. We loved it and probably went once a month since.

I went by a friend's house to drop off a picture of Shannon to be at the church for the lost souls mass next week. I feel very out of place at the church—for obvious reasons. But I think Shannon would be honored to be remembered, so I am glad this friend will take care of that for me.

Anyway, I ended up talking with the friend and her daughter for a bit. The daughter is very sharp—first time I met her, and I was impressed. Especially since she is a UGA grad! She said the word that described Shannon to her was "light." I thought that was beautiful. She said Shannon was just always able to see the positive, always able to be comfortable with what she was given, always able to go along. I agree, and I appreciate that way of remembering her. And the mom told me how once her daughter—home on school break—was going crazy with being back at home and "under mom's thumb" and all that. Apparently Shannon told the daughter she could come stay at our house for a while. The mom laughed, recalling the conversation with Shannon about "whose side are you on!" And how Shannon said, "I don't have a daughter, so you need to be willing to share yours with me." That was a nice visit.

Then I got to thinking about the "light" comment, and I remembered how hard the last few weeks carrying Reid were for her. Shannon weighed about 95 pounds most of the time. When she was pregnant with Reid, her weight went up to 140. She felt so bad because she had to wake me up at night to help her get up to go to the bathroom. She couldn't create the momentum to get up and out of bed.

And I have been thinking about love in our relationship. The more I think about the word, the harder it is to understand what it means. But even though I feel like I less understand what it means, I think I better understand what I lost when I lost Shannon. This is confusing, I know.

Shannon never accepted the fact that I thought she was beautiful, that she was smart, that she was sweet. She used to say, "Don't throw out those glasses." I insisted it wasn't about any special glasses—it was how it was.

And in fairness, I never really understood why Shannon thought I was a good risk or good company. I was glad she did—but I never entirely got it.

I guess we both thought we were 5s who somehow managed to get what we thought was a 10 to be interested in us. It makes me wonder just how important insecurity or self doubt is in a love relationship. We each lived each day wanting to be worthy of the love we got from the other. We couldn't take what we had for granted because neither one of us ever thought we'd trick another 10 into falling for us. It wasn't going to ever be better than what we had, so we committed to making sure we never lost what we had.

So I lost my 10. I lost a big part of my mission, which was to be worthy of her companionship.

This is one of the things that scares me about moving forward. I really, really hate to make mistakes. I hate feeling dumb or unprepared. I am afraid of their consequences. When I make a mistake, I tend to be really hard on myself. It isn't a good trait—at least not to the degree I do it. I understand where it comes from—it started in earlier life experiences, but recently it's because I didn't want to disappoint Shannon or to lose her, so I worked really hard to not make mistakes.

The path ahead is really uncertain, and as a result, I am going to make lots of mistakes. Life is full of chances to make mistakes. So part of what scares me is how I am going to deal with that. I don't want to be too hard on myself. But the only way to not commit a mistake is to stand still, and I can't do that, either.

If I had a mission, then I am confident I could figure out what to do in order to accomplish the mission. Shannon's happiness was my mission. Sure, some concept of doing "what Shannon would want" exists. It's so vague as to be pretty much useless.

It's hard to admit that so much of my sense of self was dependent on someone else. And it is hard to admit that I am really struggling without that someone as an anchor. But it's true. I was joking with a friend that it's too bad it isn't as easy as some plug-and-play accessory. I have every component for a charmed life, except one. And I can't just go grab one off a shelf and plug it in. Not how it works. But without that piece, the other pieces (except for the kids!) just aren't that special.

> ### 8:16 p.m.

I headed to the airport early and took advantage of the time to get a chair massage. It felt good—human contact and all that. A gang at work gave me a gift card for a "real" massage, and I hope one day soon to get over to the place. Of course, airports are sort of crappy places to get a massage—the buzz doesn't really last very long as you lug luggage, wait in lines, get smashed by people's carry-ons as they board the plane, and all that. But it was good while it lasted.

Just before I left for the airport, I got a call from the patients' rights person at St. Joseph's—more follow-up. They are doing a good job. I explained about the situation where Shannon was sort of exiled to die in strange quarters after 11 days with the same nurse team. I told her that from my perspective, the hospital had two problems because of what the doctor did. First, the nurses on the ICU were very upset. They wanted to help us keep Shannon safe as she died. That isn't good for morale. Second, when I tell people about what happened at the hospital, I have to say that while the nurses were amazing, the whole thing kind of ended in a bad manner that showed no compassion. That hurts their brand. Do I sound like a business school professor or what?

As was the case with the death certificate, she agreed it was not the hospital's finest moment. She wanted me to know that my concerns had the attention of the highest people at the hospital, that they agreed with my concerns, and that she was sure things were going to change. Something about the way she said it and the tone of her voice made me think she was telling the truth. With your help (one of you in particular!), the right people have heard the news that normally would probably have been handled—but maybe not as aggressively and with as much weight. I believe things are going to change.

A nurse friend suggested that since it isn't usual for a 48-year-old to die from outpatient surgery, it might be worth bringing the issue to the attention of the Georgia State Regulatory Agency. So I did. We will see what happens. I am told that if it looks fishy to them, they will do an investigation—again with an eye towards making sure that these places always take all necessary precautions. As I told you, there aren't protocols for people with mitochondrial disease—but maybe I can help create some motivation to at least try to get doctors and facilities to be extra vigilant the next time they meet someone like Shannon. Not that they will, really.

Off to NY for work—a leadership conference, basically—at West Point. I am glad to be going, and I hope I can perform okay. At the same time, it was hard because Shannon is supposed to be sitting next to me—not this other woman. We had reservations at the London hotel in NYC for Saturday night—we were going to eat an amazing meal someplace, visit my aunt and uncle, and enjoy the city. That's not happening now. I am coming home Friday to the safety of my too-empty house. Still trying to do something to get some voices in there.

When the "turn off all electronic devices" announcement came on it made me sad...that's the point at which I would send Shannon a text that said, "okay—shutting down—all is well—love you." Then when I landed I would send a text that said, "landed—call you when I get to the hotel." When I landed I would get a message from her telling me to have fun and that she loved me. I miss those—I have one I just happened to have saved on my phone from the last trip I took before her surgery. I can't bring myself to read her actual words, but I know I never want to delete it, either.

Her actual words are hard to take. I have a note she wrote Reid to go with a care package she never got to send. I have my "honey do" list of chores. I have all sorts of Valentine's Day and birthday cards. When I read them I just can't stop crying. It is hard to have Shannon as an abstraction—but it is impossible to have the reality of her words. I miss the abstraction a million points, and I miss the reality of her a billion points. That's cheesy, but you get the point.

Funny thing about the crying. My stomach hurt for a month after Shannon died. On bad days, that comes back. My head hurts a lot. If I am not careful, I realized I am clamping my jaw so tight all day that it gives me a headache. My eyes hurt all the time. I find it so ironic because it doesn't bother me during the day—but at night I can't sleep because my eyes hurt. It is ironic because Shannon couldn't sleep because her eyes hurt.

Her mitochondrial disease impacted her ability to move her eyeballs and open and close her eyelids. Years ago she has surgery to install slings between her eyelids and muscles up in her forehead. That gave her better ability to raise her eyelids—but it meant she couldn't close them all the way at night. I used to tease her that she was the opposite of those dolls kids have—when you lay Shannon down, her eyes open...when you lay the doll down, the eyes close. When you stand Shannon up, her eyes close.

When you stand the doll up, the eyes open.

I used to tease her that she was like a doll from the Island of Misfit Toys on *Rudolph the Red-Nosed Reindeer*. She was so okay with that. Shannon was my doll. She was great.

October 27

I feel very strange right now. I am staying at the Thayer Hotel at West Point. I am here for a meeting of the Accenture COO Circle—a function where COOs gather to talk about the challenges they face in running their company. I have been fortunate to be a part of the events since they started a few years ago.

So I feel good because it was an exhilarating day. The Accenture team members are amazing hosts, and they are extra amazing in how they take care of me. It was a day spent with people I would never normally get to meet sharing ideas and experiences—really just incredible. As someone who is fascinated by business and who spends their career studying business, it is incredible to be a part of events like this. That makes me feel great.

As I reflect on the day, I realize the versions of how this day could or should have gone. In one version, I am right now talking to Shannon on the phone to let her know how the day went and to see how hers went at home. The call makes me feel good, but it also makes me homesick because I miss her. I get to tell her I love her and that I can't wait to see her tomorrow night. That's the way the day would have ended back when our kids were younger. In the second version—how we planned it would be—Shannon is sitting here on the bed with me. She enjoyed hanging out in the historic hotel all day. She joined us for the tour of the campus and the wonderful dinner in the old train station. She joined us for the drinks at the bar. We are sharing stories of what the dinner conversation at our part of the table was. We are anticipating a wonderful weekend in New York City. In the third version, Shannon missed all that I am here writing to you.

It's hard not to think about my loss in comparison to what the brave people who come to West Point confront. This weekend is the reunion for the class of 1986. I wonder how many of the class gave their lives for the country. I think it is incredibly brave to come to West Point and to be willing to make all the involved sacrifices. I respect that so much, and at the same time it makes me feel weak by comparison.

All those kids who lost their lives before they had a chance to have what I had—all those parents who find a way to move on with daily lives while their children fight a war—all those parents and spouses who have to find a way forward after losing a loved one. Like I said, it makes me feel weak. In a way it makes me feel greedy—I got 28 wonderful years with Shannon, and I grieve about not having more. There are probably kids in that class of 1986 who didn't get 28 years of life. There are parents who had to bury their children before they found a soul mate, before they got to raise kids. I wonder how they found their way back in to the light.

October 28

10:05 a.m.

First and before I forget—I am sorry for typos. I do know how to spell reindeer, and I do know the difference between there and their. I blame it on blurry vision or being tired or getting to the point where I just have to push "post" and move forward.

It is great to not feel so alone. This morning we heard a great speaker—a professor here named Colonel Bernie Banks. West Point grad, MBA from Kellogg, MPA from Harvard, PhD from Columbia. Plus distinguished military career. Let's just say he had a few insights on leadership. Great start to the day.

I am on a short break from the program and have another reminder of not being alone. Last night/this morning, I heard from a student from many years ago. He is one of several West Point alums I have had the pleasure of getting to know during my years at Tech. He answered my question from last night. Here is what has happened to the West Point class of '86:

> *21 members of that class are now deceased, 2 of them as a result of 9/11 and the subsequent Long War. In fact, one of the two, Douglas Gurian, died as a civilian working in one of the World Trade Center towers, and the most recent death was Colonel John McHugh, who died of his wounds on May 18 of last year in Kabul, Afghanistan, when a suicide bomber steered his explosives-laden Toyota minibus into a convoy he was in as it moved through rush-hour traffic. 17 other soldiers and civilians were killed along with another 48 wounded.*

I thank them for their service to our country. I know their families are incredibly proud of them and that they miss them terribly. I wish their families peace.

Colonel Banks tried to claim that he was just an ordinary guy. I told him that was the only thing he said that I had to completely disagree with. There may be "average" students at West Point in terms of class standing, but no one here is an ordinary person. The kids who come here are special—and there is no doubt but that this is a transformational place that makes them even more precious—and I hope the families of the class of '86 and every other class always are proud knowing that, too.

8:34 p.m.

Today was a beautiful and inspiring day at West Point. I heard some new stuff—I heard some old stuff in new ways—and I got lots of good ideas. Our group spent time with Bob McDonald, CEO of Procter & Gamble. Good stuff—what a "normal" guy—West Point graduate—great leadership stories.

Fall

I am on the plane now back to Atlanta. A lot of what we talked about the last couple of days was about commitment and purpose. The focus was on work and employer-employee relationships, but it is impossible to not see the parallels.

There is a lot I need to process, but one thing struck me the most— the importance of purpose. That is something you have all heard me struggle with over the past several weeks. Bob McDonald asked us, "If you were to die today, would you be able to say you had served your purpose?" Immediately I thought about Shannon. I am convinced that she would say "yes" if the question were asked of her. She made it through college, she found me, she supported me through graduate school, she had two kids who are going to be positive forces on the world because of her love, she made me a safe home. She took some of my unnecessary rough edges off; she helped me feel safe, appreciated, and loved. She made it so I could do what I had to do to support our family. She provided me with my purpose. With Reid off to school, I think she was in a struggle for a new purpose. Like I am now myself in a struggle for a new purpose. Perhaps that's another piece of context that helps me feel less sad for Shannon. But on the other hand, it seems she deserved a time where purpose meant to explore, to have adventures, to learn, to travel. She missed out on that. She didn't just miss out—she got screwed out of it.

Over the course of the last couple of days, I spent a lot of time thinking about my purpose—my new purpose, I suppose. One purpose is to use Shannon's death to make others more safe and better cared for than they are today. I am on that, and it will happen although I realize it will be in some small measure. Another purpose is to continue to support the boys and to do what I can to help the rest of my family.

Most of the "purpose" conversation at the meeting was around purpose at work and that the role purpose played in connecting people to work. I get a sense of purpose from my writing and consulting. I get a tremendous amount of purpose from my students. I like that part of my job so much. I don't get much purpose from Tech anymore. That's been true for a while now. I am proud to be an alum,

I really like my colleagues, but take away students, and there is no purpose there anymore. That's something to look at.

Understanding a new purpose is going to be an important part of finding how to move forward. The problem is that I don't want to let go of my old purpose. I loved Shannon and I loved having Shannon to take care of and I loved having Shannon to take care of me. You have no idea how much I dread the first night sick alone in this house. It will happen, and it will be a terrible couple of days. No way around it. I am almost always listening to music—right now, because the guy next to me snores like a freakin' earthquake, and there are two "consultants" who won't shut up across the aisle. I digress. One of my all-time favorite artists in the "under appreciated" category is Taj Mahal. Check him out. His song, "Lovin' in my Baby's Eyes" just came on the iPod, and it fits what I am feeling tonight and every night—and the whole purpose problem. Simple little song and simply true.

I love you, Shannon. I miss you, and I still need you. I wish you didn't have to go. Just me and one baby a few rows back crying on this plane.

October 29

> 3:30 p.m.

Today is passing quickly—thanks in part to a very late start. In bed at 3, up at the crack of 10:30. Felt pretty good, actually.

Last night, the College had a homecoming event for MBA students. (BTW, is Tech the only school that schedules homecoming around a game where they are probably 45-point underdogs?) I was pretty sure it would have wound down by the time my plane landed, etc., but I was determined to stop by. I did pretty much get there at "last call," but I was still able to see some people and then found my way to the after-party at a nearby bar. It was great to see people I hadn't seen in a while, and I was happy for the folks who put the event on that the turnout was pretty strong.

Ran errands this morning—cleaners, broken suitcase to be repaired, need a new winter coat—that sort of mundane stuff. I found myself in a rush at Jos. A. Banks—trying to get done. Then three thoughts came into my head in quick succession:

I am rushing because I think I am missing time with Shannon who is waiting at home for us to have lunch.

I don't have to rush home (sad)—but Shannon is as "with me" here at Jos. A. Banks as she is "with me" at home (less sad, almost comforting).

Point (2) is sort of like someone saying, "Don't worry, no matter where you are in the world you will always have half as much oxygen as you need to survive." (Crippling may be a bit of hyperbole...but not by much.)

So having realized I was not in a rush—and because it is a sunny day—I decided to drive around a bit. I also ate lunch at a Chinese place. I am doing that a lot—Shannon had sort of been off Chinese food for a while. It was the one thing she could NOT eat when she was pregnant with Spencer. In fact, it is part of how she "detected" we were expecting Reid. And then recently she just couldn't eat it. So I am catching up.

I feel like I am going to have to start some sort of Michael Franti fan club or nominate him for sainthood or something. I have mentioned many times how his music is just somehow working for me. I like all his albums, but the most recent one is the one I listen to the most (*Sound of Sunshine*).

Almost every song on there makes me feel Shannon's death. And when I say feel it what I mean is that I experience it in some deep way—that way isn't good or bad consistently—sometimes I grin and sometimes I tear up. I suppose what I am feeling is that it is my heart that is remembering her and not my head. Maybe that is the best way to explain it.

Here are just some examples. It's reggae—it isn't complicated—it isn't deep—but it is real to me. One of the songs is called "Say Hey." Franti makes two great points. First, that no matter how mysterious the world or our place in it seems, true love can be a foundation. That matters to me because that I loved Shannon and she loved me was one thought that was never in doubt. It didn't matter what happened in a day—or what didn't happen. I never got confused about that or about what it meant.

The second point he makes is how at the same time you can be so surprised and so certain about love—the whole "first sight" thing.

Those lyrics matter to me because I remember the moment I knew about Shannon. We had met before—she wasn't impressed. She was a little sister in our fraternity. I was not very active in the fraternity— I worked weekends because that's when the money was to be made. I had lots of friends in the fraternity—but I was there mostly to eat lunch, watch *All My Children* (it was big), and park close to campus. I didn't go to many socials or tailgates. And I suppose at 21 or so the correlation between being obnoxious and having fun was strong and positive. I remember the story of our first meeting as Shannon recounts it, but I think she may have jazzed it up a bit to make me look even more ludicrous, and I don't want to repeat such gossip here.

Anyway, months later Shannon took a job at the Chart House Restaurant—my second fraternity, basically—as a hostess. I remember it was a Saturday, and I was the closing bartender. This meant I didn't have to get there until a bit late—maybe seven or something. As I came up the stairs, there she was at the hostess stand. She was wearing a blue-and-white-striped dress. She wore her hair longer then, and it was curled. She was smiling. I saw her and I knew. And I am not talking about love at first sight—I think if you fall in love at first sight, you are really underestimating what love is. It wasn't love then—it was a deep awareness that somehow

I had to have her in my life and to get to know her and to see what happened next. A couple of weeks later we had our towing station first kiss. And then I knew I had to have that smile to look at for the rest of my life. That just had to happen.

That was the song about then, this is the song about now. Michael Franti gets it. Another song on that same album is called "Hey, Hey, Hey." Remember—it's reggae—it isn't complicated. It is my "now" song. He sings about just trying to hold on. I am trying to hold on.

Finally, he has the song that kills me every time. All you need to know is the title. You should listen to it though—it's called "The Only Thing Missing Was You." That relevance shouldn't need explanation, either.

I went online to do some research on Franti, and I saw an interview where he explained how he wrote this album after a hospital stay where he nearly died. He had appendicitis and apparently by the time it got figured out, he was in really bad shape. So he was in a place where he was hopeful after being hurt and scared. I suppose that is why it seems so true to me.

October 30

11:42 a.m.

I have been trying to catch up on e-mail from the week. Lots of perfect sentiments—but one thing struck me. A friend who has known me since Tulane said: "I realized I never knew you without Shannon in your life." I have been thinking a lot about that. I don't remember a whole lot about me without Shannon in my life. What I would say with confidence is that if you know me from the time that Shannon was in my life then you have known a better me than I was before.

Shannon and I became engaged at a place in the New Orleans Garden District called The Versailles. It's been closed for some time, but back in the day it was one of the fine restaurants in New Orleans. I don't remember the date—Shannon would—but it was sometime in the late summer or early fall of 1984.

I had picked out a ring. I think it cost about $800, which didn't buy a whole lot in terms of diamonds—but $800 was also four months' rent. I am pretty sure the monthly payment was $28. We had a great dinner. Shannon had to know what was coming, so I don't think I really surprised her. I am glad she said yes. We thought we were being so discreet about the whole thing, and we blushed when as we were leaving three different tables told us "Congratulations!" We went to her apartment, and she spent forever on the phone calling each of her friends, her parents, telling them the whole story, describing the ring, and all that.

A few years later, we went to New Orleans for an anniversary. I don't know which one (Shannon would!). Spencer wasn't born yet—I think it was maybe our third, and I think a convention is what actually brought us to New Orleans. Anyway, I made reservations for The Versailles for dinner. Shannon was so sick that day so she stayed in bed. She wanted to go to dinner so badly, but felt so terrible. I called the restaurant and changed our 7:00 reservation to 8:00...later I changed the 8:00 reservation to 9:00...she kept hoping that just a little more rest and she would feel well enough to go.

She got up and got ready, and we went for the 9:00 time. It was a weekday night. We were the only table in the restaurant—there may not have been a table there for some time. The host, the wine steward, several bus boys, the waiter, the kitchen crew—they were all there, and we were treated like royalty. They knew they had a table at 9, and they were ready for us. Shannon ordered the bouillabaisse— it was a signature dish there. She felt that it cured her. We had a wonderful dinner, and I was so impressed with the place that they would do that for us. That was a great night.

So I am trying to practice the sort of kindness Shannon would want me to demonstrate. I was in the car from West Point to the Newark airport for a long time Friday—it took two and a half hours to go 50 miles. Needless to say, I got to know the driver. A character—but that's all they have in New York, right? The trip and gratuity and all were set up to be billed—no need for a cash transaction. But during the drive he took a call from his wife and explained that he was going to be home late because of this traffic. From what he said, I could tell she was asking him to go to the store on the way home. So when we got to the airport, I gave him some cash and told him to please use it to buy his wife some flowers from the store. He promised he would.

I hope he did it. I'd like to think that helped her day and put a smile on her face. I really miss the chance to make Shannon smile. How does something so simple and small leave a hole that is so big and impossible to fill?

10:07 p.m.

Today, Sunday, was quite a day. I realized last week that many of my Monday night students have kids—and tomorrow is Halloween. I told them that I had no shortage of time on my hands and would do a version of the class today for anyone that wanted to be able to stay home for trick or treat and not come on Monday. So I had about 40 for class today. Then two exec ed program kickoffs—one in Buckhead and one at Tech—and then the Stephen Stills show.

As to Stephen Stills—this was the last show that Shannon and I had tickets to. I did the date as faithfully as I could. I went to Serpas and had the stuff we always ordered before a show. I went to the show and got a PBR that we would have split. I listened for a while and was sure to leave before he played "Love the One You're With." Not a great song to hear when you "love the one you're without." It was nice to be there and to hear some live music and to see so many people having a good time.

One sort of random but important thought—some people have asked if I get jealous when I see happy couples. I do a little, but what really is hard is seeing proud moms with their sons. Someday I might have a date that I can try to make smile. But my boys are missing out on something that I can't offer and it isn't fair. Just another problem I am powerless to fix. They are never going to have another mom. The fact I can't fix that makes me very frustrated. I can't get them ever again the feeling of "making mom proud."

As I think about it, that might be the very worst part of the future. It's probably true that they got as big a thrill out of putting a smile on Shannon's face as I did. They aren't going to have that chance again either.

I have been adjusting medicine—with doctor approval, I promise. I have found the combination that seems to do the trick. When I get really close to Shannon, it still hurts. But most of the time I can find a way to be okay. Being okay is good—I have to work and function and all that, but it made me wonder if the not feeling pain is somehow cheating. I feel guilty if I don't hurt. I am supposed to hurt.

That made me think of Spencer's birth. Another irony—Spencer was born about 200 yards from where Shannon died. I used to love to drive across Interstate 285 and think: "That's where Spencer was born!" Now when I have to drive there I think: "That's where Shannon died."

Anyway, I remember Shannon's water broke around 2 in the morning. She woke me up and off to Northside Hospital we went—but not until after she showered and shaved her legs. Spencer wasn't born until 6:48 that night—Shannon had a long and difficult labor. In the end, Spencer actually was showing signs of distress, and they had the OR ready—this was the "last push" to see if he would come out. His shoulder was caught on her pubic bone. Two nurses had climbed more or less on top of Shannon to push Spencer down to see if they could dislodge him. He made it out on that last push. I remember now how the doctor and 3 nurses stayed long after their shift—they said they were not leaving Shannon until the baby came. Maybe nurses do this stuff all the time, but I would like to think they did it because they knew how much Shannon appreciated them. Maybe they do it all the time because lots of patients are appreciative of the work they do. That'd be okay, too.

I did have a point here—I promise. At one point around 9 in the morning I was trying to comfort Shannon through contractions. She hit one—it was a hard labor—and I was sitting next to her being pretty useless—the guy role. She had a hold on me by both my ears and was basically shaking my head back and forth through the contraction. At that moment the doctor came in, saw what was happening, and said to the nurse, "She looks rather uncomfortable, let's get her the epidural." They left, and I said to Shannon—who had finally let go of my ears—"YOU look uncomfortable—what about me!" She smiled.

Shannon got her epidural, and she didn't have to feel ALL the pain of delivering Spencer. Some women think, I guess, that the pain is part of the process—and an important part. I can respect that, but Shannon and I felt that the pain was something to get past to focus on the important process—teaching a child to love and to live.

I suppose I should not feel bad that there are pills that make my pain less severe. I don't think a mom should feel guilty because she somehow didn't "hurt enough" when having her baby. I suppose I shouldn't feel like I loved Shannon less because the sight of her nightgown doesn't disable me like it did a couple of weeks ago. But sometimes I do. On the one hand, I know Shannon never wanted me to hurt. On the other hand, I don't want anyone to ever think that this has not been devastating. Do not try this at home.

October 31

Monday is the two-month anniversary of Shannon's collapse—the anniversary I am observing. I expect to spend some time over the next few days reflecting on what has happened and what I have learned in those two months. Not ready to write about that yet. I can say that the longest I ever had to do without Shannon was about four days—I was in Moscow and didn't have a way to be in much touch. I still can't believe I lost her. But I did.

I had to pack my own suitcase for West Point—haven't done that in a while. I did have to pack to take Reid back to school, but that was just tossing some jeans and polo shirts in a bag. This trip required dress clothes, etc. I can't do it nearly as well as Shannon could—but I think I managed. It reminded me that back when we were first married I was traveling a lot. I would set out clothes, Shannon would pack them, she would harass me about whatever I forgot. When I got to my destination and unpacked, I would find a card she snuck in. Just something silly and sweet—an unexpected kindness that made me feel good and miss her a little less. She took good care of me.

When I think back on our time together, one thing that strikes me is how much more I miss the little things—like the card in my bag—those are such good memories. I suppose the "big stuff" we expect from our spouse as part of the deal of being married. The little stuff is so clearly discretionary—and the fact that it gets done makes it—the little stuff—more special than the big stuff. That is how it feels, anyway. So that's my recommendation—do some little stuff for someone tomorrow. Make one of those little things a habit. You will make someone grateful forever. For as long as I live, I'll never unpack a suitcase and not think fondly about how sweet Shannon was to me.

I learned at dinner and the concert last night that I am definitely going to have my patience tested with this being alone. When being alone is a choice for a night it isn't bad—in fact, it can provide some comfort. When being alone is just a reality, it isn't very comfortable. I was talking to a friend today about it—it's clear I am not in any position to be anyone's company, and I am not very happy being alone. I miss sharing things with someone special. Someone special isn't going to happen soon, and it might never happen. So that's the next struggle. And I have to be able to handle it for as long as it takes. Right now, that is my big fear.

I have a lot to say for someone who didn't have much to say. A last thought I am trying to work through. Lots of people encourage me by saying some version of "you should do what Shannon would want" or "Shannon wouldn't want you to be miserable" or something similar. I agree—she wouldn't. I promise you that she would feel miserable if she knew how miserable I felt. She would do anything to be un-dead if she knew how badly I hurt.

That made me think about what exactly I did that made Shannon proud. I can't answer that for certain. She wasn't impressed with any work accomplishment. She was worried about how I felt. She didn't care what I did as long as I felt good about doing it. I think that is amazing. When, for example, I was happy to have a book published, she didn't care about the book—she cared that I was happy. So although I am thinking that I am supposed to throw myself in to finishing the book number three project to make Shannon proud, I realize she doesn't care about book number three. She cares if I am happy. What I do isn't important to here; how I feel is.

I have invited my MBA students to come over for gumbo and red beans a week from Sunday—the Saints play the Falcons. Should be a fun game and it will be nice to have a house full of good people. Spencer may help cook…and I think the Thanksgiving for Thanksgiving orphans is on for the 20th or 21st. Those are two events to look forward to.

November 1

The neighborhood moms are gathering in the pool parking lot across the street waiting on the elementary school bus to pick up their kids. Our neighborhood isn't that big...but I guess the kids are little to do too much finding their way home.

When Spencer was in middle school, he was really, really hard to get up in the morning. We tried everything—alarm clocks that run around the room, alarm clocks that shake the bed, yelling, squirt guns, rewards, you name it. It was a struggle every single morning. He is a night person—has been since he was a baby. Shannon would go to sleep around 9 and Spencer and I would stay up and watch Letterman, SportsCenter, whatever until around 2. Then he would sleep.

One morning Spencer missed the bus because he couldn't get up. Shannon told him she wasn't taking him to school and that he should call a taxi. He was so pissed. He said he didn't know the number of the taxi. Shannon tossed him the phone book and said, "You know the alphabet—you can find it." He was so pissed. He called a taxi. Shannon asked him how he was going to pay. He trudged to his room to get money. He was so pissed. The taxi came. He was so pissed. Shannon called the school to explain what was happening just in case they became too worried. Shannon got in the car and followed the taxi at a distance just to make sure Spencer got to school safely. Spencer got out of the taxi and went off to school. He had a bunch of kids say, "Hey—I didn't know your dad drove a taxi!" They just figured I dropped him at school on my way to work.

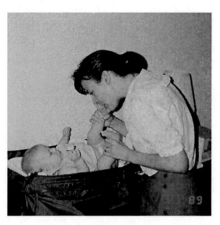

Shannon came home. Spencer never missed the bus again. Sometimes she struggled to find the right thing to do with these big, loud, stubborn kids of ours. But sometimes she nailed it. And she never quit trying. The picture is Shannon with Spencer at 3 months—the week before we moved to Baton Rouge. They are both cuties.

9:34 p.m.

Met this morning with lawyer, financial advisor, and accountant. We made all these connections—at Shannon's insistence—so that if something happened to me there would be people who could help her. Instead we are all together so they can help me. In a way, there isn't that much that needs to be changed. I am worried that if I died tomorrow the boys are still a bit too young to inherit what we have. So we are coming up with a plan that will be good for a few years. Then I will need to make a plan that is the "now the kids are out of school and adults" plan.

Shannon wanted to be ready for a long disability—and because of her mitochondrial diagnosis she was denied all sorts of insurance coverage. Our plan was to have to fund this out of pocket—should it come to pass. The good news is that our current saving plan involves saving a lot of money that Shannon won't need. I could save less and have more now— but more money is not what I want now. For now I will keep saving it.

On Sunday night, a student stayed behind to ask a couple of questions. We got to talking and the Stephen Stills concert came up as my next destination. She said, no kidding, "Who is Stephen Stills?" Wow—immediate flash to the Steely Dan song "Hey Nineteen." I have reached that age.

After explaining the significance of Stephen Stills to her, I told her I had extra tickets and that she and her boyfriend should go. She took the tickets.

While I was at the show, I got ane-mail from her explaining that on their way in, a couple was desperately looking for tickets. They said "none for sale" initially, but when they saw the sadness in the couple's eyes, she said they thought Shannon would want someone who really appreciated the show to see it—so they sold them the tickets.

She went on to explain that she wanted to give me the money—or if I wouldn't take it to use it to get pizza for the class or something. I told her that what Shannon would really like is if she and her boyfriend used the money to have a great date—so that she should keep the money and do that. She said that her boyfriend is pretty good at finding great dates—so she is going to give the money to the Mitochondrial Disease Foundation in Shannon's name. What a great kid. I know she should probably be referred to as a young woman...but if you don't know who Stephen Stills is, you are a kid!

So that's a story with lots of happy endings—the people who got to see a show they really wanted to see. My student did a great thing for Shannon. Good stuff.

And—how can your day be bad when you get a note like this one below. Frankly, I think the author is misguided...truly. The e-mail is from a former student...

> ...I took your organizational behavior class...it was a class that I expected to be incredibly boring and preachy, but was anything but. The class was inspirational, exciting, and useful, and you're the best instructor I've had at Georgia Tech (that includes my years as an undergrad here).

So as a wise guy, my first response is that it is a great example of the "power of low expectations." But my real response is a simple "thank you." People in the MBA program have to take my class—it is required, and I have been the only one teaching it for years. I am honored by the chance to do the job—and I am glad they show up week after week. I know I am not everyone's cup of tea as a professor—but I am glad it works for some.

It makes me sad that I have started to let people know about my plans to leave Tech for Georgia State. I will really miss the MBA students at Tech. They are good people, hard workers, and I will always vouch for them. Quick story—When I pass back exams at Tech, students e-mail me to let me know I made a math mistake. And it isn't that I gave them too few points—it is that I gave them too many. They are letting me know that I need to lower their score in my grade book. You should know that I always manage to forget to do that. I am so forgetful.

If you ever have to choose between a Tech kid and any other kid—take the Tech kid.

November 2

10:11 p.m.

Last summer, one of the wonderful trips Shannon and I had was to Napa to "celebrate" my 50th birthday. Control freak that I am, Shannon put me in charge of planning my "surprise." It turned out great. I am thinking about it today because the first shipment of wine that we ordered out there arrived today. I don't have to tell you how much I am going to miss sharing it with Shannon. I'll think of her each time I open a bottle. But I think about her when I do most anything.

The trip out there was with our friends, Wayne & Ginny. Wayne was the best man at our wedding—I've known him a long time. Ginny and I have the same birthday, so every few years we have celebrated together. We did a great trip to New Orleans. One year we went to Dallas and saw Eric Clapton. This past summer it was Napa. I am going to miss those trips—but I don't think friends need me to tag along on a birthday celebration!

The wine trip made me think of Wayne—and Wayne made me think of Shannon's death. Many of you met him—he was one of the many people who dropped everything to come help us. I am fortunate to have so many friends like that. The crew of people I met in the early 1980s still contains my closest friends. Even people I see once every five years at a Jazz Fest I bet would do about anything for me if I called. I know I would do anything for them. When Shannon collapsed, one of this group drove from Denver to Boulder to get Reid and take him to the airport to get him home to Atlanta. Another friend hosted a wonderful dinner for everyone the night before the service at a restaurant here in town. It goes on and on. It's a bit of hyperbole, but I was surrounded by people who for two weeks did nothing but throw themselves on figurative grenades to try to protect Shannon, me, and the boys. Thank you all for that.

I really, really hope that Spencer and Reid are so lucky to make friends as true as the ones I made when I was their age.

I was thinking about the service today. I felt a strange comfort by the fact that the overlap between the attendance at our wedding and the attendance at Shannon's service was so high. Somehow it feels good to know that nearly everyone who saw our marriage start was there to see it finish. I am glad to have kept all those people in our lives.

The afternoon when we all knew Shannon was going to die, my "pit crew" decided that since Spencer was with his girlfriend and okay that I should spend some time with Reid—who was otherwise alone and not that interested in being at the hospital. So one of my best friends and I took Reid for some lunch at a sports bar near the hospital. It was

133

as good a time as could be expected. As we were leaving, I got a text message from Wayne saying that Shannon seemed to be slipping away and that we should get back. Reid took my car and headed off to see his friends; my friend drove me back to the hospital as fast as we could.

As I rushed in, I was running to the elevator at the same time the on-duty clergy person was running to the elevator. I knew Shannon was dead and that I hadn't made it back in time. We rode up together, and she confirmed what I suspected. I got to the room as fast as I could. Wayne was with her when she died, not me. I think he felt terrible that I couldn't be there. In a way, I do—but the bigger feeling I have is that I had lost Shannon already 11 days earlier—and that she would have wanted me to be trying to help Reid. There wasn't anything I could do for her. We had spent the entire previous night together holding hands and talking. So we were okay. And an equally big feeling is that I know Shannon was with someone who cared about her deeply.

I know this likely sounds weird, but if you have friends dear enough that you trust them to stay with your wife as she dies then you have really good friends. And I have a few dozen people like that who have been with Shannon and me for over 30 years. That makes me lucky.

From: Nathan Bennett
Date: Wed, 2 Nov 2011 09:03:18-0400
To: "mbalists"
Subject: Thanks

Class,

I would much prefer the chance to thank each of you in person, but that is clearly impractical. I actually have a lot to thank you for, but this particular thanks is for your thoughtfulness, kindness, and generosity during Shannon's hospitalization and since her death.

I knew all about the wonderful food that was arranged for us—and for frankly the entire nursing team at St. Joseph's ICU—Shannon had a well-fed army looking out for her, and as OB veterans I know you all know how important that is. I also knew about those of you who came by to sit with us a bit. And I also knew about your patience with me as I figured out how to get back to work—and with my colleagues as they jumped in to try to keep courses moving forward.

I recently learned about your generous gift to the United Mitochondrial Disease Foundation. Mitochondrial disease is really rare and not well understood—your contribution will no doubt help lots of families down the road. Shannon would be embarrassed by and grateful for your contribution. I'm just proud of all of you. You make this a great community and I am lucky to be part of it.

Thank you!

November 3

9:17 p.m.

It's been a very busy week, but there are some thoughts I'd like to share. First is that I have had three decent days in a row. A "decent" day is one where I can get some stuff done, I can behave like an adult in public, and I can do my job duties basically okay. It is a day where my head wins over my heart. I think the medicine has a lot to do with that. I do think the help and support I get from people helps with that, too. But what I miss is feeling with my heart. How is that for something? I want to complain about feeling too deeply, and I also want to complain for feeling nothing. I feel detached from emotion most all the time. So I hurt less about Shannon—but that is replaced with nothingness. I suppose for now that is okay, but I do miss knowing I have a heart.

Second, today the professional organizer that I hired came over. I am optimistic she is going to be of great assistance—there are things she will take on for me, and there are things that will be easier if I am scheduled to do them.

We took on two projects. We cleaned the pantry. Finally got rid of the cornstarch that was best if used before 2005. It's a job Shannon and I talked about but we always found something we'd rather be doing. The food in my pantry is now commensurate with the number of people living here—and his palate. I will never need to buy mustard again. She brought a bunch of food to Must Ministries here in Marietta and the trash is, well, in the trash. That felt good.

Next, we took on the bathroom. Boy, do women have lots of products. The stuff that was usable went to Must Ministries. I also sent them a ton of towels. I think there were about 40 washcloths—most brand-new—in a drawer. Must have been a sale at Costco. You don't want to know how long I could make that last before washing any of them. The stuff that would not really pass on quality we threw out. I saved Shannon's soap—it smells good and sometimes it's nice to remember her that way. I also kept her hair dryer rigged to the wall for her post-surgery "no, I don't need your help, Nate" hair-drying technique. I somehow like seeing that. Some things just remind me she is gone—but this reminds me she is gone and was a beautiful, selfless, and clever person. That feels good.

Finally, in cleaning up we were very careful to keep an eye out for jewelry. She has it stashed everywhere—and not where you might think. I found, for example, 43 cents in a felt robin's egg blue pouch from Tiffany—but no jewelry.

In about 1992 or so, the Associate Dean at LSU came in to my office and said, "Get your passport—you are taking the EMBA students to Europe." I was excited. Only later did I realize this was not entirely an honor! A few people before me said "no"...My mom and Shannon's folks each took a shift taking care of Spencer, and Shannon and I went. I have great memories of the trip. First, in Lucerne, Switzerland, Shannon and I went out to dinner. After, we waited for the bus back to the hotel. It came. It stopped. The doors didn't open. It drove off. What the !#$@, we thought. So we took a cab. Found out the next day when the bus stops, there is a button on the outside of the bus we were supposed to push to open the door. Oh well. I am more considerate of confused people here as a result.

In Zurich, I bought Shannon a watch that became one of her favorite things. My helper found it today in Shannon's drawer—a Bucherer nurse's watch. It is a fine watch, and it is meant to hang from a pendant or a chain, and it is built "upside down" so when you pick it up to look at it, it is right side up. Shannon really loved it and wore it for years. When kids got older and time mattered less, she wore it less. But for me it is so "her" that I am going to keep it. I think I might even get a little chain and box to display it in.

My second great memory is of a night in Munich. I talked to the concierge at the hotel, and he got me two tickets—front row—to the Munich Symphony—they were playing Tchaikovsky. I was very excited. Shannon was too tired and wanted to stay in. We have always been good about letting each other do what we wanted—so I went to the show with one of the EMBA students, and Shannon stayed in at the hotel. The concert was amazing—the conductor actually sweated on me—I was that close. I came back to the room and found Shannon. She was in bed in pajamas—too cute—watching sumo wrestling with German announcers and eating room service. Too funny. She said it was her favorite night in Germany. I loved that we could be together or be apart—but end the night together with great stories. She never held me back, and I hope I never held her back.

A few weeks ago I wrote about being in Boulder and imagining Shannon with her tea relaxing until it was time to pack. So I found this picture of Shannon in San Francisco with her tea relaxing until it was time to pack. When I look at it, I can feel my heart. So that is why I am sharing it with you—even though she would be embarrassed for you to see her so early in the morning.

November 5

Some people have asked about my decision to move from Georgia Tech to Georgia State. I want to make sure no one thinks this is a rash PTSD decision—it wasn't. I began talking to them about a position last summer. I actually got a FedEx the day after Shannon collapsed with the formal job offer.

For those of you who don't know, GSU is a very big operation. It provides some different challenges and opportunities, and the job offers me a role in helping to make the place even stronger. They are building capacity in Buckhead, they are building a new school downtown, they are active in international campuses. The business school is one of the jewels on the campus where at Tech it is a bit in the shadows. And they value someone who cares a lot about teaching MBAs and EMBAs. They have a very good faculty, and their EMBA programs are very well regarded.

For the first part of my time at Tech I got to be part of a great ride upwards—I think the GSU job is going to provide a similar great ride. The decision was made before I lost Shannon—losing Shannon hasn't made the opportunity less intriguing. Although it has made my love for Tech and the people there more on the surface. So the thought of leaving has become much more bittersweet. But as I wrote in my book (that not enough people have bought), you need to take an opportunity seriously when it is something you feel like running to—those are probably better than the ones where a current job is something you are running from. I am not running away from Tech—I am running towards something where I can once again offer input, have impact, and add value.

Some random thoughts for you...

I keep getting e-mails from Ashley Green—she is from Norway and wants to meet me and be my special friend...I wonder if she knows the dude in Nigeria who wants my help getting money out of the country. Someone shoot me if I e-mail her back.

Widower shopping list: Cascade, trash bags, Rx, bank, milk, pretzel chips. You know the saddest thing about that list...that I have to write it down. I think that's the medicine.

Backing the car out of the garage last week, I caught the passenger side rearview mirror on the wall, and the mirror popped out of the housing. When I drive around, I look over there where Shannon used to sit and realize something's gone. I sort of don't want to get it fixed. It feels right that it's gone.

6:43 p.m.

I have that old Sam Cooke song ("Another Saturday Night") stuck in my head...the younger of you will know it as a Cat Stevens' song...and the even younger of you won't know what I am talking about! You can Google it. It is lonely here without Shannon. We would have had a good day today, and we would have had plans for something fun tomorrow. It's a pretty easy case to make that sitting here is less of a good time. It makes me very glad that the next two weekends—maybe actually the next three—will be pretty busy.

During the day I thought of several things I wanted to share, but I would rather write about them when my spirits are better. So for tonight I will have some supper, have a glass of wine from what Shannon and I ordered last summer, and I'll think about her. The picture is Shannon at Larkmead—a fascinating winery visit. I know I wrote a while ago that I panicked about forgetting her voice. I was thinking about that today. I remember absolutely everything about her. I have forgotten nothing. And that makes me happy, and it also really hurts. I know I can feel better, because I have. So hopefully I will again soon.

November 6

7:52 a.m.

When I was at the funeral home making Shannon's arrangements, the director explained to me that at some point down the road, I would be getting a survey from J. D. Power to evaluate their work. That survey came this week. I have to say I find that distasteful. Am I supposed to evaluate my wife's service like I would evaluate a new car or a new dishwasher? I filled it out—the people there were great, and I don't want them to get graded down. But I think it is tacky. On a scale of 1 to 10, how would you rate how your loved one looked in the casket? Really—I have to answer that? She looked shitty in the casket. She looked a lot better sitting here in our living room or across the table at a restaurant. It is a stupid thing to ask, yet I went along. I am not sure if I am more pissed they asked or that I answered.

And this week I got a check "to the estate of Shannon Bennett"—$350 from Discover. Her "cashback bonus." I mention this because they would not have sent me the money if I hadn't asked—so know you or someone you care about will have to be proactive on this stuff one day. They called me a couple of weeks ago because the Social Security Administration reports deaths—probably something they sell to credit card companies. So Discover called to make sure that Shannon really was dead. Then they asked me if I would like to have an account in my name. I said no. They were ready to hang up, and I asked about the cashback credit..."Oh, okay..." Got to love that "take care of the customer" attitude, Discover. Screw you.

I promise this won't be such an angry note. Sorry about that. Weekends are just bad—they are the days where Shannon being gone is just so obvious—for so long. It makes me worry a bit about spring because I won't be teaching a regular schedule. I need to find a way to make sure I am busy.

Right now I have 8 pounds of red beans on the stove. Getting ready for the MBA game-watching party next weekend—Saints versus Falcons. Should be fun. Gumbo still to fix, but that is for another night. House smells good.

Plans to go to dinner with Spencer on Tuesday; I am obviously looking forward to that. Reid gave me a one word text reply to a question and then disappeared again...I hope I'll hear from him later. It is hard—texting lets you invade your kids too much. If he'd call once a week, I wouldn't feel the need to text...who knows.

Listening to Dave Matthews today—the song "Jimi Thing" is supposedly about Jimi Hendrix and LSD. I think the lyrics sound exactly like me and my relationship to Xanax. Went for a walk—still not doing good on the cardio, so I wanted to do something. Halfway around the neighborhood, the James Taylor song "Something in the Way She Moves" came on. I think the lyrics to that song come really close to how I felt about Shannon. Happily for James, he is singing about someone who is with him nearly "all the time now." My someone is past tense. Still a sweet song. So I mention halfway on the walk because I really didn't want to cry—and there was no short way home if I did!

Back to Dave Matthews...we went to see him at Philips Arena this past year. I had to teach, so I wasn't going to be able to go until 9:30 or so. I asked Shannon if she just wanted to meet me at Tech and then go over together. She said, "Isn't Trombone Shorty opening?" I forgot her secret crush on him. So we made plans for her to go to the show to catch Trombone Shorty, and I was to head over after class.

I got to the show just a few minutes before Dave Matthews started. There was Shannon, sitting quietly with her Coke, reading some trashy book on her iPad. Next to her was my seat; next to my seat was some middle-aged guy. He looked grumpy. After the show, Shannon explained that the guy next to me was paying a lot of attention to her during Trombone Shorty. He was another five trying to get the attention of a 10. Sadly for him, he was 26 years too late. I don't blame him for looking grumpy. He missed out on something great.

So—like I promised—not too sad, not too angry. Hopeful about the week; hopeful next weekend won't involve quite the same decline as this one did. Most of all, I hope a path forward begins to clear. There was nothing to do this weekend that felt like that—and that is just hard for me.

November 7

> 7:41 a.m.

Today marks two months since Shannon's collapse. The date I am observing as the day I lost the best friend I ever had—and that is saying something because I have amazing friends.

Over the two months there is less and less I need to do because of Shannon's death. I miss having things to do because those things were of service to her. And I miss being of service to her. And those things provided some comfort because they allowed me to hide in my sorrow and to focus on what happened in the past.

So as those things resolve, I now have to turn my efforts to the future Shannon would want me to have—and frankly that I want to have. Grieving interrupted by work is not sustainable for me. She knew me better than I know me, so it would be great to have her help in figuring out what that means. I get parts of it—but there are lots of uncertainties, too.

Sunny day, classes to teach, students to visit, time to remember Shannon, time to think about what I am supposed to do now. I hope it will be a good day.

8:22 a.m.

Ironic story in the Atlanta paper today. It turns out one of the sons of the Atlanta Braves GM is a student athlete at Tech and has mitochondrial disease. I am going to reach out to the young man.

November 8

8:42 a.m.

So now it has been two months. Someone who had been through something like this explained to me early on that it had felt like to them that they were going through life wearing one of those lead aprons the dentist puts on you during x-rays. I think that is about right. I am really tired. But moving is better than sleeping or lying around. Lying around feels like defeat, and I don't want to be defeated.

I have been working on trying to put some deep thoughts together— yesterday being a milestone of sorts—but things aren't quite falling in place. So I guess I am about to write something else instead...

I have been thinking a lot about the holidays coming up. Not too excited, to tell you the truth. I am very glad to see the boys—but it isn't like we are "celebrating."

Shannon used to complain about how hard I was to shop for at the holidays. She never accepted that I really didn't want anything I didn't have already. I had a different problem—when I bought her something I couldn't wait for the holiday to give it to her. So she started getting Christmas gifts in November. With the kids, we had a different problem— we would buy stuff, hide it, and then not remember where we hid it. I am sure that somewhere as I clean out the house, I will find a Nerf gun or a video game or something.

Anyway, one year when she was complaining about how there was nothing to get me, I told her that all I wanted was a list from each boy of their favorite memories of things I did with them. Reid was probably a freshman in high school, and Spencer would have been a freshman in college. I have them right here—and it is the best present I ever got. It might be a neat thing for you to do for a parent—or to ask for. The boys were supposed to present it (according to Shannon) in some "nice" form. Reid's is torn out of a spiral notebook; Spencer's is on a piece of construction paper—I guess he took the idea a bit more formally.

Here is Spencer's list:

> College search road trip; seeing the Bruins play in Montreal; walking around Boston in the snow; leaving UNH and UMass early because they sucked
> Spring break lacrosse trip to see Johns Hopkins play Duke and Navy play Maryland
> Youth hockey road trips; early morning drives to the rink; everything about Baton Rouge Youth Ice Hockey
> Late night walks around New York City when we would go for Thanksgiving
> Being your little chef

Here is Reid's list:

> Going to California to see Manchester United play...
> [he included a drawing of the famous "Randy's Donuts" place we went to]

Running away from the alligator at the Louisiana rest stop
[true—we had to escape—long story]
Crawfish boils at the house
Watching the World Cup on the big screens at Georgia Tech
Going to 6 Flags with you to celebrate Father's Day

They are great lists. Shannon didn't give me one—I didn't ask. I wonder what would be on it though. Sort of wish I had asked. This would be mine for her.

Watching her be an amazing mom
The way she always made me feel safe and never alone
Her selflessness
Her spirit of adventure that made it possible for us to do anything we wanted—combined with her contentment that made it possible for us to do nothing at all
Hugs

That's it.

8:46 p.m.

Thankful for a couple of better days. One grumpy realization I have is that I am so tired of the term "bittersweet"—not from others, from inside my own head. All these memories and reminders and thoughts and events are bittersweet. Bittersweet is just a euphemism for "sucks."

That aside, I had a chance to have a "real" conversation with Reid last night. He sounded like Reid. I got a chance to give some parental advice that I think actually helped him. I told him I loved talking to him but that I was worried about overparenting. Good kid that he is, he said, basically, "Dad, call as much as you want...if I can't or don't want to talk to you, I won't answer." They've had a little snow in town; he says school is keeping him busy; some fraternities are doing a spring rush, and he is trying to decide if he wants to be part of it. He missed it during the fall because of Shannon's death; he isn't sure he wants to be in a fraternity, but he wants to check it out.

Busy day tomorrow. Class in the p.m., electrician in the a.m. to install some recessed lights to make the living room more inviting—it's always been kind of dark. Computer guy coming in a.m. to help me pull stuff off Shannon's computer. Helper coming over to deal with Shannon's art room and whatever else is next on the list. Tomorrow night or Thursday I have a lot of gumbo to cook for the MBA party at the house Sunday. So lots to do.

Still think about Shannon endlessly. Even though I have come to understand why she is gone—and even though I have some peace that in a way she would be okay with being gone—it is hard to have her gone. Being in this situation makes the whole "make a deal with the devil" completely understandable. If someone could give me one dinner out with Shannon, they could get me to do just about anything.

I remember various times in my life when I had the realization that "it could be over any minute...you need to live each day like it could be your last so you don't have any regrets." That's not possible—it's an exhausting way to live. Unfortunately, it was over for Shannon and me in a minute. I am glad that somehow we lived in a way that I don't have regrets about anything other than time. I feel good about what we did with the time we had. I just wish we had more. 26 years isn't very long...until I think about what to do with my next 26. 26 years with a great girl goes by in a blink of an eye. The thought of 26 years alone sounds terrible—2 months has felt like an eternity.

On this point—last night on my way to my 6 p.m. class, I stopped to talk to a colleague. His class ends at 6, so we always cross paths in the hallway. He made a special point of telling me that he had been talking with a mutual friend who had been asking about me—he wanted me to know. I told him that I had been thinking about this mutual friend,

147

as well, and was glad he reminded me I needed to pull the trigger on finding a way to meet. A couple of hours later—while I was still in class—my colleague had an "event"—like Shannon's "event"—fell down some stairs, injured his head, and died in the ambulance on the way to Grady.

Shannon collapsed on September 7. My PhD student days' office mate had a stroke on his way to Tech on October 7. My colleague died on November 7. I really have had enough of this.

November 9

> 8:11 p.m.

Listening to Warren Haynes and Vusi Mahlasela sing "Soulshine." Great performance. If you don't know Mahlasela, check him out. Great story, very unique voice.

There are now three kinds of days. More accurately, there are three ways I feel. Most days have some amount of each. One way of feeling is hopeless, sad, and empty. That was Sunday. Another way of feeling is so busy that I get lost in whatever my activity is—it's like a vacation from hopeless, sad, and empty. That was Monday and Tuesday. It is a hard way to feel because it is more like I have forgotten my situation. It is good while it lasts, but when I finally "remember," I sort of crash. The third way of feeling is what I think the goal is—I am functioning, and Shannon is with me. That was today.

So the disc jockey knows I am writing about Shannon...the song now? Robert Randolph playing "Dry Bones." She was a sucker for slide guitar. We went to see him at the Buckhead Theater last winter. It was a hard night for Shannon—she stopped in the restroom, and I went ahead to grab seats. On her way to me, she took her eyes off the floor to find me, hit a step that is really poorly designed, and fell hard. She was so embarrassed, and she hurt. Her knee swelled up and later turned purple. But she wasn't going to miss the show. We treated it with scotch on the site to get her back in the game and then with ice at home. It was hard for Shannon because of the pain, but also because it was another assault on her confidence with her mitochondrial condition and her vision. She didn't have much downward gaze and to see me and take a step was basically a blind step.

The disc jockey really knows I am writing about Shannon—now Galactic. Great New Orleans band.

Progress this morning. Got more things packed up. Went through Shannon's office. Found some things she had written—it's going to be nice to read them one day soon. I know there will be some things there to share with you. I am going to have to be a bit stronger first. Found some sketches she had done. Really good—interesting. I am so disappointed that she wasn't more confident in her art. She would have done more of it if she had been. Worked on getting the computer files stored in the cloud and all that. Lights installed in the front room. Shannon would approve. Wish we had done it sooner.

The Audubon Institute e-mailed: Shannon's tree will be planted next week. I am going to try to shoot down there and watch them plant it. Then I am going to Dom's for an oyster po'boy. In fact, I may get it and bring it to eat under the tree. The tree isn't going to be tiny—but it may be optimistic to think I will really be eating "under" it. You get the point. One day. I have to think of the words for the commemorative plaque. Everything I think of sounds like a headstone and that isn't what this is. That's cool—I am excited about it. I am glad to have a place that anyone can go that is pretty and special to Shannon.

8:11 p.m.

I had a couple of conversations today with people who thanked me for what I was doing with this journal. I can't tell you how good that feels. It is a little hard to believe, though. I told one friend that (I need some poetic license here again) the writing was almost like putting out the trash. My head becomes full of thoughts; I have to purge it and set it out by the curb so I can move on. So you make me feel like a celebrity in Hollywood who has paparazzi going through the trash to look for something interesting! I don't entirely like the analogy—but at least it isn't depressing. My point is that this is a way for me to have a release—and you all add so much value to the process when you share that you have found something decent in it. In a way, you are offering me something like what my students do—every once in a while, someone shares that a point we discussed in class really helped them solve a problem at work or understand something that had been a mystery. It's a feeling I miss—to be helpful. So thanks.

I did reach out to the Tech student with Shannon's condition—he sent a really nice note back. I think between his dad's connections and the reaction to the article in the paper, he has all the support he needs. But I appreciated that he wrote back. He sounds like a super kid who doesn't deserve an obstacle. Just like Shannon.

November 10

3:54 p.m.

Today I am thinking about the best age to become a widower. The question came to mind because I found myself thinking that from where I stood, the grass was greener in every direction. I hate the self-pity—I really do. So I was trying to work my way through it to get past it. The widower book I read had stories of people of all ages—so that was my "data" for this analysis.

If I was younger, I might not have Spencer and Reid. Or I might be in a severe struggle to try to raise them right. Or I would have lots of mobility restrictions. But if I was younger I would feel like there was still enough runway ahead to use to launch something great.

If I was older, I might not feel as frightened about spending the time I have left alone. I might be able to just work myself to death. I like my work—so that isn't as bad as it sounds. But 30 years of working myself to death is too long.

I think I am a widower at the worst age. I am a 'tweener widower. Too old for round two, too young to throw in the towel. So much for working through the self-pity!

Of course if I was thinner, wiser, richer, etc., then all my worries would vanish.

Changing the sheets today. The thought passed through my Spock-like brain that I could wash the sheets half as often if I slept for a week on my side and then a week on Shannon's side. Think of all the water I would save the planet. I could be an eco-hero. I quickly realized that I am careful when I go to bed, when I wake up, when I walk around the bedroom, to NOT look at Shannon's side of the bed. I have her side of the bed covered with pillows. I think part of me is trying to "hide" her side of the bed from the rest of me. So I don't think I'll be sleeping over there any time soon.

The final deep thought for the day was that my bad moments come in two different flavors. I am not sure I understood them this way before. One is when I am overcome by loneliness from missing Shannon. I get very, very sad. That is a curl up in a ball and wait for it to pass thing. The other is when I am overcome with fright about being alone. That is a get up and do stuff to be distracted thing.

So today was a frightened about being alone day. Boy, was I busy. Bank, carwash, tailor (she said "it's good to see you," not "how are you?"), Reid's bank, FedEx shop, lunch, grocery store, liquor store (for party Sunday). Came home, unloaded the car, put stuff away. Still frightened about being alone.

What could be more fun to do when you are missing your wife than to drive to the courthouse and probate her will? So that's what I did. What a blast. I swear the women who work there see me walk up, assume I am in the wrong place, ask how they can help. When I explain I am there to probate my wife's will, they immediately switch into

kindness mode. It feels good and bad when they do that. It cost $264. So much for her Discover Card cashback bonus.

Came out to the car, turned on the car. Song playing on the radio is "Miss You" by the Rolling Stones. Really? Not fair.

9:58 p.m.

Just sat down after cooking two huge pots of chicken and sausage gumbo. It tastes pretty good—and will taste better after it sits for a day.

I got a call from the Sister at St. Joseph's who holds the position of "Director of Mission Integration." She wanted to know about what happened to Shannon, so I told her. I told her that the doctors who apparently were responsible for her never spoke to me in 11 days (except at intake). I told her about them sending Shannon away to die. I told her about the month-long death certificate escapade. She was (in my opinion) properly disappointed. She asked what she could do. I told her to make sure nothing like that happened to another family. She promised me that what we experienced is not what the hospital is trying to be about and that she would make sure this case improved things.

I feel bad when I write dark notes. I prefer the chance to share stories about Shannon and about what she taught me about life and love and how she made my life more than I deserved. That is what I planned to do when I sat down. But that's just not what I am feeling tonight, so I am going to stop writing. I'll share a story when I am less angry. Maybe the sun will be out in the a.m. and that will start the day off right.

November 11

> 7:55 a.m.

The sun is shining—the sky is an incredible blue. No clouds. First two songs on the radio were Bruce Springsteen's "Radio Nowhere" and Needtobreathe's "Drive all Night." If you know them, you know they are well-paired songs about a guy missing a girl. Sometimes songs like that feel good—I played them turned up loud.

The only thing I wanted to say this morning is that last night is the first night Shannon came to me in what I would call a dream. During her hospitalization and maybe for a month after she had been in nightmares; I was often shocked awake by vivid, horrible still shots of her full of tubes, of her dying, of her unnatural brain-damaged efforts to smile, her in the coffin. Last night, she was just there in my dream like she was in life. I don't really remember anything special about the dream—we were just living life—but I remember as I slept being so surprised and happy to see her. I'd like to think it means something, but nothing means anything anymore—or at least anything obvious.

Today I learned something that I need to remember. I learned that it is a very bad idea to go back and read what I have shared here.

When I post something, I read it many times on that day. It really is a "centering" sort of thing—"this is what I am focused on." Then I move on to whatever spills out next. But until this afternoon I have not gone back to September. I don't know why I did today, but it was a bad idea. As I read those early entries, I can see that I had hope. Not much hope, but some. Now that's over. Then I can see myself organizing and trying to be a good host. Then I lose Shannon.

I have been thinking a lot about the five stages of grief/dying—denial, anger, bargaining, depression, acceptance.

I think the true model is much simpler. There are only two states (not stages): anger and defeat. Anger is the root of denial and bargaining; defeat is the root of depression and acceptance. Calling something "acceptance" is really overselling it. What you are accepting is defeat.

The words in the model are attempts to make the situation less dire and to make you feel less helpless. Bargaining implies you can play a role in changing an outcome. Trust me, you can't. Acceptance implies peace with an outcome. There is no peace after losing a loved one. I can hear you saying, "It takes time." I am willing to bet it doesn't. Those are two things I know right now—I will never be angry at Shannon, and I will never "accept" that she is gone. I will never be "at peace" because she is gone. Why would I even want to be at peace with that? It is a horrible thing.

So as I sit here and write this, I think about the toll it must take on the people who have to sit and read it. I worry that people will run out of patience for me to get better before I get better. I know I ran out of patience with me a few weeks ago. I am not going back again to read entries for a long time, but I don't think there is less vitriol today than there was a month ago. All I can say is that being honest with you is helping me. Thanks for helping me.

To end on a better note...not going to say "bittersweet." Shannon really liked her orthopedist. Before the surgery, she took me to a visit to meet him. I like him, too. Each of the examination rooms had 8x10 pictures of famous people he had helped in one way or another— Bobby Bowden, Braves, Falcons, you name it. Autographed pictures with notes to the effect of "thanks, Doc!"

I hatched up a scheme, and Shannon was very excited by it. When she got better, we were going to have her sign a 8x10 photo with some similar sentiment—like, "Thanks for getting me back in the game," and the picture was going to be of her with her iron at the ironing board. I am really sorry we didn't get to do that. I think he would have liked it. I know Shannon would have.

10:37 p.m.

Feeling a little better. Went to the Tabernacle to see the Trey Anastasio Band. Was very happy to secure "our spot" by the bar. The last time I saw that band there was with Reid—and he and I texted a bit about it. He is going to a ski place tonight to snowboard tomorrow. Very happy for him.

Shannon was funny about performers. In order for her to like the show, the performer had to look like they were having fun. It was good if they also interacted a lot with the audience—but they had to look like the concert was play, not work. Shannon loved Trey Anastasio because of the goofy smile he wears the entire time he plays. I doubt she could name a single song of his—or Phish—but she still loved watching him play and smile. She also liked the crowd that seems to be attracted to his shows. So it was nice to sit there in the right spot and imagine how much she would be enjoying the show.

On the way home, I stopped at the OK Café. That wasn't exactly a tradition—but it was a frequent post-concert stop. I ordered what she would have. Turkey, avocado, bacon, and sprouts sandwich on wheat bread and pot likker/liquor (not sure how to spell that—not southern enough, I guess). It was good.

Now I am home enjoying a glass of wine from what we ordered this summer in Napa. Going to watch *Burn Notice*—a cheesy show that somehow we got hooked on. So it will be a night just like she was here except that she isn't. But she is being so, so fondly remembered and sorely missed. That's all I can do for her now.

From: DS
Date: Fri, 11 Nov 2011 11:44:16-0600
To: Nathan Bennett
Subject: Dreams

Dear Nate,

I do believe that Shannon came to visit you last night.

It is hard to understand these things, but I feel as if I have "proof" that such things do happen. Here's why:

About a week or so after my mother died, I dreamed about her. In this dream, she turned to walk down the hallway to her bedroom.

As she walked away, I asked her, "Mom, tell me—can you hear me?" (Meaning that I'd been talking aloud "to her" ever since she passed away.) She replied, "Yes, I can hear you—and tell Lynne I got the poem."

I found this to be a bit odd and called Lynne to relay to her what I had experienced.

She immediately started crying. When I asked why she was crying, she said, "Because last night I was reading through a book of poems and I found one that I liked for Mom and I copied it on to a sheet of paper for her."

I don't know how these things happen, but I could never have known that Lynne copied this poem down for Mom had my mother not told me so.

Visits from the other side do exist.

November 12

Today was a good day. I was invited up to Highlands, North Carolina, for the day—hung out with friends, spent the day shopping in exactly the sort of stores Shannon would love—without freaking out. I didn't try to buy her something by mistake, so I guess I am learning. I did buy a few things that I thought she would buy for me. It was a day she was with me in a good way.

The only bad part of the day surprised me. They often do. We went to look at a pretty cool waterfall. As we were walking back to the car, a young guy was posing his girlfriend for a picture with the falls in the background. I said—as most people would—"Would you like to be in the picture, too?" So I took their picture for them. No big deal—I have done it for lots of people before—so have you. People did it for me and Shannon, although Shannon usually resisted. She didn't like being photographed because she was self-conscious about her eyes. It was crazy—there was nothing wrong with her.

157

Anyway, I handed the guy back the camera—they looked at the picture to make sure it turned out—they were happy and said thanks. As I turned to continue on to the car, I got a sudden fear: I was hoping that one day he didn't find himself posting that picture to CaringBridge and telling a story about his departed wife and the neat day they had exploring the falls. It was really hard to not let that overcome me. It still hurts now. Stupid stuff. Hate it. Hurts.

Otherwise, it was a really nice day. Tomorrow 30 students or so for gumbo and red beans. Will be nice to have a noisy house. I mentioned that Dr. Shoffner put me in touch with a local organization working on mitochondrial disease, fundraising and research and all that. I gave them some money—a woman who is prominent in the group is going to come by and see me Monday. I look forward to knowing how I can help. The more I learn, the more I realize I won't be able to do much—but I will do what I can. The reason she is on campus is that Sanjay Gupta (CNN) is coming to do a special on the kid at Tech Colby and mitochondrial disease. He will be able to do more with that one show than I will in my life—but that's great!

Almost 5 hours in the car alone. Lots of time to think. Lots of songs. Lots of memories. One (maybe) deep thought. It struck me that maybe nothing changes a life more than a death except for love. So Shannon put both of those in my life, and my job is to figure out how to make that all net out positively. She made me much better by loving me. And I have to figure out how to be "more better" after she is gone.

November 13

5:24 p.m.

This weekend would have to really deteriorate quickly to be as bad as last weekend. So even I am willing to express some cautious optimism.

The secret—be with people. Not difficult. So I am making changes. For a while, I was making "Tech days" as full as I could and protecting some days to be "work from home" days. Since "work from home" has turned into "be bummed at home," revision is in order. I am going to try to make sure I have a reason to go to Tech every day. Even if I am just there a few hours, have lunch with someone rather than alone, and then come home, it will make the being home better. It isn't rocket science—unless you are impaired. Took me a while to get to the obvious.

30 MBA students, Spencer, and Andre just left. It was a great afternoon. It wasn't my best gumbo or beans, but they were okay. As I expected, it was wonderful to be in a noisy house. Two toddlers who joined us—it made me miss Shannon because she would have been all over those kids. But it was a good miss, not a bad miss. I am really disappointed I didn't get to see Shannon be a grandmom. She would have been awesome at that.

The Saints/Falcons game was a good one. Not really exciting, but very close. The better team won, what can I say?

What I can't say is enough about my students. They are amazing. People came early to help me set up—and they made me make the calls about how to set it up that Shannon would have wanted (but where I would have cut corners). As the game was winding down, the clean-up took form. The house was clean within minutes of the end of the game. I told them I appreciated it—but that they sort of blew my plans for the evening...with all that done, now what am I to do all night? I have said it before and I will say it again and I will say it forever—if you ever get a chance to choose an MBA hire, take the Tech kid. It isn't because of what we do...it is because of what they have had to do to have the chance to be at Tech. They are just good people. They do the right thing.

I was sitting in the basement for a while during the game—me, Spencer, his dog Andre, and about 10 MBA students, and one of their daughters—not sure how old she was...more than 1 but less than 2, I guess. Spencer was joking with the MBA students...the little girl and Andre were totally entertaining each other. I flashed back to Baton Rouge when Shannon and I would first have MBA students over—burgers in the fall and crawfish in the spring (with the now Father Michael as sous chef/party planning assistant)—and it was Spencer who was the baby. Spencer is almost the age of my students.

Where did that time go? It is hard for me to wrap my head around the idea that the "average-age" student in that room was born the year Shannon and I got married—or since. I guess it is good that I don't feel that old. I have spent a huge percent of my life with people who are 25–30, so maybe it rubs off...except on my knees.

On the down side, not sleeping is back. Maybe three hours each of the past two nights. Honestly, the thing I hate the most about the not sleeping now is that it is just plain boring. Too tired to read, too tired to work, nothing engaging on TV—but can't get over the edge on sleep. It isn't a big deal. Just boring.

Psychiatrist says I need a hobby. I said no, I have work. He said one day I won't have work. I disagreed, he disagreed. I explained that Shannon was my hobby. He didn't disagree, but pointed out that she was gone. Oh well. Hard to pull one over on him.

The things I like are not good for me—I miss hockey, but when I played in my 30s I remember it was the guys who were 50 who got hurt. I don't need to break an ankle or a wrist. And hockey is not something I can do "casually." I could pick tennis back up, but I met a lot of jerks playing ALTA. I am sort of about the process, not the outcome. I just want to play. I really don't need to win an ALTA match to feel good about myself...some people here in Atlanta clearly do. Maybe golf—I used to object primarily because of how long it takes. But I have time now. It is outdoors, I could do it for a long time. Don't like the outfits, though.

Donovan Frankenreiter on the stereo now—"Life, Love & Laughter." Yup. The chorus pretty much sums it up.

Thanks to all my students who kept me company today. Company is a simple thing to be and really a great gift to offer.

A final piece of good news is that last week I started to be anxious to get back to writing...not this—the academic stuff that is apparently less compelling but more instrumental in bill-paying than this stuff! The next few weeks are nuts with the holiday, then finals—I don't expect I can really get back to it until January, but it felt good to want to do it.

November 14

> 9:23 p.m.

Today was complicated. Some days I feel like I need new words. Maybe words that really are just sounds—umpf, argh, eeks—stuff like that. It's too much work to find the right words.

The main reason for the day's complexity was two-fold. First, I had too much wine last night. After everyone left, I was simply enjoying the wine too much. So that made getting started a bit difficult. Second, since Shannon's death I have not gone anywhere without a Xanax in my pocket. Today, I inadvertently left home without one. I panicked a bit. Most days I don't take the pill—but knowing I couldn't was hard.

On the way to work, I was thinking about how odd it is to feel guilty when I have a good day. I want so much to feel better—but when I feel better, I feel like I am dishonoring Shannon. Yet I know she would want me to feel better, and I am actually committing a greater dishonor by not trying to have a good day. Having a good day is the right thing to do—but it makes me feel guilty. I can think of lots of instances where doing the right thing is hard, inconvenient, embarrassing—but not guilt-provoking. Guilt is supposed to be connected to getting your hand caught in the cookie jar, not to feeling like you managed to execute your job or handle your business like an adult. Stuff like this gives me a headache—especially when I already have a headache.

The day got off to a rocky start—but it did get better. One highlight was meeting with two women who are in key roles with the Atlanta-based Foundation for Mitochondrial Medicine (http://www.found-mm.org/foundation.php). They stopped by on their way to meet Sanjay Gupta and the CNN folks for the taping of the segment on Colby. It was great—they have a ton of energy, great ideas, and have made a lot of progress in terms of raising awareness, etc. Their strategy is right on—mitochondrial disease impacts very few people, but research on lots of conditions (Parkinson's, etc.) all can shed light on it. The challenge they want to attack is getting these researchers to better share with one another—it's like a siloed business where the left and right hand are not in sync. They are going to stay in touch about ways I can be involved and help—after the holidays.

One thing they shared struck me as pretty cool—researchers have found that the enzyme in the tail of lightning bugs—I think it is luciferase—can be injected into a cell, and then the glowing indicates the efficiency of the cell in producing energy. So theoretically, they could one day test someone like Shannon and have a much better idea of how compromised her system was. And one day they will be able to use the technique to see if treatments are making a difference in how well a cell is working. Really cool stuff.

Thinking about these things is comforting—but it's hard, too. I don't remember who said it, but the line is something about how horrible it is to be the last soldier killed in a war. I am sure you all know someone who died from something that now is treatable. I would never want someone else to die like Shannon did. But I can see how hard it would be for the mom, dad, husband, or wife of the last soldier killed to be okay with that. I wish she was still here.

This is the story I wanted to tell when I thought this morning about writing. I was listening to the radio, and the Ray Parker Jr. song

"Ghostbusters" came on. It reminded me of two of Shannon's all-time favorite dates.

In 2006, I had my first book come out. To celebrate, my co-author and I took our wives to dinner at a place called Aria. It's one of our favorites in Atlanta. Just after we were seated, we were presented with a bottle of very nice champagne. Shannon and I didn't exactly understand who it was from or why it had arrived—our friends did, but we missed the conversation. We just were happy to have it.

We finished dinner, and our friends said we needed to go out to the patio to say thanks to the person who sent the bottle—so we did. Turns out the bottle was sent by Earl Klugh, the jazz guitarist. Shannon and I both love him; turns out he and our friends go back a ways. Shannon felt so special that someone famous was sending us champagne. He later sent us some kindly signed CDs and all—really nice. Shannon felt like she had a friend.

So what does this have to do with Ray Parker Jr.? A couple of years later, we went to see Earl Klugh in concert at Georgia Tech. He has played several times as part of their jazz series. He seems sort of a reluctant star—he clearly loves to play but doesn't like being the center of attention. Whenever we have seen him he does something to put the spotlight somewhere else. One year, he had kids from a high school here he sort of adopted play with him—they were quite good. This particular year he invited Ray Parker Jr. to play with him.

Parker is not exactly a jazz person—the audience was mainly jazz lovers. As I recall, it was Valentine's Day. So what is the first song Parker plays? "I'm in Love with the Other Woman." Not your typical Valentine's Day song. What does he do next? A very extended version of "Ghostbusters"—he worked hard to get the 60+-year-old audience to sing along. Ugh. Shannon loved the absurdity of it.

Our favorite Klugh CDs are two that he did which are solo guitar. On each one, he does his own stuff and some covers. On one, he does a version of "Ding Dong, the Witch is Dead." Shannon used to joke she wanted it played at her funeral. I told her there were people where I would find the song appropriate, but that she was not one of them. So if you were at her service, you didn't hear it.

And that makes me think about promises you make, promises you keep, and promises you break in a situation like mine. So far, I am pretty happy that I think I can keep all the promises I made her about what I would do to take care of her and her things if she went first. I was pretty sure I would go first, so I could have gotten myself in a fix— but thankfully I don't think I did.

November 15

6:59 a.m.

On the plane headed to New Orleans for the planting of Shannon's tree. Neat it is the 100th posting. Good it is commemorating something wonderful. If I was on a trip and she were home, this is when I would text her and say this: "on the plane, looks on time, shutting down device. Love you and see you tonight." She'd write back, "love you, too—have fun." I miss that. Today is a good day in the new normal but not really that great overall.

1:30 p.m.

Sitting under the shade of a live oak in Audubon Park. It is mid 80s and sunny. Lots of ducks, sound of the street car going by, bells chiming at Loyola to mark 12:30. I am sitting on a bench dedicated to Annie. Annie lived from 1980 to 1994. About 30 yards from where Shannon's tree will go. Tree was going to happen at 11, but apparently the crew got so worn out after the first tree of the day that they took an early lunch. So I went and grabbed an oyster po'boy. I am promised there will be a tree in the ground before I have to leave for the airport, but to tell you the truth, I am not that worried. I like being here. It's a good spot. People walking, jogging, biking, pushing strollers. Sound of wind in the trees (that is unusual in New Orleans—usually the air is too heavy to move). Only downside is the occasional mosquito. The tree will get planted—I'll be here next month.

9:29 p.m.

It was a nice day at the tree planting. Shannon's cousin met me at the spot this a.m. and hung out for a while to see if the tree would arrive. When we heard it wouldn't, she had to head back to work. I grabbed an oyster po'boy and a Barq's at Parasol's (Domilise's was closed for the week). Headed back to the park in time to read the paper, relax, enjoy the people watching. Then it was like a procession—backhoe, truck with guys, flatbed truck with tree. They don't waste time once they show up. The tree is in the ground. The spot is wonderful—you can hear nothing but happy sounds and New Orleans sounds. I am really excited to have a place to go and remember Shannon—I think she would be really, really honored—Ginkgos can live hundreds of years, so it should last me. I appreciate my friends so much for doing this for us. I finally decided on words for the plaque that will go by the tree. I struggled to come up with something that didn't sound like a headstone. It should be installed by the time the boys and I go visit in December.

Most of you know how much Shannon loved New Orleans. Background—Spencer is our Jazz Fest baby—he was born April 25—basically always Jazz Fest. Reid is our Mardi Gras baby—he was born January 6th, which is the first day of the Mardi Gras season. What more evidence could you want of a cosmic New Orleans connection than a woman who gives birth on two of the biggest days the city has each year?

The year Spencer was turning 21, we splurged and rented a house in the Garden District over the two weekends of Jazz Fest. We had a wonderful time—one weekend was family (Spencer let me buy him his first legal beer at midnight at the Rock 'n' Bowl); the other weekend was friends and family. In between weekends, Spencer and his friend went to Pensacola for a couple of days. Reid and I came back to Atlanta for school duties, and Shannon stayed in New Orleans. Mind you we were at a rental house. She spent much of the time while I was gone working in the yard of the rental house. I remember coming back, and there she was weeding the flowerbed. I asked her what she was doing, and she said, "The dirt here feels so good." That was all I needed to know. That was Shannon. Connected to New Orleans.

I had planned to say a lot more—but I sort of like this ending. So that's it.

November 16

> 8:56 p.m.

I just made a list of things to write about. I am finding that my memory is—well—I am not sure how to explain it. It isn't that I forget things—but I have to be very deliberate to remember them. Recall is irregular. I think the medicine is the culprit. At least I hope that is what I can blame it on. The medicine will end one day, and I need my memory to come back.

The list has 16 things on it. Too much for a night, that's for sure. Particularly given everything else I need to do tonight.

So first I will tick off some easy ones. Here are some things that are funny if you are a believer in karma.

Shannon's tree in Audubon Park is coincidentally at the end of Benjamin Street. Shannon's first apartment was on Benjamin Street.

The woman who runs the Mito Foundation in Atlanta started Tulane the fall after Shannon graduated in the spring. She was in the same sorority as Shannon.

Right as the guys finished planting Shannon's tree yesterday, it started to rain.

That's three—that was pretty easy.

Had lunch today with a friend from the Chart House days—he was passing through Atlanta, hadn't been able to go to Shannon's service, and wanted to check in on me. About a year ago he went through a divorce—and it's still tough for him. I got to thinking about the expression "misery loves company." That is wrong—at least for me. My misery just wishes fewer people were miserable. I have heard so many stories about divorce and loss over the past couple of months—maybe it is the same rate at which I have always heard them, and I am just sensitized. Regardless, life is hard enough. I wish people had less misery.

Shannon just qualified for a credit card—$20,000 limit. I think I'll get it...and Lena, a librarian in Russia, wants to be my special friend. She is cute—at least in the picture she provided. She seems oddly posed for a librarian. So maybe I can use some of the $20,000 limit to bring her over...ugh. I swear I get one of these a day—some entrepreneur must be combing over obits or something. Did not get them before I was a widower.

That's three more. On a roll.

Shannon was worried that I listened to music too often and too loudly and that I would be deaf in my old age. So her plan was for us to learn sign language. I told her I learned all the sign language I need from Boston cab drivers. She was not impressed. So I have a sign language book, but no longer the motivation to learn.

I have opened all the cards. I read some of them over each day. Mostly, I just like seeing the pile of them. They are all great, but this is one of the ones that really struck me. It is from a guy who was an MBA student here at Tech almost 10 years ago. I had him in my organizational behavior class.

Here is part of what he wrote:

> *Although it has been years since we have spoken, and I don't think I ever met Shannon, something you mentioned in your OB class has stuck with me to this day. You asked us to try and define love, and I remember your insight as 'the feeling we get when someone does so much for us and we are so thankful that we want to do even more for them.' It was clear at that time that you understood something that I had yet to know. When our first of two children was born four years ago, I began to understand what you meant and have thought about it almost daily. It was quite clear that you shared something so special with Shannon that someone like me, having no direct experience with it, can be a lucky beneficiary of the incredible energy. I have heard and read countless definitions of love, but this was the one that stuck and helps me understand what it is I feel for my wife...*

That is a ridiculously beautiful thing for him to have shared with me. Okay—you are wondering, "What the hell are you doing talking about love in a business school class?" I guess my answer is that we go where the road goes. As Forrest Gump might say, "OB is like a box of chocolates..." Personally, if this guy got a takeaway that helps him appreciate his wife, I count that as a big, big win. The other stuff we talk about is trivial in comparison. There are a million things I love about that note: that he was kind enough to send it, that he remembered something important from my class, that it has helped him be better in his life, that he appreciates how lucky I was.

A lot of professors don't like teaching MBAs. I can't imagine doing anything else. I am going to miss this group so much—it's going to leave another hole in my world. Considering everything, moving on is the right thing for me to do. But the fact is that in 20 years of teaching MBAs— nearly 3,000 students—I have developed a fondness for the "type."

So that is two more—half the list. Enough for now. I know I have said this before, but this is worth repeating. Please find someone tomorrow who may feel you take them for granted and give them a boost. Because there is enough already in everyone's day that is pushing them down. And because there is nothing worse than not being able to do something for someone you care about.

November 18

6:57 p.m.

I had a friend share with me today her concern that I could be putting myself at risk with what I am posting—that mentioning wine and prescription drugs might create an opening for someone who wanted to be a jerk to, well, be a jerk. This is a good friend—someone I have known almost as long as I have known Shannon. So I take her concern very, very seriously. And I have thought about it a lot this afternoon.

I have a lot of people looking out for me, and I am grateful for that.

On the other hand...each day when I wake up, my first thought is that my dear wife is way prematurely dead, and I am alone. So I challenge any jerk to make my day worse. From that moment forward nothing is going to make my day worse. I am bulletproof. I don't mean that in a James Dean car stunt kind of way. I am psychologically bulletproof. There are bad moments every day—but nothing like that first moment. Once I sit up and put my feet on the floor, my day gets better and really can't get worse.

And on the third hand...I have found myself almost wanting someone to try to upset me. I have a lot of rage, and I would love a target. It has been hard when well-intentioned people frustrate me to not go off on them. They don't know they are frustrating—they are just barely doing their jobs; they aren't trying to piss me off.

I am managing it, but it's hard. I want to get the rage out, but I suppose that if it does I'll just make more—like tears. I wish I could just get the tears over with, but I make more.

And on the fourth hand...let's see...I lost my wife, and I am taking an anti-depressant. Anyone surprised? Anyone think that is a bad idea? Anyone want to suggest I should be ashamed of that? And one night in the two months since my wife died (2 months today, by the way) it was a little hard to get out of bed because the wine was really good the night before. I didn't miss a thing I was supposed to do that day. And it wouldn't be hard to get a lineup of people who would say that I am managing to function.

For this to work, it needs to be honest. For it to help me—for it to help anyone else—and for me to honor Shannon, I need to be honest about what it is like to live without her.

But I appreciate a reminder that I also need to be prudent.

I am pretty sure I am keeping myself safe, and my friend's concern will remind me to be thoughtful and careful. But in the meantime, let's remember Dirty Harry's line for any troublemakers out there..."You have to ask yourself one question...do I feel lucky?...Well, do you, punk?" I don't suggest anyone poke an angry widower with a stick.

To all my friends, especially the one who prompted this post, thank you for caring about me, for looking out for me, and for wanting to make sure I keep all four wheels on the road. I will. I promise.

Good progress in the basement today. The hard thing was that somehow the picture we took of Shannon's hand the night I gave her the engagement ring was out loose for me to find. That was very hard. It says in her handwriting on the back "THE RING March 1985." There is a lot of stuff down there I am happy to be getting rid of, but boy are there a lot of memories, as well. Those I am less sure how to process.

November 19

3:08 p.m.

This morning was a difficult one. It was very cold and gray, and I am just tired of being alone. People will say—to help encourage me to be patient with myself—that "it's only been two months." I understand this is a not a situation with an easy fix—but that doesn't mean I don't wish for one. The "only been..." expression cuts both ways. Yes, it has only been two months, and it is unrealistic to think things would be "fixed." So I should be patient. But it has been a very dark two months—"minimizing" two months means there is a lot of suffering to endure.

The day got better when some students came by to help with getting ready for tomorrow. I am excited—the final count is 26, we think. We have 26 seated places ready. I have knocked out cornbread dressing, traditional dressing, asparagus casserole, and cranberry sauce. Dirty rice and oyster dressing and gravy tomorrow morning. All I have to do tonight is get the turkeys ready. Although if I don't go to the concert, I will make the oyster dressing.

Fall

It feels great to be doing something for someone—because people have been doing so much for me. Of course, I can't do it without neighbors lending me chairs and students coming to help me lug tables around. It's a whole helping circle...

The reason I sat down to do an entry now—other than that I don't have time to do another dish before I head out to get Reid—is to share a memory. The first time we did a Thanksgiving for students was several years ago. We did a seated dinner for 20 something. Shannon was amazing. She set beautiful tables. She spent time the day before cutting out a couple of dozen little turkeys out of construction paper to make place cards. Each table had a beautiful fall arrangement of little squash, dried leaves, and so on. She was always 100% in on these things.

I was thinking—hey—they are students—it's free food—no worries— whatever. She made it elegant. I am glad I got used to letting her just go crazy with that stuff. I thought she was working harder than she needed to—she knew it was a chance to be doing something for someone else—and I needed to just let her do it.

So I am thinking nice thoughts about her and all the good stuff she added to my life. And I am trying to do things in a way that she would approve. Everyone gets a cloth napkin—no paper. Everyone gets a real plate. I ran to Target and bought some inexpensive flatware— everyone gets real utensils. We don't have to eat in shifts.

It is going to be tremendous to have Reid home for a bit. I wonder if I will see him! I hope he isn't too uncomfortable here. I hope he enjoys seeing friends and getting a break. I am so sorry the boys are having to deal with this. It is hard to be helpless with them.

It is going to be a good weekend. Things at work are going well. I have lots to do. The boys are around. I have so much good stuff in my life— I wish it were enough. It's not. I have been spoiled.

6:39 p.m.

Right now in this moment, life is good. Reid is home. I made sure to have some leftovers that he likes. He walked in the door, he ate, we talked a bit, and he went to bed. I am to wake him up at 8 p.m. so he can be ready for the concert tonight.

I met him at the airport earlier—there he was at baggage claim—wearing pajama bottoms, a hoody sweatshirt, and a Green Bay Packers knit cap. The kid could not look more like a college student. He said he just didn't feel like getting dressed this morning. If Shannon were here, she would have been anxiously waiting for him to come home. When he walked in the door and she saw that outfit she would have been appalled—and she would have laughed—and she would have given him a killer hug.

It is good to have him here. But it is hard to deal with the elephant in the room. We'll talk at some point this week, but I want him to enjoy the nap and seeing some of his old friends.

November 20

11:43 a.m.

A quiet few moments in between tasks. Tables are set. Turkeys are in the oven. Giblets are simmering away to start the gravy. Just oyster dressing to cook. That's next.

The house smells really good.

Reid is upstairs in bed. Who knows when he got in. He went to the concert in the same pajamas he flew here in.

Fall

This morning I remembered how I have missed what Shannon and I referred to as "evidence" that we could examine each morning. "Well, it appears he ate…" and, "It looks like he fell asleep the first time in this chair (with the empty glass next to it)." So this morning I got to be the detective a bit.

It is nice to have the house smell like a holiday, and I have enjoyed cooking the past two weekends. But it is sad to not be doing this with Shannon. She always worried about things like this up to the day of—but they always came off great. Today will, too, because of what she taught me. It won't be quite to her standard, but like a lot of things around here, I just can't do it like she could.

Thanksgiving is going to be hard—everyone agrees. How can I frame the classic "what do you have to be thankful for" question positively this year? I'd really rather just not have to answer. Of course I am thankful for the joy Shannon brought me and for the boys she raised with me—and a good job and friends.

But it is as if that stuff exists on the surface of the earth, and I am standing at the bottom of a well. I can't see any of that stuff. I am surrounded by darkness. I know the good stuff is there—but I can't get to it, either.

The only thing the stuff on the surface does is help you want to get out of the well. But there is no ladder, no rope. Just waiting.

7:37 p.m.

Today was as good as it gets. I should get in bed now!

The dinner was wonderful. We had turkey, ham, oyster dressing, cornbread stuffing, herb stuffing, some other stuffing, broccoli casserole, asparagus casserole, squash casserole, gravy, cranberry sauce (canned and homemade—both are necessary), dirty rice, brussel sprouts, green beans. Everything tasted great. Then there were the desserts the students brought—wow. We sat 26 people at three tables in three different rooms in the house. My student co-hosts were tremendous in coming over yesterday to get the tables set—and to do their share of the cooking—and more than their share of the dishes.

Spencer came over a bit early with Andre (his dog) to help me cook. He paid me the highest compliment—he said I can still cook. It was fun to send Andre up to wake up Reid. Reid finally did shower and get out of his pajamas. When he woke up, people were already here, so I haven't heard much about the concert last night yet. He is down in the basement playing video games and is about to head over to Spencer's house for a while.

The students had a really good time. Many of them have never had an American Thanksgiving. Some of them are of other nationalities but live here now, and their families celebrate US Thanksgiving with their own native cuisines—so Indian food, Chinese food, etc. Not turkey. Spencer and Reid like meeting the students—and I like the students getting to meet them. They are part of some of the stories I tell in class, and it is good for them to have a chance to defend their reputations.

I thought about Shannon—all night—but particularly as I watched the boys proactively introduce themselves, shake hands, and all that. Just as Shannon would have wanted.

As I mentioned, I have a ton of dishes to do. And I have a little work to do to get ready for class. I know I have been writing sort of dark stuff, and I wanted to let everyone know that some days are okay and some hours that are pretty good. And that's good—and hopeful.

November 22

It was a nice morning. The sky was blue, and it was warm enough to be on the porch. It was one of those mornings where I would have told Shannon I was going to leave her in the family room and take my coffee outside to work. At the end of each of her cups of tea, she would have come to the door to check on me while the next cup was steeping. She would open the door and be there in her pjs, robe, and socks—always socks. She would smile at me and tell me I was crazy to be outside in the cold (65 degrees). She'd fake a shiver and head back inside for the next cup of tea.

That's just one example of the dozens of little things that used to be in my day and don't happen anymore. Depression by 1,000 cuts. A conversation about what to do for dinner—having someone interesting to sit and converse with over a meal and a glass of wine—sharing a story about one of the kids—having someone show interest in how my day went—seeing that someone handled something for me—seeing the smile on their face because I handled something for them—all gone and missed.

Reid is still allegedly here. One more pair of his shoes here at the bottom of the stairs. He did laundry because my stuff was moved out of the dryer. That provided more evidence of Shannon's good work. When Reid empties the dryer he doesn't dump the pile on a bed or chair. He lays everything out flat so it doesn't wrinkle before I have a chance to hang or fold it. We are going to do "something" this afternoon. Supposedly going to have dinner where Spencer has picked up a shift tonight. Tomorrow we head to Florida for the family Thanksgiving celebration. Will be good to see folks and to be on an adventure with the boys.

Today one realization and one recollection.

The realization:

The realization isn't really new, but it was front and center in my mind today and helped me stay in positive territory for most of the day.

I am lucky in that I can tell a story about Shannon's death that makes some amount of sense and that (okay—karma...The minute I mention Shannon's name the radio starts playing Trombone Shorty with Widespread Panic) helps me know that Shannon would accept the way she went out.

Here are the basics:

She didn't suffer, best I can tell.
She didn't become a burden on me—something she feared greatly.
She got to get both her kids "on the path" to being independent.
She didn't experience that much decline from her condition to lose much quality of life; driving may have been over, sometimes eating and swallowing were hard, her eyes had long been a difficulty. The last months of her life involved great trips to London, to Napa and San Francisco, to Boulder, to New York for a play. She enjoyed all those things fully.
She was worried about her world getting smaller because of her condition, and she was afraid of living in a small world.

So I can tell myself that she got most of the good stuff and avoided most of her fears. I was thinking today about the family of one of Reid's friends. He died in a car accident at the beginning of senior year in high school. The accident was a freakish thing. I don't know how someone makes a story in a situation like that to try and find peace.

Some people might see a horrific accident like that as part of God's plan; some people might find comfort because the boy is in a better place. I don't have a lot of beliefs. I am pretty focused on data. So I consider myself lucky to have a way to understand what happened to Shannon that helps me know she would be okay with it. She would want to squeeze every minute she could out of being with me and the boys—I know that. But I heard her say a thousand times that she just really wanted to go out like a light before her quality of life declined and she became a burden. And that is pretty much what happened. I just wish we had a few more minutes.

The recollection:

I know this is no one's fault—but it is something that could be better. In Cobb County, the "office" that handles probating wills opens on to one waiting room. The "office" that handles marriage certificates opens on to another waiting room. These two offices are actually one—if you are standing at the window to probate your will the perpendicular wall has similar windows for people getting marriage licenses.

It is hard to be at the window to probate your deceased wife's will while you watch and listen to the chatter around the anticipation of a marriage at the perpendicular window. It probably doesn't need to be that way.

November 23

3:07 p.m.

Arrived with the boys at my dad's house in Sarasota. Just finished some work that had to get done. About to go and do some serious prep work to make tomorrow's cooking easier. As you would all expect, it is hard to be here without Shannon. It is going to be a day and a half with 9 people who miss her terribly and are trying to move forward. It's hard—we want to hold each other up, but none of us really has the strength to hold ourselves up. That's a bit of an exaggeration, but I think you understand my point.

9:25 p.m.

This is a time it is just impossible not to be thinking about Shannon. Just got back from a family dinner. The first time this group of nine has been together in years. First holiday without Shannon. My family is great. Every single person is a character. Shannon truly loved that— she enjoyed everyone and the color they added to the family canvas so much.

So here is a story. It is silly. It is dumb. But I think it is also fun. It is a good memory, and I think it shows how easy it was to be Shannon's husband. A couple of years ago, Shannon and I went to see Paul McCartney at Piedmont Park in Atlanta. In consideration of Shannon's situation, I thought it would be a good idea to get a hotel room at the Midtown Hotel in Atlanta—it's about 6 blocks from the park. We could park, hunker down at the hotel, walk over when ready, and all that. Then we could just take our time getting back to the hotel and crash. It wouldn't be too much on Shannon. So that's what we planned to do.

About halfway through the concert, it started to pour down rain. We stuck it out for a bit, but eventually we were plenty wet. So we headed back to the hotel. We were 100% drenched by the time we got there.

When we had checked in, we realized the hotel was not what it once was, and we weren't that sure we wanted to get between those sheets. Shannon had a plan. Those of you who knew her well will not be the least bit surprised. She sent me to the bar to get some Grand

Marnier, and she headed up to the room. I got doubles. I got back to the room, and Shannon was there with the ironing board out. She was blow-drying her bra with one hand and using the iron to dry her pants. Once her stuff was dry, she took my clothes and did the same. It took about an hour, but at that point we had warm, dry clothes and had enjoyed a drink together talking about the concert. We called the valet to bring the car around, and we drove home.

It was one of thousands of great nights. I can't even exactly tell you why it was great. I suppose the point is that a lot of people might consider a night where you missed half an outdoor concert because of rain—and that you had to walk through this downpour to get to what had become a sort of seedy hotel—a bad night. But when you are with someone you love those are adventures—and you find a way to make them cherished memories, not disappointments.

There is just nothing like the feeling that comes from being so comfortable with someone that you are happy to sit tight with an after-dinner drink in a seedy hotel, wrapped in a questionably clean towel while they iron your underwear dry! How's that for a Thanksgiving story!

I am so thankful that Shannon and I found each other. I said this earlier, but thanks again for supporting me. Sometime last week the counter on this site hit 20,000. I can't believe that. To know that people have basically checked in on me that much is incredibly comforting. It is great to feel heard. And I am thankful for that this Thanksgiving, too.

November 24

8:03 p.m.

I am sure we all feel the same right now—relieved, full, and worn out. Those words certainly describe me. The dinner came out very nicely. Spencer made brine for the turkey, and it soaked in it all night. I handled getting it in the oven this morning and then dealt with various side dishes. Things went smoothly, and it really all tasted good. It was great to be with family.

What I really want to write about is simple: I couldn't be more proud of Spencer and Reid. I started to say "they really stepped up to the plate," but that would make it sound like it was unusual for them to be that way. It isn't. And it is all to Shannon's credit. They can be a pain in the butt when they want, but when it matters, they are great conversationalists, they get along with everyone, they help all over the place without being asked. They don't complain; they take things in stride. They work until the job is done. They aren't selfish—like their mom, they are good at seeing what can help others, and they do it.

My uncle very kindly said to Spencer—as they were getting ready to leave—that the meal was the best Thanksgiving meal he had ever had. My aunt tried to correct him to let my uncle know that I had really cooked the meal. Spencer said they didn't understand. I was the sous chef—so I did the work. He was the chef—so he was to take the credit.

The boys got me through today. As Spencer left with Reid to go out to catch a movie—or as Reid said to go to Target just to have the chance to trample over some people when the store opens—he asked me, "Are you going to be okay here?" That is something I used to say to Shannon every time we walked in to a hotel room, every time I had to leave her someplace. It was strange and sweet to have my son ask it of me.

So as I said yesterday, I am thankful that Shannon found me and said yes. I am thankful for the boys she left behind and for the work she did to make sure they always get the big stuff right. She would have been so, so, so proud of how they handled themselves today. But she was proud of them every day.

I hope you are all content, and that your families enjoyed a peaceful day together.

November 25

9:13 p.m.

So that is what it is like to do a holiday without Shannon. There are a bunch more ahead over the next couple of weeks—Christmas, New Year's, Reid's birthday, Shannon's birthday. Those all fall in a 15-day span. I think Reid's birthday will be the hardest. The boys are sort of over Christmas from a kid standpoint. New Year's will be hard for me, but the boys will be out with friends. I have had Shannon to kiss at midnight New Year's Eve since 1983. I don't like thinking about that. That is going to be a really crappy night to sit home alone. Good preparation for Valentine's Day, I suppose.

As for Thanksgiving, what I found interesting was seeing how my assembled family interacted without her. Everyone loved her—and because she was genuinely not self-interested, she was like a tremendous shock absorber whenever we were together. She didn't need to talk, be entertained, work, not work—she just moved in and out around everyone. If someone was alone, she went to talk to them. If someone was upset, she told them they were great and helped them feel better. If there was work to be done, she did it. When I was tied up with one thing, she jumped in to take care of another. We did okay without her, but it wasn't nearly the same.

The boys and I got home around 8. Spencer grabbed his car and headed out. Reid found that some friends are headed to a concert so off he went. I am alone again in the house. I've had lots of family time over the last 48 hours, and there is a lot to do around here in terms of getting all the kitchen stuff I used last weekend back down to the basement. And the boys were just tremendous and certainly merit a night out with friends.

Some updates—the Sanjay Gupta special on mitochondrial disease featuring the Tech kid will air in December on a segment called "Human Factor." It is also supposed to run 6–7 times each on CNN and Headline News. I asked my attorney to send a letter to the Pulmonary and Critical Care of Atlanta practice expressing my concerns. He wrote a great letter that deserves a response—but I don't expect much from them because I am pretty sure they are sub-human. I am going to report them to the State Board next week—I am told that has been threatened before, but no one has done it. I will. I also plan to CC the CEO at St. Joseph's the letter the attorney sent so they are in the loop. If the doctors' practice doesn't respond in a positive, honorable way, I am next going to the Internet and the various sites that review physicians. I'll keep going until I get their attention, an apology, and a credible explanation of how they are going to be compassionate in the future. That bar is too high for them, but I am going to get them to try.

November 26

4:05 p.m.

One advantage of being a Tech fan is that often you don't have to watch the second half of a football game. It is a gift—90 minutes of my life back. I just finished a quick game of lacrosse catch with Reid. That was good. He was excited that early this a.m. I grabbed him some

Krispy Kreme glazed donuts. I just didn't think it would be an official trip to Atlanta without one or twelve.

I am realizing that one of the reasons I am tired most of the time is that I feel like every relationship I am in is being redefined, and that's requiring a lot of energy to sort through. Some of this is not new—everyone my age or older has parents who are older and can use some help. That's par for the course. And I have written about trying to find a way to redefine the way I think about Shannon so that she is honored and appreciated by—and supportive of—all of us left behind. And I have to learn to relate to the world as a widower. Neither of those are par for the course, but both are necessary. That's a lot of psychic work.

Then there are relationships with our friends that came to us via Shannon. And then there are relationships with Shannon's family. And relationships with basically anyone who knew Shannon. All being redefined somehow. More work.

The relationships I am struggling a bit about are with Spencer and Reid. These relationships were in a transition anyway—the whole separation thing. Then we lose Shannon, and now that is a new variable in the equation. It is hard to figure out how to handle normal separation issues, loss of wife and mom, and being a single parent (although I recognize my "case" of that is nothing like what someone with younger kids would be struggling with).

I feel like I have a great relationship with each kid, but in many ways Shannon was more the direct and blunt one. She would just "barge in" to any child-rearing topic; I have always more nibbled around the edges. Sometimes her barging in made all three of us uncomfortable—"oh, Mom, not the condom talk again!"—but at least it got issues out on the table. So my style may not be as direct as I need it to be—if the boys "seem" okay, I assume they are. I am afraid to ask directly how they are doing without Shannon.

It is a lot of work to figure out how these things are supposed to be and what the path is to get there. One nice thing is that I am not sure before Shannon died the boys and I ever regularly told each other "I love you." We do that every phone, text, or meeting now. I've always known it—and they've always known it—but it is important to say it. The relationships are good—I just wish I better knew how to be there for them in a way that respected their independence and wasn't just a cave in to my neediness.

I don't know if I mentioned that the neighborhood here has made a nice spot in Shannon's memory near the pool and playground. I am going to upload a picture. The picture is sort of crappy—the spot looks nicer in real life than the picture conveys. And it is still a bit of a work in progress. It's right across the street from my house—a tree and flowering bushes that were among Shannon's favorite. The neighbors have been great. I was gone for a couple of days for Thanksgiving. I try to be good about suspending mail and paper delivery, but I sometimes forget. If I do, I always find when I got home that a neighbor has brought them up to the door. If it is a trash night, someone pulls the can up close to the house. If the mail stacks up, my mailman—he is great, too—takes care of it for me. Simple kindnesses like that are so good to receive.

Tonight Reid and Spencer are going separately to a concert at the Fox—each with friends. I have a ticket to see Shawn Mullins at Variety Playhouse. We saw him at Eddie's Attic here a couple of times. He is a really underrated songwriter. So I will go and have a PBR and listen and think about Shannon for a while.

I am finding that what has happened over the last several weeks is that some of the rawness of my hurt is going away. It is like the death created a big, raw hole in me. The hole is still there, but the edges are starting to heal. At least it feels that way most days. The existence of the hole sucks—don't get me wrong. I guess that is what people mean by "the new normal"—it is life with a big hole in it.

185

The stages of grief I wrote about earlier—I still think Kübler-Ross is wrong—or at least the labels are. To be fair, she was writing about dying, and the work was stretched by others to grieving. I don't think the model fits. So far, the stages feel like anger, defeat, and detachment. Anger is anger. Defeat is admitting complete and utter uselessness. Detachment is like a Viking funeral. Shannon and her things being gathered up and sent out to sea in a burning boat to become memories. Not sure what comes after that, but I will let you know.

November 27

9:38 a.m.

This will clearly be the Shawn Mullins edition. The concert last night was tremendous. I really, truly do not know why this guy isn't more famous. And he is from Atlanta and the place was still not sold out.

The two times Shannon and I saw him it was at a really small place—just him and another guitarist. This was the first time I saw him with a full band. Shannon would have absolutely loved it. It was a little hard driving there—it requires driving through a neighborhood we seriously considered looking at moving to, once we were empty nesters. In town, New Orleans uptown vibe, and all that.

Shannon and I experienced music differently. As you might have figured out, I am really into the lyrics. Shannon was more about the feeling. I guess that's just another reflection of how we were different. My brain, her heart. We would hear a song, I would ask her what she thought of the lyrics—she wouldn't be sure what they were. She just knew how the song made her feel.

Anyway, Shawn Mullins writes great songs. And where I am they really resonate. A couple of examples—they were so powerful last night when I heard them again.

First, from the song "Can't Remember Summer." Shannon's service was the first day of fall—so "Can't Remember Summer" is sort of appropriate. I wonder how he gets it—what was his tragedy? Because I don't think you can just make this up—and if you can, you are incredible. Another one of his songs is called "Shimmer."

Reid goes back to school today. I can tell I am on antidepressants because when I came down this morning he was not here, the car was not here, and there were no messages...I did not panic. I sent him a text. He was on the way home. He said, "It was a fiasco involving me locking my keys in another kid's car and not being able to find that kid." He called Spencer who went to get him and bring him home. So all is well that ends well. It has been good to have some family time.

Tonight I will be alone again. I know I will be trying to avoid self-pity around the whole "what is the point of feeling better when you know you are just going to feel bad again" thing. Why not just save yourself the trip and feel bad all the time. It's the crap car/good car metaphor I vaguely remember using weeks ago.

That's the defeat stage talking. And on that—anger isn't a stage—it's chronic. That bothers me—I really don't see not being angry ever again. I have talked with others who lost people "inappropriately" (if that phrase is okay) and a lot of them still seem angry.

What makes anger go away? Maybe nothing, but if I had to pick something I think I would pick justice. And there isn't going to ever be any justice here. Maybe people get tired of being angry—that's defeat, too. The challenge is learning how to live with anger—not learning how to move past it. Without justice, you can't move past it.

One thing the holiday makes unmistakable is that Shannon is truly gone. During each "regular" day, I tell myself what I consider micro lies. I'll be going to the store and will start to feel bad, and I'll tell myself, "Shannon's just at home." Or I will be moving the wash ahead, and I'll tell myself, "I can do this to help her out." I know it isn't true as I say it, but it creates a brief memory and enough positive energy to knock down the negative energy that was building up. It works because I went on errands without her; I went on trips without her; and so on. But there is no way she would not be with me for Thanksgiving. There is no lie that overcomes that. That's going to be true for each of these holidays. Oh well.

I mentioned that I had some great e-mails. One was from the spouse of a former student. She is a teacher herself, has been reading along, and shared that some of what I have written has helped her help one of her students deal with the loss of a family member. That feels really, really good.

Another was from a former student. Shannon knew her and thought she was great—and Shannon tended to be right about that sort of thing. Anyway, this woman is always good to send messages intended to lift me up. That is no small task—I am literally and psychologically pretty heavy. But she tries.

She asked me if I knew about the expression "Tebowing." She said she is on a campaign to make doing something nice to someone mean they have been "Shannoned." I think it may be hard to get equivalent media attention, but I appreciate the effort, and it did crack me up. "Have you Shannoned someone today?" I can see the T-shirts and billboards now...

Finally, I got one from an old friend who shared my sense of the wonder it can be to play the "You know you are on antidepressants when..." game. They had some great examples. It is an odd feeling to have something happen that you know would normally totally make you crazy and it just doesn't. The emotion is there, but it can't get any traction, and it slips away.

November 28

9:24 p.m.

Finally I got the picture of Shannon's spot in the neighborhood to load to the website. What an ordeal! Like I said, it looks better in person than I captured it here. I am so honored the neighbors did this for Shannon—and for me. Even the boys think it is kind of cool.

I keep buying concert tickets—always two, actually. Some habits are hard to break. Going to see Anders Osborne next week at a bar here in town. He is now a New Orleans-based guy, and we have seen him at Jazz Fest. I like him okay—his musical style really ranges. The song I have been listening to is called "Got Your Heart." I am not trying to turn this into a song lyrics website, but it just is a big part of what I do each day that helps me think about Shannon, what she meant to me, and what it means that she is gone. Some people simply say it better than I can. Or their words help me understand. I guess different people are inspired and comforted by words from different places...

So anyway—in the song he is telling his girlfriend/whatever that he knows the world is a hard place, that he knows they have tough times to get through, and that he knows she is scared. He is telling her not to fear—that he isn't going to abandon her—that he knows they can get past whatever obstacle is in their way and that she shouldn't worry because he has her heart.

I like that line a lot—"I've got your heart." It's like a giant step above "I've got your back." I felt that Shannon and I thought that about each

189

other. It feels tremendous to be trusted with taking care of someone else's heart—and that feeling might be surpassed only by knowing that someone is taking care of yours. I have been thinking all day today about how honored I was that Shannon trusted me with her heart. And I appreciate her taking care of mine for so long. I really like that line.

A few weeks ago, Shannon was in a dream. Just that once. Nothing special—it was a pretty dull dream about daily minutiae. She hasn't been back. Not sure what that means—if it means anything. I certainly think about her plenty when I am awake. Maybe it's the detachment stage. Viking funeral. I am coming to appreciate that imagery.

November 29

7:33 p.m.

Today was an interesting day. This morning my helper came over, and we took on the second of the two disaster storage rooms in the basement. Tremendous progress. Lots more logically packed, lots to give away, lots to throw away—all piled up and ready to go. The room is navigable again. Friday a professional organizer is coming to help us with the final push.

Today's tasks involved going through old pictures—the boys' school photos, our wedding album, all that. I have set all the pictures aside— Wolf Photo is going to take them from me and digitize them. I was doing it with a little scanner, but it would take years. It is worth some $$ to just get it done.

What was encouraging is that I could touch the wedding album without my hand or stomach catching on fire. I wrote a while back that each day I woke up with basically a punch to the stomach about what happened to Shannon. Most mornings now I instead wake up with a dull sadness about being alone. Progress, right? There is evidence that I am doing the rewiring I need to be doing for Shannon to be in the right place as I move forward, I guess. More often than not, I can look at pictures and feel good. Or at least better. Maybe my feelings now are 60% "sweet memory," 30% "I miss her so much," and 10% "disbelief and shock." Months ago it was 60% shock and 40% miss her and 0% sweet memory.

I also found a journal of Shannon's—she didn't have formal journals—I will be finding bits and pieces forever in various notebooks. I was thinking about what I wrote yesterday—if she trusted me with her heart, I guess she trusts me with her journal. It is hard to read—she didn't journal regularly; she journaled when she was hurting one way or another. So the entries aren't really much about happy memories. They are about struggles—with the kids, with her parents, her body, and with me.

I know we struggled—these entries were from a few months' time in 1995. Spencer would have been 6, Reid 2. It was the year I was going up for tenure at LSU. Spencer was not easy to raise—but remember (a) it isn't supposed to be easy and (b) he is worth it. But he was probably almost as big as Shannon by then—a bit ADD, and highly oppositional. Hard for her to contain! And Reid was a terrible two. And I was stressed out about work. We had money problems. She wasn't working and felt bad that she wasn't able to solve the money problems. It was hard—reading about how bad she felt was hard. And reading about her description of mitochondrial issues—nearly 20 years ago—was a harsh reminder of how much she overlooked physically and didn't complain about.

We were getting counseling—that was a good thing once we found the right person. I think it was important that we had about four years of being married before we had kids—it cemented us together. We knew what we could be together. It made it so our approach was "how are we going to work through this?" rather than "can we work through this?" We knew we were both committed to the whole "until death do you part" thing.

Another way Shannon and I are different (I am still here, she is gone...am I supposed to say "were different"?) is that she had a really hard time leaving baggage by the side of the road. She carried so much baggage, and she was such a petite person. It was more than she should have been expected to carry, yet she couldn't put it down. I have what is usually a blessing, but can be a problem. I honestly wake up each morning with a sense of a clean slate. I just am not bothered by yesterday anymore. It isn't some skill or effort—it just is how I am.

I recently came across a Will Rogers quote that captures it—he said, "Don't let yesterday use up too much of today." I am lucky that yesterday uses none of today (death of a spouse aside—I am talking "regular crises"). That's a blessing because I don't carry much baggage. It is dangerous because I assume everyone else operates that way—and they don't. So I couldn't always understand why on a Tuesday Shannon was bothered about something that happened on a Sunday. I had to learn to remember she handled things differently so that I could be sensitive.

So the journal reminded me that we weren't always happy—but I at least always felt happily married. I hope you can understand the difference. I knew she wasn't going anywhere. I knew I wasn't going anywhere. We just had to find our way through it. And we did. I am so glad Shannon got some years "on the other side." Kids doing fine, kids being fine young adults, no debt, money in the bank, fun trips. Being a mom to two boys is no picnic. And while I like to think I worked pretty hard to be a good spouse, I know I am no picnic either. Believe it or not, I can be grumpy, obstinate, opinionated, rash, impatient, and angry. And when I am not like that, I am whiny and needy!

So coincidentally today I got a link to pictures from the trip we made this summer to London as part of my consulting work. We had a private dinner at the Tower of London—here is Shannon and me talking to (not quite in the picture) Michael Jackson—he was Deputy Secretary of Homeland Security—the first to hold the job, appointed after 9/11. He is a great guy and Shannon enjoyed his stories. A long way from the dark days in the journal from 1995. I am so, so glad for these brighter years.

November 30

9:36 a.m.

Woke up at 5:30—felt rested and energetic. Odd. But I went with it. I did more before 9 than even the Marines. Fewer pushups (0) but way more e-mails, etc.

Last night I gathered up all the cards, legal papers, and medical papers that were strewn about on a chest in the front hall. I organized it all very neatly. I had gone to The Container Store to get a nice holder for it as an interim home. It felt good to read the cards again. Now on the dresser I have in a nice vase the dried roses from the flowers from Shannon's service. I have my favorite card there—it's the one that always cheers me up because it convinces me I can still do good in the world. That's all. Right underneath great pictures of the boys. It is a better presentation to remind me about Shannon than the mess that was there.

Here is something that Shannon would be okay with me sharing. It's dated July 29, 1997. Spencer is 8 and Reid is 4. Since we are revealing ages, Shannon would have been 34, and I would have been 36. We were staying at my childhood home in Concord for a couple of weeks wrapped around a convention I was attending in Boston.

Spencer is on a platform/raft in the middle of the shallow part of the pond. The same pond that Nate played in when he was little. I can't believe that Spencer is actually laying still for this length of time (30–45 minutes). He is on his belly—spitting into the water to attract fish.

The wind is strongly rushing through the trees. I'm afraid I will get sand in my eyes. Reid has a metal shovel and has been digging in the sand for an equally impressive length of time. The water is cold and dark, yet clear. The sand is warm from the sun.

They are both trying to skip rocks across the pond. Reid has resorted to dumping handfuls of sand in to the water...Ker-Plunk. I love them so much. They are frustrating, miraculous little angels with curiosity and a stubborn streak.

Shannon and I loved to fight about where they got their stubborn streak. I guess the fact we each vehemently blamed the other meant we were both right. More later—gotta go to work—the Marines are catching up with me in terms of work done.

Today was a good day—enjoyed with caution. Saw a bit of blue sky and am hopeful about tomorrow. Boys both in contact; both seem in fine spirits. Spencer is nursing his dog a bit from a scratched eye; Wednesday is Reid's longest class day. So they were having some challenges but hanging in there.

Enjoyed dinner tonight with my old fraternity brother—the lawyer who has been helping me out with my issues with the various medical facilities. It was great to get caught up. I have truly been fortunate to have so many good people in my life. And I am glad now that he is back in it. Shannon thought he was great, so I wish I knew he had been here before.

Best part of the day—I learned that Spencer, Reid, and I will be joining 27 Tech MBAs to go to St. Bernard Project in a couple of weeks—by far the largest turnout we have ever had. I am so proud of them. I have always bought a nice dinner as a thank-you for the students—dinner and drinks for 30 is going to hurt (in a good way). It's the least I can do for what they are doing for New Orleans. And, the boys will get to visit Shannon's tree. Last year, Reid and Shannon came along. Reid worked with us—that was fun. He enjoyed trying to convince the students they were nuts for ever listening to anything I said. Sometime I need to share the story of the lunch we all had at Parkway Bakery. Shannon joined us for dinner—hanging sheetrock was not a good idea for her. I am glad she got to meet some of the students. I wish she had met more.

December 1

> 6:33 a.m.

Well that didn't take long. Up too early again today. I mentioned about not having Shannon in a dream—should have kept my mouth shut/fingers off the keys. She was back last night in a bad way. Woke me up and couldn't go back to sleep.

It is so eerie how this stuff happens—I start typing about Shannon and a perfect song starts playing..."Complicated" by Yonder Mountain String Band...Shannon loved the lyric where the singer insists he wasn't born so complicated. I love that lyric, too. Shannon was complicated. Not going to venture guesses on how she got to be. And anyway, complicated and interesting often are synonymous.

The day starts with two wheels on the road; two wheels in the ditch. I am going to try to get all four on the road. Trying to match yesterday's early morning productivity. Lots of good things on the schedule today—including psychiatrist. So he can help me interpret the dream...not that it really is much of a mystery.

I feel like I have turned some important corners over the past month, but I can see there are a whole lot more I need to turn in the months ahead. Wish I could get to wherever I am going a bit faster. I wish there were more markers of progress. On the whole turning corners imagery...four right turns—or four left turns—brings you back to where you started. Hope I am mixing the turns up so I move forward. I don't want to go back to where I was in September.

December 2

I remember when Shannon and I got married there was a period of maybe a month or so where most every day when we came home from work there would be a package at the door—a wedding gift from someone. Each was a neat reminder of our new status—and it was nice to be cosmically sharing that with whomever it was that sent the gift. After a while, the packages stopped coming—everyone was going back to their normal life; our status was not new anymore. And we had to settle in for the "long haul" as just another married couple.

Now it is a bit like I am unwinding that—it is a process in reverse, but with similarities. When Shannon collapsed, when she died, at her service, in the days that followed, there were reminders every day of my new status. People sent cards, people sent food, all that. Now my status isn't new anymore. Friends are going back to their lives, and I have to settle in for the "long haul" as just another widower.

This isn't a complaint—it's just an observation. My friends—all of you—have done about 400% more than I could have asked or imagined. So there is no need to send food!

At the psychiatrist yesterday, he made a point about this that should have been obvious to me, but I hadn't gotten to it yet (or maybe I never would have). The point was that everyone in my life is having to change the way they think of me. I am not half of a couple anymore. I am different and that means all my friends have work to do. That's interesting—obviously I have to figure out my situation—how to act, what to say, what do to; but I guess all of you do, too.

You all may be confused about me just like I am confused about me.

Yesterday ended well—I have rarely been so glad to see the sun (and it is back today). Had a chance to work with some students on a pro bono consulting project they are doing—that was fun. Then a beer with a friend. It was nice to be out in a bar with a friend having a beer and talking about whatever. It was something "normal" to do. I am going to try to find more ways to do stuff like that. It is weird to stay out late on my own.

Today is going to be a good day. Helper and organizer coming over to begin the final phase of basement clean up. Decided to add some more music listening capability to the sitting room—the sun in here is just irresistible on a pretty day—so home theater people coming.

Something sweet from Shannon's journal—July 30, 1997—the same trip to Concord...

> *Quote from Spencer yesterday—he had caught a dragonfly in his hands and was holding it by the body/legs and crouching at the water's edge—he dunked the bug underwater and then let it go. He exclaimed "It lives—it's a witch!" Warped, yet still I laughed. Poor creature!*
>
> *I will wash whites today. The bright light from the window woke Nate early on. I have scary hair. The coffee smells good.*
>
> *My kids have so much energy. I wish I could match their enthusiasm and stamina.*

4:24 p.m.

Wow. I have been organized. It is like a reverse action tornado hit my basement. I have a TON of crap to haul upstairs for trash and Goodwill.

And what is left is sensible, seeable, and retrievable...I sound like an infomercial.

It is a great relief—the team is coming back tomorrow for a short day to 100% finish. Shannon would be amazed and would certainly approve. She would sit in the keeping room, imagining the mess one floor below her, and stress out. I wish we had done this when she was alive, but like I said, in the moment we always had something better to do. Right now, I don't. So trying not to feel like I cheated her out of it.

I joined in a bit, but mostly they took care of it. I had to decide "trash or keep," mostly. One of my jobs was to begin the process of sorting through the pictures to make the pile to be digitized. It was really nice to do today. I know it will feel worse other days. So, so many great memories. And it was good to see so many of Shannon's smiles—especially after reading her journals (which she wrote mostly when she was feeling down). It was odd to see the pictures of her before her eye surgery—with her lids drooping down—I had forgotten she looked like that. And I came across the pictures of her right after her surgery—when it looked like someone had hit her across the bridge of her nose with a baseball bat. She was so tough, really.

I got my first two Christmas cards today. One from someone who was with me when Shannon died, one from someone who does not know. The latter is such a casual acquaintance I feel like I can just ignore it. It made me think about my situation—"To Christmas card, or not to Christmas card...that is the question." The answer is "not to Christmas card." I usually write a wiseass letter. Sometimes we send a picture card of the family. Don't think I am going to do it this year. People will understand.

Sitting on the back porch with a hard-earned beer—nice to be able to do that in December. Listening to Widespread Panic on the new speakers. Sounds pretty darn good. Sun going down to my right, moon rising to my left.

I peaked too early. Friday night with nothing to do. Or at least nothing I feel like doing. It is funny to me how much it matters that it is Friday or Saturday night—or Tuesday. In my life, the nights really are not any different. I am not dealing with getting kids to school, I work pretty much 7 days a week on something—my work is what I do; I write all the time; I teach at night and on Saturdays. So every night is pretty much as consequential as the next. If I was sitting here and it was Tuesday and I had nothing to do I wouldn't care. It's like Friday and Saturday are somehow insults. Isn't that weird. If I stay home, I am angry that it is Friday and everyone else has something neat to do. If I go out, I am angry that everyone I run across is in a couple. I am a wimp.

I went to a new kitchen store that opened in the neighborhood this week. I found some cool pots and some kitchen odds and ends. I bought them. As I was paying, the nice woman at the register said, "Good for you for getting your wife's gifts early!" I was glad I didn't fold on the spot. I handled it well, but it hurt. I wish I had Shannon to shop for. I don't even really have the boys to shop for. So here is where I would like to ask for your help. When our boys were little, their schools/daycares would "adopt" (that isn't the right word...whatever) a family that needed help—so we would be assigned to find a basketball for a boy or whatever.

I can always give money to charity, but what I would like is to know if any of you know a family that needs some help at Christmas. I would like to know their situation, and I would like to shop for them and wrap the stuff and then arrange for someone to deliver the stuff. I don't want to be there. I just want to know it happened. I don't have a network that will make it easy for me to find something like that. If you know a family that needs a Santa please let me know.

It would feel good to have someone to take care of. I definitely peaked too early today.

5:23 p.m.

I like your idea of finding someone to help. Sometimes churches have lists of people in need. We live in a very poor area—our club is adopting a family who lost everything in the spring tornadoes. Schools also have lists of families in need—they would keep their names confidential most likely, but would tell you what is needed. Georgia Department of Family Services will also have lists of needy. Plus you may have friends in local clubs who are sponsoring families. Good luck and God bless.

CD

6:09 p.m.

I was in the shower cleaning up from all that basement work and became angry that I had written such a whiny entry earlier. I got sidetracked by remembering the cooking store. I handled it at the time much better than I handled it today. I prefer to write something nice about Shannon as an ending—so here it is.

Working in the basement today, one of the major decisions was, "Given that every bed upstairs has a full complement of pillows on it already, how many of these 8 additional pillows in the basement do I need to keep?" If my count is right, I live alone in a four-bedroom house that has upstairs 24 pillows already.

If you heard Father Michael at Shannon's service, you know that she was famous in her small circle for her hospitality. There was no type of pillow she didn't have. I really don't need any of those 8 pillows, but in her honor I carefully examined all of them and picked the 5 that together offered the best variety for any upcoming guest.

Her consideration of others hardly stopped at pillows. One of the things I found to give away is a metal bar/handle that bolts around a tub so someone with injury/disability can more easily get in and out. Shannon ordered it from a catalog years ago when my dad was coming to visit. He had recently had a hip replacement and was having trouble getting up and down. She wanted to make sure he felt safe in the shower.

But her consideration of others did not stop at bolt-on tub devices either. She had a plumber come to remove a perfectly good toilet and replace it with a taller one designed to be easier for people to get off of if they have difficulty with their hips. Just for my dad for his two-day stay.

That was Shannon. She took good care of people whenever she got a chance.

December 3

6:12 p.m.

Blue Cross sent me an interesting letter today—just a form letter, but it basically asked if Shannon's event was related to a job-related incident or an accident...I guess they are trying to see if a 100K hospital bill might be someone else's responsibility.

Lots of good things going on today. Organizing is now 93% done. I cannot believe the difference. I told the organizer that this was great progress and that now I have room for a lot more crap down in the basement. She didn't like that strategy. Most of what remains is just carrying up the giveaways whenever I can arrange a pickup. The trash is all stacked in the front hall ready to go out tomorrow. The 7% that remains are all the pictures and a couple of boxes of memory stuff that I need to weed through.

I have discovered some treasures. One mystery box contained stuff from Reid's Christening/birth and all that. I have the *Wall Street Journal* (Dow at around 3,300) and the Baton Rouge papers from the day he was born, lots of other little artifacts—hadn't seen them in 18 or so years. The very best thing, though, gave me the biggest smile I have had in a while.

Reid was a C-section delivery. Spencer had been a very tough delivery for Shannon; her doctor didn't want that sort of thing to happen again given her condition. Plus, Spencer was just barely over 8 pounds at birth—the estimations on Reid put him at 9 and a half.

So because it was a C-section, I was in an operating room with her—not a delivery room. And because it was surgery I had to wear scrubs and all that. I sat up by her head and did NOT look over the curtain placed across her chest. I remember the doctor telling Shannon that if Reid didn't come in at least 9 pounds she was putting him back for a normal delivery. He did come in at 9 pounds, 8 ounces...pretty good estimating.

After the nurses got Reid clean and were starting the paperwork they covered Reid's feet with ink and called me over—they pressed his feet on the chest of my scrubs—right where my heart was. The best treasure in that box today was the neatly folded scrubs top with Reid's tiny footprints right there on the chest pocket. That was such a cool thing to find.

I received lots of good suggestions for secret Santa-ing—I think there are about four of them I can do. I appreciate your help in making some great connections and finding me that outlet. Christmas is going to be better if I can imagine there are some smiling kids out there who might be having a better day than they would have otherwise. It will be nice to have a more specific idea of who than I would get from just sending $$ to a charity. It's going to help a lot.

Ending with a Shannon story...one of the things I found was the old list she made titled "BABYSITTER INFORMATION REVISED JULY 1997." The list is encased in plastic—it was posted right by the kitchen phone in our Baton Rouge house. The first thing that cracked me up is that in those days, people didn't have cell phones—they had car phones. So the list has a "Van phone number" and an "Explorer phone number" on it. It has my pager on it.

The list then has home, work, and/or car/back-up phone numbers for four relatives, four doctors (during and after business hours numbers), the pharmacy, the vet, 911, police, fire, sheriff, EMT, hospital, pharmacy, ambulance, cable, gas company, and time.

Then the list has numbers, addresses, and names of all household residents for 6 different neighbors.

Finally, the list contains the boys' various allergies. I think most people would see the list as a sure sign of OCD. But Shannon wasn't OCD. She wanted to anticipate every single possible thing that might make a dear child who was babysitting uncomfortable and then have a fix for it so they wouldn't be uncomfortable. It was how she took care of the people who were taking care of her kids. That's sweet.

December 4

9:23 a.m.

It is a bit cool here on the front porch, but I am burning up—just hauled a sick amount of trash to the curb—properly sorted, of course, in to recycle and dump. I am pleased with the fact I am convinced I have significantly reduced clutter and restored order without in any way compromising my ability to be the sort of host Shannon would want me to be. You want pillows? We got pillows! Need to seat 25 people for dinner? I found the rest of the matching everyday dishware—no problem. You want a waffle—coming up! Heading to

Chastain for a concert? Got your seat cushion, wine cooler, battery powered fan, poncho, can huggies, and classy plastic wine glasses all right here ready to go. Want to see cute stuff about the kids...that's over here...

I did get to see most of the second half of the LSU game—after watching the Bruins trounce the Maple Leafs on "Hockey Night in Canada"...I used to drive Shannon nuts with that. Saturday is Hockey Night in Canada...the CBC does a featured game nationally—one of the Canadian teams. On Saturday afternoon, I'd ask Shannon, "What day is it?" She'd groan. I'd say, "That's right, hockey night in Canada!" She'd groan again. We were hysterical.

Now that I am gaining momentum in organizing my stuff in the physical world, I am beginning to think about the virtual world. I am trying to save some of Shannon's e-mails—so to do that I log in to her account, export data, log out, go to my account, log in, import, etc. Except it doesn't work because of version compatibilities, so I need experts, etc. Anyway—in trying to make sure I was "in" her account I sent a test message to my account. How dumb is this—it felt good to see her name pop up in my in-box. I miss that so much. More than so much.

There are also people who sent her wishes via Facebook—so I am trying to thank them. While I was in her account, I "liked" the post I made referring to Spencer's link above...I knew it was a true sentiment on the part of Shannon's spirit. Then I realized I didn't want to freak Spencer out...so I immediately had to log in as me and leave a comment that "fixed" it. Then I realized that Spencer is not an idiot and would figure it out on his own. Oh well.

Shannon also had a friend request from one of Reid's high school friends. I sent her a note—Shannon would have been thrilled to have been included that way—and this girl has continued to be a good friend to Reid, and she would have appreciated that, too.

It is harder to deal with the virtual world stuff than the real world. Maybe I should leave it alone—but then again it is about done. I don't want to lose any memory that might be a precious one.

8:33 p.m.

I am in DC at a client site with a fussy Internet connection—matters of national security, firewalls, and the like. So I have to be quick...

Doesn't take a psychiatrist for me to understand why the basement clean out was so meaningful. It was undeniable, demonstrable progress on something. That's good—feeling like I was taking steps forward has been rare. Mostly feel like one foot is nailed to the floor, and I am walking around in a circle.

On the plane today I was thinking about work and writing. I have been focused a lot recently on careers—what makes for career success and the like. Some things commonly come up when talking to successful executives. One regards what the execs would probably be comfortable labeling a crucible experience—lots of pundits have used that term. These are events where the person feels overmatched, somehow succeeds, and as a result is a better person.

I have had three previous crucible experiences. Very short versions of the stories—the first was when I was a camp counselor at 16, charged with the care of a sailboat full of twelve 10-year-olds for two days at a remote, undeveloped beach reachable only by boat. I was told that as long as I brought 80% of them back, I had done okay.

The second was at Exeter, where I was so clearly academically average. It was a tremendous shock after public high school. I have never had to work that hard in my life. One example—my sons went to what is considered a very strong public school here in Marietta. In English, they spent about a month reading one of Shakespeare's plays. In one semester at Exeter, I read everything he is said to have written. When we were doing the plays we read two a week, and had a paper due on one of them every Monday. One play in a month is rigorous? Really? I was so overmatched there.

The third was in my early days as a Chart House dishwasher. I wanted to quit so badly—especially one night. A friend who was a waiter smuggled me a beer in a Styrofoam cup. I stuck it out, and I am glad I did—I have the best friends possible from that experience.

In each of these cases, I was seriously overmatched, overwhelmed, you name it. In each case, somehow I got through—or it ended—whatever. I can point to specific things about how I think and work that are better because of surviving those experiences. I can point to people I have in my life because of surviving those experiences. So they weren't always much fun while they were going on—but I can't deny they made me better.

I used those experiences many times every single day of my life.

Losing Shannon is my fourth crucible experience. I am again seriously overmatched, overwhelmed, you name it. Somehow I will get through, and I will find a way for it to make be better. I will find a way to live every day differently in a good way from having had Shannon in my life.

After that I may be as good as I am going to get. I don't feel up for a fifth crucible experience.

December 5

Just back from DC. Thanks to the neighbor who brought up my papers for me, whoever you are! Trip went well—I thought I taught well, but the crowd seemed a little behind all day. Some days are like that.

Wasn't going to write tonight—it is late, and I have 23 hours of teaching to do in the next four days. Lots to do—rest sounds good. But I had an odd experience on the way home that I want to get recorded.

I had to tell a lie—I guess I had to act a lie tonight. I was on the train to baggage claim at the airport. A guy next to me noticed my platinum medallion status baggage tag and asked, "So do you live at the airport?" I laughed and said, "Not quite, but I do visit it a lot." He said, "When I made silver medallion, my wife divorced me."

I had to work so hard to choke back the words, "My wife is dead so I guess I am safe from that." Boy, would that have been awkward. I said instead, "Recently, I've made a lot of trips with my wife, so that makes it better." That is sort of true—playing a game with verb tense.

After the exchange it was odd—I know that by handling it the way I did I saved him feeling pretty crappy. But instead I felt crappy because of what it reminded me of and even more because I had to quickly find some way to deny the thing that is defining me these days. I didn't like doing that—but what was the choice? No good comes from shocking someone else or embarrassing them. I guess I could have said, "I'm sorry that happened to you."—but that sure wasn't what started to form on my tongue at the time.

December 6

5:45 p.m.

Front porch—65 and drizzly. I'd rather sun, but then it would be too cold to be out. The drizzle will have to be tolerated.

I was just catching up on e-mails—lots of e-mails. Then a song by John Butler Trio came on, and I just had to get to where I could think about Shannon. We got to see them with friends in Central Park a couple of summers ago—fun night. The song that came on is called something like "I'd Do Anything Just to Be with You." When his girlfriend is gone, nothing is or works right. I like the discombobulation the lyrics imply.

The important stuff...I went to the rheumatologist today for a checkup—that's who treats my psoriatic arthritis. He is at Emory—a teaching hospital. It is busy, you have to expect to wait. Normally it takes 20 minutes to be called back. The resident sees you pretty quick; the doctor usually takes another 30 minutes to arrive.

I like my doctor there—I have been seeing him a long time—he is a solid guy. It was weird to have to change my emergency contact information from Shannon to Spencer.

The resident came in and asked, "What's new?" So I told him. He was kind, we went through the exam, etc. He said, "Okay—I will go talk to the doctor, and we will be back." It couldn't have been more than 3 minutes before the doctor came in. He expressed his condolences— we sat down and talked about Shannon, her situation, etc., for 15 minutes. Then he examined me. That's 15 minutes more time than the critical care doctors who treated Shannon gave me during the 11 days she was their patient at St. Joseph's. It's 15 minutes more time than they gave me during the month they jerked me around on the death certificate. I now have about 30 years, hopefully, to make them re-member that was a bad way to practice medicine. They'll quit medi-cine before I quit reminding them.

The other important thing—the piece on the Tech kid with mitochondrial disease has begun to air on CNN. I haven't watched it yet—that's for later tonight. But he is a Tech kid, so you know I expect he nailed it.

Finally, tomorrow is the three-month anniversary of losing Shannon. It is the two-month anniversary of my friend's stroke. It is the one-month anniversary of my colleague's death. I hope the sun is out. It is going to be sort of a miserable day.

8:22 p.m.

I was going to share some stories, but I have lost interest for now. I watched the interview, and as I predicted, Colby did great. He is heroic. What brought me down was reading the comments people have posted in response to the story. If you read the comments, you will see how much pain and suffering this disease causes people—that's hard. People with bad cases are in really, really terrible shape. You will also see how people seem to blame Colby for not being sicker—that somehow his struggle is not worthy of the attention when compared to what their families are dealing with—that "sicker" people must be featured to raise awareness—that Colby makes it look "easy" to have mitochondrial disease. I understand the frustration, but that's really pretty ugly behavior. And then there are comments from people who I think are able to see the bigger picture—that every case is different, and every victim worthy of compassion.

Shannon was kind of like Colby. She was sick—it impacted her every single day of her adult life. But she still had a good life. She found ways to live with it, to let it "win" when she needed to rest, to fight it when she wanted to have kids, and so on.

So lots of families dealing with the disorder might not be very sympathetic towards Shannon, either. Well, if it makes them feel better, the disease killed her three months ago. So you can see why I am not really in the mood anymore to share silly stories. I hurt for those people—but I find their comments ugly. I have to turn those feelings around.

December 7

10:18 p.m.

Today is three months—90ish days. I was working on a syllabus tonight for the class I am teaching in the spring. Ironically, the main book's title includes the phrase "your first 90 days." It's about your first three months in a new job—how to make sure you get off on the right foot and all that.

So this has been my first 90 days in my new job. The job really sucks; I'd rather quit it and go back to my old job of being married, but I think I am doing okay. The boys are hanging tough, my work is going okay and trending in the right direction, bills are getting paid on time, the house is in good shape. I feel like I am doing okay on the stuff I can do. The stuff I can't do is a bitch. But at least today I am not angry, I am just admitting defeat. There is a huge hole in my existence that I can't fix. As I told a friend tonight, I really miss having someone to tell "good night."

I had tickets to a concert tonight at a bar in town. Worked late, grabbed some pretty bad Thai food at a place that was really good in 1988, and then went to the show. Stood around for an hour waiting.

Alone. Didn't even have my iPhone (left it at work by mistake). So it was waiting old school style...nothing to do, no Facebook status to update. I just people-watched and daydreamed. When you go to a show alone a major consideration is how badly do you want to keep your spot...if you go to the restroom, you have no one to hold your spot for you.

After waiting an hour, an opening act came on. I made it through 1.5 songs and left. I wasn't going to listen to that for 45 minutes, then sit through the break-down/set-up of equipment, etc. to hear Anders Osborne.

One Shannon story. Maybe it is an "us" story—or maybe it is even a Spencer story. When Shannon was pregnant with Spencer, we went to the doctor for an ultrasound. I have the tape around here somewhere. The tech asked us if we wanted to know if it was a boy or girl, and we said yes. It was a boy. Then the tech captured a really neat profile shot of Spencer. She froze the image, looked at it, looked at Shannon, and said, "Wow—he has your nose!"

I looked at Shannon and said in a matter-of-fact voice, "Well, I guess that settles the question of maternity!" Shannon laughed so hard she told me later she was sure she would have an accident on the table. I told her I thought I was pretty funny, too. She agreed it was a good line, but what she said was funnier was watching the technician try to understand just how big an idiot I was.

Shannon always hated her nose. I thought it was pretty cute. Spencer's nose has evolved, but it did look just like Shannon in that picture. That was a neat day—seeing him in there growing.

December 9

I have tried to explain my view that in some ways Shannon would not be all that disappointed with how things played out. I found this piece of paper a couple of weeks ago, started to read it, and had to put it down. I felt strong enough today to pick it up and share it with you.

There is no date on it, but from the full contents I am pretty sure Shannon would have written this in 2007 or so. This is part of what she wrote:

I am afraid (terrified?). I realize that I worry about ending up conscious inside of a useless body. I worry that the Mito will kill my physical abilities, and the mind will still be aware. I will be trapped. I will be forgotten. I will be alone, unable to communicate.

That sounds like a crappy way to die—and it sounds like a really hard fear with which to live. She had a great last summer. She didn't suffer this ending. So that's good. That makes me not so sad. But then she ends the note with this:

I am already trapped in an ineffective body. My joy is Nate. Poor thing...such a burden. I know that the strain of that burden is not sustainable—nor should it be. He should be as happy and vibrant as he is—always. I drag everyone down.

That makes me very, very, very sad. We talked about this all the time, but I could never get her to understand that she didn't drag me down—she propped me up.

It is so much harder for me to be me without her.

December 10

It's been a very busy week. Maybe that's why I am a little less disappointed this week with my Saturday night filled with errands and domestic bliss. I will try to limit myself to just one negative comment... add beautiful sunrises and full moons to the list of things better enjoyed with someone special. We have had both this week.

Tonight I finished my secret Santa shopping. I have to say it was a lot of fun. On the way home, I stopped for gas. As I was pumping, I heard the "Excuse me, sir?" that you know is going to be followed by a request for money. I turned around, and it was a guy—maybe 40— who looked like hell. He was walking towards me from a pick-up truck with an older guy who looked similarly wiped out sitting in the driver's seat. He started with his hard luck story and wanted to know if I could give them a couple of dollars for gas.

Well, I didn't have any cash. I asked if he had a gas can, and he said he did. I told him to get it, and I would fill it up after I filled my car up. He was excited and ran to the truck. He had the tiniest gas can I have ever seen. It might have held enough gas to get him to the next gas station. So I told him to bring the truck over—I swiped my card and put 20 dollars' worth in his tank. You would have thought I cured his cancer. I got handshakes, tipped caps, the whole thing. That felt good, too. Not even going to make a joke about the guy's UGA hat.

Two useful stories from school this week. On the way to lunch one day, I walked past one of my new students—just starting with his group this week. He was sneaking a cigarette in before heading to lunch. He is of Middle Eastern origin, I think. He said, "Professor, I wanted to tell you that I really enjoy your class and that you have a much better sense of humor than most Americans." I laughed. Then he said, "I love your sarcasm—I hope you keep it up." I laughed again and said I didn't think he had to worry...that I didn't think being sarcastic was a choice I made. It's just me.

I appreciated that interaction because, like the others in this new class, he did not know me before I lost Shannon. So if he thinks I am teaching well, if he thinks I have a sense of humor, and if he gets my sarcasm, then it means I must be doing okay. I don't think the students who know about my loss are lying to me when they say I seem to be doing well at work—but I also know they want me to be better and may be wishful thinkers. Somehow this was like independent confirmation that I am doing well at work.

The second story is bittersweet (remember, euphemism for "sucks"). One of my students lost his stepmom last week. He wasn't sure if he would make class, etc. It was the first time I was the "experienced hand" and I was comforting—rather than being comforted. He talked about how he wasn't sure how to help because his dad kept insisting everything was fine. He said he just wanted to know what the plan is so that he could start working the plan. Sound familiar? And I knew how to slip in to my role, and I knew what to say. And I think it helped. And the rest of the week when I saw him I said it was good to see him. And I told him I was thinking about him and his dad. And I am.

Finished the basement clean out today with the help of my "team." My front porch is crammed full of the stuff for the donations truck coming by on Monday. Now that I am back from shopping, my Saturday night will involve moving laundry ahead and polishing a silver bowl. The bowl is special to me—it was a gift from my mom, dad, aunt, and uncle to my dad's parents on their 40th wedding anniversary. They were the sort of cute little old couple Shannon and I looked forward to being. I know that's what Shannon wanted—but I also know she was afraid that her life was not going to be a slow, peaceful glide to the end, but rather a tumble down a steep, rocky slope. Anyway, after my grandparents died, my aunt had the bowl. She recently gave it to me and Shannon. It's been touched by everyone on my side of the family, and I think polishing it up will feel good.

December 11

The most important thing today was a very sweet event here in the neighborhood. Some neighbors gathered mid-day to share a glass of wine and to "install" the "In Memory of Shannon Bennett" plaque at her tree. I got a lot of hugs and handshakes—that's great. Lots of smiles and well wishes—that's great, too. And they brought ornaments to hang on the tree to dress it up a bit. On the one hand, it looks a bit like the Charlie Brown Christmas tree—but on the other hand, it's beautiful because of the sentiment.

There was other good stuff today, too. Some neighbors took me to an unusual and neat lunch; I went by the restaurant before the dinner crush and visited a bit with Spencer. He looked good. Lastly, my front porch looks a bit like the Sanford and Son set from the old TV show— but hopefully that stuff will all be carted off by the AKF tomorrow. Right now, it might be the first time in a few weeks where the inside of my house looks better than the outside. Progress.

It was the sort of day that should leave me feeling pretty good. The week behind was good, and I am very much looking forward to the things on the calendar for next week. At the same time, the heaviness I had avoided all week is back. I have three months of data on this, and I am about to conclude there is no pattern; there is no discernible cause and effect.

I've written about my doctor explaining that I needed to be comfortable being selfish for a while. The most selfish thought I have is of course that none of this had happened. When I think about that particular selfishness, I feel bad because after reading Shannon's journal entries, I realize how hard things were for her—at least on the bad days. Wishing she was back is in part wishing for her to have more fear, more pain, more anxiety, more frustration. I wouldn't wish that on her. So wanting her back is selfish in a way that isn't going to help.

The next most selfish thought I have is about wishing for ways to be happier tomorrow than today. I'm told—and I've observed—that there isn't a proven plan for doing that. I am about bad metaphored out, but what struck me today was that my relationship with Shannon provided the mortar that kept my bricks stuck together in a coherent fashion. Now I am a barely organized pile of bricks. I think there may be some potential in the pile, but it is kind of hard to tell! So the second selfish thought isn't going to help, either.

It's taken me over an hour to write the last two paragraphs—so I need to back up and regroup and try something else or I will be sitting here all night.

Ironically, what may be frustrating me is feeling so much better about how work is going. I am experiencing an "unbalanced recovery"—perhaps that is the way to think about it. I am hopeful about where the boys are, work is coming along very well. The rest of my life isn't really. The discrepancy is obvious and my impatience returns. How's that for selfish—2 out of 3 ain't bad—I wish I could be more patient.

Phew...finally.

December 12

> 5:53 p.m.

Sitting here in my hotel listening to the iPod after a solid workout. I don't know if any of you know of Eva Cassidy. She has a beautiful voice. Sadly, she died from cancer at 33 and really became more famous after her death than she was before. It was listening to her music that led me to check out Blues Alley in Georgetown—now a required spot whenever I go up there.

Anyway, here is the song that came on—it's called "I Know You by Heart." I had forgotten about it. It's been on my iPod for years, and I've always liked it. Check out the lyrics. It's brutal and comforting to me at the same time because it's true down to the seasons. It came on, and I grabbed my keys (with my wedding ring on them) and held on to them so I could make it through the song. Hard to listen to, but didn't want to turn it off. You can find it on YouTube—you'll love it, too.

10:49 p.m.

I had a lot of time today to think about the "being selfish" thing. In the end, I think what it really means for me is that I have to lighten up myself. I have been so indulged by everyone else—in basic interactions no one tells me "no"—people help, people check in. There isn't more I could ask for. Being selfish around others isn't necessary—people are so good to me.

The problem is me. My experience is that problems are solved when you use your head and then work hard. This "problem" is resistant to that strategy. When I fail to see "progress," I feel like I have failed to be smart or to work hard. I think for me, the being selfish means I need to give myself a break. Wish me luck. Not really how I am wired. I am becoming a bigger believer in the role of personality in determining behavior with each passing week.

Today had some great moments. Trip to Minneapolis was smooth. I got to the gym. I had lunch with a friend I haven't seen in some time. Catching up was fun—we always have good laughs. I had dinner with another friend I hadn't seen in even longer. It was great to linger at a table with a glass of wine in a nice place talking about whatever. I could have sat there a long time. Normal stuff feels so good. I'd like to think these were moments to build on—that they created some momentum—but I know better than that. It's good to experience normal, but tomorrow will be its own adventure entirely independent of anything that was accomplished today.

Speaking of tomorrow—very much looking forward to the teaching. I have tickets to see Ryan Adams in concert. One for me and one for my coat! Should be an interesting show...I've read that if he doesn't like the crowd he just walks off...I had a professor like that at Tulane.

December 13

11:32 p.m.

Last night, I got to have dinner with a friend. Pleasant atmosphere, food was okay, conversation was great. Tonight, I ate alone. Pleasant atmosphere, food was okay. No conversation—Sunday *NY Times*. Lots of time watching people. Absolutely blew my mind to see couples with nothing to say checking their iPhones to pass the time. Last night, I didn't even think once about my phone. Same at lunch with a friend. When I was out with Shannon, the only time either of us checked was when we knew we expected a text from one of the boys as to their activities. Don't they care about the person sitting across the table from them? Can they be out of things to say? Do they not realize how lucky they are to have someone to share a night with?

Concert was surprisingly good. Great venue, quirky artist. No one could enter except between songs, no bar service, everyone hushed like at the symphony. The songs are all sort of depressing—which he acknowledges himself. I listen to lots of male singer/songwriters—most of them are passable singers and good poets. Adams has a voice I can only say is pretty. Odd thing to say about a guy's voice, but it fits.

219

On this next point—please don't write me now. If I am wrong, you can one day say "I told you so." I'll be in a better mood to hear it then. I have to accept the fact that Shannon and I spent 28 years building something. It's gone—my personal Hurricane Katrina and all that—I am not able to do what needs to be done to go back to square one, and relationships don't start in the middle. So I need to refocus myself on work. I don't want a hobby. I don't give a shit about learning to play golf. I am not about to start painting miniature soldiers. I can't make any difference with any of that. I can't make a difference for Shannon anymore. That leaves work. That's the only place I can make a difference. My doctor will be mad at me on Friday, but so be it.

For whatever reason, the other day LinkedIn recommended a "you might know" to a guy I used to work with at LSU. He has been gone from there a long time—we've been out of touch. So I sent a request. He accepted and replied "...and just when I thought you were dead." Well, I'm not dead, but Shannon is. I know he didn't know any better, but still.

December 15

10:29 p.m.

I wanted to not write today, but I am drawn in regardless. Sometimes writing makes me feel better, sometimes it makes me feel worse. I guess I am hoping for a lift tonight. We'll see in a couple of paragraphs.

I had been looking forward to this week—and there was a lot in it that was fun. But somehow it nets out in the red. There are only two explanations. One is simply holding unrealistic expectations about how much will be accomplished, how much progress will be experienced, how much relief will be felt. The second is the point I shared earlier in the week, which is that a lot of how I feel is based on stuff that is not going away. I'm connected to it forever. It feels like that sets a ceiling on just how good a day or week can be. Sort of like high school—I eventually came to understand that I simply couldn't earn an A at Exeter. It wasn't going to happen. When I forget the ceiling is there, I set myself up for disappointment.

Expectations are something I can control, so that is what I need to do. I need to have more realistic expectations about the future that take in to account my varied limitations—motivational, emotional, physical, spiritual, etc. I had already crossed skydiving out, a hockey comeback, and moving to a shack on an island somewhere. Now I need to cross out some things that I thought were realistic, but that I am learning are not. As I wrote the other day, what is going to be left on the list is work. So I am very lucky to love what I do.

Speaking of work—did a lot of it today. Took a break on the plane home. As usual, got caught up in some lyrics. I'll boil them down. First, back to Dave Matthews' song "Jimi Thing"—He is singing that he has what he needs, but that what he wants is what he's without. Yup. That's true or I guess it needs to be made true or accepted as true by me. I don't expect to fill wants—not sure that crater will ever be filled. But I have more than I need if I can reorient myself to be satisfied with it.

One of my favorite bar bands—actually my favorite bar band—is from New Orleans—Cowboy Mouth. Their energy is just amazing. I talked Shannon into loving them, and we saw them many times. One of their not-quite hits is a song called "Easy." The lyrics explain that it's easy to label all that's wrong or missing in your life; that it is much harder to be happy with what you have, but that it's worth the effort. That fits me this week, too.

The boys got me interested in the band Foo Fighters—their song "Wheels" flashed across the iPod today on the plane home. The song recounts a couple's beginning coming to its end. But it ends hopefully—expressing that there will be another round to go.

Fall

So to the first sentiment—my beginning with Shannon came to an end. Yup. To the second bit—it's hopeful, but I can't go there. Isn't going to happen. A friend used a "winning the lottery" metaphor—in a hopeful way, of course. My problem is I already won the lottery, and no one wins twice. No one. I can wish and want all I want, but I know there isn't another round for me. I am better off doing something else and staying away from the lottery. Gotta know when to hold 'em, know when to fold 'em, and all that, right? I got dealt a great hand and played it, but those cards are gone.

I sound depressed, don't I? Probably most people would say I am. Depression is an interesting concept. I've always figured depression is irrational—it is when you are sad in the face of circumstances that would predict happy. Recognizing when things suck and labeling them as such is not depression—that's just paying attention. So I am just paying attention.

Or depression comes from frustration over the inability to meet important expectations. I am learning to refocus them on things I can accomplish. I am realizing some can stay high and be useful motivators—others just aren't going to happen and need to be let go.

I am sure the doctor will see it differently tomorrow. He'll tell me I am depressed. In the end, I don't care what it is called. The name doesn't change how it feels or how little I can do about it.

Today is, plus or minus one (I haven't counted) my 100th day without Shannon. I don't like it, and I can't fix it, and there isn't even a "plan B" to turn to. We had about 10,000 days together. I could live 10,000 more days. There will be some good days, but I am not really that excited about the rest of them.

So you have had to put up with yet another fairly grim essay. But this is what I would like for you to try to take away from the downbeat entries. I feel the way I do now because I was so lucky to have Shannon in my life. You have a chance every day to make someone in your life feel as lucky as she made me feel. That's a tremendous gift, and I hope you use it to its full extent.

December 16

2:57 p.m.

I have smart friends and a smart psychiatrist—that's good.

First of all, apparently lots of people have won the lottery more than one time. Okay—I give on that one...sort of. But to win the lottery you have to be willing to spend the money to enter. It isn't clear to me that I will ever feel like I can risk the buck to enter. I may feel differently some day down the road. Everyone I talk to is sure I will—I am not sure I will. I don't want more hurt, and putting yourself out there leads to hurt—sticking with the metaphor, you usually have to buy a lot of tickets before you win. Lots of losses accumulate—and you don't know if you will ever win. I just don't see taking the risk. There isn't a clear path to a win, and what path there is will be full of yuck.

The doctor asked me today how I would feel if I met someone, had 20 years of wonderful wedded bliss, and then lost them like I lost Shannon. What would I prefer—the next 20 years alone or 20 years of great company and then to lose it in a New York minute? I know I am better when I am with someone, but right now I am not sure what I would pick. Does it get easier to be left behind? Does anyone even want to be part of that experiment?

He knows that I know the answer is of course I would suffer this again if it came after a great run with a partner. But there are lots of things I know I should do that I can't do.

On the other hand, there are reasons I still buy concert tickets in pairs. The practical reason is that if I decide not to go it is easier to scalp a pair than a single. The emotional reason is it gives me a millisecond to imagine how much fun it would be to tell Shannon about the show we were going to see, to see her excitement and smile. The hopeful reason is that maybe one day the second ticket won't be for my coat. So don't think I am without hope—I just don't think the smart money is on me.

10:33 p.m.

Enjoyed the chance to attend the EMBA graduation party this evening. Not enough time to visit enough with everyone—but still a good thing to do. Reid spent some time catching me up on things. He made me smile a bunch—but at one point in particular. He was doing laundry—of course he came home with all dirty clothes. I heard an exasperated sigh from the laundry room and then the exclamation, "I miss having a laundry expert!"

I laughed and walked over to the laundry room and asked if I could help. He has a seersucker sort of dress shirt that he was hanging to dry. He said, "Mom had some way of doing something with clothespins so the shirt wouldn't curl up when it was drying...I don't know how she did it." I don't know how she did it, either. So now Reid's shirt looks like a porcupine with about 50 clothespins sticking out of it. Maybe some 10 of them are in the right place...

There is a new book out, I guess, called *The Top Five Regrets of the Dying*, written by a palliative care nurse about regrets of the dying. It's getting a lot of play on Facebook. Shannon didn't have any communicative moments while she was waiting to die, but I think I can confidently address these on her behalf.

Regret 1: *"I wish I'd had the courage to live a life true to myself, not the life others expected of me."* I feel good about this because I think she learned to do this—as did I—through our marriage. I think we were both really good at wanting the other person to be who we really are/were—that's who we loved. I don't think she would list this as a regret at 48. She would have if she had died at 28.

Regret 2: *"I wish I didn't work so hard."* I have to editorialize a bit—I think working hard is not something to regret. The people this author is writing about are really talking about a regret of not having enough time for family. The two are not the same thing. Anyway—we were lucky—though Shannon went back to work for a while after each boy, she mostly was able to be a full-time mom. Hard enough work. I don't think she would list this as a regret. She would regret that she didn't have more energy—but that's a different story.

Regret 3: *"I wish I'd had the courage to express my feelings."* See Regret 1. We helped each other do this. It's easy now—you've been reading mine for 100 days. Shannon helped me not be afraid of expressing my feelings. Not sure Shannon would be blogging if it were her in my situation—but her best friends would all know how she felt. She had a different style for doing it, but she had places and people that made it safe. This would not be a regret.

Regret 4: *"I wish I had stayed in touch with my friends."* Of the top five this is the one she might have felt. She really missed some of her high school friends—and college, too. At the same time, we just spent Jazz Fest with a krewe of people (that's New Orleans for crew). We spent my birthday with friends in Napa. We visited friends in DC. We had plans to go see Peter Frampton in Houston with friends. So my final score is that while there were some people she indeed missed that no, she would not have this regret.

Regret 5: *"I wish that I had let myself be happier."* More editorializing by me first. Saying that happiness is a choice bugs me. I think it is a sort of blaming the victim thing. But let's cooperate with the author for this one final regret. I think Shannon was too hard on herself, that she had a hard time accepting how loved she was by me and the boys, and that she did not feel worthy of what she had. She was stubborn, and I worked on getting these points across for many, many years. I also know that there was nothing in my world as great as her smile, as comforting as holding her hand, or as powerful as her celebratory hug. So all I am saying is I wish she had the chance for more happiness. But that's my regret, not hers.[4]

So let's say these are indeed the top five regrets of the dying. It's of considerable comfort to not just believe—but to know—that Shannon wouldn't have felt them much.

December 17

> ## 8:29 p.m.

What night is it? It's hockey night in Canada! Insert Shannon's groan here.

I have never been the kind to pick at scabs. Until now. I can't leave well enough alone. It was a very full and interesting day—this is the first quiet since early morning. Reid just left with a friend to go find something to do. I could sit here and get in to the game—it's a good one. But instead I go down to Shannon's art room where all the

---

[4] Bronnie Ware, *The Top Five Regrets of the Dying: A Life Transformed by the Dearly Departing* (Carlsbad, CA: Hay House, 2012).

memory stuff to sort is. I just wanted to find something that would help me spend Saturday night with her.

After Reid was born, Shannon's mom sent her something called *A Mother's Journal*.[5] Each page has a quote or reflection about motherhood and then there is space for the mom to share her reactions. Shannon did it for a while, and then I expect life got in the way. I wish there were lots more entries, but what's there is neat. Here are a few.

The quote is: "I actually remember feeling delight at 2 o'clock in the morning, when the baby woke for his feed, because I so longed to have another look at him."

Shannon wrote:

> *Truly a fantastic feeling. It was a time of sweet quiet joy with both of my boys. Then the fatigue set in and then the magic was dispersed until that tiny little hand wrapped around my finger again and began gulping down the bottle. Then it was all so very treasured again.*

I think the only better feeling than the one she had at those moments was the feeling I had when I looked in on the two of them.

The quote: "Jennie smiles for the first time—a gentle parting of her lips into a contented, happy crinkle, and we are filled with delight and excitement."

Shannon wrote:

> *That first smile from either boy was more valuable than gold, or even sleep. The wonderful thing is that it is still one*

---

[5] Mary Engelbreit, *A Mother's Journal: A Collection of Family Memories* (Kansas City, MO: Andrews McMeel Publishing, 1993).

of my greatest rewards from my children—and they take it so for granted.

The quote: "Being a mother enables one to influence the future."

Shannon wrote:

What a frightening thought!

December 18

11:26 a.m.

New picture. Spencer baked this birthday cake for Shannon. Her birthday was the 9th; Reid was born on the 6th—this was her first day home from the hospital.

Right now, it is Sunday morning. I am leaving for New Orleans in a couple of hours with the boys to volunteer at the St. Bernard Project with about 2 dozen students. It's going to be great.

One of my charges on this trip with the boys is to take care of Shannon's ashes. Today is three months since her death. I feel good about the timing.

When I picked up the ashes, the attendant was careful to give me some warnings. She said that it isn't going to be like it is on TV. It isn't necessarily a fine powder—there may be bits and pieces. That's a little disturbing, and I was glad for the heads up. She also described how the ashes were secured and the tools I would need to untie them.

Good to have that heads up, too. Would be a drag to get to the spot and then find out you needed a Phillips head screwdriver instead of the flat head in your pocket. And she described how it worked to fly with ashes in terms of TSA. Another good heads up.

As I was getting things together to pack, it seemed like I should sort of verify that everything was as described. So I unpacked the stuff from the funeral home. No matter how ready you might think you are to see your wife reduced to a pile of ashes, you aren't. Took my breath away. Not in the way she used to.

So I was ready for a nicer memory and that's why I changed the picture. It captures a lot. Spencer as a chef before any of us knew it. Shannon as a proud second-time mom. Spencer as a proud big brother (he wore that "I'm a big brother" t-shirt forever). And I like the most that they are holding hands.

That's all for now. I am saving this as a draft. I wanted to write it while it was raw, and I will finish the story tonight in the hotel. Time to pull myself back together and get ready for a great trip. Maybe better to think of it as an important trip.

It's Sunday night now. I gave the boys the choice of coming with me to do the ashes or to miss it. They both agreed to come. I think it helped them to know another friend would be there. I think maybe they were worried they would be stuck with me in a crying heap.

Now Shannon has been returned to New Orleans—in the same sort of dirt she loved to play in. I was really happy that it wasn't freaky. It was much freakier to look at the ashes at home this morning. What we did tonight just felt right. That was a relief. The boys each took a turn holding the bag of ashes—one joked it felt heavier than she did in life. The other agreed.

I feel like we have done right by her and that she would completely approve. That means a lot to me, and I am thankful for that. I will say that as I sat on the plane with her ashes in a bag at my feet that my main thought was that it just wasn't right that this was going on. This isn't how it is supposed to be. But it is, so I have to continue to work to be okay with it.

Winter

December 21

7:18 p.m.

Today the boys and I made it to Shannon's tree to see the plaque that had been installed Monday. The boys both approved. It was a beautiful day in the park—73 degrees, dry, blue sky. We walked over to the lagoon and watched what had to be a half dozen different variety of ducks splashing around. Lots of people were out enjoying the day. The sights—all the families enjoying the park—and the sounds—the ducks, the streetcars on St. Charles, the bells at the clock at Loyola—are great. It is a perfect spot, and I am so thankful to everyone who made it possible. Shannon would truly be honored by the whole thing. I know she can't enjoy it, but I can. I am glad to have a special place that I can go and think about better times.

December 22

I have a lot of time to myself—lots of that time is spent trying to reconcile what has happened, why it happened, and what it means. The first part—what happened—is pretty clear. The second part—why—is something I am choosing to be clear about, though it may never really be clear. The third part—what it means—is still pretty hard to figure out. So the efforts to reconcile are ongoing.

I spend a lot of time generating metaphors as ways to get to this reconciliation. Here is the one that hit me today.

When the kids were little and we lived in Baton Rouge, they loved to go to "Kids' Night Out" at a gymnastics place. One of their favorite things was "the cheese pit." The pit was the hole under some apparatus—I don't remember which one. It was about 15 by 15, maybe 10 feet deep, and filled with 8-inch cubes of foam rubber. It was a place where the gymnasts could land after a trick without really having to think about landing. Of course, the kids just jumped in and started whipping foam at each other. Endless laughs.

So it feels like I am constantly tossed into this pit. All the people I have helping me, all the other crutches I have like medicine, and time are like cubes of foam. In the beginning, I had no idea how many cubes of foam were in the pit, and I knew I was going to land unprotected on a hard concrete floor. Frightening. Now I am learning the pit is really full of lots of cubes of foam, so maybe I don't have to be so afraid of how I land on any given day.

When I was in Minneapolis last week, I went to a hockey game. I got a call today from a young woman who was doing a follow-up on people who just attend one game (as opposed to people who buy packages), I guess to see why they don't attend more. We chatted for a long time. She must not have had many other people to call. We chatted about where she grew up, where I grew up, why hockey is the only sport that should matter, the Thrashers leaving Atlanta, my accent or lack of accent for someone from Georgia—oh, and the game experience. She asked about what my wife and I were doing for the holidays, and I mentioned that Shannon had passed away. It was reflexive—usually I don't say that because the result is predictable— the other person feels terrible and I have to switch in to consolation mode so that I am making them feel better about my wife being dead. Weird.

What I realized is that my reflexes are changing. I am not reflexively married anymore. I am reflexively alone now.

I do like symmetry, and I do like odd coincidences. So for symmetry— completely unplanned, but I like that Shannon's ashes were returned to New Orleans on the three-month anniversary of her death, and I like that the boys and I were able to first see her plaque on the three-month anniversary of her service. For odd coincidences, the restaurant some friends bought in New Orleans (Charlie's in Kenner) and where I ate with the boys on Wednesday is on Shannon Lane. I always thought the address was Jefferson Highway.

I posted a picture of the plaque at Shannon's tree on Facebook yesterday. I noticed today that something like 60 people have "liked" it. I clicked on the list, and it made me feel so good because there were people from my high school, Shannon's high school, our college life, my colleagues from LSU, my colleagues from Tech, former students, current students, neighbors, friends. I feel very lucky that so many people are in my life.

A lot of people have sent such kind cards for Christmas. Everyone hopes we will be okay. I am going out on a limb to say that maybe Christmas won't be so bad. I think if the kids were little it would be crushing. New Year's Eve will be bad because no matter what I do it will be quite obvious I won't have Shannon to kiss at midnight, as I did for the last 28 years. But it is really a dumb holiday—people say it is a fresh start and symbolizes hope and all that...okay, but I try to feel that way every day. The hard one will be Reid's birthday on the 6th and Shannon's on the 9th. I am sure it will surprise none of you to know that I am going to see Shannon's tree for her birthday. Arrangements have proven a bit complicated because that is the day LSU and Alabama play in New Orleans—but I got it figured out.

To end on a funny note—it was so great to have the kids in New Orleans for the St. Bernard Project work. Spencer went to hear Rebirth Brass Band at the Maple Leaf—it is a must-do thing in New Orleans— Shannon would be so pleased he did it. Not really his music, but a great dive venue—the kind of place you can't help but have a good time. Apparently there are pictures of Spencer up on stage with the band at some point...not sure I want to see those!

And Reid...wow. I have traditionally bought a dinner for the group as my personal thanks for the work they have done for the people of New Orleans. Usually, there are between 5 and 10 of them. This year, it was a party of 30. But a deal is a deal, so I took the 30 of us out to eat. We were at four different tables—I purposely did not sit with the boys. They need their break. I noticed at one point in the meal that Reid, who is 18, was enjoying a nice glass of wine...fine by me, but I was surprised he got served. Whatever. Then at the end of the meal, I see a snifter of cognac delivered to him. Again, whatever. I learned later that he used the cognac to toast, as he put it, "the memory of my homey, Kim Jong-Il." Needless to say, both boys got along fine with the students.

It made me remember one of the entries in Shannon's journal. The quote is, "Nothing else ever will make you as happy or as sad, as proud or as tired, for nothing is quite as hard as helping a person develop his own individuality."[6] Shannon basically agreed with that thought. And I think she did a great job of creating individuals. I love looking at each

---

[6] Marguerite Kelly and Elia Parsons, *The Mother's Almanac* (New York: Random House, 1992), xiii.

boy—it is so clear to me that there is some of me in there, some of Shannon in there, but also that they are who they are. She did a great job of building independent-minded, loyal, strong, and sensible young

men. She'd have been really proud of them this week—up on stage at the Maple Leaf Bar or boldly toasting a dead dictator with a fine cognac—or spending the days helping someone get back home in St. Bernard.

December 25

10:00 a.m.

If I was someone worrying about me, I would appreciate some sort of update that the holiday was moving along in an okay fashion. But then again, I overthink things! This is for those of you who might also overthink things...

I have been writing, but not posting until this is all over. For now, it is Christmas morning. It's quite beautiful here on Jekyll Island—very quiet—nearly boring, but not quite.

December 26

7:02 p.m.

It feels good to be back home. Spencer and Andre have headed off; Reid is off to the mall with friends to spend gift cards. So that leaves me with some time to kill before the Saints-Falcons game.

We have survived the first Christmas without Shannon. The advice was to do something "really different" and so we did. It's all chronicled below—but I do think it helped to not try to make it how it would have been. We have a wreath on the door that a friend sent, a poinsettia delivered by another friend, and a stack of holiday cards on the front chest by Shannon's roses. Other than that, not a single sign of Christmas in the house. I am glad the kids are the age they are. This would have been a brutal thing to do with a 6- and 10-year-old, etc. As it is, we hold each other up, don't require much, and expected less—so this degree of holiday difficulty was pretty low compared to what it might have been.

Here is the holiday rundown as recounted in "real time":

Friday

Lesson learned: don't let someone who just lost their wife drive 6 hours alone to spend a night alone in a strange house—especially a strange house with a funky smell. First the car—that's just too long to have just the company of my own head. Enough said. Then the house—it really was sort of okay—I wanted the boys to come when they were rested, and I totally told them to come Saturday was fine. But it was gray, sort of cold, and kind of nasty in the house. Easy situation to feel sorry for myself.

The happier thoughts on the drive were Christmases past…I remember one when Spencer got an LSU football uniform—he especially loved the helmet. I have a great picture of him eating a chicken leg through the helmet's facemask. Not an easy thing to do, but he wasn't going to take that helmet off.

And my favorite with Reid is the year he was almost 2. He opened a present and was content. He just wanted to play with that toy. He didn't open another gift until the next day—and then he just played with it. Drove Spencer absolutely nuts. Reid opened his last Christmas gift on January 6—his birthday—when the whole process continued

236

until those gifts were exhausted. Reid is just content; Spencer has to see what is next. Always been that way.

I remember our first "assembly free" Christmas and what a relief it was. I remember making lemon bars for Santa every year. I remember when we started having to record the Yule Log channel because the boys insisted we open gifts "by the fire" and they slept so late the channel would have already gone back to normal programming.

As for the house, being with Shannon prepared me for rental houses with funky smells. Three cans of Lysol spray, open all the windows, turn on the fans. That helped. Then the dishes—I just washed all of them to be sure they were clean enough to use when the boys arrived.

Van Morrison is great—his song, "Have I Told You Lately" came on while doing dishes today. He writes about how thankful he is at the way his lover can ease his troubles. That was Shannon's job for me. I miss her. I went to dinner at the Jekyll Island Club. Shannon and I stayed here for a conference many, many years ago. It hasn't changed. Lots of gray-haired couples, an entire wait staff from Hungary, and me.

Saturday

Beautiful sunrise this morning. I am making the most of the location. Took a good, long walk on the beach—didn't see a soul. Strange to be somewhere so pretty and so alone.

On the one hand I am anxious for the boys to get here, but on the other I really want them to be having the day they want to have. I don't feel I can ask for anything from them, beyond expecting them to work hard, be nice, and all that. I can't ask them to take care of me. This work is hard—and it doesn't seem to have an end. A friend who lost a son many, many years ago says it hasn't ended for him. He just keeps on. Ugh. That's hard to comprehend.

Finally I am ready for the boys. Presents wrapped. I am a really bad wrapper. Stockings are plastic grocery bags. I had thought about bringing stockings but am sticking with the "Christmas like no other" motif.

The rental house is replenished each morning with mouse droppings. Sort of depressing. At least it smells better. Andre will keep any attack-mice at bay, I am sure. The location is terrific, so it is worth it.

Boys arrived after lunch. We had a great afternoon with Andre on the beach, wonderful dinner, lazy night just sitting around watching bad football, watching boys play Words with Friends, etc.

Spencer made a tremendous dinner. He brought an immersion circulator and a vacuum sealer thing, and we did a filet sous vide, finished on the grill with mushrooms, baked potato, and grilled asparagus. Delicious. He has taken over my role as the family cook. I have taken over Shannon's role as the dishwasher. The food is better, and the dishes are not as clean.

Sunday

Hanging out with Andre and waiting for the boys to wake up. I have taken him on three walks already. He is really grumpy with me for letting Spencer sleep in. It reminds me of taking Spencer to feed the ducks at LSU so Shannon could sleep in.

Fell asleep last night to sound of waves—great to sleep with sliding door open.

Before I went to bed, I watched some of *It's a Wonderful Life*. What would be different if Shannon hadn't lived? She didn't eradicate disease, erase poverty, or bring peace to the Middle East. But neither did any of us. She brought thousands of kindnesses into the world. She made my adult life what it's been. And she got two kids off to a great start. I can't even begin to articulate what an impact she's had on our family. That's just the impact her being here has had—her being gone is shaping an entirely different set of circumstances.

Thinking of all the Christmases and how different it is without Shannon—we knew we were thankful for one another, but had no idea just how thankful we were—is there any way to feel and appreciate something that you may take for granted? It sucks if it takes losing something to really help you see how special it was.

After presents—long session with Andre and the boys on the beach. They use their lacrosse sticks to throw the ball as far as they can, and Andre fetches it. That dog can really run. Wow. Nice day—warm—clouds come in and then out. Boys liked their gifts—I liked mine—candles that don't smell sissy for the house, hockey game date with the boys. Perfect.

The boys operate like being without Shannon is just a fact—the way I wish I could operate. Of course, I am faking it, and they are probably kind of faking it, too. But we are together. Everyone is pitching in and behaving and taking care of each other. Boys off to Jekyll Island Club; I am dog-sitting.

Boys rejected for lunch at Jekyll Island for no reservation even though Spencer insisted there were about 25 open tables. Not to be deterred, they went to gas station for groceries, and we had beanie weenie and Ramen noodles for Christmas lunch. Spencer poached eggs to sit on the Ramen with some green onion. That was better than the "to go" they were going to bring me from the Club.

More good beach time with Andre. Spencer made a great pork dish in the sous vide machine. Boys now sitting on opposite couches video chatting by laptop—Spencer's Christmas present was a laptop. Reid is helping him set it up. Cool to watch. Andre is very confused to see Spencer "live" and on Reid's computer.

Not a bad day, considering.

Monday

Up early for coffee, waiting on the boys to hit the road. Another beautiful sunrise over the beach. I could get used to the sunrises—the rest gets old, quick. People say you need to do something different on a holiday after losing someone. This was pretty different. Shannon's name came up a few times in great stories, but you could tell she was at the front of everyone's mind the whole time. The boys miss her, too.

Looking forward to watching the Saints tonight from home. On to the next holiday.

Monday Night

So that's what happened for Christmas. It worked. We laughed and smiled and got through. Drive home sucked about as much as the drive there, but the other choice was to kidnap Reid, and I prefer he and Spencer spend the time together.

Been thinking about when or how to end this. I would like to not feel a need to do this anymore. I would like to stop after Shannon's birthday. I am going to see if that works. A motivation for me in the beginning was that people were saying it was helping them understand similar situations, and I don't feel like I am breaking new ground. It's like I have drawn the background on one of those old, old cartoons and the characters are "running" past the same scenery over and over. Once you know that trick, you can't accept the effect anymore—you sit there, watch, and count the rock formation every time it cycles by. I will eventually bore myself. If this doesn't end naturally, then I have to just pick a date and stop.

December 27

I had lunch with a friend in Minnesota a couple of weeks ago. She told me that I looked like me and I sounded like me, but that she knew I really wasn't me. And I got a holiday card from someone who said it seemed like I was doing fine. At first, I thought those were such contrary views, but now I see they are both right.

I am learning to act like me. That's not the same thing as being me. And that is why I am so tired. Not sleepy—physically and mentally tired. I am playing a role rather than just "being." I play it for other people. I play it for the kids, and when I am alone, I play it for myself.

I am "doing fine" to the extent I can act like I am doing fine. I am not doing fine. I am miserable. This sucks every day. There is a huge dissonance between how I am and how I act. But the choice of giving in and acting like I feel isn't palatable. I don't want to be with that person. Who would?

This makes it hard for other people. Should you go along with my act? I don't think you have a choice. Who would say, "Nate, stop laughing, stop enjoying that meal, stop working...don't you realize Shannon is gone? You are supposed to be miserable!"

So I don't have a choice but to act. And you don't have a choice but to act. It makes me tired, and it's going to make you tired, too.

December 28

I received a lot of much-appreciated notes this past week. One suggested that I was a strong person to be handling things as well as I am. I've written about the "handling things" notion—all depends on definitions. And I'll admit that it's only when I am really being hard on myself that I can say I am not handling things okay.

But I have been thinking about the "strong person" part of the statement. What I am learning about myself now is how weak I am, not how strong I am. I defined so much about my life based on how someone else received my efforts. The boys and I used to joke, "If Mom isn't happy, no one is happy." But as I have said, she was my barometer. It wasn't just a joke to me. It was a "key performance indicator" in MBA-speak.

Now Shannon is gone. I pay too much attention to whether or not people read this. I take it personally if a Facebook post I make isn't "liked" enough. Teaching is sort of selfish that way. You get lots of feedback about whether or not you are doing okay. It is weak to depend on others for validation, and I am doing too much of that.

I had an e-mail exchange with a friend who has been single for a while after a divorce. She has been supportive in terms of sharing her experience that being single really is okay. I think she is strong.

Last night, I had tickets to see Rebirth Brass Band. I had forgotten about the tickets for a while—bought them long ago—Shannon and I were looking forward to it. They were supposed to start at 10. I know that when 9:30 rolls around I won't leave the house. I need to be in town already to make that work. So I left early, went to see *Girl with the Dragon Tattoo*, stopped by the office to do some work, then had dinner, then headed over to the show. I was still early, so I stopped at a Starbucks to read the paper. A liquor store was right next door, so I grabbed a mini-bottle of Grand Marnier. Tea is way, way, better with some GM in it. Being alone for all that was okay. Finally, I headed over to the concert. So many Saints T-shirts, Jazz Fest T-shirts, etc. I left before Rebirth came on. All that work to get there, but after spending 30 minutes watching couples hanging out, watching gangs of college kids having fun, and seeing about a dozen sad sacks like me standing around with their hands in their pockets, I just wasn't having fun. So I left. None of that would have bothered me if Shannon were here. That's weak. That's what I am learning.

From: DF
Date: Wed, 28 Dec 2011 21:02:46 +0000
To: Nathan Bennett
Subject: Hi there

You are not a weak man. We all borrow some functioning from our spouses, and when we lose that, our flaws and cracks are more visible. You're doing as well as you can, and that's pretty damn good. However, this journey will not always provide a positive self-assessment, or the validation you want.

In that same vein I saw a movie last night that was highly personally relevant and sad, and also made me think of you—*The Descendants*. The story line is about a successful man who loses his wife to a boating accident. But, it's way complicated and even sadder in some ways than anticipated. I lost my brother to a boating accident, and the wife looked just as comatose as my mom at the end, I suffered. However, the story about the man is compelling for almost any middle-aged guy who has enjoyed professional success and struggled with emotional connection. Despite being a great guy, he must confront his weaknesses—it's really good stuff. It reminded me in a funny way of *Little Miss Sunshine*.

It would be very raw for you right now. Put it on the list for a rental when you are ready.

I am on the up tick from surgery, and grateful it's slowed me down enough to just sit still these past few weeks!

See you in January.

DF

December 29

1:30 p.m.

I feel spoiled by the weather. Another December day when I can sit out on the deck in the bright sun. Weatherman, who has never let me down, tells me I have three more of these to come. The sun helps so much. House was quiet last night—Reid was out at a concert, Spencer was just AWOL. I went down to the basement for a change of venue to watch some hockey. Found myself drawn to Shannon's art room— all the pictures and memory stuff from the basement organizing task are in there.

I spent a couple of hours sorting stuff out—basically getting it organized enough so that it was ready to be dealt with more permanently. I found some great stuff. Shannon tried to keep cards and letters; she tried to do all the notes you are supposed to do in your kids' baby books. We both did. The work is imperfect, but what exists is so sweet. What precious memories. I found our dried wedding bouquet in the glass jar Shannon put it in years and years ago. It sits now on the chest by the dried roses from her service.

I found some old correspondence. Letters to Shannon from her mom and dad. I don't read those—those are private. Letters to Shannon from high school suitors—I do read those, sorry, Shannon, and sorry, suitors! They are sweet in an odd sort of way, I suppose. And letters from me. I used to send her letters from the road whenever I travelled—no cell phone, no e-mail, phone calls were expensive. I apparently sent one from a Ramada Inn in Michigan in 1984. It basically said: "I can't wait until we can do trips like this together— though I don't think Detroit is ever going to be high on your list." We barely made it to that point—and no, Detroit was not high on the list. Ramada Inns anywhere were not high on our list.

So the room was all ready to be attacked. My helper came over today—we did the rest of the closets on the main floor and have what I think is the last stack of donation stuff on the front porch. Then we went downstairs to deal with the pictures. I lasted about 10 minutes. Couldn't do any more. Verge of weepy breakdown.

I had a realization about how to describe this personal unreliability that I find so frustrating. I thought it was very clever and then I found out it is the title to a book so I can't really take credit for originality. Anyway, the phrase is "mentally incontinent." That's me.

Around the house all that is left to do is the hard stuff. Shannon's closet, the pictures, and her hair dryer still wedged up against the wall so that she could dry her own hair after surgery.

December 30

8:02 a.m.

Radio is playing Warren Zevon's "Poor, Poor Pitiful Me." Great song— you've probably heard Linda Rondstadt's remake. Trying not to have it so loud it bothers Reid, though after a semester in a dorm, he can probably sleep through most anything.

Sleep is very unpredictable. I have always had a hard time falling asleep. Once I am asleep, I have no problem sleeping through the night. Shannon was always the opposite. She fell asleep quickly but had trouble sleeping through the night.

As I waited to sleep last night, I remembered how much I miss our routine. We'd turn out the light. Shannon would reach over and scratch my back. She'd do that until she fell asleep. Sometimes I would fall to sleep first, but most of the time I could lay there and "feel" Shannon drifting off to sleep. Her momentum would slow, the range of motion would constrain, and then eventually her hand would stop entirely. If I stayed still a few more minutes, I could hear her breathing change into a sleep pattern. Then, I'd roll over and hold that hand until I fell asleep. That was better. Took longer than Ambien, but it was better.

10:20 p.m.

Spent a lot of time today thinking about New Year's. If things were right, Shannon and I would be planning to go to dinner tomorrow— probably 4th & Swift. Then we would head over to the Fox to see the band Cake. Shannon loved that band, and they put on a great show. Then we'd have come home to wait anxiously for Reid to get home safely.

In years past, New Year's Eve provided some nice family time. We started a tradition way, way back of playing board games and eating fondue. I am not sure where the idea came from. I have a vague recollection that maybe my family did it when I was a kid. Anyway, as should be no surprise in our family, the food element took over from the board game element. The fondue expanded to be three courses—first a bread and cheese fondue, then a meat and veggie fondue in oil, then a chocolate fondue with strawberries and pound cake. And then each year more sauces were added, tempura batter for the veggies was added, and so on. I was reminded of all this when cleaning out the basement. I have four fondue pots—probably four more than I need now, but I kept them all. One year Reid gave me fondue plates for my birthday—the first truly "thoughtful gift" he picked out all by himself. Perfect.

Fondue is a ton of work—so much prep and so many dishes. We would eat a course, Shannon would clean up, and I would prep the next course. The kids would play video games. Then rinse and repeat—you get the drill. We were lucky to have the dishes done by midnight for a toast. But what a fun tradition. Lots of good memories.

In the years before that stage, Shannon and I were living in Baton Rouge, and we loved to celebrate East Coast midnight and then go to bed. Too late to stay up to "real" midnight. When the kids were really little and we were really tired, we joked that we should just celebrate London midnight and go to bed.

Several people have said I must be glad that 2011 is over. The calendar is just arbitrary, but I know what they mean, and I agree with the sentiment. I do hope nothing as bad ever happens to the boys or me again. Maybe the worst thing that will ever happen to me has already happened to me. Maybe not. No way to know.

I do know that a lot of great things happened in 2011. Reid graduated high school with honors. Shannon and I had some wonderful trips. I had exciting work. I learned just how good my friends are. I learned there are a lot more good people out there than I would have guessed. I cleaned up the basement. So I can't really blame 2011 too much.

I went to a minor league hockey game with a friend tonight. Team lost—fortunately I really don't care. It was good to be out. He cracked me up when he said, "I haven't been able to read your blog for a few days, so

247

get me caught up." Like when I used to go to lunch at the fraternity house and say, "I missed the last episode of *All My Children*...someone catch me up." It was a good reminder of one of the ways this effort has helped me.

I am going to visit some friends for New Year's. Reid is heading up to Nashville for a concert with some of his friends. Spencer is going to a show here with friends. Cake will put on a great show without us. Maybe I'll listen to that CD on the way to my friends' house.

Driving home from the game, a couple of thoughts came to mind. I have been thinking a lot about Shannon's service—I can't help but do a "post-action review." Isn't that sad..."The next time I have to plan a service, what did I learn from this service that would help me do it better next time?" That's how my head works. I can't complain about the service. I am thankful to have had Father Michael's help. So many decisions with absolutely no point of reference. So I guess the first thing I learned is that it really is important to have either done your own homework or bring someone—like Michael—who has (sadly for him) lots of experience.

The second thing I learned is that at least for me the open casket was important. The funeral home did as nice a job as you could hope for— given they didn't know Shannon—of making her look okay. She did her makeup—or mostly lack of makeup—better than they did—but they did fine. So in some ways, it was weird to see her not quite look like her. But—there are still at least 3 or 4 times a day when my brain forgets she is gone—I can quickly bring back the image of her in the casket; I can quickly remember how cold her body was—and it makes it simply impossible to deny the loss. I appreciate that.

The third thing I learned is that shock is great. I have no fear of being in shock. Shock is a lifesaver. When Shannon died, supporters sur-rounded me, but I was also surrounded by people who were pissed, hurt, sad, whatever. I was also confronting something impossible personally—and I was also so worried about my kids. If it wasn't for shock, I would have simply gone totally crazy. Shock is great. It makes it possible for you to smile at people who hurt, to thank people for coming, and all that. I am a big fan of shock.

Today I filed an official complaint with the State about the doctors that jerked me around on the death certificate. I also "rated" them poorly on a website that collects that sort of information. I plan to follow up with the hospital and surgery center to ask if they really have made changes. I am not optimistic, but who knows. If I ran a hospital (or similar) I would make sure that I followed up with people to let them know promises made were promises kept.

For the most part, I hope to be able to leave as much baggage as possible in 2011. That said, I am not taking anyone off the hook. I am trying to think of resolutions—why, I don't really know. I think the one I am most serious about is getting in to a position to do something more than writing a check for mitochondrial research. I'd like to find other ways to help—and to be well enough to do it.

January 1, 2012

3:40 p.m.

I was invited out to Lake Oconee to visit some friends last night—a great diversion from New Year's Eve. The drive out was tough. During the first month or so after Shannon died, a long drive was therapeutic. Now, time in the car—long drives—are difficult. No matter where I try to force my thoughts to go, they end up with my "situation."

On the way to the lake I had the memory of how when I was a kid— junior high age, we all had bikes with "banana seats"—I think that's what they were called. Long, narrow seats that made it possible for you to have a friend ride along with you. So that in turn created the image of Shannon riding along with me with her arms around my waist. That's nice enough.

The next thought is remembering how light the bike felt when your friend got off. And the very next thought is how heavy the "bike" I am on now feels that Shannon got off. It was easier to pedal with her on board than it is without.

January 3

8:18 a.m.

It's nice to have a chef in the family. Last night Spencer came over to cook for some friends and us. He fixed beet salad with goat cheese and arugula, homemade pasta with a pea/prosciutto cream sauce, seared salmon over black lentils. Pretty tasty. My first attempt at homemade pasta—turned out okay. He cooks, cleans up, won't let me give him money for a beer as thanks. He's a good kid.

I was feeling pretty good about surviving the holidays, and then last night Shannon appeared in my dreams. Just the third time that's happened. I can't remember all the details of the dream, but the theme was that she was telling me that if I wanted her back badly enough, she would come back. That woke me up with a start. I wish it was that easy. She'd have been back a long, long time ago.

Yesterday, some wine racks I found on Craigslist were delivered—from a wine store that went out of business. This completes the basement project. I feel both good and bad about it. The reason to feel good is obvious. But I feel bad because I know how much the nightmare mess down there bothered Shannon.

For her it was a symbolic representation of her fears of things being out of her control and overwhelming in her world. That makes me wish I'd been able to get it done when it could have offered her some peace. That's certainly the biggest regret I have—the list of things that I could have done in a more timely way so she had less to fret over. It was just a messy basement—it wasn't some big deal—but still. In my head it is a missed opportunity to have put another smile on her face.

8:43 p.m.

I received an e-mail from my attorney friend today. The critical care doctors replied to the strongly worded letter of disappointment he sent them a few weeks ago on my behalf. The letter says in part:

We are indeed sorry that the delay of the submission of the death certificate caused significant inconvenience to your client. There are multiple system-based issues that we have identified since this occurrence, and we are working closely with St. Joseph's Hospital to have a more efficient manner of dealing with deaths in the intensive care unit.

The letter then goes on to explain their practice a bit and says:

Although Dr. [Redacted] was the admitting physician and I myself had taken care of Ms. Bennett, we were only part of a larger team taking care of her and were not involved when she finally expired.

Right. Because your partner strategically moved her off the ICU to die and become someone else's problem.

Then it says:

> *As a result of this recent event we are in discussions with the hospital to ensure that an appropriate death packet is instituted at the time of death, so that the attending physician at that time who is taking care of the patient correctly and accurately takes care of the death certificate in a timely manner instead of it going to an arbitrary person named on the chart who has no accurate and up-to-date information...*

I appreciate the doctor wrote back. Even though there is a fair amount of excuse making, the letter suggests an effort to deal with some of the concerns I raised. So I can put something in the win column. I am going to write a cover letter and send it with this letter to the CEO at St. Joseph's...just in case the letter is fiction from the imagination of the critical care practice.

On a different front I went out to the kitchen store to get some more toys and then to get sushi. More time with the '70s channel. Ringo Starr's song "Photograph" came on. It's a break-up song, not a lost your wife song, but the lyrics of the opening verse are pretty spot-on—all he has left to remember someone is a photograph.

I didn't cry—don't really anymore. I leak. I look like someone with bad allergies as I drive around listening to sappy songs.

But it did remind me of the last photograph I have of Shannon. It's just my hand holding her hand just after she died. I never look at it, but I am glad I have it.

And that reminded me of something Shannon said that made me laugh. She was talking about aging, and she said, "One day I put my arm in the sleeve of a sweater, and my mom's hand popped out the end!" I thought that was great.

January 4

I should be at the gym, but the sun is out. It's January 4, and I can sit on my back deck and work. Pretty nice. The sun will be down in a bit, and I will go to the gym then. I've just filled the bird feeder up and a stream of species constantly visits me. When I am out here, they appear in a pretty predictable order—oddly it is pretty much the tiniest who are the bravest. They show up first—titmouse, wrens, nuthatch. Then cardinals. Then the woodpeckers. All the other species will harass each other for position on the feeder—but when a woodpecker is there, the others all wait on the nearby branches.

There was an article in *The Wall Street Journal* yesterday on research that has found people with folic acid deficiencies have trouble getting benefits from antidepressants. Shannon, as is apparently common in mitochondrial patients, had a folate deficiency—and she had trouble finding antidepressants that helped. When the folate deficiency is treated with supplements, the antidepressants start to work. So I sent the article to Shannon's psychiatrist. She was glad to get the note and shared with me that Shannon was on her calendar for an appointment this week that they'd obviously made months ago—she was sad she wouldn't be seeing her. I know how she feels.

I have received so many special notes over the past few months—and particularly over the holidays. I like sharing bits of them because I think all of you have such beautiful, inspirational things to say—they deserve a wider audience than just me. And you have heard me brag about Georgia Tech students, so I won't do that other than to say this is a note from one of my former students. It's wonderful. I haven't even been able to reply to her yet, because I need to find the right words myself.

I started reading back in September because I felt very sad about your loss and wanted to read along to see how you were coping. I continued to read because I realized your blog was doing to me what watching Oprah for years hadn't done! The more I read, the more I saw how much life you and Shannon got to live in the years you spent together and the more I was inspired to live my best life. Little things like you talking about the music you shared, the food you ate (most of which I never heard about before), the places you visited, made me realize that "living" isn't when you go to the same restaurant and eat the same dish every time!

My husband now knows your story (he had to pick a different restaurant, and we had to try new dishes when we went out two weeks ago), my best friends have read your blog, and my sisters have read too. All because I can't stop talking about my professor who managed to stay present in his life and how my heart prays that yours will find peace soon.

That's just a beautiful note—and I hope I haven't made her husband's life too rough with all these new restaurant rules! She goes on to say that she won't forget Shannon because Shannon's service was on her birthday. I am going to ask her to please, please, please not let Shannon ever be a cloud on her birthday. That would make her miserable. I hope instead she and her husband will make the day extra special.

When the weather gets cold, the music venue shifts to Variety Playhouse. Big Head Todd, G. Love & Special Sauce, Matt Kearney, O.A.R., Railroad Earth, and Yonder Mountain all in the next few weeks.

Looking forward to getting out for those shows. Shannon would be very excited about BHT and G. Love and would be patient with me to come to the others. She was a great date because what we did didn't matter. That made her a pretty easy person to take out.

So it turns out that in spite of my best efforts to be truthful here I sometimes lie. It was a lie when I said the other day that I don't cry anymore. My cue to go to the gym.

January 5

1:12 p.m.

For the past two weeks it's been hard to sleep, each night for a different reason. Last night, I was convinced some neighbors were outside arguing. I went out on the porch, and it was a group of three owls "talking" back and forth. I listened for a bit—it was cold but fairly entertaining. First time I have heard owls since we moved to this house 10 years ago.

Some of the sleep issue is likely that I haven't been taking as much medicine. I just prefer to only take the minimum and sometimes I guess what I hope is the minimum is not quite enough. The holidays are probably not the time to decide to cut back. I thought it might be okay because I don't have as many duties I have to perform, but turns out not to have been the case. It's like the line in the movie *Airplane*..."I picked a hell of a week to stop sniffing glue!" So Ambien tonight.

Today was a day to see the psychiatrist. He and I have very different views of my future. We each produce data—and interpret data—in very careful ways to support our side of the argument. We are each quite certain that we are correct. In his view, I am not alone forever, but I will get angry with Shannon—among other things. In my view, I am alone forever, and I never get angry with Shannon—among other things. So although I am pretty sure I am right (I have lots of data), he is pretty sure I am wrong (he has lots of data). To hedge my bets, these futures are like two trips I have to pack for, psychologically. He actually says I should not pack anything at all...I should just go and get what I need when I get there...metaphorically speaking.

That made me remember how Shannon used to pack for a trip. I swear we always had what we needed, unless it was a deliberate choice to get what we needed when we got there. Shannon would ask me to print out the weather for the days we would be at our destination. She would then draw a little grid for each day. Then she'd ask, "What are we doing each day?" I'd go through that with her, or we'd plan it out together. Then she'd go make outfits, get supplies, and organize brochures. She was not a "don't pack and get what you need when you get there" person. I'm a little more comfortable with it than she was, but still sort of prefer a plan.

I finally—with lots of help—was able to move Shannon's e-mails over to my machine. She didn't save much, but what she saved was important and is quite organized. Lots of it doesn't matter anymore, but some of it is just so wonderful. I read one last night that was something she sent to Spencer when he was a freshman in college. It was great to read her words of encouragement to him—to really make the most of the experience.

We don't write letters much anymore—but I know when I was in school it was mostly phone calls. As a result, I don't have much in the way of a record of communication with people. Now with e-mail, I am glad there is at least something here of Shannon that I can organize and share with the boys.

And in thinking about the e-mails that I just said don't really matter, I realize that isn't a fair way to label them. They do matter. One of the things I miss the most is how I used to hear from Shannon 5 or 6 or 20 times a day—and I could touch base with her similarly. Short e-mails, text messages. Virtual pats on the back throughout the day. Little kindnesses that help you feel like what you are doing matters to someone—that someone is looking forward to seeing you at the end of the day. In some ways, missing those is harder on a day-to-day basis than the more symbolic "now you're off on your own adventure" messages.

January 6

Happy First Day of Mardi Gras and Happy 19th Birthday to Reid.

Reid's birthday is a very sad thing to do without Shannon. Worse than Christmas or New Year, for sure. I always tried to spoil Shannon on the boys' birthdays—it wasn't just an anniversary of their birth, but also an anniversary of something incredible that she did. So I miss her tonight a little more than usual.

I used to get Shannon a card, too, along with one for Reid. This morning I went to Publix to get Reid's card, and I remembered how much fun I used to have picking out something for Shannon. One of the cards I opened at the store today said something like "You know what they say about people your age?" on the front and then on the inside it said, "At least you're not dead!" That might have been funnier last year. I put that one back. Sort of odd to think that someone else will buy it, thinking it's funny.

Since Reid was born on the 6th, he's always had a King Cake as his birthday cake. When he was little he had no choice, but Shannon and I were both glad that when he did get old enough to express an opinion that he clearly wanted nothing but King Cake. This year, some dear friends again arranged for one to arrive today. That was a nice tradition to carry on. These same friends are on the road and ran 5K races today in Shannon's memory—add this to the marathon a friend did in November, and it is clear that many more miles have been run in her memory than she ever ran in her life! Running was not something good for her condition at all. That was something she wasn't sorry to give up.

Just Reid and I went to dinner. We had a great meal and conversation, but it was just so wrong that there were only two of us. He even left his iPhone in the car and went totally unaided to dinner with me. Brave young man is he.

Reid is now out with friends, and I am alone in the house. Spencer called to check on me—he is doing a really good job of that. He has been working very long days on the cookbook photo shoot. Sounds like he is having a great time at it. Spencer and his culinary exploits were also featured in a local magazine here this week. Fun to see.

Tomorrow will be four months since we lost Shannon. It doesn't get any less tragic with the passing of time. The hurricane metaphor does seem to work. The water has receded. The power is back on. Everything is a mess. Now what? Things are different now than they were after one month. A few things have improved, some clearly haven't, and others are just different.

On Sunday I am going to New Orleans. Shannon's birthday is Monday. She would have been 48. I'll stop by the tree for a bit and then come back to teach Monday afternoon. Hopefully that will be a good day.

January 7

8:46 p.m.

Four months ago tonight was the longest night of my life. I was terrified about Shannon. I was worried about how to handle things with Reid who was just getting settled at school.

I was thinking about that tonight and two thoughts came to mind. The unpleasant one is how the difference between tonight and that night is on that night I had hope. I don't have hope anymore. That feels tough, but then I realize what I had was false hope—Shannon wasn't going to get better—she would have been back with us by that night if she was just reacting to anesthesia. Somehow losing false hope is easier to take than losing hope. Doesn't change what I am doing tonight, but it is a little easier to take.

The other, much more pleasant thought regards what had previously been the longest night of my life—the night we waited for Spencer to be born. I had hope then, too—and it was well-founded. I remember that after Spencer was born—nearly 17 hours of labor—Shannon was having a hard time resting in the recovery room. Every hour or so a nurse would come to check on her. What really bugged her was the door to the room was terribly squeaky. After a bit, she asked me if I would please get her some things from the house. And then she asked me to go to Kroger to get WD-40 and to Chick-fil-a to get a lemonade. So that's what I did. She drank the lemonade, and I oiled the door hinges for her so the room would be less squeaky. She gave the can to the nurse in case any other doors needed attention.

That story reminded me of the time Shannon lost her wedding ring. I wrote a while ago about losing mine, but I don't think I shared the story of when she lost hers.

For the last two Jazz Fests we rented a house in the New Orleans Garden District. The first year we were there, Shannon came to me in a panic because she had lost her wedding ring. Her actual wedding ring is a tiny gold band—that's all. She was so despondent. It had rolled off the bathroom vanity when she was washing up and disappeared—it was a perfect shot, apparently—down a cutout in the floor for the sink drain.

I went upstairs to check it out. It did not look good, but then I realized the drain did not line up with the wall below. That meant the pipe did a 90 degree turn in the ceiling between the floors—and that meant the ring was likely sitting on the sheetrock between floors—it hadn't slipped down an interior wall.

I called the rental agent and explained the situation. I told her that I had checked it out and that if a plumber came and unhooked the vanity from the wall and slid it out, the ring should be reachable inside the ceiling. I asked if we could hire a plumber to do that at some point—we'd obviously pay for it. She said her handyman would come take a look. He did, and he somehow was able to snake it out without even moving the vanity. Best $50 I ever spent.

Of course the best part of the whole thing was being able to reunite Shannon with her ring and to see that sense of joy and relief. If we had to go the plumber route, I bet that would have cost more than replacing the ring—but she wanted the one Father Buddy had blessed—the one that really wasn't round anymore from years of abuse. I still have it—it sits in Shannon's purse.

The part that is just "so Shannon" is that the next year we rented the same house, and before we went Shannon purchased a nice dish meant to hold things like rings while you are washing up. Of course, a Tupperware container would have worked for our stay. But Shannon shopped around, found something that worked with the other decor in the bathroom, and brought that to use and leave behind. I teased her about it. She said, "This is a nice place, and this is just something it needs." That was her contribution to the house. She just did stuff like that all the time. It was so sweet.

Sitting here thinking about her ring, I am going to get it and put in on my keys with my ring. Maybe that's a step backward, but it isn't like I am going anywhere fast. A step backward is not a big deal. A step backward is at least movement.

Finally on the ring theme—I have been obsessing with the song "Give Me Something" by a band called Scars on 45. The singer is desperately wishing for something to help him know the relationship is real; if there was some evidence, he'd wear her wedding ring. I understand about making wishes that aren't coming true, I understand wanting something to hold on to that links me to Shannon—maybe that's the boys, and I understand about wanting to wear a ring for a lifetime. I just thought it would be my lifetime, not hers.

January 8

12:02 p.m.

On Facebook this morning, Father Michael posted from the Disney Marathon:

Waiting in the corral to begin the last leg of this journey. Running with my dear friend Shannon on my heart today. She was here last year, on her birthday, to support me. Love and miss you! Thanks for all your prayers and support folks!— with Shannon W. Bennett.

I just now got a text from him with his picture wearing the medal he got for completing the marathon. That's terrific!

Shannon's birthday present last year was to go to Disney in order to be part of his "pit crew." They had T-shirts, got up at some ungodly hour; they rode the monorail and buses from check point to check point to wave signs cheering him on. She had a blast. It was a memorable birthday for her. Her favorite part of the trip was her effort to beg from hotel staff a wine opener and plastic cups so they could celebrate with everyone in the hotel lobby—New Orleans habits, like "go cups," don't fade away. She was also so happy that on her birthday—though everyone was exhausted—Michael summoned up enough energy to go with her to a nice restaurant so that she didn't have to settle for fast food alone. Those of you in Atlanta will remember the ice storm—it kept Shannon stuck in Orlando for an extra day, and it made picking her up at the airport an adventure. She'd been gone 3 or 4 days and that was an eternity for me to be without her.

I am very proud of Michael. I don't like even driving 26 miles. And I am sad whenever I am reminded that someone else is suffering about Shannon being gone. I promise that I feel miserable enough for all of us, although I know that isn't how misery works. When somebody goes, we all take a bit of the bullet. It would be better if misery came in known and finite volumes so that we could figure out a way to work together and process it through.

From: DS
Date: Sun, 8 Jan 2012 18:40:36-0600
To: Nathan Bennett
Subject: Tomorrow

Hi Nate,

I realize that tomorrow is going to be a very tough day. I don't know how, but I remembered that tomorrow is Shannon's birthday. (I really surprised myself when I went to FB and checked...)

Anyhow, I just loved—love!—that girl, and the impression she left on me will last forever. Clearly, she made a big one.

You're in my thoughts and I hope that all of this—even from afar—somehow reaches you and helps you.

Much love and peace to you.

January 9

12:16 a.m.

Eastern time, it is Shannon's birthday. I was wrong before—it's 49, not 48. Can't do math. I can't explain how nice it was to be able to sit by her tree for a bit tonight. More later on the night. Tired. You will see the new picture. I left her a rose. I really don't want the tree to feel like a tombstone, but I couldn't bring her nothing.

I had 11 roses left. Trying to stay in proper spirit I got back to the hotel, gave the car to the valet, and tipped him. I asked him, "Do you have a girlfriend?" He said, "I have a wife." I said, "You about to be off?" He said, "Yes—I am off in 5 minutes." So I gave him the roses and said, "Please give these to your wife." He was so incredibly thankful. His valet partner said, "You just made this guy a hero." That felt good. Shannon would approve.

The roses cost $9. It is such a deal. For nine bucks, I could leave a rose for Shannon, I could make the valet guy—who seems like a solid young man—happy that there are nice people in the world, and I could make his valet partner smile. And then his wife will be happy when she gets flowers for no special reason. For 9 bucks. I feel like I should just do that every time I leave my car with a valet. Why not?

10:41 p.m.

Time is winding down on Shannon's birthday. I can't begin to explain how thankful I am to have such a perfect place to go and think about her. As I sat there in New Orleans last night, I was trying to find the right word for how it feels. I start to think it feels good, but it doesn't. It would feel good if I were sitting there holding her hand. What it feels is right. "Right" means "good for the circumstances."

When I landed in New Orleans I went by and picked up Shannon's cousin. We went to the tree for a bit and then grabbed a bite to eat. I dropped her home and visited with her family a bit, and then I headed back to the tree. Earlier, I had bought the roses and a bottle of wine. Ever prepared for events with Shannon, I had grabbed the plastic laundry bag from my hotel. Since it had rained during dinner, the bag came in handy as a seat.

I got to the park around 9:30 or 10. As I approached the tree, I could see it was surrounded by dozens—maybe even hundreds—of what I guess were all ducks. They were everywhere—and loud. I made a recording of them on my phone. I just got the biggest grin because my first thought is how much Shannon would love the company. She had pet ducks when she was a little girl. I imagine they are there shouting every night.

The ducks cleared enough room for me to sit on my plastic bag and have some wine. There were a few joggers, even at that hour. About every 15 minutes, the Park Police would drive by. As I saw the headlights coming, I would get up and stand behind a tree (I can't yet hide behind Shannon's). I wasn't doing anything wrong, but just didn't want to deal with them if they found me a curiosity.

I sat there and was very quiet. I tried to think of things to say, but that doesn't work. First, there is just the practical matter of the fact that she can't hear me. But more importantly, I know that she already knows anything that comes to my mind. She knows how I felt about her and how appreciated she was and what I miss and what I regret. So I don't have to say it. Once I realized I didn't need to say anything, it was nice to just sit. Every 20 minutes or so the sound of a streetcar; the constant cacophony of the birds; every 15 minutes go hide behind the beautiful live oaks that surround and protect Shannon's Gingko...not a bad routine.

The day could be viewed symbolically as a foot in the past (at the tree) and a foot in the future (the new semester). I have been thinking about 2012. My initial reaction to the new year has been like most people's—it has to be a better year for me than 2011. After thinking about it, I realize that is very, very wrong.

It is true that chances are good nothing as bad as losing Shannon will happen in 2012. But 75% of 2011 was magical. Especially in hindsight. The trips, the progress of the kids, how well we were working together, my work, our lives. I had 75% of what was a tremendous year.

2012 will have 0% Shannon; 2011 had 75%. So that sort of changes the way I am thinking about 2012. Maybe 2011 wasn't such a bad year.

Thanks to all of you who sent well wishes today. I saw some nice notes on Shannon's Facebook page...I was scrolling down and found this entry—she wasn't a huge Facebook person, but she was learning. This is something she posted a couple of weeks before she died when we were at a Grace Potter concert in Charlotte—it just sounds like Shannon so I wanted to share it with you:

> We r the 4th oldest here. Entertaining music and scenery—especially the young couple in a full body lip lock behind us. Ahh to be young and not care...

January 10

As I was driving to the airport, I was listening to the song "Steady as She Goes" by the Raconteurs—there is a fitting lyric in the song about having too much time to think. It couldn't be better said than they sing.

On the plane yesterday, I was thinking about Reid's birthday. We had a nice time, but I feel so bad for him. Two years ago, Shannon and I took Spencer, Reid, and two of Reid's friends to Fogo de Chao. One of those friends died in a car accident at the start of Reid's freshman year. So last year, Shannon and I took Reid and two other friends to Fogo de Chao. Now Shannon is dead.

We didn't go to Fogo de Chao this year. Just Reid and me for oysters— I guess that's the anti-Fogo de Chao menu. I know in his head he was remembering past dinners, just like I was. He shouldn't have had to deal with all this at 19.

Packing this morning I gave myself a compliment. My dress shirt is going to look great tomorrow. I am glad I studied Shannon's technique, and I am benefitting because I am bored enough to take the time necessary to get it right. That made me think about how one act—learning independence—can be so freeing and so depressing, depending on the situation. My kids are in a process of learning to be independent from me. They've pretty much done it. And it's something natural to celebrate. I have to learn to become independent of Shannon, and that is nothing to celebrate at all.

January 11

8:47 p.m.

Shannon's birthday has come and gone; I am still writing, but I somehow do feel the end coming. But I've been wrong before. I did get a letter last week from the State Medical Board indicating there was enough evidence of "oddness" to open an investigation against the critical care practice that did or didn't treat Shannon at St. Joseph's. I have some other follow-up to do in order to feel the case is closed on the entire medical event.

As I look more broadly at my situation, I suppose the new normal is setting in. The boys seem to be finding their way. Shannon's situation is essentially resolved. My job situation is well on the way to being resolved. I am trying to learn to find comfort in what I have and not to focus on what I don't. The number of times a day that I feel really miserable is just two or three. When a bad time comes, I just ride it out. It feels right to be miserable; I know it will pass; I just let it happen.

I actually find it harder to stay happy than to stop being sad. Happy just doesn't feel right. Even if the immediate circumstances are 100% consistent with being happy, I quickly am reminded of the rest of the story and lose whatever rush I had. Maybe it's a stage I am going through.

I found a talented person who is integrating all this writing in to a document—for now, I suppose just for posterity, but who knows. That's nice to have underway.

This was one pretty dull note, but it is late, I am on my fourth plane of the week, and it is only Wednesday. Looking forward to sleeping in my own bed, to maybe seeing the boys, and to some music this weekend.

January 13

I don't think tonight is going to be one to remember, but I am going to try.

Yesterday, I went with Reid and a friend to one of the neighborhood places Shannon and I used to frequent. Most of them I don't go to anymore, but this one I thought we had stayed anonymous enough at to make it work—and I had been there a time or two since Shannon died, and no one had said anything. I thought it was safe.

When Reid and I got there, we had to wait while they bused a table. Reid ran next door to do another errand. While I was waiting, the waitress came up and asked where my wife was. Ugh. I was really glad Reid had stepped out. I need to have a better-rehearsed answer for that question. I probably should say she just couldn't make it today. Then I could never go back there and that would be that. And it isn't a lie.

But I don't do that; I tell the truth. The waitress becomes sad and embarrassed and from my table I could watch the news spread through the bar. Now they are all a bit sad.

Today I had the closing on a refinance of the house. Got a great rate and all. I show up at the attorney's office and he comes in, shakes my hand, and says, "Where is your wife?" Here we go again. This time, "She couldn't make it today" isn't going to work. The office had a death certificate—all this was supposed to have been handled—and they admitted it. But what was supposed to take 20 minutes took two hours because the bank had to reissue documents, etc., without Shannon's name. So that sucked.

The best part—and believe me, I am laughing and crying at this—is that I have more data to help me win my argument with my psychiatrist. Not sure why I want to win so badly. I remember Shannon teasing me about what a burden it must be for me to be right all the time...I would tease her back that it was hard, but at least it beat being wrong.

Anyway, the data. I created a profile on match.com as an experiment. I found that I can eliminate 100% of the women on the site using just six criteria. The six criteria are not very stringent. I will reveal three as evidence of my reasonableness...no smokers, roughly my age, and within 30 miles. I do get lots of "winks" from very pretty 20-something-year-olds. I suspect they come from the same place some of the e-mails I have been getting are from. The pictures are all shots from above of a woman looking back and up over her left shoulder. Hilarious.

The doctor will counter with, "If you are looking in the wrong place, you shouldn't expect to find what you are looking for." And he's right—but it's the next round of our debate. And I really am not looking anyway. I want Shannon back. What I want in this experiment is to feel justified in my hopelessness about the future. How is that for depressing? I am getting good at it.

So tonight is Big Head Todd and the Monsters at Variety Playhouse. I am going to dinner at Serpas, one of our usual pre-concert places, with my Kindle. Then I will go over for a PBR or two and listen for a bit. Shannon really liked BHT. I have liked them for years, but she got hooked when we went to see them at the old Roxy Theater in Buckhead several years back. In fact, the string of text messages from Shannon that I am saving began the night in Boulder where I went to see Todd—the main guy—play at the Boulder Whole Foods parking lot in the rain while she stayed safely ensconced in the St. Julien Hotel. I was giving her play-by-play about the concert.

I had to vent all this—but after sharing a bad day I feel like I walked in a room full of you happy people and farted. That's a good sentence—vent and fart. Sorry—I take laughs where I can. So the picture—Spencer just sent this to me—it's him clowning around with a tuna. He had the cookbook photo shoot last week, and this is one the photographer took. It's funny, Shannon would have loved it. What is amazing to me is that Spencer knows exactly what to do with that giant fish to turn it into an incredible bite.

January 14

11:45 a.m.

Making pasta from scratch for lunch. Going to grind up a perfectly good steak to make meat sauce. House is very clean, except for Reid's shoes all over the place. Painter still banging around upstairs. Sun is very bright, but it's cold. Did get the front porch furniture cushions back and ready to go, so as soon as it hits 55, the front office is in business.

I cannot begin to describe how tickled I am by match.com. If you ever find yourself nostalgic for the pettiness, shallowness, and self-promotion that characterized all you hated about high school, set up a profile and just watch. It's like dangling a hook in crystal clear water. Watch the fish approach and dart away...watch other fish hang out in a corner too busy to be bothered. It's like you get to be in your own reality TV show. Everybody describes how wonderful and desirable they are and then behaves like an ass.

It's funny until you realize that for some people it may be the best way to meet people. Then it is fairly depressing. To continue the experiment, I am going to fiddle around with the profile a bit and see what changes. I need to find that picture of me from when I was in the movie *300*—those abs could kill.

Big Head Todd was great last night—as was dinner at Serpas. At the restaurant it was lots of couples and me. I took a break from reading and was enjoying my meal. I started thinking about the movie *Date Night* where Steve Carrell and Tina Fey go out to eat and try to figure out the stories behind the other couples in the restaurant. I wonder what people are trying to figure out about me—it's easy to know you are noticed. I bet no one guesses widower. Not sure how to feel about that.

January 16

7:49 p.m.

It's been a busy weekend. I've had a lot of work, painters came over and painted, Reid has been in and out and around, and some friends stopped over for a night on a road trip. The prep and clean-up from all that also kept me busy.

Now the friends are gone, Reid is on a plane back to Boulder, the house is clean, and really, really quiet. I won't see him for about a month. I had to take Shannon's hair dryer down for the painter. I will put it back as it was for a little while. It won't be the same because it won't be just the way she left it anymore. It will be a prop, not a part of her. That's okay. It will make it easier to take down later.

These little things are hard. Two related stories. Shannon has never really cooked. She had no confidence there at all. The truth is that she could cook pretty well—but she was just slow. Early on in our relationship, she got tired of me hovering and sort of abdicated the kitchen duties to me. That was okay—I like to cook.

Somehow over the past couple of years she became addicted to soup for lunch. It's easy to fix and with her condition, it was not something hard to chew. She developed a specialty with ramen noodles. She would get a pack of that terrible stuff out of the pantry. She'd open it up and throw out the seasoning mix. She'd boil fresh chicken stock, add mushrooms, spinach, green onion, hot sauce, and the noodles and eat that. Sometimes she'd throw in an egg. I begged her to fix me a serving once. It was pretty good.

For Christmas—I think two years ago—I gave her a special bowl I found at maybe Crate and Barrel. It was an Asian design soup bowl with chopsticks. I told her the soup would taste even better in that. She loved it and agreed. The bowl had a special place in the cabinet, and she used it a couple of times a week. Since she died, I saw that bowl every time I open the cabinet. It was really hard to see. When Spencer was over here helping me cook for friends the other day, he knocked the bowl out of the cabinet by accident, and it broke. I was so relieved. I could throw out a broken bowl, but I couldn't throw out Shannon's bowl. He was disappointed he had broken her bowl, but really he did me a huge favor. I don't have to see it anymore. Now that I have written about it, I don't have to think about it anymore.

It's really hard for me to look at pictures of Shannon now. I can look at a picture—say from our London trip—and have the best memories of her and of being there with her. But it really hurts to look at a picture of her. Maybe this is a stage of her going from a reality to a memory. I don't know. But it means all those pictures in the basement are going to be sitting on that table a long, long time.

January 17

This morning, I went to check progress on the piece of furniture Shannon and I are/were having built. We worked with the furniture maker to design it just a few days before Shannon went in to the hospital. It is pretty much built—I was down there today to pick the right stain. It is going to be beautiful. I hope it will make me happy every time I see it. It's an expensive mistake to go ahead with its construction if it ends up making me sad every time I see it.

I also talked with the guy about Shannon's memory box. Months ago, when I told him about Shannon's death and asked if I could commission him to build the box, he insisted he do it for free. Today he was describing the box to me. It is now a chest of mahogany with inlaid work, brass finishes, etc. I said it sounded like more than he should be giving me, and that we should cut back on features. He said no, he wanted to make sure it was really special. He met Shannon twice, and he was tearing up. He said it would help if I could contribute to materials because brass finishes were expensive. I told him he was being ridiculous—of course I would pay—mahogany is not cheap, either. So we agreed he would provide his time for a kindness, and I would cover supplies. I'll over-reimburse him. The box is going to be gorgeous. In it will go this tome to Shannon, one of her teacups, and a few other things of hers I want to keep.

A few days on match.com and you realize how lucky you are to have real friends...what a trip. No kindness there! Darwin at work. It is great that we have found a way to use technology to create a superficial and demeaning environment. No need to waste gas driving!

I wrote a bit the other day about the profiles—so funny. Talk about a lack of product differentiation. On the plus side, all the drop dead gorgeous girls who you daydreamed about in high school—the girls who wouldn't give you the time of day—are alone and on the site. Justice prevails. On the minus side, so are you. And they still won't give you the time of day.

I often don't play well in situations like this—I have the petulant child version of a profile. "You can drag me to match.com, but you can't make me like it!" Oddly, it works for some people out there...they e-mail me and tell me I am funny. One person wrote "Your profile made me LOL." okay—I get the abbreviation...but when you are 50, don't try to sound so cool; LOL in that context makes me G-A-G. LMAOROTF!

The best part of the day was a picture I got in e-mail. The friends that stopped over Saturday night made it to New Orleans—their next stop. They sent me a picture from Shannon's tree—the white rose I left on her birthday is still there, and they left a fresh one there with it. So kind and so beautiful! Just a wonderful way to end the day.

January 19

5:12 p.m.

Today was a day to see the psychiatrist. Interesting discussion related to how I move on in the world.

I commented as to how I felt like I would never finish saying good-bye to Shannon—or more precisely to the concept of Shannon. The material good-byes are somewhat obvious and straightforward. She is gone; I said good-bye. The Viking funeral continues—when the bathroom got painted I again was impressed with the volume of "product" I won't need anymore and threw out. That's a concrete sort of good-bye. One day, I need to take care of her clothes.

But saying good-bye to Shannon's things is different than Shannon as a concept. Maybe a way to say it is that it's a lot less clear how to handle her spirit. He isn't telling me to say good-bye to her spirit—and I hope I never do. I'd like to have that with me forever, and I suspect I will. What he is asking me to think about is how might some woman down the road feel about my unwillingness or inability or what have you to let go of her spirit.

As an example, I had told him about visiting Shannon's tree for her birthday and leaving a rose. He, being a reasonable guy, thought it was sweet. He's right about that. But he said—and these are really my words, not his—he is more diplomatic—in five years are you going to explain to a then-girlfriend that you have to go to New Orleans to put a rose at Shannon's tree?

I said no, I wouldn't do that. But it is something to think about. I would like to think that if I met someone in the future they would mostly think that it was a good thing to remember a loved one. Wouldn't they want to be remembered? So if down the road I end up in a relationship, how much of Shannon comes with me before it gets creepy? And if she can't come along, how do I say good-bye to her spirit? Those are hard questions to answer.

Earlier in the week, I had to get the car from the shop. I have been using a guy—a taxi service—for trips like this since Shannon died. The guy is remarkable. In the taxi Monday we were making small talk, and he shared with me that he had hit a string of bad luck. He hurt his back badly and needed an operation. He has no insurance, so he has a $60K medical bill. He couldn't work for 2 months this fall because of the recovery—so no income. During that time, the bank foreclosed on his condo. He paid $130,000 for it years ago, and now it is worth $40,000. His lawyer told him to declare bankruptcy. In November, his dad passed away from complications of diabetes. The bank just recently kicked him out of the condo—but he was okay with that because his taxi had been towed away twice—the condo rules allow no commercial vehicles. He has a Lexus 300 that just had a logo and a phone number on the door—it isn't some big truck. And, while he was moving, he hurt his back again.

Here is the thing. He told the entire story with laughs, grins, and a sort of "oh well, stuff happens, I'll get by" point of view. Amazing. How does he do it? That's what happened to him in the last three or four months, and he is as upbeat as someone could be. I consider it a good day if I just manage. What makes some people so resilient, and where can I find some of that?

January 21

> 5:06 p.m.

At dinner with Spencer the other night, he was telling me how he and Reid had shared stories about what I suppose are "awkward" situations they've been in. You might remember boys that age making cracks about one another's moms. Spencer told me that Reid told him only about four other students at CU know about Shannon's death. He has kept it to himself. There have been several times where someone starts cracking jokes on Reid, and one of his friends that knows has had to intervene and get them to back off—to explain. It's happened to Spencer, too. Same thing—friends who do know step in. It makes me angry this goes on—but I can also remember being that age and pretending when someone teased me that my mom really HAD died. I'd keep it up until I made them feel terrible for making the joke. Not so funny now.

Finally, I went on a couple of dates this week. They were nice. I try to be good company. I am not going to talk about that in this forum (or any forum!), except to say now that the one good thing I can say it does for me is to force me to think about the future. I spend most of my time—probably way too much time—pining for the past. I really want Shannon to be with me. It's easy to imagine her here getting ready for this concert. I want to watch her eat room service eggs benedict while she reads her book tomorrow morning while I beat away on this laptop. But that isn't going to happen. The laptop part will, I suppose.

January 24

12:25 p.m.

It's interesting to meet new people. People my age and single are such a diverse group—there are so many more things to consider when you are trying to figure out who will be good company. The last time I was trying to find good company was 1980 something. We were all pretty much the same—same age. The school we attended screened us a bit; the circles we hung out with screened us more. And we all knew we were at the beginning.

People I meet now are not like that. People with kids at home, people with kids gone, people who chose to never have kids. Which of those three am I more likely to find as good company? People who are self-made, people with lots of education, people who have worked, people who have been stay-at-home moms. Which of those am I likely to find to be good company? We are all at very different places. It's harder.

I had a surreal experience earlier today at match.com—I somehow found my way to a wormhole or something. I was replying to a note from a woman. When I sent it, it came to me. I backed up a page, and the screen inside the frame of my account said, "You have successfully sent your note to Nate. If you like Nate, you might be interested in these others." And there were 6 pictures and short bios of guys "like me." So bizarre. So I looked. I didn't think they were much like me.

They were like the boy versions of the girl profiles I just skip past. So I am sure they will find someone soon.

I have received a lot of books and book suggestions from friends over the past months. I have been pretty good about chasing them down and checking them out. There aren't many grief books that aren't based on a belief in God. It makes it a little harder to process the advice when the foundation is something you don't share—at least not in that way. It's made me think about my beliefs. Would I be less hurt if I thought there was a God? Would I be less sad if I believed Shannon was in a better place? Would I be less lonely if I thought I would see her again one day? Who knows.

What I have come to realize is just how powerful hope is. I believe in the power of hope. For a while, hope helped me deal with Shannon's collapse. Now, hope that I haven't had my last fun night out is helping me deal with being alone. The question then becomes, where do you find hope? Maybe it would be easier to find hope if I believed in God. But I don't, so I have to find other sources.

I find hope in my kids. I was driving to work earlier today, and I passed a mom out teaching her little boy to ride his bike. I found hope in that.

I find hope in a great song and the energy of a crowd at a concert and in front of a class and in the kindness of friends. I hope that's enough hope.

January 25

> 4:20 p.m.

Just as I opened this link, Pandora served up Etta James singing "At Last." It's sad that she is gone. What a great performance.

On the music front, riddle me this...why is it that the two musical groups I have NEVER skipped or changed the station on since Shannon died are Tom Petty and the Bee Gees. Figure that one out and you get a big, big prize.

And, I am loving a book called *Love is a Mix Tape: Life and Loss, One Song at a Time*. It's by a guy who writes for *Rolling Stone*—Rob Sheffield. I wrote him—not sure the e-mail address I have is very active, but it would be great to hear from him. He lost his wife after just five years of marriage.

Yesterday was the first time I can remember that writing didn't bring some sort of relief. Sometimes writing has been energizing. Sometimes it crushes me, but even in doing that it provides some relief. That didn't happen yesterday. As is often the case, I got the two fairly random e-mails that filled in the hole that blogging couldn't. That was great.

There is a lot going on—a lot. But what is happening now is so much more complicated. It's difficult to write about—I haven't a clue how to begin. As I write that sentence, Pandora served up the Beatles "Let It Be." I listened. Now back—I am not sleeping again. Seems like whatever is going on—for better or worse—means I don't sleep.

Yesterday, a neighbor undecorated Shannon's tree. Of course, this didn't just happen—she checked to make sure I was okay with it. It's nearly February—the ornaments can come down. I appreciated her checking. I went about my business, and I later found the ornaments on my porch neatly placed in a box tied with a ribbon. That's nice.

I was thinking about the day we put the ornaments up. It seems like a year ago. It was a warm afternoon, there was a nice turnout of neighbors. I remember one neighbor shared a sweet story about Shannon and then offered to let others chime in. No one did. I think people found the pause awkward. I didn't. That isn't who Shannon was. I think it is actually appropriate that no one had a story; she didn't seek to be story-worthy. She did so many things that no one knew about. She wasn't about credit.

In Baton Rouge one time, she was upset at me about something and decided to exercise her frustration and used our edger to edge the neighbor's yard while they were out. They never knew how it happened. She figured something good might as well come from her being angry.

So now Pandora has served up James Taylor's "Fire and Rain." That's a good way to end—and this will be the second time in a row that writing hasn't worked.

Miss you, Shannon.

January 26

9:36 a.m.

January 26, 2012
Mr. Howard Watts
St. Joseph's Hospital
5665 Peachtree Dunwoody Road, NE
Atlanta, GA 30342

Dear Mr. Watts:

I am writing to follow up on our conversations regarding the care my wife, Shannon Bennett (DOB 1-9-63), received at St. Joseph's last September (admitted 9-7-11).

As I am certain you recall, I shared several frustrations with you and your team at the Hospital. As the process unfolded, it became clear to me that many of the frustrations were better directed at the medical practice contracted to provide care in the CCU, Pulmonary and Critical Care of Atlanta.

In the time since, I have been direct in sharing my frustrations with them. I haven't found the experience very satisfying—but it's clear that doesn't trouble them.

I have attached a letter they shared with a friend who has been helping me work through this process. In the letter, they offer assurances that they are working actively with St. Joseph's to make sure practice is improved. I am sharing the letter with you in the hope that you can tell me unequivocally that the efforts they claim are underway truly are underway.

It would be a comfort to know that lessons learned from my family's experience were not wasted. Sadly, Drs. [Redacted], [Redacted], and [Redacted] have given me no reason to believe their deeds would ever match their words. For that reason, I would appreciate some validation from St. Joseph's.

Thanks in advance for your assistance in this regard.

Cordially,
Nathan Bennett

GUESTBOOK

11:06 a.m.

NEVER NEVER give up this fight.

PM

January 26

> 2:45 p.m.

I don't know what is up with the weather in ATL, but I am not going to complain. The sun helps—probably the one constant, besides medication, that helps. And Tom Petty and the Bee Gees, apparently.

Pandora played Bill Withers's "Ain't No Sunshine" today—a while back I had put the song on the "don't play for a month" list. I guess it's been a month; I made it through.

I have had people e-mail me to say that I seem to be doing better, and I have had people express concern that I seem to be pretty miserable. You are all right. I think what is happening is that the thought of being happy without Shannon is too much for me to comprehend somehow now. When I find myself happy, I basically start to question everything, and it is overwhelming. So I suppose I am still sort of bi-polar, but maybe with a higher average score.

I got a letter from the State Medical Board today. They have completed the investigation of the surgi-center where Shannon had her procedure and collapsed. They did surprise visits, etc. They found there was no evidence Shannon was overmedicated or not properly attended after surgery. They also found no evidence that the facility did not have proper protocols in place for her care.

I suppose most people who get that letter are disappointed. I am so happy. I really am. I don't want to be angry with them—I don't want to think they mistreated Shannon—and I don't want to think that other people are getting bad care. That's really good news.

They are still investigating Pulmonary Critical Care—but those doctors are, I am sure, Teflon. I don't expect much there.

January 30

On my way home from DC for the second time in four nights. Ready to be home—an entire two weeks without a trip. The woman boarding the plane ahead of me had on a nice coat. The flight attendant said to her, "What a beautiful coat!" As I got on, I said I was sorry—my coat wasn't much to look at. She said, "But you have a beautiful coat of hair!" I said, "You should see it on my back!" She laughed. If Shannon were with me she would have hit me. I would love to feel that exasperated gesture of love again.

There was a story in the *NY Times* on Sunday about the power of blogs and how blogging has helped teenagers cope with the stresses in their lives. The article points out how much more the "being heard" adds to the experience—when compared to a private diary or the like. I agree. You all have helped me so much.

I have said that I feel this winding down. The main reason is that I don't get the same cathartic rush. I was thinking about that today and why it might be. I think I figured it out. I have been able to be very open here because I truly felt we all were sharing the loss of Shannon. What I wrote was personal, but it involved us all. Now the things I struggle with feel more private. They really just belong to me. I am not so comfortable sharing them. No sharing, no catharsis.

So I was thinking about what the right way is to end. I wanted to write about how my life has been different because of Shannon—both having her in it and losing her. It is such a big topic. I don't have any concept of what my life would have been without her. Because of her I experienced unconditional love and unwavering trust. I had someone in my corner 24/7 for so many years. Even when she was pissing me off, I know it was based on her efforts to take care of me. What am I like without her? I am more empathetic. I am an even more outrageous tipper. I am terribly sad. I still have some thinking to do.

Here is an example of what I can share...but it's hard. Tomorrow, I am getting a new bed. Tonight will be the last time I sleep on the bed I shared with Shannon. It's just a mattress, but when I take all the sheets and stuff off it in the morning, I will see the little crater she made there on her side for the last time. That makes me so terribly sad.

From: AS
Date: Tue, 31 Jan 2012 12:23:42-0500
To: Nathan Bennett
Subject: your blog

Nate,

In a very selfish way, I have enjoyed reading your blog and getting to know Shannon better. I never saw her without a smile on her face, and I now know that it wasn't a fluke. She wasn't being polite—she was a genuinely warm and caring person. Regardless of where you go in life and what happens to you, Shannon's smile, her laugh, and her joy will be a part of you. For those of us who have followed these months of your journey to start the process of coming to terms with your new situation, you have been inspirational, funny, and have made me cry. I am sure that as difficult as this period has been, your next steps when you have to internalize this and come to terms with it will be even more challenging. I thank you for sharing Shannon with us.

I do hope we keep in touch when you leave for Georgia State. That will be a sad day.

Please know that a part of me will always remember Shannon and that hearing her name will always bring a smile to my face. She was fortunate to have you, but you were one of the luckiest men in the world to have her, and Spencer and Reid are two others.

February 1

	12:07 a.m.

Today was a good day. So what better way to handle that then to go back and revisit entries from the last several months. Three things came to mind. First, my boys and I had (and still have) a ton of support, and I am so thankful for that. Second, even though I feel a little better, it doesn't take much to make me feel bad. You might remember a quote I shared weeks ago—it had something to do with the memory of a loved one fading or becoming obscure like a shape becomes obscured as it is covered in a snowfall—the edges soften, etc. I actually think that is a better description of my pain than of my memory of Shannon. I remember her vividly. I remember how she felt, what she smelled like, every curve, everything. What is covered in snow and is obscured is my pain. All it takes is someone to brush it off and there it is—right at the surface. Third, and this won't be news to any of you, life isn't fair. Shannon, more than anyone I know, deserved some carefree, happy time. She never got it—or at least she didn't get her share. That just sucks, and there is nothing any of us can do about it. Except maybe to just spoil someone else to make sure they get their share.

February 2

8:00 p.m.

I finished the book *Love is a Mix Tape* last night. It was a good read. Right at the end the author wrote about his reflections on kindness— something I have been struck by and tried to recount. He says it better than I have:

> *That was one of the strangest things I learned as a widower— how kind people can be...You lose a certain kind of innocence when you experience this type of kindness. You lose your right to be a jaded cynic. You can no longer go back through the looking glass and pretend not to know what you know about kindness...People kept showing me unreasonable kindness, inexplicable kindness, indefensible kindness. People were kind when they knew that nobody would ever notice, much less praise them for it. People were even kind when they knew I wouldn't appreciate it...I had no idea how to live up to that kindness.*[7]

The book was good—but these words were perfect. That's exactly how I have felt. He got the dark side right, too. He shares a quote from an essay Ralph Waldo Emerson wrote about losing his son that is dead-on: "I grieve that grief can teach me nothing." I have felt that.

Sheffield, this book's author, goes on with this theme and again his words nail it:

> *It's the same with people who say, "Whatever doesn't kill you makes you stronger." Even people who say this must realize the exact opposite is true. What doesn't kill you maims you, cripples you, leaves you weak, makes you whiny and full of*

---

[7] Rob Sheffield, *Love is a Mix Tape* (New York: Random House, 2007), 164–165.

yourself at the same time...Whatever doesn't kill you makes you incredibly annoying.[8]

I have felt that, too.

Shannon would be thrilled to learn that her favorite, Trombone Shorty, is the subject of the 2012 New Orleans Jazz Fest poster. I am going to take this year off from the Fest, but I did order the poster. The trips we were able to take these past two Jazz Fests were some of the best days of my life, no question about it.

February 4

4:22 p.m.

I found the apparent courage this week to start to handle the things in Shannon's closet. A while ago, a neighbor had volunteered to help, and I was glad to take her up on it.

I found more treasures—notes she wrote to the boys, one of Reid's baby teeth in an envelope he addressed to the tooth fairy, some drawings she did and tucked away, and some old photos. I think we were able to get it about halfway finished. There are some things I am keeping, there are some things I am sending to her sister, and some things are give-aways. And there are some things that are trash.

The trash category is interesting to me. Some of the stuff is just properly trash. Underwear is not meant to be passed on. But some of the trash is stuff I don't want someone else to have. I don't want it—

---

[8] Ibid., 190.

it isn't really something to pass on—it just needs to be returned to the earth.

I also found it interesting as far as what hurt. Shannon's trousseau, for lack of a better word, was easy to get rid of. I thought that would be hard. The things that were hard to even touch were the things that she loved to wear—one pair of flannel pajamas in particular. The thought that I'd never see the grin on her face when she broke them out each fall was unbearable.

The things that gave her joy are the things that are hardest to part with.

Among the odd scraps of paper, photos, and all that were tucked into this and that was a fortune from a Chinese restaurant. It said, "You will live a long and happy life." Maybe she kept it for the lottery numbers on the back, because the sentiment on the front was way off.

I can't get over how unprepared Shannon was to die. We left the house that morning with every reason to believe we would be back that afternoon. If you knew you were walking out of your house for the last time, what would you finish? Shannon would move the wash ahead. I know that.

February 5

9:50 a.m.

I heard good music at two venues in town last night. It was good to get out. People watching helps distract me from what is going on in my mind; time listening to music lets my mind run. The back and forth is therapeutic and tiring. When I start thinking dark thoughts I just try to find someone to watch. Before I can be sensed as a stalker I have to let that person go, and letting go gives my mind a chance to exercise.

So what did I think about? I just still can't believe Shannon is gone. I know it is true in a million ways, but I can't believe it. Took me back to pondering about religion. If I know Shannon is gone in a million provable ways and can't believe it, what are the odds I would ever believe in something that can't be demonstrated nearly as unequivocally in a million and one ways? Might have been the deepest thought going on in the crowd at the Railroad Earth show.

I thought about how sad it is that when I am old and looking back on my life there will probably be a third of it that I have no one who shares my memories. What memories could matter more than raising your family? The person I did that with is gone before the memories really became memories. I thought about how much during that time of my life I was relying on Shannon to remember for me. Those memories are gone with her forever.

And I thought about how cool it would be if material possessions could vaporize like memories—if loved ones didn't have to touch your things and make decisions about them and all that. What if when you died all your things just evaporated? I thought about how great it would be if your physical stuff went away, but all your memories somehow became documented. That's what I want from Shannon—her memories, not her stuff.

And that was probably the deepest thought at the Mike Doughty concert—although Doughty is a pretty quirky guy.

Who knows what goes on in his head?

And I thought that after nearly five months it doesn't get better. I am finding ways to treat the symptoms. Just like sometimes aspirin dulls a headache or a glass of wine takes the edge off a hard day, the treatments help. Medicine, exercise, sunshine, work, music, a rare good night of sleep, hearing from my kids—they treat the symptoms.

Imagine being uncomfortably full from a meal...the relief you get from loosening your belt is about right. You are still uncomfortably full, but at least your belt is not making you in to a figure-8 shape.

I think I am always going to be two people from now on. The one who lost Shannon and the one who is trying to figure out what to do next.

February 7

4:47 p.m.

Today is five months since Shannon collapsed. Not a very meaningful milestone; no real deep thoughts have revealed themselves to me. I suppose none of the monthly anniversaries will be that significant until it's become a year. I have Spencer's birthday, my birthday, and what would have been our 27th wedding anniversary to deal with before then. After that, no more "firsts without." I guess the open question is, "how much better are seconds without?"

I sent the signed offer letter back to Georgia State today. That's another page turning. I am looking forward to new challenges, but I have a lot to finish this spring before heading over. The main project is the book on leadership succession...how is a smooth transition from one leader to another best made? It is fairly ironic that every single thought I have as I work on it in some way applies to trying to understand how to make a transition from one partner to another. These aren't love relationships...or they aren't supposed to be. But character, trust, shared vision for the future fits.

Dating is strange. I have heard a few more stories of failed marriages, and it reminds me of how fortunate I was. I went for a walk this afternoon—too pretty in Atlanta—the cherry trees are all as confused as I am and are in bloom. On the walk, I was thinking about these stories and about Shannon. For us, it was a lot of work to get to a relationship that was really easy. Apparently there are guys out there who are kind of lazy. The conclusion is that what made me fortunate was not that I found someone easy to be with; it was that I found someone who was willing to work as hard as I was to make it easy.

February 8

7:22 p.m.

Letter today from the CEO at St. Joseph's...

Dear Dr. Bennett,

Thank you for taking the time to forward the letter you received from Dr. [Redacted] with [Redacted] Care of Atlanta. I sincerely apologize that anyone at Saint Joseph's involved in the care of your wife has given you any reason to doubt their word.

Please rest assured that your voice was heard and I have asked my team to improve how we handle situations such as Shannon's in the future. Dr. X, Medical Director Intensivist Service, has been working with Ms. Y, Director of Patient Safety and Quality, to identify and review the practices that were in place. Their review has brought to light several improvements that are being put in place to ensure no other family has to go through what you experienced.

Again, please accept my sincere condolences on the passing of your beloved wife. If I may be of any assistance in the future, please do not hesitate to contact me.

I am going to consider that good news and close that chapter of this adventure.

February 13

I have been wrestling with questions for several days without success. The process is brought on each time I walk through the living room and pass the stack of bags filled with Shannon's clothes. I can't get a pick up scheduled for a bit. That timing didn't turn out well. Once you feel ready to part with things, the things need to actually go.

The thought is about good-byes. I am lucky that someone I met online turns out to be good company. Not to rush things—I'm not—but obviously a lot of future scenarios play out in my mind. I am trying to understand how it works when someone new enters your life. The question starts as: Is room in your heart finite? To make room for someone new, do I have to let Shannon go? I am crippled by that thought. But as I process it, I think room in your heart is infinite—people with 2 kids love them; people with 10 kids find a way to love 10. Then I realize that my issue is going to be more with my head. How can I wrap my head around the thought of having someone else close where Shannon used to be? That's really the question.

February 14

Another first has snuck up on me—the first Valentine's Day. We always complained about greeting card holidays—things we were "told" to celebrate. And we liked to insist "every day is Valentine's Day around here." And thankfully that felt true a lot of the time.

I say it snuck up on me—I saw it coming last week at the grocery store when I was looking for cards—my dad's birthday is February 14. Seeing the holiday cards was one of those moments where suddenly my heart was in my throat. I can't say there are fewer of those—but I am better at handling them when they surprise me. I used to get Shannon two or three cards, and she would do the same for me. We'd each on our own go through the same process. We'd find a sweet one, a smutty one, and a silly one—not be able to decide—and just get all three. I have a lot of those cards tucked around the house.

Thinking back on the holiday, though, what I remembered more than dinners out or cards was how, when the boys were little, Shannon would get them ready for Valentine's Day. She would get the little packs of cards that are made for school kids, a bag of Tootsie Pop suckers or something, and the class list. She would sit at the kitchen table with each boy helping them assemble and address cards for everyone in their class.

That's a wonderful memory of a great mom, and I am glad the holiday brought me that. I hope you all get your Valentine a sweet card, a silly card, and a smutty card.

February 17

Today was a beautiful day in Boulder. Blue sky, sun, warm enough to feel okay walking around. I am at the St. Julien Hotel again, so I changed the picture to the one I took of Shannon here last summer. That mountain in the background is fairly snow covered today.

It was hard to be at this hotel without Shannon the first couple of times, but now it feels like my Boulder home. One thing I noticed about nice hotels—they treat me just like people treated me as a new widower. No one says "no" to me; everyone appears happy to see me. Everyone helps me solve problems. I see it as a testimony to the quality of my friends and neighbors that they have 5 star hotel quality service capabilities!

It was great to see Reid. I picked him up after his morning class, and we grabbed lunch at a great dive near campus. Then, he took me past the house he and friends rented for next year. It looks just fine from the outside—great location for campus, near bus line but walkable, too. Near the action on "the hill" but not really "in" the action. Looks a lot like places I lived in college.

He also took me by his fraternity house...I was waiting on this revelation. Spencer had heard Reid received a bid, but Reid had said nothing to me. I told Spencer I was sure I would hear from Reid just about the time the first check was due. So Reid has joined a fraternity. They all sound like decent guys. He has been elected president of his class—they aren't pledges...they are "associates" like at Wal-Mart. Nothing like a good euphemism to take the edge off hazing.

I dropped him back at class, ran back to the hotel for a quick nap, then picked him back up. He came to the hotel with me, and we worked for a couple of hours, grabbed dinner, and I deposited him back to his room. He has the paper to finish and quizzes in economics and math tomorrow. I met up with some of Tech students who are here for a school competition, and we went to hear Phil Lesh and Warren Haynes. I love Warren Haynes.

I was struck tonight about how much Reid reminds me of Shannon. Maybe I am looking harder for it now; I don't know. He looks like me, but he behaves like Shannon. He is really low maintenance, but loves good things when they are available. He had oysters on the half shell, duck, and pork belly for dinner. Shannon would have been all over that spread. A sense of contentment about life simply emanates from him. And he is reflexively gentle and kind. He sure doesn't get any of that from me.

Shannon would be thrilled with this report about Reid. I wish I could call her and share it.

February 18

11:23 p.m.

I am in Chapel Hill, North Carolina, tonight. A friend had me up for the UNC-Clemson basketball game, and then his wife made a great dinner. It was a good day.

This next week is another anniversary of sorts—though I will admit I am stretching to make too big a deal of it...the first Mardi Gras. I have so many great memories of Mardi Gras. First when Shannon and I were falling in love and then when we brought Spencer, then Spencer and Reid. I remember driving from Baton Rouge down to Harry's Ace Hardware in New Orleans to buy the official "ladder box" that you installed on top of your ladder, so your kid would have a safe place to sit up above the craziness. We caught a LOT of plastic crap using that box, the boys and I. I was glad to bequeath it to a colleague with young kids when we moved from Louisiana.

I remember one year when Spencer was maybe 2 years old that after a long day of parades we stopped at a McDonald's to get him some fries for the drive home. He literally fell asleep in the middle of a fry—it was hanging from his mouth like a cigarette for the entire drive to Baton Rouge.

I remember Shannon making a bed for Reid out of towels and blankets in the gutter of St. Charles Avenue so he could grab a nap between parades. And I remember that no one thought there was anything wrong with that.

I remember Spencer insisted—after months of failed potty training—that he was finally ready to go without a diaper the Mardi Gras of his third year. We begged him to wear a diaper for the day, and he refused. "I want big boy underpants!" You don't want to have to find a restroom quickly for a kid on Mardi Gras. Thankfully, we ended up parking near some entrepreneurs who had a port-o-let installed on their driveway—for $10 you could have privileges all day—and they cleaned it after each guest. Best $20 I ever spent—I paid for me and Shannon, and they threw in Spencer for free!

I remember the two boys in the ladder box with me standing on the ladder behind them one year—a guy on the float threw me a teddy bear. I caught it and immediately had the dilemma—which boy to hand it to? It was so funny because the minute I had that thought, I looked up and the guy—the float heading down the street—realized he had sort of screwed me by getting me one bear. You know he was a dad. He had another—he pitched it to me, and I caught it. Each boy got a bear.

I am really thankful to have had New Orleans in my life. No denying my life is richer for it. I'll never get the city off my waist/mind.

Since starting this blog, several people have said I should find a way to turn it into a book. It is hard for me to know what to make of it because I am surrounded by encouraging people, not harsh critics. I would love though, for example, to do something that could increase awareness of mitochondrial disease, to perhaps raise some money that would help research, and—most of all—that might offer comfort to men who lose their wives.

I spend a lot of time thinking about this—is it just an indulgence or could there be some value? I've mentioned that a friend is helping to organize things in a way that protects everyone, but explains what I think is really the story—how a community of sorts comes together to get one another through an unexplainable, horrible, wrong, and untimely loss.

One day last week, I contacted a friend from high school who has done a much better job than I of staying in touch with friends from high school. He noted that a woman who was a year behind us worked in publishing in New York City. I found her e-mail, we exchanged notes, and she read some of the blog. She was kind—and she gave me an interesting piece of advice. She said I had to be very clear about the promise I was making to the reader—and then I had to be very sure to keep the promise.

I like that for lots of reasons. First, it is very actionable advice. And reasonable advice. Second, it's what Shannon and I did for each other. I like the thought of "ending" with a promise the same way we "began" with a promise.

The trick is that none of this started with much of a promise other than the one I made to myself—to be honest and to try to say things that were "useful." So I have been spending a lot of time thinking about the promise I could make that these writings would keep.

February 22

9:55 p.m.

I had a chance today to talk with a friend who lost her spouse about a year before I lost Shannon. There aren't a lot of people I know who are in this club, but it is very useful to know some. You can quickly feel comfortable knowing that they know what you know they know, and so on. It is one reason the advice I haven't taken—to find a support group—is probably good advice.

The timing of the visit was perfect because I have been trying to sort a few things out—and my psychiatrist is on vacation. These things all have to do with coming to terms with how women may view the challenge of trying to enter in to a dating relationship with a widower.

When I first meet someone, the fact I am a widower is viewed as a positive thing. It means I am not bitter about relationships, I am not stalked by an ex, there is no ex for me to suddenly decide I want to go back and be with, and the like. I am like the "quality pre-owned Lexus" I hear so much about on TV. Then, after a period of time, what had been to my benefit may become a disadvantage. Women may realize that I didn't leave a relationship, and they may worry I might never fully leave it. They will hit a wall of sorts when they realize they have to deal with the fact that I still love Shannon.

It is hard for me to think of Shannon as someone's competition—it just wasn't her style. But it will be natural for a woman who wants to get to know me to see her as such. As I think about all this, the issue (at least for me) isn't about how someone compares to her—it's about how strongly I feel that they will help me feel the way I felt when I was building something to be as proud of as I was of our relationship. I want to feel like I felt when I was part of a great team; that is all.

The irony is rich—it's as if I may have a hard time getting my next job because I was successful with my first job. If my first job had ended in flames, that baggage might be easier for someone to accommodate in a next job.

And those of you who knew Shannon will quickly agree that there wasn't a less intimidating person than she was—unless you messed with her kids. But in her death, she may become a force to be reckoned with! More irony.

February 25

10:49 a.m.

It's been a very productive morning, and I see sitting here now and doing this as an earned indulgence. That is another sign of progress for me. Months ago doing this was all about release—I had to do this in order to then be able to do what I needed to do to pay the bills. Now I can do what I need to do to pay the bills and use this as a reward.

When I was talking to my widowed friend last week, one of the things I shared was how I currently found myself grieving. It's different than it was months ago. It's like I have found a way to have "all things Shannon" in a room in my head. The door stays shut, and I go about my business. Sometimes, though, I feel like I need to go in that room. Actually, I want to go in that room. So I do. I can surround myself with all that is there and in my head I experience it with all my senses. I just go with it. It is miserable, and it feels really good. After a time, I pick myself up, leave the room, close the door, and get back to my business.

Sometimes someone else opens the door. On Valentine's Day I was flying back from visiting my mom. Upon arriving in Atlanta, I was the only passenger in the shuttle bus back to the parking lot—so naturally the driver and I got in a conversation about whatever. As we were pulling up to my car, she said, "Now don't forget it's Valentine's Day!" All the stuff just burst out of the Shannon room in my head. I didn't even have time to think. I automatically stuck my hand in my pocket, found our wedding rings on my key chain, and rubbed them. I took a breath and said in a surprisingly calm voice—around the heart in my throat—that I "had it covered." When that happens, it takes me a while to get all the stuff back in the room and to close the door.

I had some oral surgery last week and my mouth is not a real happy place. Seems like a proper occasion to break in to Spencer & Shannon's chicken soup, so that's for lunch. Hurting is a drag, and I certainly missed Shannon's hovering. The soup will be a good comfort but no substitute.

February 27

11:26 p.m.

Today was a hard day because I found myself stuck in a pity party— thrown for me by me and attended only by me. My mouth still hurts— though the good news is the tumor was benign. I haven't heard from the boys in a long time—other than monosyllabic texts. So all that is a bit of a drag.

Shannon was in my dream last night—just the fourth time since she died. In the dream, we were going through "normal life" stuff, but she was leaving me—the whole dream was about her getting ready to leave me. There was no upset, there was no fighting—it was never clear in the dream what the leaving was about—but she was leaving. That certainly didn't help with my mood today.

I wrote earlier about my revised model for stage of grieving:

Anger
Defeat
Detachment

The fourth stage is confusion. Confusion sets in as you detach—detaching creates a giant void in your life. The confusion is about how you try to figure out what to do with that giant void.

On 2/28/12 12:27 a.m., "AJB" wrote:
Subject: Thoughts from your journal yesterday

Hey Nate,

Just sending you a quick note about your mention of dreams in your post yesterday...It was another "me too!" moment. I very rarely remember my dreams about John, though I think we dream of them more than we realize...we just keep them in the very deepest parts of our sleep so we don't have to face them when we don't want to.

One of the very first dreams I had was of us on a boat, on vacation sailing around somewhere. Except I couldn't see his face...very similar feeling like your comment that you knew she was getting ready to leave. I knew he was leaving, but I couldn't turn him around.

The good news is that now some of the dreams are about him coming to say hi to me or to give me a hug. The hug dream was amazing. It was just what I needed. I think you'll get a hug from Shannon soon, too.

March 1

	10:20 a.m.

In a couple of weeks, I have tickets to see Bruce Springsteen here in Atlanta. I don't remember how many times I have seen him play—I remember some of them—one trip to Mobile when I was in college in particular. But the last time I saw him was with Shannon here in Atlanta—about 10 years ago. We had to leave early because of our babysitter's curfew. Time flies and things change.

I have written here how when it comes to songs I am more about lyrics, and Shannon was more about feeling. Springsteen is oddly one performer where the lyrics really worked for her. I guess in a previous life she was a teenage boy from New England.

We both thought the song "Tunnel of Love" was cleverly composed and so true about how scary it is to start a relationship—I'll always think of her when I hear the song. It came on my iPod as I was flying home from Minneapolis last night and in my head it sent me to Shannon's room.

There sure is a lot to be scared of when you are starting out. Then, after a few trials by fire, I stopped being scared. That has to be one of the best parts of a strong relationship—you aren't really ever scared and even when you start to slip that way someone there with you can "talk you down from the ledge."

It might be that freedom is the absence of fright.

Now I am at a place where being scared is back in the portfolio of emotions, and I have to learn to deal with it myself. And when another person enters my life, Shannon is going to be part of all the stuff that makes it the three of us. She never would have seen that coming. She would not want to haunt anyone.

I also wrote early on that moving on is difficult because Shannon was the person who I could count on to help me with the hard stuff—so how I am supposed to do it without her? I want to be able to write that she is with me in this—that somehow what she taught me, or the experience I had with her, or something "prepared" me for this so that she IS helping me now. But I can't write that—it doesn't feel true. Sometimes when a person leaves it does make things better—the whole "addition by subtraction" phenomenon and all that. But that isn't the case here. It is just plain subtraction. No other way to do the math.

I am looking forward to the concert. Springsteen is having to get along without his long, long, longtime bandmate Clarence Clemons. Wonder how he is doing at that?

March 4

9:53 p.m.

This is going to be a hard week because Thursday will be the six-month anniversary of losing Shannon. I have plans to go to Nashville to see a hockey game. To paraphrase Tom Hanks in *A League of Their Own*, there is no crying in hockey. Maybe being at a game will be a good thing. On the other hand, it means 8 hours, round trip, in the car by myself. It's a conundrum, all right. Right now, I am betting I don't go.

Some friends had me to dinner last night. On the way, I had to pass by the neighborhood where Shannon and I lived during the first year of my PhD program, so I drove thru. It has aged about as poorly as I feel I have. She was so brave. I suppose the truth is we both just didn't know any better. The place looks terrible, but I have such good memories of living there. We moved there about a year after we got married, but in a way, it was our first "new home." We had left New Orleans together for this adventure.

At dinner, my friend told me about a Garth Brooks song that he thought fit the things I've been thinking and writing about. It's called "The Dance," and though I haven't listened to the song yet, the lyrics are indeed perfect.

I think Garth's girl just left him for another guy, but that doesn't make the words any less right. I am glad I didn't miss the dance. It's funny when being so glad makes you so sad.

March 6

8:58 a.m.

Shannon has been gone nearly 6 months (tomorrow), and I swear that when I typed the last sentence of the paragraph above I typed "the last time all four of us are..." Had to go back and change it to three. Speaking of Reid—he called Friday. I suspect Spencer guilted him into it after he and I had dinner Thursday. Reid was on his way to an outdoor music festival—Snow Ball—in Vail...or maybe Aspen. Three days of the bands he loves, outdoors in winter, with a bunch of his high school friends who made the voyage out for the weekend. Sounds like a really good time. He will pass through ATL on spring break, but mostly will be in Florida with friends.

On the way to dinner last night I was thinking about the 6-month anniversary and what struck me is that for all that time—a long time—one thought has never left my mind—a disbelief that Shannon is gone and my marriage is over. I never saw it coming—as a friend said, six months ago today I was certain I was going to have Shannon as my partner for another 30 years. Six months tomorrow that was gone. And for the six months since, I have tried to make that make sense.

I don't think I have ever carried a thought for so long. Sometimes I am not sure I have carried a thought from one day to the next. I tried to think of when someone might. The only thing that I can see is even close is perhaps a woman who is pregnant. For 9 or so months, the fact she is pregnant likely never leaves her mind. She thinks about it when she orders food, buys clothes, talks to friends, takes prenatal vitamins, or lights up another Marlboro.

I know Shannon carried that thought for all that time for each boy. She started making decisions based on what was best for them LONG before they arrived in our family.

And I suppose people who face a terminal condition feel that way, too. Their diagnosis can't help but define them—and to continue to fight for the best real estate in the mind of the victim and their family—for as long as the fight goes on.

In the end, it is so incredibly exhausting to have a thought for six months. It's heavy, it doesn't get lighter, it doesn't surrender. It is difficult to find the way to carry it while at the same time having enough free hands to do what it takes to move your life forward.

March 7

> **11:05 p.m.**

So this is what 6 months looks like. We all made it. I never want to do it again. I would never wish it on someone, but it will happen to lots of someones no matter what I wish. Maybe we are all in a better place to help those someones when it does happen.

I worked hard to make today just a day, and that went pretty well. I am not going to Nashville. I need the time to deal with work and taxes—just can't justify another personal day now. I decided instead to go to New Orleans next week for a po'boy and a visit to Shannon's tree. Perhaps there will be signs of spring on its branches.

I am fortunate not just to have friends but to have wise friends. I have received a lot of good advice over the past 6 months. I have listened to all of it, I have thought about all of it, and I have taken some of it. I think all of it would have been good to take, but I tend towards stubborn. And some of it isn't so much advice as it is insight. Insight is very useful because I can't always get there myself.

One insight that was great was from a friend who told me today I was, in their mind, so different from a few months ago. I asked for some explanation—I don't remember the exact words, but basically it was that I was clearly more engaged in the world, more able to think about the future—that sort of thing.

An insight another friend shared today was that I was, to their mind, still married to Shannon.

They are both a bit right. Shannon didn't volunteer to leave me; why would I volunteer to leave her? I guess I am not happy with "until death do us part." That vow is not sufficient. I don't want to leave her behind. It's more than that—I am not going to leave her behind. I know that if she died first that she would not leave me behind. While technically her death ended our marriage, it didn't end our relationship. The relationship was so much better when she was around, but I think it can still help me be a good person.

So yes, I am still in a relationship with Shannon.

At the same time, I have to go forward. So in some ways, I have made progress. In other ways, I am in exactly the same spot I was in 6 months ago: how do I keep Shannon in my heart while I move ahead?

That's a rhetorical question. There is no answer. It's just my struggle—
that's what it has been and that's what it is going to be.

March 9

> 10:56 p.m.

There were three occasions today where I realized what a new feeling
was. I've sensed it just very recently but only today understood it.
This afternoon, I went to the Y to exercise. It tends to be, for me, a
solitary experience. Just me and *The Wire* on the iPad. About halfway
through my cardio, Shannon's friend and Pilates teacher came in. She
asked if she could keep me company while I finished and got on the
elliptical next to me. I was truly glad to see her—I've wanted to visit
the studio—even headed there a couple of times, but could never
walk in. We talked about my kids, her kids, and, of course, Shannon.

Later, I spent a good amount of time on the phone with a friend I
haven't spoken to in a long time. We had lots to catch up on—and, of
course, some of that was Shannon.

And in between, I got an e-mail from a new friend—someone who
hadn't known Shannon. She had looked at the pictures on this site and
shared with me how happy Shannon looked. I realize I haven't posted
pictures of irate Shannon—frankly, I never had the nerve to take any.
But it was still nice to hear.

The common experience across these interactions was that I finally
understood I felt something warm inside when I was recalling
Shannon. I still recalled dread, sadness, and heaviness...but there was
something nice in there, too. So that's good. Maybe that will grow.

My plan for after dinner was to drive out to Duluth to hear Shawn Mullins. It's a haul, but he's worth it. On the way, I listened to a live broadcast of Bruce Springsteen from the Apollo Theater. After a few songs, he stopped to introduce the band. After naming everyone there, he asked the audience if he had missed anyone. The audience started screaming Clarence Clemons's name.

Springsteen also lost his long, long-time keyboard player, Danny Federici, to cancer a few years ago. So he was "introducing" both of them to the crowd—he said, "As long as we're here and you're here— they're here." Perfect. I'd like to feel that way about Shannon, too. I had to pull over for a bit because I was leaking about the eyes again. So that was another nice, but hard, thing to deal with on the drive.

Finally, I made it to the concert. Neat little venue—the downtown of Duluth is much cuter than it was the last time I was there (1987?). Mullins was great, but after about 45 minutes I realized the songs were just bringing me down even further. He writes beautiful, but sad songs. Wasn't the right night for them. But that was okay. I'd had a cold beer, listened a bit to a talented guy, and headed home.

Somehow the fact that I recognized the music wasn't working and I knew to leave picked me up. Then on the way to the car I got a text from Reid—he told me he and some friends were off to hear Umphries McGee—one of the bands I love that he introduced me to. He wanted to know if he should get me a poster or a T-shirt. That picked me the rest of the way up. So thanks, Reid. Not that you're reading or anything...maybe one day.

March 12

Heard a bit from Reid—he wanted to know if he had registered with the government upon his 18th birthday—there was a hold on his registration at Colorado that required him to be registered with the government to register for class. It made me laugh—it was a HUGE deal in the house with Shannon harping on him to register. How could he not remember that? I guess that's something he gets from me. Stuff that bugged him on Monday just isn't that big a deal on Tuesday.

I had lunch with Spencer today before I left. He seems really good— he is excited about San Francisco, working hard to figure out how to do it, and chasing down all the right leads.

It's good to see him and to hear from Reid—that doesn't usually happen in a few hour span. The entire lunch with Spencer, the Everclear song "Wonderful" was playing in my head. It's a song about divorce written from the point of view of the child, who is talking to one of the parents. I can't help but think about one verse whenever I am with Spencer or Reid. It describes a child's frustration with the parent's effort to convince the child that it will all be okay one day. The child just wants things to be the way they used to be. We are all that child. Obviously there is no growing "in a different way" as the song describes the failed marriage involved here, but I do wish I could make this something the boys didn't have to deal with. I wish I could make their life like it used to be. But I suppose that is the good thing about where they are in life—their lives are supposed to be changing all the time for the next few years. They have no expectation of "the same."

As I was driving from dinner to the hotel tonight, I remembered a story from days in New Orleans. Actually, this happened before Shannon and I were dating—she wasn't involved in the story, but whenever we passed the neighborhood where it happened she made me tell it.

One summer, the Chart House crew joined a restaurant and bar softball league. Games were played after work—we started at 1 or 2 in the morning. Somehow, the city would actually turn on the lights at fields for us. Most of these were in pretty bad neighborhoods and frankly I was surprised we were allowed to be out disturbing the houses that ringed the field. People would come out on their stoops to watch us. We'd have a keg of beer, various bottles of various things, players, and cheering sections.

The part Shannon loved (re)hearing about was a safety precaution we implemented. The lights were okay in the infield, but the outfield was pretty dark. If someone hit the ball in the gap, it could roll into complete darkness. So we had an outfielder buddy system. We had three outfielders and three buddies. The buddies could not touch the ball. They held the outfielders' beer, and if a ball went in the gap, they followed the fielder to make sure nothing bad happened to them in the dark of the outfield.

I remember how none of us felt like the safe choice was to not be playing in the first place. She won't ask for that story again, and that makes me sad.

Tomorrow I will see Shannon's cousin for a po'boy, and then I will go and sit by her tree. It is spring-like enough here that there may actually be some signs of life on its branches. The park will be pretty, anyway.

I never really know what to do at the tree. I sit. I've tried talking, but that just is silly. What works best, so far, is to spend some time taking in the park. I am so unequivocally convinced that if Shannon understood where she was that she would be thrilled. It really is perfect in every way. So it is good to listen to kids play, to watch people walk, to bird-watch. Then, I spend some time just trying to feel. No better way to explain it than that. So that's what I'll do.

Backs

March 13

	8:24 p.m.

Back from New Orleans. The park was great today, as expected. Lots of sun, ducks, dogs, bikers, joggers, birds, walkers, and strollers. Sounds of all that, plus streetcars and the church bells at Loyola—all happy sounds.

It was pretty wet from Monday's rain, so I sat for a bit on Annie's bench and read. And I remembered to snag the plastic laundry bag from the hotel so I sat for a bit on the wet ground at Shannon's tree and was just still. And I remembered a white rose, so I left it. The tree has produced just one cluster of a few leaves. It's on its way, but the older gingko next to it is just about full of green. Shannon's cousin was quick to point out that Shannon was a late bloomer, so why shouldn't her tree be the same way? Makes enough sense to me.

The best part of the trip was that Reid "liked" my Facebook post about gumbo for dinner Monday. It was great because it gave me a connection to him—however superficial—when I really wanted one. And it was great because he is still using that amazing black and white picture of him and Shannon as his Facebook photo. It was good to see it—and to help me remember that he remembers her.

I plan to go back to see the tree for my birthday. It should be full of green by then.

March 17

It's a pretty St. Patrick's Day in Atlanta. I was getting groceries and across the street the fields at the YMCA were full of kids playing soccer. It's the kind of spring day where years ago we'd all come home sunburned from a long day of either soccer or baseball.

Shannon's tree here in the neighborhood has just started to put out some green. That's cool.

Shannon always referred to herself as an ethnic "mutt," but she was quick to claim Irish as the predominant strain. I suppose it would be hard to NOT do that when your name is Shannon. And she stamped Reid with it as his middle name is Patrick. So I am thinking about her for lots of reasons today. Would be nice to have a houseful for corned beef and cabbage, but I don't. Instead, I am headed to Atlantic Station to hear Better Than Ezra. I suspect it will be a zoo, and I won't hang around too long.

With my doctor's blessing, I have weaned myself off the antidepressant. It's going to take a few weeks to really leave my system, so if I seem nuts around April 15—for some reason other than taxes—someone dope slap me, and I'll get back on it. I am optimistic that it will be okay. So far, the only difference I have noticed is that I can work up a good road rage again. Didn't have that for many months!

On the stages of grief, I am still in the confused stage, but I think the fifth (final?) stage is going to be "acceptance." So anger, defeat, detachment, confusion, acceptance—ADDCA. Not a very catchy acronym.

Confusion is okay as a stage—confusion makes me think and wonder and I like thinking and wondering. I have been confused many times before and I usually am able to work my way out of it. I am sure I can do that here, too. Eventually.

While confused, I have been thinking about what's next—that's where acceptance comes in. Acceptance is going to be very complicated. I have to try to accept a lot. I have to accept Shannon is gone, I have to accept that she isn't coming back, I have to accept that there will be a nice way to go forward. I have to accept all sorts of things to move forward. And so on.

Spencer and Reid have to accept a lot in their own lives, but they will also have to try to accept the choices I make as I go forward. I had lunch with a colleague yesterday, and he shared that his mom died when he was about the boys' age. He said he managed it acceptably until about five years later—that's when it really hit him. I wish there was a way for me to protect the boys from that, should it happen. That's another thing I have to accept—I can't. And it's another thing they have to accept—that it will likely happen.

Other people in my life will also have to try to accept the choices I make. That's going to be interesting. I think about how I have acted when I have been in their shoes...I have tried very hard not to be judgmental—but I have been judgmental nonetheless. It is entirely possible that my friends are better people than me...but it wouldn't surprise me if they also struggled not to judge. I don't think friends judge a widower, but that status has to start defining me less and less as time passes. I haven't been judged for quite some time. That's another thing I have to accept—disapproval. No one has disapproved of me in a long time. In fact, I have experienced quite the opposite.

And, if I end up with someone, they are going to have to accept in me a lot of baggage and at least a handful of actual flaws.

So acceptance is going to be interesting.

March 18

| 2:35 p.m. |

Just a couple of hours until the Bruce Springsteen concert. To get in the proper frame of mind, I read the interview he gave Jon Stewart for the March 14 issue of *Rolling Stone*. There were a couple of things in it that resonated. I am not sure any of the thoughts are original, but sometimes his words strike me as particularly well-chosen. And it made me feel good to read them—just another time when it feels less lonely knowing that someone truly gets it. It isn't just that they hurt for you—it's more than that.

Stewart asked him how he was dealing with the loss of his friend of 40 years. Springsteen said, "Losing Clarence was like losing the rain. You're losing something that has been so elemental in your life for such a long time. It was like losing some huge part of your own psychic construction—suddenly it's just gone, everything feels less."[9]

Springsteen was talking about the making of his new album, too. He had called Clarence and asked him to come to record the saxophone parts. Clarence said his hand was bothering him and would it be okay if he went home to Florida to have it checked out first. Springsteen said it was the first time Clarence had ever not been up for playing. Clarence went home to Florida, had a stroke, and never had another conversation with Springsteen.

When Springsteen went back home after the funeral, the record's producer told him how sorry he was about Clarence, and he told Springsteen he had found some live tracks where Clarence had played

---

[9] "Jon Stewart Interviews Bruce Springsteen," by Jon Stewart, *Rolling Stone,* March 29, 2012, http://www.rollingstone.com/music/pictures/jon-stewart-interviews-bruce-springsteen-20120314.

the necessary parts. He found a way to add them to the record. Springsteen said he cried when he heard it.

That is so easy for me to understand. When I lost Shannon there was so much unfinished business. And I am so, so glad whenever there is something that can be salvaged. In cleaning up my office the other day I found some piles of stuff that were hers. Things that can be salvaged. I am looking forward to going through them—but I am also not in a hurry to do it.

He's excited about the tour because he wants to celebrate Clarence and he wants to miss Clarence. It's like he has a place to go when he wants to feel that. He's got a stage where he can go to deal with Clarence's stuff; I've got a room in my head for Shannon's stuff.

If you have heard Springsteen live—or a live recording—you have no doubt heard the story of how Clemons came to be part of the band. It's told with great flourish at every show. In the *Rolling Stone* interview, Springsteen said, "Our relationship was just this immediate chemical connection that happened that first night in Asbury, as he was walking toward the stage: 'Here comes my guy.'" It took them a while to make it all work out, but it did. It's absolutely parallel to how I remember that first time I really "saw" Shannon.

I had someone try to convince me that I was romanticizing things. To their mind, it couldn't really have been like that. Their view was that if I could be more honest about my memories those memories wouldn't be so hard to get over.

If I try, I can see a logic in that—if what you had wasn't that great, it shouldn't be so bad to lose it. But then I think about what Springsteen said about wanting to celebrate what he had with Clarence. If you choose a strategy of minimizing the relationship, then there isn't anything to celebrate.

The greater flaw, I think, is the thought that what mattered now was somehow the way it "really" was. I don't have what it really was and won't again. I have a memory of how it was. In fact, all I have is a memory of how it was. I don't want someone trying to take that from me. That's what it feels like when someone tries to help by getting me to minimize Shannon, me, our relationship, or anything else. I don't think anyone is trying to convince Springsteen that Clarence was "just a saxophone player."

March 19

9:41 p.m.

The concert was great. It's tremendous that a guy can still be at the top of his game after more than 40 years. Still making great new music, still incredible energy, still really cares about people. He introduced the band the same way he had at the Apollo concert. I was glad I had heard it so that I knew what was coming. Still, I cried a bit when he talked about his lost friends. It was plenty dark, so that was okay.

A week or so ago, I told my doctor about the dream where Shannon was telling me good-bye. He asked me what I thought it meant. I told him that I thought it was my subconscious mind trying to tell me that it was okay to tell her good-bye back. He asked why I didn't think it was actually Shannon telling me good-bye—giving me encouragement to keep moving forward. I took it for a rhetorical question.

He was undaunted and went on to tell me about the concept of (and this might be a bit wrong) *ohana aumakua*—something from Polynesian culture. It's a belief (this might be a bit wrong, too—still investigating) that the departed are still a part of our experience—protecting the family and all that. That message shouldn't necessarily be a surprise; that they should be taken as just that—messages from loved ones who are still "around."

So how do I feel about that? On the one hand, if I believed it there would be some comfort to feel like Shannon's spirit was around. On the other hand, I really don't want to hear her tell me good-bye.

Spring

March 24

> 3:42 p.m.

Beautiful day in Atlanta today. Other than the pollen. Reid is supposedly on a plane to come home for spring break. In spite of my best efforts, I have no idea at all if he is on the plane. He is becoming more and more communication-impaired. It's as if the more choices he has to stay in touch, the less he is able to be in touch. I'll head to the airport just for kicks—maybe he will be there, maybe he won't. Maybe he'll be in pajamas again.

What I really think about is how sorry I am that Shannon isn't here to be so excited to see him. She'd have spent time in his room getting it right. I didn't—it looks fine to me. She'd be thinking about all sorts of things he might need or want to do—doctors, barbers, dentists, fortune tellers, whatever, would all be on hold. I didn't. She'd be so happy for a chance to take care of him one more time. He'd resist, he'd fuss, he'd cooperate a little. It was the dance they did.

Shannon's tree in the neighborhood is starting to leaf out nicely. It's a very pretty scene right now with all the wisteria in bloom behind it.

Spencer had a good couple of days in Boulder with Reid. He met some of the kids in the fraternity. He allowed that most of them seemed okay; the others really didn't. But Spencer is pretty hard to please. He also met most of Reid's roommates for next year. That group he approved of without exception. He told me he was trying hard to make Reid cut class to hang out and that he wouldn't. He assured me Reid appeared to be taking school pretty seriously. He told me some stories about Reid's dorm that make me happy he'll be in an apartment next year. It's cool when one kid can fly across the country to harass the other kid—and that they both enjoyed each other. That was the best part of a week I am happy to turn the page on.

March 27

8:56 p.m.

A big disappointment for me every day is the inability to spoil Shannon over the half of her life she didn't get. It's strange to feel guilty for enjoying what sometimes feel like the spoils of someone else's work. I wouldn't have what I have if she hadn't done what she did. I get to enjoy it. She doesn't. I truly hate that.

Anyway, one tiny thing I could do for her was to get help with cleaning the house. Sometimes, her cleaning supplies got confused with the cleaning crew's supplies. No one was trying to pinch her Lysol—things just get mixed up sometimes. I guess it didn't really matter to her—except when she needed something, and it was gone. So she started putting her initials, SWB, on the tops of the cans so it was easy to tell what stayed in the house and what stayed with the team.

Today, I grocery shopped, and I needed to get Lysol. I swear I took it out of the grocery bag, found the marker, and reflexively put "SWB" on the top. That's just what it is supposed to say—the minute I finished and understood what happened, I was a bit freaked out. That's the sort of day it was.

I went to the psychiatrist. That usually gives me plenty to think about. He does a good job of knowing how much and when to support me and how loudly and when to call bullshit on me. I appreciate that. Everyone needs someone to do each of those things.

We were talking about how things were going. Another useful to me analogy came up from our discussion. We agreed that for the first four or five months, I was in a place that I couldn't even bring myself to (figuratively) watch TV. That is, I really had no way or desire or ability to engage with the outside world—other than for work. Over the last month or two, I have had that desire, but what I am doing is like watching a show with the color turned down so the picture is black and white. It's rudimentary what I can do—it's without much feeling or emotion—it's colorless.

He says that one day, I will walk over to the set and turn the color back up. That will happen when I allow myself to feel something other than bad. Allowing that means allowing for more hurt, among other things—it's risky. I think I can't be hurt again. He thinks I can't be hurt again as long as I watch TV in black and white—that's safe. And he says he couldn't blame me if I wanted to do that—but he thinks it would be sad, and he thinks I won't want to do it. He thinks one day I will want to live life in color again and that I will be willing to risk being hurt again. He says I shouldn't feel in a rush, but I should know that day will come.

I get it. But I don't know about turning up the color. I don't know if I have to decide to do it—that's what he thinks. He thinks it's a choice, and that it's fine that I am not ready to make it yet. I don't think it's a choice. I agree it might happen, but I think it will just take forever.

That example—of steps in coming back to the world—just fit for me. I can remember playing with the "color" and "tint" dials on our old TVs to do just that—to bring the color in. One day.

He told me again—when he told me before I thought it was hyperbole, but now I think he is right—that I have to remember I have essentially had a serious brain injury. My head is messed up, and it is going to take a very long time to overcome it. Nothing about the rest of my life is going to be the way I thought it would. The past offers nothing but sadness. Sometimes it's sweet sadness, but still. So all I have is the present. Each day has the potential to be a good day. That's as far ahead as I want to think.

11:04 p.m.

One of my Facebook friends posted this yesterday—some form of it has been floating around for a while—and of course there's a dad version, too:

At 3 years, "Mommy, I love you."
At 10, "Mom, whatever."
At 16, "My mom is so annoying."
At 18, "I wanna leave this house."
At 25, "Mom, you were right."
At 30, "I wanna go to Mom's house."
At 50, "I don't wanna lose my mom."
At 70, "I would give up EVERYTHING for my mom to be here with me."

I am sure that most of us read something like this and laugh and get it. If it's true—and we all know it is a little—it means Shannon died at a really inopportune time. In between "I wanna leave this house" and "Mom, you were right." That makes me angry. And it makes me feel sorry for the boys. Those things, and the fact that no matter what I do, Pandora won't stop playing John Mayer, are pissing me off.

Since I am down, there is one more thought that has been eating at me for a couple of months now. So far, I have made the choice to not write it down, but it won't go away. So I am going to write it down. If I were you, this would be a good time to stop reading and to check in on me later.

A couple of months ago—I don't even remember now when or with whom—I was an observer in a conversation about someone who had to deal with a very sick pet. They had to put the pet "down" because it wasn't going to get better. I just can't hear that—or type it—or think it—and not become very upset. That's what I had to do for Shannon. We say we are going to just withhold life-sustaining treatment and then treat for pain, but we know that isn't really what is going on. We are putting our loved one down. That sucks so, so bad. I can't even imagine anything in the neighborhood of how badly that hurts.

I am changing my advance directive (again) because I don't want my friends or my sons to have to do that for me—even if it's what I want, it's still too much to ask. I didn't know it then—neither did Shannon—we had no way to know; but I know it now. That I had to do it for Shannon kills me a little bit every day, even though I know it was her wish. I am going to let the doctors make the decision for me. If it is written the right way, they will do the right thing. Maybe now that I wrote this here, it will stop haunting me.

Told you to stop reading. At least Michael Franti is now on the radio. So there is hope for tonight. Like him, I'm just waiting for this storm to pass.

From: PM
Date: Fri, 30 Mar 2012 08:48:47-0500
To: Nathan Bennett
Subject: RE: post

Your experience with Shannon, my experience with my mom, of taking someone off life support, putting them down...it haunts. Some days it torments. I cannot tell you the thousand times I've asked myself whether we paid close enough attention, should we have caught it earlier, would even 48 hours sooner have saved her life, was I too willing to let her go because I loved my dad best and she had been both a tormenter and a supporter to me (how's that for brutal truth). One thing I will say is that changing your advance directive probably will only change what Spencer and Reid have to go through, not fix it, if the time ever comes. My mom didn't have one at all, so all I had to rely on was her cantankerous, attention-seeking proclamations throughout her life about what she did and didn't want. In the end I know I did the right thing because by the time I got there, she was too far gone to save. I get to live with, "Should I have gotten there sooner?"

These horrific events bring home how media, TV, movies, etc. gloss over this crap and make it all look so noble. Sorry to sound angry. It came home for me about seven years ago when the young daughter of a friend of ours was in a terrible wreck right outside our neighborhood on Perkins—she was a new driver and made a mistake, ended up with a snapped neck, on life support, and eventually died. There was the whole organ donation thing. I had NO IDEA how it was done. Had always been such an advocate of it but had never thought through the actual mechanics of it. Still don't know if I know exactly what happens or if it happens the same way every time, but I did come to understand the obvious. Talking later to a friend whose niece had died and whose brother had to make that call, she said, "Well, what did you THINK was happening? It's not like in the movies."

Ain't that the truth. This shit's not like it is in the movies.

March 31

> 12:31 p.m.

I came out to the front porch after some kitchen experiments—to sit and read the paper before going in to clean up the rather impressive mess. That became more involved than I expected. The paper had a story about what most would call a "murder-suicide." I am not sure what I want to call it. An 81-year-old man apparently killed his Alzheimer's victim wife of over 60 years and then himself.

You can read a bit about the story at: http://nyti.ms/H2TVqG, but the real story is in the piece the man wrote a few months ago for the paper.[10] I can identify with a lot in what he wrote about the falling in love part. It's a sweet story, but it moves me a bit more because I can see pieces of Shannon and me in it.

He wrote:

> *When I was a sophomore I went on a double date, to a Cedar Crest College sophomore prom, with a girl whom I had never seen before, and who was, shall we say, not to my liking. At our table was a simply marvelous young lady: ravishingly beautiful, bright, well-groomed, well-spoken, mannerly, disciplined and circumspect. Her name was Adrienne Celeste Angeletti.*

> *What a wonder. She was, unfortunately, on the arm of the Yalie who had come to Cedar Crest College for the dance as her date. That Adrienne was the girl that I wanted, the girl that I needed to bring into my life, and the girl that I had to marry became very clear to me quite soon. So I began an*

---

[10] "The Life Report: Charles Darwin Snelling," Charles Darwin Snelling, *The New York Times: The Opinion Pages*, December 7, 2011, http://brooks.blogs.nytimes.com/2011/12/07/the-life-report-charles-darwin-snelling/?src=tp.

energetic pursuit of this sweet young lady. She was a psych major and she used to say that I was her case study! She was diligent and very suspicious of my undisciplined ways. I pursued her with all the vigor at my command. First I had to get rid of the Yalie, and I did. Adrienne was studious, so I had to pretend to study. She used to go with a blanket and her books into Trexler Park to study. I would bring my blanket, books and notebooks to pester her.—"You're not studying," she would say, to which I would retort: "I'm studying you." Not a good answer, according to her. Usually we would make a treaty. Adrienne would study that afternoon if I would go away and leave her alone and be profligate, and then we would meet for dinner. Perfect!

And later he added this, which I think, is perfect:

The love affair was only beginning. Adrienne was teaching me something about which I never had even a clue. She was teaching me about unconditional love! I could hardly imagine such a thing. The lady loved me, good or bad. She did not measure her love for me by performance. She discouraged me from being bad, and encouraged me to be good, but she loved me just as much, good or bad. Who could imagine such a thing?

I can.

April 1

> 7:22 p.m.

I sold Shannon's car today. It never really felt like her car though. She took my car over so I could get the Jeep. I cleaned it out for the new owners and found five things of floss tucked in various compartments.

326

She had some in the front—and some in back because that's where she liked to ride when one of the boys was with us. That's an indicator of sorts that it was at least the car she used. I also found the paperwork for the body shop repair after her July accident. That was really hard for her. She felt terrible ruining someone else's day—the woman she hit. She was scared that she needed to stop driving, and she didn't know how we would manage if she couldn't drive. And she was embarrassed to have had the accident in the first place. I know—because we talked about it—that she saw it as a window into a future that involved confronting new limitations all the time. Frightening for her. I tried to convince her we were up for the challenge, and I know she wanted to believe me.

I was excited to get an invitation to a wedding for the daughter of an old New Orleans friend. I was relieved that the invitation was addressed just to me. It was from one of Shannon's friends that I was terrified had somehow not been in the loop about what happened. Clearly she was included. I can't go—but I am thrilled for their family.

I spent some time in the yard today. Everything is suddenly blooming and sprouting and growing. It was the sort of morning where Shannon would have spent hours slowly walking the yard, crouching down every few steps to check on a plant, to figure out what sort of critter was crawling around, to pull a weed. When she came in her cheeks would be bright red, and she would be full of stories about what she saw. She loved spring—I think everything in the plant world showing energy helped her feel like she had some energy.

Some friends stopped by Audubon Park the other night and sent me this picture of Shannon's tree. It has many, many more leaves than when I was there at the beginning of the month.

It's become clear over the last couple of days that the antidepressant is gone. So far, it's making me want to take on some things that I was happy to leave alone. I am not sure if taking things on will end up productive or destructive.

April 5

10:09 a.m.

Lots of thoughts have piled up over the past few days. Each time I sit down to write, I get frustrated about not knowing where to start, so I don't start. And more thoughts pile up. This time, I will get at least some stuff down.

I still haven't found the title for Shannon's car. It's my fault. I put it someplace special. In looking for it, I have come across more treasures. Shannon has to have the record for "journals begun." I found another from her high school days. She was given nice journals each Christmas, at some point in the next few weeks decided to give it a try, wrote a bit, and then got distracted and never went back to it. This one is pretty short—but it also had a bunch of pages tucked in from other times.

This particular page wasn't originally dated, but Shannon at some later point wrote "1983" on it. She and I would have been in some pre-dating stage, I suppose. It's what she was thinking when she was deciding what to do with me, I guess. She wrote:

> *...Nate—I have this compulsive tendency to jump right in the middle of a relationship...I need to control my urges in that situation—I will only hurt him and myself. Sometimes I wonder if I'm capable of ever honestly caring about someone and not have some bizarre extenuating circumstance to cause problems or use as an excuse—I think I'm basically scared. I hope that Nate is as sensitive as he seems. People are sure undependable sometimes. It hurts the most when they're the people you care about and they just walk on you.*

I wonder if that "Nate" is the first time she ever wrote my name. Might have been. From that pretty tentative start, we did pretty well. The last time she wrote my name was on a "notify in case of emergency" form. That's a thought I wish I could unthink.

So you go to find a car title and instead you fall down the rabbit hole.

The second thought to get out is that whoever is doing your laundry is not being adequately thanked by you. One of my fictional heroes is a character named Jack Reacher. He buys clothes, wears them a few days—pressing them as needed at night between his mattress and box spring—and then throws them away when they get covered in blood or whatever else life throws at him. Usually, he walks in to a store in one set of clothes and just walks out in the other. It's a tempting model. Why did Shannon never complain about doing laundry?

When Shannon was in the hospital, the MBA students at Tech were a tremendous support. In a heartbeat, they raised $5,000 for meals for me and the "team" at the hospital. I cry every time I remember. Anyway, Shannon didn't make it as long as their generosity would have allowed; a lot of money was left over. We talked about what to do with the money. The student leaders wanted it to go to good use; they didn't want to stray too far from the premise that motivated the donors. Good kids. The final decision was to make a generous gift to the mitochondrial disease foundation in Shannon's name and then to use the rest—still a quite generous amount—to endow a fund that would be used to provide assistance to any member of the Tech MBA community that had an emergency situation—it's simply called "The Community Fund." They wanted to make sure that was okay with me—since the money had been raised for Shannon.

One of the other topics I haven't been able to move out of my mind since going off the medicine concerns organ donation. It was another learning experience that is changing how I look at my plans—it wasn't like it looks on TV. So while what follows may not be news to some of you, I'd hate for someone to be surprised—and then upset—like I was. Writing about the "putting down" topic helped, so maybe this will help, too.

Shannon and I are/were both organ donors. Neither one of us had a problem with the concept. I still don't have a problem with the concept, but now that I understand how it works, it's become more complicated for me. No easy way to write about it, but here goes.

Near the end, a person from the pastoral care office at the hospital came to Shannon's room. She noted that Shannon was an organ donor and wanted to talk to me about when they could come take her for "harvesting."

What we didn't understand (because they don't tell you) when we became donors at the drivers' license office is that to use your organs, they have to take them from you while you are alive. I thought—and I think Shannon did, too—clearly naively—that you were allowed to die "naturally" and that then you were rushed off before anything "spoiled."

What this meant was that Shannon wouldn't die in what I would consider a peaceful way. She would die from a parts shortage. I would have to send her away breathing, and then I wouldn't see her again until the service. I didn't want her to die that way. Not that there is a good way.

If it makes me a bad person, I'll take the rap—but I couldn't go along with that. My shock and horror were evident; a nurse in the room mentioned to the person that as a victim of mitochondrial disease, Shannon's suitability as a donor needed to be examined. After all, it wouldn't be fair to make someone who had waited a long time for an organ to get one that was compromised. I was relieved to find out from the doctor later that day that indeed Shannon should not be an organ donor.

Even though I was spared the choice of going against Shannon's wishes or doing something unthinkable, I have felt very guilty about the whole thing. She would have loved being able to help someone— no question. She would have felt terrible "sticking someone" with a defective part—she would have exclaimed that it was bad enough her life involved defective parts—why should someone else's. And knowing Shannon, she would truly feel guilty that she saved $5 every time she renewed her driver's license for making a promise she couldn't keep.

I would like to still be an organ donor. I still like the concept. I am not sure I like the reality of it, though. Then again, I suppose I am doing a good job of compromising most of my organs. I guess they could be used to keep someone alive that society wanted to punish a bit longer.

It's a new day and age...I got an e-mail "from" my new Jeep letting me know it had been built and was on its way to me. And I got this video with the progress on Shannon's memory box. The wood is mahogany—it's gorgeous. And as you can see, it even has a lid. Just needs some finish and a bit more hardware:
http://www.youtube.com/watch?v=EALKL5Fs7kA.

7:14 p.m.

The thing currently stuck in my head concerns the role of widower. How long does it last? I know it lasts forever—I guess the better question is how long should it be your major defining characteristic? Obviously in the days, weeks, and months after you lose your spouse,

331

it is your major characteristic. People rightly relate to you based on that. And I know that I wanted that to be the case. I hurt so badly, I couldn't function very well—and I needed people to understand why I was the sort of person I was. It was so unbelievably hard to try to interact with people who didn't know I was going through.

On Saturday, it will be seven months since I became a widower. Most of the people I deal with on a daily basis know my situation—even the checkout people at the grocery, the tellers at the bank, most everyone. I live in a small town inside a big city. For all of these people, my status as a widower is no longer central. Our conversations are about the boys, about life, about pollen—not about death and loneliness. That's good.

However, I still come across people—maybe once a week—who haven't had a chance to tell me they are sorry that I lost Shannon. Sometimes, they have told me in a card or e-mail, but they haven't had a chance to tell me in person. They want to start our relationship—or renew our relationship—where I was seven months ago. That really hurts. I don't want to go back there. Lots of people have done lots of work to get me past that.

So that's the problem—they need to say what they need to say. It will help them, and they think it will help me. I get that. But I'd rather stipulate it and talk about the Red Sox chances in 2012 (they're not good). There has to be a point in time where losing Shannon isn't what defines me. Even as I type that I realize it's wrong. Losing her is always going to define me to a great degree. I need it to not be how other people define me. That's better. How do I respect their need without it just being a sting for me?

April 8

One day last fall, I was walking the neighborhood and a song came on that cracked me up—and cheered me up. It's by a group called Nappy Roots—most of their songs are way past my taste, but this one called "We're Gonna Have a Good Day" was on this morning again—it still cheers me up. The chorus is sung by a group of school children—a contrast against the rap style of the Nappy Roots.

That song was playing while I was cruising Facebook—so many pictures of little kids discovering what the Easter Bunny left for them. Really cute, and of course it brought up all sorts of memories. It was a good way to start a good day. Shannon did Easter well from the standpoint of the Easter Bunny. I remember one year when Shannon's folks had their little house in New Orleans that we went there for the weekend. Spencer was probably about to turn two. He loved the game of searching the house and finding all the plastic eggs Shannon had carefully stuffed with Cheerios.

The whole Easter Bunny thing changes as kids grow up. Shannon loved to protest that she was "tired" of being the Easter Bunny—yet last year she made a basket for Spencer, a basket for Spencer's roommate, and a basket for Andre the dog and delivered them to Spencer's house. She would have done that this year, plus she would have schemed to get something to Reid in his dorm. I started to buy some stuff at the store last week to give the boys and then decided I didn't want to. Some things we'll just do without as we are doing without Shannon. It's part of how we can miss her.

It seems wrong and sad to me if the world doesn't change because someone is gone.

Last week I had a chance to "Shannon" someone. It had been too long, and it felt really good. There is a custodian at work who, among other things, empties my trashcan. Most days that I am there, I see him. He passes by pretty predictably around 4:30. He is a friendly guy; we usually exchange some small talk and off he goes. Most days, I haven't even made any trash. All my work trash is in electronic form.

One day, he asked me, "What do you know about Garrett Popcorn?" I said I didn't know much—I had ordered a box for a colleague who loves it to thank her for helping me with a program. He said he had been emptying the trash, and the box caught his eye—he is from Chicago, loves the popcorn, and hadn't had any in many years. He saw my name on the address label and was just curious how I knew about it.

So off he went to the next office. I went online and ordered a tin of it for him. It came in Monday or so. The first time I was in and saw him was Wednesday. He came to my office to see if I had made any real trash. I hadn't, but I gave him the tin. He was dumbstruck. His voice was literally cracking, and he had trouble getting words out to say thank you. It's really easy to do something nice to help someone else have a good day. I miss having Shannon as my target.

It turns out there was one more difficult thought in my head. I have struggled a lot over the past couple of months with what to do about the orthopedist who operated on Shannon. I think he is a really good guy and a really good doctor. He was careful—he tried so many non-surgical treatments first. He consulted with neurologists, he wanted nerve studies done—he truly made every effort to make sure surgery was not a rushed option. He was so excited that the surgery had gone well. He had talked to Shannon in the recovery room, and she was glad to hear she had a good result. He came to me with pictures and explained the whole thing, how well it had gone, how much better Shannon was going to be. I don't think people who do shoulders, elbows, hips, and knees have many patients die. He was clearly struck. He came by every day. He gave me his cell number, and we texted several times each day. He reached out to experts to get additional information. He tried to help "referee" the medical team at the hospital.

Anyway, I feel badly because I want to thank him and make sure he knows I don't hold any sort of grudge or anything. But I can't bring myself to go there or to call or to even text. I know that in the beginning, some people in his office were reading the blog. I have no way to know if they still are. I am going to hope so, and hope that they can pass this thought on to him. I keep thinking I'll get strong enough to do it myself somehow—but I don't think I will.

April 12

8:59 p.m.

I've been off antidepressants for long enough time for me to really be sure I am off them. On the good side, it is causing me to take on thoughts, feelings, and concerns that I think are reasonable and appropriate and necessary to address in order to heal. I can tell I am angrier. Not postal angry.

Somewhere in between the good and bad is that just as I feel angry more vividly, I also feel good more vividly. When I get involved in something, I can tell that I am experiencing more of it. But when I am alone or tired, thoughts of Shannon and her fate and our fates rush in to fill empty space. Then it feels a bit bleak.

And on the bad is this example from last night. It's a little involved—and really began on Tuesday. Tuesday night, Spencer and I went to see the Red Hot Chili Peppers in concert. It was a great night—he regaled me with great stories about his California plans on the drive over; the band was great. The entire time I had in my head that this was the last time I would ever really DO something with just Spencer.

And I thought about all the places he, Shannon, and I went—and all the experiences we had together. That's over now—for some normal and some terrible reasons. The normal reasons I try to accept, and the terrible ones—well, they're just terrible.

Anyway, while I was working through those happy thoughts, the band started playing a song called "Under the Bridge." The singer never wants to feel like they did on some fateful day and is pleading to be taken to the place they love.

Those were hard lyrics to listen to. The whole thing would have been an easier setting if I was still medicated. Because I wasn't, it was unavoidable that I spent some time thinking about "that day" and wondering if there even was anywhere a place I love anymore. I am not sure if there is.

Then on Wednesday, I had given in to a nap while doing some reading for work. I was listening to the stereo and sort of half sleeping—drifting in and out. While I was asleep, the Van Morrison song "Tupelo Honey" came on. It's a beautiful song, and in my semi-dream state, I felt like nothing bad had happened—that things were as they were supposed to be. It was a magical sort of trance. Then something snapped me out of it, and I was "back on that day." It was a terrible way to wake up—it was like I woke up every day just after Shannon died. All the loss and hurt and worry just hit me at once—7 months of upset focused on one breath. That was brutal. That would have been a good time to have been on drugs.

April 16

I met with a student from one of my classes today—he's having a problem with a team dynamic, and we were talking about it. The student is a nice kid. He's lost a lot of weight and is to be congratulated for that. He mentioned to me that he lost 95 pounds this year. I thought to myself, that's about what Shannon weighed, so I did, too. Weird how things like that come up.

Tomorrow the last "official" purge of Shannon's clothes will take place. I saved just a couple of things. I saved a skirt that Spencer and I sought out for her in Paris. While we were there, Spencer had noticed Shannon admiring one like it. He just had to get her one. The day before we had to come home, he and I went on a lengthy expedition to find one. Shannon loved it a lot.

In the spirit of progress, I also finished going through her desk. I found a lot of information on her medical history—she really had those records organized. I have a lot to look through, but all the non-essential stuff is taken care of and ready for giveaway. Mostly what amazes me is that as early as 1985 she was struggling with swallowing, with incontinence, and of course her vision. She was entitled to complain so much more than she ever did. She lived with those miseries a long time.

The summer concert season is gearing up. It will be different this year. I broke out an Eagles CD—they are playing in a couple of weeks. A few years ago when they were here they also played outdoors; we had to leave early because it was so cold. We hated to—it was a great show. Anyway, beautifully depressing lyrics are something Don Henley has a knack for—listen to the song "New York Minute" and you will have a sense of where I am today.

April 19

Well, that's enough of that. I am going back on Lexapro. The past seven days have held some truly positive, special things, and I just don't find myself caring enough about them. I don't want to talk to anyone. I don't particularly want to go out, and I don't particularly want to stay in. Bad dream about Shannon last night—some deranged couple in a hotel was holding her away from me. Not a mystery as to my diagnosis.

While I am where I am, I might a well share some observations from the bottom of this well.

Many months ago, a friend who had lost her husband wrote me and told me how she would go and lose herself in his closet. The sights and smells of his things connected her to him. I bet it felt awful and necessary at the same time. For the most part, I stayed out of Shannon's closet—I have other ways to get that same awful and necessary feeling. But now that her closet is finally empty, I do go in there every day. I am amazed with how empty and sterile it is. She is really gone and not coming back.

I think the half-life of volunteer helpers is about two months. In the weeks after a tragedy, 100% of the people you know will drop everything to help you. After two months, only 50% can make it a priority. I am coming up on eight months, and if I am doing the math right, it means only about 6% are ready to help. I absolutely do NOT say this as a criticism—people aren't here to be on call for me, AND I have received more kindness than I will ever be able to put back in the world. I say it because I think people who are in my position need to be aware that if their healing is happening more slowly than this half-life phenomenon, they need to be ready with some other way to get the help they need. And it means that for me I will put a date about 8 months out whenever someone I know has a similar tragedy. It will be good for them if I can be there then.

A few weeks ago when it was seven months since Shannon's collapse, it was six months since my friend and colleague had his collapse. I visited his CaringBridge site—it looks like he is recovering nicely and will be able to come back to work at Tech in August. I am so, so glad for him and for his wife. They are just sweethearts. Shannon and I used to get a kick out of running into them at one of the neighborhood restaurants—Shannon liked to send them each a shot of Irish whiskey on our tab. I suspect I'll get to run into them there one night soon. That's going to be nice.

I haven't been me since about 2 p.m. on September 7, 2011. That's a long time. Not that being me was ever a picnic, but at least I was used to it. I don't want to get used to whatever I am now, and I am worried that I don't have a choice.

April 26

> **10:56 p.m.**

Today I went to the doctor. There wasn't really that much to talk about—familiar ground all around. So I learned that it is better to go in with a full agenda—otherwise, he asks hard questions. Today he asked: "What do you miss about Shannon?" I can say that no one else has had the nerve to ask me that.

I thought about it; I started leaking a bit around the eyes. Every little thing that came to mind sounded so incredibly trite that it wasn't even worth saying. The first thing that comes to my mind is supposed to be something consequential. After a few minutes, I just said all I could say—"I miss her." And that's true—I miss the whole thing.

He let me get by with that answer. I thought about it some more. Here are just some of the things I miss.

I miss the way her hand fit in mine.

I miss the way we fit when she climbed up a step and hugged me.

I miss the way her whole face lit up when she was happy.

I miss the truly unique way in which she saw the world.

I miss how when I was cold her hand felt warm and when I was warm her hand felt cool on my skin.

I miss how truly easy it was to be me around her. I was so accepted, and that's an amazing gift.

That's a start. But at the same time, that's enough.

Tonight I was invited to a gathering of some alumni from maybe three or four years ago. I love these opportunities even though currently they are a bit hard. None of these people had seen me since Shannon died, so I knew how the conversation was going to go. Parenthetically—I think this is safe to say—if you are seeing someone for the first time, and they have had a loss many months ago, don't say anything. They know you know and that you are sorry. Just give them a really big hug or whatever and tell them you are glad to see them. Don't be part of a processional that makes them recount time after time that "Yes, it's been a hard year...blah blah." They will know you are in their corner, and that's what matters.

Anyway, I got there early—as is my usual. They straggled in a bit late—as is fine. So I got to spend about 40 minutes at the Tilted Kilt by myself. It's sort of a Scottish Hooters—exactly my kind of place. I was well looked after by a very kind and tattooed young lady. When the invitation came, I did almost ask that we meet somewhere else, not because of any prudishness on my part, but because this is the same place a friend and I took Reid for "guy time" as Shannon was passing on. I still have the texts on my phone from another friend letting me know it was time to hurry back to the ICU—that Shannon was crashing. I thought about those text messages, but I didn't look at them. I know they are there.

Anyway, Shannon died as I was leaving this bar to try to take care of Reid but also get back to her. So there I was again.

April 29

1:18 p.m.

On my way home from a work meeting yesterday, I was stopped at the toll on GA 400, waiting for my turn to pay .50. Just like everywhere else, I have a knack for picking the wrong line. If you see me at the grocery store checkout line, pick the one I am not in.

The "Cashier" line was pretty short, so even though I had exact change I picked it. Things were looking good until the car in front of me pulled up. The body language was clear; she didn't have .50. So she put her car in park, got out, and walked back to my car where she very apologetically explained her situation and asked if I would give her .50. I Shannoned her with the money; she was embarrassed and relieved. I had to give her a $20 bill—I had two quarters for me, but no other change. Why I didn't give her the two quarters and hang on to the twenty myself, I can't say. She said, "Should I just tell the attendant to give you the change?" I said that sounded like a good idea. Off she went.

As I pulled up to drop my .50 in the bucket, the attendant had my change ready—she handed it to me and said, "That's the girl you should marry, if you're single!" And then she said, "Hurry up—go after her!" She sounded so earnest—sort of like a fortune-teller who really believed in her powers.

I am still not sure what to make of that. Maybe I just missed "Ms. Right."

April 30

> 7:28 p.m.

Sitting on the back patio listening to Big Head Todd and thinking about Shannon. Their song "Bittersweet" was one of our favorites—sad song about a relationship falling apart. The irises across the yard are in close to full bloom. They are special because we've moved them house to house all the way from Baton Rouge—they actually started in her dad's yard in Houston. On the side of the patio is a plant—I forget what it is called—but Shannon was trying to train it to climb up to the porch above. She'd be excited that this spring it finally made it. It smells great and makes sitting out here all the more pleasant.

Today, some friends were installing the landscaping around the outdoor fireplace. It turned out great. It was a hot day—I asked them if they wanted some water and they said no, they were okay. So I brought them water anyway. Big glasses with ice and all. I handed them the water, and one said, "Shannon used to pack us a cooler!" I had to laugh. I love it when she is remembered that way—because that is who she was. And I don't ever plan or even want to be as good at it as she was. I actually enjoyed taking crap for not quite going the full distance. It helps me remember and feel one of the things that was special about her.

May 2

Last summer when I turned 50 I gave in to Shannon's insistence and went for a physical. I know it is wrongheaded, but my view has been that it's just like with a car—you take it in for some minor service, and they find 5 other things wrong. So if nothing is broken, stay away. I went and one of the prizes for going was to be told to get a colonoscopy. I was going to do that last fall but for obvious reasons didn't.

I set up an appointment a few weeks ago for the initial consult with the doctor my primary care physician recommended. Yesterday was that day. On the way, a truck threw a rock up and broke the windshield of the new car—not even 600 miles on it yet. Then, the doctor turned out to be in the same building where I had to go rescue Shannon after her wreck. Of course, all recommended cancer doctors seem to be connected to St. Joseph's, where Shannon died—so that's where they all are. I was not in good spirits by the time I got in for the consult.

So the doctor is explaining the prep and the procedure to me. After a bit, I asked him what the harm was in delaying this test. I explained why. He was very kind about it. He acknowledged that the use of age 50 to get a test is pretty arbitrary and that if I wanted to wait until fall he understood. He did say—thanks, malpractice—that I should know that if I happened to have a polyp that was about to go all crazy on me, there was a risk in waiting. I set up a test for the fall. In the meantime, I am going to see if I can find a good practice located somewhere else. I just get chills going to St. Joseph's.

Strange thought—I never adjust the showerhead settings because the knob is a little hard to operate, and it was set the way Shannon liked it. After eight months, it occurred to me that I could change it. The shower feels much better now, but it isn't much of a trade.

I have spent a lot of time in the house over the last few days—grading. I was thinking that it is starting to feel to me like it must have to Shannon. I can see how, without driving, the thought of being here could get hard. We are fortunate to have a very nice house—it isn't like "hard time" to be here. But being alone here is hard.

I understood that when the kids left it would be lonely here—but I also thought it would be liberating. The problem for Shannon was that because of her physical state—and the role it played on her mental state—she didn't feel she could take advantage. Her world wasn't going to get bigger, it was going to get smaller. That's why she loved so much to go out—and the more people to watch, the better. It was tiring for me sometimes, but really important for her. I am glad I was smart enough to go along with her on that. If I had said at night, "I'm tired, I just want to watch TV," I would feel so much worse now.

May 6

6:58 p.m.

If things were as they should be, Shannon and I would likely be in New Orleans at Jazz Fest right now. It's 6 p.m. there; the Neville Brothers just started. That's the stage where we'd be camped—after hearing Galactic and Foo Fighters. We'd be sunburned, hot, dusty, full, and excited from a day with friends. We'd cut out a bit early on the Neville Brothers to get a nap and get cleaned up. Later tonight, we'd be at One Eyed Jacks in the French Quarter for Eric Lindell—a "last Sunday of Jazz Fest" tradition of which we only were able to observe together for two years.

But things are not as they should be. Instead, I was able to enjoy graduation yesterday at Tech. The class of 2012 is a very good bunch, and they were so good to me. It was special to be part of their celebration and to meet some parents and other significant others. I can't tell you how many graduations I have attended, but I can tell you this was the first one I was sad to see wind down. My last official Georgia Tech act, I suppose.

I have heard from friends who went to Jazz Fest and stopped by the tree to say a prayer for Shannon that it is looking very tree-like. I'll be in New Orleans Thursday to volunteer with the MBAs at St. Bernard Project—if I don't get to the tree then (I am sure I will), I'm looking forward to going on Mother's Day.

Last week, I spent some time on the front porch grading and grading. There was a couple walking around the neighborhood—they did three laps. I miss walking that loop with Shannon. She was funny; she'd begin by insisting that we make sure we were walking at least 2.5 MPH. I guess at physical therapy they had told her that was what she needed to do, given her constraints and goals. She'd turn to me and ask, "Are we going 2.5?" Like I'd know. About halfway through the lap, she'd grab my hand to hold, stop worrying about 2.5, slow down, and start pointing out landscaping she liked, landscaping that needed rescue, critters running around, whatever. I'd ask her, "What happened to 2.5?" She'd just groan and we'd up the pace—but she'd keep holding my hand. I still walk the neighborhood and think about 2.5. It is just one of a million things that isn't the same.

Anyway, the couple walking. The couple was together, but they weren't walking side by side. The first time they passed my house, the man was perhaps 6 steps ahead of the woman. The second time, he had increased his lead to maybe 15 steps. The third, 25 steps or more. I obviously know nothing of this couple, but it made me sad because I knew how much the conversations Shannon and I had on those walks meant in our day. I hope that couple is getting that meaning some other way.

May 10

7:23 p.m.

Back at the Hilton in New Orleans after a good day of sheetrock mudding for the St. Bernard Project with some MBA students.

A friend passed on this blog to me: http://www.injennieskitchen.com. It's a food blog—coincidentally, the writer lost her husband nine months ago. She writes about food, but she writes about her efforts to cope since his death. She writes well. As I read it, I had that experience of truly understanding what someone meant. We say we understand each other all the time—but this is a deeper sort of feeling. Here's a piece of what struck me so strongly:

> *If you're coping with the death of your partner, husband, wife, soul mate, then it's important to remember you're also coping with the death of your dreams. This doesn't mean you can't build new ones. I gave myself a permanent reminder to do it every day. It just means you need to let yourself mourn the loss of the old dreams to make room for the new ones.*

Losing Shannon was the death of dreams.

A while back, I mentioned that one of my colleagues at Tech has a child with mitochondrial disease. I heard today that she just died. I don't know, but I am guessing she was maybe 5 years old. The funeral is Saturday. I feel so badly for that couple. They have to bury their daughter on Saturday and Mother's Day is Sunday. That's just terrible.

Shannon's been gone eight months. The day came and went. I was traveling for work. I think it passed without much attention because I am starting to think about measuring this in years rather than months.

May 12

While I was in New Orleans, the final letters from the Georgia Medical Board came. I waited to open them until this morning. The Board found insufficient evidence to take further action against the critical care practice. It's the outcome I fully expected—my goal was to apply some pressure that would hopefully improve the experience others down the road have with that group. I didn't think the State would do anything more.

I think I counted earlier that in the 8 months of 2011 that Shannon was alive, we went to live music about 50 times. In the 8 months that she's been gone, I have been to see about 30 shows—all but 4 or 5 by myself. Last night was Mayer Hawthorne. Shannon would have loved that show. I was thinking about it—he is someone she never heard at all. I became aware of him after she died. That realization felt strange—to be experiencing something she never experienced.

The day was a bit odd overall. I did some work at the hotel in the morning and headed out to Shannon's tree in Audubon Park. It was raining, so I didn't stay long. I stood by the tree a bit—I took a leaf and put it in my wallet. A connection to Shannon. I sat on Annie's bench a bit—the live oak that shades it also does a pretty good job of providing shelter from rain.

Finally, I went to grab lunch at a friend's restaurant that's out near the airport—the one ironically on Shannon Lane. The event requires background. It's a long story that I'll try to tell quickly.

Years ago—before I started dating Shannon—a guy showed up at the Chart House. He worked at the Baltimore location and was riding his bike across the US as a summer adventure. He wanted a place to crash, so my roommate and I offered our couch. I don't remember how long he crashed on our couch, but I do know he never left New Orleans.

He married one of three sisters—his wife got pregnant around the time Shannon was pregnant with Spencer. We weren't incredibly close—we were in Atlanta by then—but we did stay connected during the pregnancies—and more so after we moved to Baton Rouge.

One of the other sisters was married to a chef—the three sisters all worked together in his restaurant. Shannon and I have been regulars there—whenever we are in New Orleans—for twenty some odd years.

I had lunch at their new endeavor—a really great po'boy and gumbo sort of place. Yesterday was seafood gumbo and seafood stuffed eggplant. Amazing. Their restaurants are the only place I still get recognized in New Orleans—it's comfortable and feels good that there is still some semblance of a connection for me to the city.

Ever since Shannon died, I had a bad feeling that maybe somehow in all the confusion these folks hadn't found out. I had an old e-mail address. On the other hand, the last time I went no one asked after her—as they predictably would have—so I thought it was maybe safe. Turns out it wasn't—one of the sisters came and sat with me a bit in between my gumbo and my eggplant. We talked about all sorts of things that weren't Shannon—my kids, their families, and so on. When the eggplant arrived, she said, "I'll leave you to your food!" And then she asked as she was getting up, "How's Shannon?" I gulped and panicked and just said something vague like, "Things at home are going fine." In that moment—a full restaurant, a friendly face, and taken by surprise—I couldn't find other words to say. How could I drop that bomb in that moment? Now I've created an awkwardness that can only be addressed by never going to eat at either of their places again.

So after lunch I flew back to Atlanta. I had time to kill, so I went to see Five-Year Engagement. A chick flick all by myself. The theater was full with women—it was interesting to see the parts where they laughed.

348

I watched until the predictable happy ending was arranged and then headed over to the Variety Playhouse for Mayer Hawthorne. He put on a good show.

I was glad to find the new landing page picture this afternoon—it's Spencer feeding Shannon cupcakes in bed on Mother's Day, 1991. He was 2. I remember how excited he was to wake up early with me to bake them for her. He insisted she have them in bed. So for Mother's Day, Shannon had to change the sheets. I don't think she minded.

May 15

10:02 p.m.

Mother's Day was harder than I expected. It might have been the hardest milestone yet. I spent a lot of energy worrying about Spencer and Reid. It helped when I was able to text a bit with Spencer—he seemed okay. Reid stayed off the radar. We've talked since and he is fine, but it was difficult to just be worried about him Sunday.

I used to whine about how Mother's Day was the boys' problem to cover. But I always got something for Shannon—sometimes just a card, sometimes something more if I found "just the right thing." It made a lot of sense to me—what she went through in becoming a mom and what it did for me is a much bigger thing to celebrate than a birthday or anniversary.

So it hurt Sunday to not be able to thank her for all that work. Watching the boys take their final steps into adulthood is something I wish she could see. All the work she did over all those years is going to pay off, and she won't know.

On the plus side of the ledger, I continue to be thankful and amazed for so many good friends. Apparently while I was out on the porch watching hockey last night I got a phone call. The phone rarely rings here, so I don't often check the messages—I didn't notice last night's message until earlier this evening. It was a call from the friend I mentioned in Saturday's post—at the restaurant. The only way that call happens is that someone reading along had the nerve to do what I didn't have the nerve to do and called them for me. I am thankful for that. It's still going to be a hard call to return, but it will be so much easier than any alternative I would have come up with on my own. And I will be so glad to not have to just avoid some of my few remaining New Orleans friends because I was cowardly. So thanks.

May 17

Suddenly, there is a lot going on. Reid reports pretty good grades for the spring. He is definitely on track and that's great. He is in Maymester now and home in a couple of weeks. He's made big plans for next summer, but hasn't a clue what he will do this summer.

On the way home from work today, a Bob Seeger song came on that I hadn't heard in a long time. Shannon and I saw him last winter, I think. He is not a young man, but he put on a good show anyway. I heard he has a young kid and that he flies home to Michigan every night after the show so he is there in the morning for the kid. Then whenever the next concert is he flies out to do it…and then flies home.

Shannon laughed when Seeger took off his jacket or shirt—whatever he had on—to reveal a short sleeve undershirt. He was there clapping his hands over his head and Shannon said, "His batwings are worse than mine!" That got her fixated and she determined the best arms in the band were on the backup singer playing tambourine—that was going to be her cure for batwings…if the Pilates never kicked in its effect, she was going to take up tambourine and find a band to tour with.

The Seeger song on the radio today was "Trying to Live My Life Without You"—great mood music, right?

I am trying to find an article I want to send to the cardiac care practice—wanting to preserve the learning opportunity for them a bit longer. I had to read it years ago—it was about the effect that apologies from doctors had on patients, their families, and the likelihood of legal action. Doctors don't want to apologize because that would admit fault and could cost them their license. I get that. But in Shannon's case, the bad behavior on their part was just being inconsiderate jerks. Now that the State Board has found no basis for any action, they should feel free to apologize, right? I am not holding my breath. Honestly, if they called, I wouldn't pick up. Their prior acts tell me what they believe.

From what I have read, there are four things that matter. People want to know what happened, that responsibility was accepted, that actions would be taken to improve future practice, and that someone is sorry.

Ironically, the funeral home did one for me, the hospital did two and three and four for me. The offending physicians haven't done anything. They did send a letter to the lawyer helping me out explaining their "side of the story." But they've never shown me anything. So I am going to show them some research on how good practices operate. They won't get it—but they'll get that I am still angry.

I talked with my friend at the restaurant in New Orleans today. That felt so good. I don't want to lose any friends because I get brain freeze in an awkward situation. I didn't mention it earlier, but she lost her husband to cancer about 10 years ago—so she completely understood about how hard it is when someone somehow didn't get the news. I am so thankful to have had that conversation.

I had more to share but it's dark and I don't feel like going there now. It's a nice night—one of the last few where it won't be too hot or too humid to enjoy sitting out, so I'd rather do that. I will just leave with one dark question and then go about my business. Does grief leave on its own accord or does it have to be pushed out? You know how it is—sometimes houseguests need to be guided to the door so you can do the dishes and go to bed. Is that what my grief is waiting for?

May 18

> 5:37 p.m.

There continues to be a lot going on. Today was a good day—a really good day. Around noon, I was driving back from the gym. The top was off the Jeep, I felt good from working out, my other morning business had all gone well, it was 75 degrees outside, the sun was shining, and Michael Franti was playing on the stereo. It felt so good—the next thought through my head was, "This is probably how someone feels right before they wrap their car around a telephone pole." So I dialed everything back a bit.

I just finished a burst of packing here at my office at Tech. Since Shannon died, I have found the office to be a safe place to be—it wasn't someplace I'd expect to see her. I am surrounded by people that I associate with work, not personal life—I suppose that's a benefit of having a bit of a wall between the two. Of course, it isn't something that was planned.

Anyway, as I packed I kept being reminded of how silly it was for me to think that my office was a place that wasn't connected to Shannon. Right over my computer are pictures from shows we went to together—James Taylor, Derek Trucks, Better than Ezra, Pearl Jam, Cowboy Mouth, Little Feat, Doobie Brothers, Earth, Wind, and Fire, Eric Clapton, Jonny Lang, Steve Winwood. Every one of those with Shannon by my side—except for Pearl Jam where a sick crowd made it impossible for me to find her after I went on a beer run. For that one, she stayed with a friend.

Behind me on the shelf were some mementos from LSU. For a while, Shannon was working at the Athletic Department in their accounting office. She loved that though she claimed she couldn't balance a checkbook, she was in charge of the football team's. She loved to intrigue me with questions like, "Do you know much 500 jock straps cost? I do—wrote the check today!"

While she was there, the team had a football player named Nate Miller. He was very good at LSU and went on to have a short pro career. Shannon told me at the time the word was he was too nice to be a pro player—lacked a killer instinct.

Since we shared our first name, Shannon thought I'd like a signed football from him. The coaches said that was fine—that she should come down to the locker room and that he'd be fine to sign it. I never could get the full story of just how it all played out—she just turned red whenever I brought it up. I have been in enough locker rooms to have a pretty good guess as to why. Anyway, she braved her way into the locker room, was introduced to Nate Miller, and he signed the football for her. She gave it to me for Christmas that year, and I've had it on my shelf at work for 20 years—it says, "From one Big Nate to another."

And, one of the most rewarding things I was able to do in Baton Rouge was to work with some parents to start a youth hockey league. I have a T-shirt we used as a fundraiser one year that Shannon had framed for me. She gave up so many hours of time with me so I could do that for the boys. And so I could enjoy it myself. It was great—we grew it to where over 200 families were involved. Spencer loved to play. He was coached by Pierre McGuire who does analysis now for NBC. He was coached by Dave Schultz—one of the people I hated the most when I was growing up—he was the tough guy on the Flyers— archrival to the Bruins. He was coached by Bob McGill—long the tough guy for the Toronto Maple Leafs. It was a great experience, and I know it is one of Spencer's fondest memories of growing up. Shannon made it all possible by being a good sport.

May 20

Michael Franti was Michael Franti last night. What fun. He spends a lot of time running through the crowd, and he came bouncing down my row—so I got a good handshake. Shannon would have loved a high-five from him.

Friday was Madeleine Peyroux. I went to Serpas, my usual spot for dinner beforehand. They used to know Shannon and me. There's been some turnover now, and the people who work there now know me as the single guy with the Kindle who needs a table with decent light. I get extra attention—it's a restaurant that gets it.

As I was sitting there, a cute couple in their 20s was seated a few tables from me. I wasn't stalking, but I couldn't help but see what was going on. They'd been sitting there just a minute, and I could tell the girl was cold because she was dressed for 85 degrees outside and was sitting inside in an AC blast zone. It was something I check out of habit from all the years with Shannon. She was always cold. So I watched. It took the guy about 10 minutes to notice, and he quickly changed chairs with her. Good job, I thought. There's hope for him.

When he was doing his paperwork, he was told there is a benefit there that you can name a significant other and if that person—whatever their relationship to you—has a medical crisis, you can take one month off WITH PAY to help them. This is, I'm guessing, an unheard of benefit to anyone working in the restaurant industry in Atlanta.

I am in Sarasota at my dad's. He has back surgery tomorrow. My first time back in a hospital since Shannon died. Glad I can be here for my dad, but so not looking forward to tomorrow.

May 22

9:33 p.m.

I have just returned from Sarasota. My dad had some chest pains the night before the back surgery was to happen, so it was delayed. Today we went to the cardiologist to make sure it was nothing—appears it was. I expect to go back soon when it is rescheduled. It wasn't too bad to be in the hospital—different hospital helps. I certainly wasn't going to fuss that they were being too careful.

I really missed Shannon down there—between being the daughter of a doctor and her own experience she was so good at medical stuff. She was just also very good at helping anxious people be less anxious. We all could have used some of that.

As I was getting ready for bed the first night, I went into the closet to grab something I knew would be there. They use feather pillows on all the beds, and Shannon was allergic. We went out years ago and bought her a special pillow for her to use on her visits. I knew it would still be there, back in its plastic bag. I used it this trip.

When I got home tonight, I watched the last episode of *House*. It's a show Shannon and I enjoyed. She loved to sit and watch and as they would roll through the various possible diagnoses that were inflicting that week's patient, she would be like someone at a Bingo Parlor…"Yes, they thought I had that…Yes, they thought I had that, too!" Funny.

As the show was ending, they used an old Warren Zevon song that I hadn't heard in forever—"Keep Me in Your Heart for a While"—so sad and so sweet. It's a great song by someone else who left too soon.

May 25

Tonight I was invited to attend my goddaughter's high school graduation. It was so enjoyable to be part of a family celebration. She attended high school in a small town here in Georgia—the small-town nature of the graduation was so entertaining—sitting out in the football stadium and all. She was Shannon's godchild, too, and I know Shannon would have been very proud to have been there. As a graduation gift, I gave the girl one of Shannon's favorite necklaces. She was very excited, and so in a way, Shannon was there.

Shannon was certainly with me on the long drive there and the—hard to believe—equally long drive home. Time in the car is a time she is always in my thoughts—driving and then trying to fall asleep at night. Other thoughts do try to crowd their way in—with varying degrees of success. As I said above—it was comforting to be doing such a normal family thing. At the same time, those "normal" moments are when it is so painfully evident that someone pretty important is missing. Thanksgiving was like that—I was with my kids and surrounded by family. That was great, but it made the missing piece so, so obvious. Christmas, the boys and I were nowhere near where we were "supposed" to be. The expectation of Shannon being there was just itself not there. That made it sadder, but easier—if that makes sense.

May 28

My psychiatrist asked me last week how I was doing. That's a much more complicated question than it used to be. I thought about it a bit and told him I thought I was operating at about a 6 most of the time, but that it didn't take much to drop me to a 3.

So he asked for an example. I told him about something that had happened that same day. When I go to the gym to lift weights—and when I was married to Shannon—I used to take my ring off because I wasn't comfortable gripping the bar with it on. It was the only time I ever took my ring off—other than to clean it. To be safe, I'd untie my shoe, pull a lace out through an eyelet, feed it through the ring, back through the eyelet, and then double knot it. I knew it wasn't going anywhere.

Just about 100% of the time I'd forget to put it back on after the workout. I'd get in the Jeep to drive home, and my hand wouldn't feel right on the wheel because the ring was gone—I'd have a moment of panic and then remember to check my shoe. It was always there. Sometimes, I'd pull back in a parking space to put it on; other times I felt I could make it home before I put it on.

I don't wear a ring anymore, but just about every time I get in the car after the gym I notice it's gone and have that panic. I start to look at my shoe and then remember it is actually gone. That drops me to a three.

And I told him how the other morning I awoke with a start to a loud voice in my head telling me I was going to wake up alone for the rest of my life. That drops me to a 3.

He called them "bumps." That they are.

I was driving home the other night from my goddaughter's graduation and a song that Jonny Lang does—I don't know who wrote it—came on the radio. I've decided it's the perfect widower song. At least it's the song that perfectly describes being at a 3. It's called "Still Rainin'" and it's worth a listen. He can really play guitar.

May 30

7:16 p.m.

Today was my last day at Tech. It went unnoticed, which was my wish. I did go to a new restaurant to mark the occasion on the way home, and it would have been nice to have Shannon's company.

Since it was the last day, one of my tasks was to clean off my work computer. After Shannon died and I got ready to get rid of her computer, I was very worried about losing her files, so I backed them up in lots of places—including at work. So today I took them off. I tried to just delete or move files without looking at them, but that was not 100% successful. I found a letter she wrote to one of the nurses at the ortho's office. Shannon was, as discussed, never a simple case and there was lots of back and forth to make sure the right path forward was being taken. Shannon, being Shannon, felt badly—like she was requiring too much as a patient. So she got a gift for this one person and attached this note to it. Two weeks later she collapsed.

Tuesday, August 23, 2011

Dear Allison,

Please accept this as a token of my thanks. Each time we have spoken, you have been cheerful, willing to listen and very patient with your answers, advice and time. These attributes are not a regular occurrence in most medical offices these days. Your kindness and promptness in answering my calls has eased my worries more than you will ever know. The professional and welcoming approach of you and your co-workers helps give me confidence that I am in the proper office and best doctor's care. Even though the entire office has demonstrated this friendly professionalism—somehow, I have pestered you with the greatest frequency. Thank you so much for helping me and providing much needed clarity and direction.

Sincerely,

Shannon Bennett

That's pretty classic Shannon. A completely unnecessary and nice deed.

June 2

6:33 p.m.

One year ago today, Shannon and I packed for last year's version of the trip I am about to go on. I do a weeklong program for a client in DC this week every year. The first two years it was hard to be gone from Shannon and Reid for the whole week. Last year, I was excited that Shannon could come with me. She went with a friend to Trombone Shorty at Wolftrap on the Sunday afternoon (tomorrow) while I worked; the two of us went to see Frankie Valli there later in the week. We had a good week in spite of the fact that in our absence Reid "entertained" at the house in a way we weren't very excited about. A little sheetrock, a little paint—it's all taken care of. Maybe it was a little too soon for us to think Shannon could be with me on all my travels!

I'll stay a different hotel this time—the one I stayed at when I did the trip alone. That will help avoid some bumps.

I've been reflecting on the last post—the unnecessary acts of kindness that Shannon used to do. I remembered how, early in our marriage, it sometimes frustrated me that she wanted to do all these things. She got gifts for every doctor every Christmas, for example. I didn't understand why we were taking the time, spending the money, and so on. One year, to save money, she said we should bake pecan pies. So that year I baked (when she said "we" should cook, I knew what that meant) 21 pecan pies. I think I could fit 4 at a time in the oven. It took a while.

Anyway, my point is that my life became so much better when I learned to just accept that about her. I don't know why it was easy for me to accept the kindness that she showed me and at the same time it was so hard for me to accept that she wanted to show kindness to others. Once I got myself okay with that idea, our relationship was so much better. And over the years she taught me to show that sort of kindness myself. I am not nearly as good at it as she was—she just was that way. I have to work to be that way. But work on it I do.

June 5

11:06 p.m.

I've been in DC now a few days. The work part has been going pretty well. The CEO came by class on Sunday early, found me, and brought me up to his office so he could share his regrets. He'd already done that in a beautiful card months ago, but this was the first time we were in the same place at the same time. I appreciated his effort—it wasn't something he needed to do. Even more, I was glad that I could talk about losing Shannon and the events of the year without too much choking back of tears. I can't do that every day, but I could do it Sunday.

The days here are very full, and the nights are rather empty. I guess it is better to say they are lonely—I have had stuff planned every night. Saturday was hockey at the Cheesecake Factory bar. Sunday was the first night of the program, so that night was full. Monday was a concert at the Howard Theater. Tonight was dinner with a friend from the Baton Rouge days. Tomorrow is a baseball game. Thursday is the "graduation" dinner. Lots of events, but still lots of down time to think about how much more fun this trip was last year with Shannon's company. I've come to realize that I don't laugh when I am alone. I need other people around in order to laugh and laughing is important to health.

Some of the thoughts I've been jotting down—they are fairly random.

1. I am trying to understand whether or not I can tell the difference between being excited to have someone else's company and the excitement that comes from just not being alone. Are my feelings because the person is special or because I am not alone? I need to be able to tell the difference. I bet a lot of the widowers who remarry quickly decided they didn't care which it was—they just preferred company to no company. But I want to know.

2. Shannon would have loved the drummer last night. He had, in addition to the normal drum kit, a Nazi soldier helmet on a cymbal stand and two hi-hat cymbals made out of the stainless covers hotel room service uses to keep food warm. Pretty funny. They played a great version of the Talking Heads song, "Burning Down the House." She loved that song.

362

3. A dark one—I was realizing that will never forget the temperature of Shannon's body in her casket. It was so unnatural, so wrong. I can just think about it and feel that temperature in my fingers.

June 9

6:06 p.m.

Shannon was in my dream last night. I had very bad blisters on my feet, and she was trying to help me deal with them. She told me she was trying to decide if she was going to come back or not. That's all the dream was. When I have a dream like that, I wake up very confused because for those first seconds it's not clear what was the dream—the life I have been living without her or the dream that I was having with her. Then I figure it out.

Last week in class, I used an example from my sailing days to explain a concept we were discussing. On a break, one of the students said that if I liked sailing, I might like this book called *First You Have to Row a Little Boat: Reflections of Life and Living*. I ordered it, and Amazon had it here by the time I got home last night. I read it this morning, and I did like it. Basically, the author uses his experience learning how to sail as a child as a way to describe how he learned about life. And he used that he didn't pass sailing on to his kids as a way to talk about his regrets in life.

After the events of the last now 9 months, there were a couple of quotes that stood out to me. Here's one:

> *I found out, almost after it was too late, that my children weren't born to learn from my experiences; they were born to learn from their own.*[11]

---

[11] Richard Bode, *First You Have to Row a Little Boat: Reflections of Life and Living* (New York: Grand Central Publishing, 1995), 4–5.

I agree—my kids weren't born to learn from my experience, but that doesn't mean they won't. I wonder a lot about what I am teaching them now that they are gone and I am alone and trying to get better. That was on my mind because someone shared a quote with me earlier in the week that I thought was special. It's attributed to Theodore Hesburgh, president emeritus of Notre Dame: *"The most important thing a father can do for his children is to love their mother."* I did and, as futile as it is, still do. It's really hard for me to talk to them about it, so I hope they know it.

June 11

8:41 p.m.

Today I am in Sarasota visiting my dad. He is recovering from the neck surgery he had last week. He always has a lot of trouble coming out of anesthesia; this time was no exception—lots of confusion. I was thankful to find him today in much better shape than I feared. We had a good chance to visit in between occupational therapy, physical therapy, and speech therapy. My stepmom and I kept him company for dinner, and then I brought her home so she could rest. I went back to the hospital—the plan was for him and me to watch the Red Sox game for a while.

When I arrived I was not entirely surprised to see him asleep. He stirred enough when I sat down to smile and give me a wave, but then he went back to sleep. I put the game on and watched Josh Beckett give up three runs in the first inning. I was glad my dad was sleeping through it. During the second inning, I could hear nurses outside chatting. It was shift change so the day nurse was filling the night nurse in on my dad. They didn't know I was in the room—I heard the day nurse say, "Mr. Bennett is really sweet. He came in really disoriented, but he is doing much better today." My dad is a good guy, but it was funny to hear him referred to as sweet.

After three innings, I was thinking about how well I was doing just hanging out in the hospital. And I was—until that moment. I think I used to be scared of hospitals because I really had no idea about how to understand all the commotion. Spending 11 days there with Shannon was desensitizing. Now I ask nurses better questions, I think I can tell the real answers from the rote answers—at least better than I could—I wouldn't have thought there were rote answers before what happened to Shannon.

Anyway, at that moment, sitting in the dark with my dad asleep, baseball on, and thinking about how unfreaked out I was brought to mind last fall, sitting in the dark, football on, with Shannon uncommunicative beside me, totally freaking out because I knew what a terrible thing was happening; slowly happening. And I recognized how completely powerless I was to do anything about it. I had to leave.

The day did bring some comfort—my dad ate in a common room on the floor with the other patients; many had family keeping them company. As I looked around the room and saw how many of the patients were really struggling—and I had the sense their prognosis was not as hopeful as my dad's—I thought again about how Shannon would feel if it was her in that chair and me feeding her. It's easy for me to romanticize it now—and of course I would have been there for her. But it would have been hard for me, and it would have been her worst nightmare fulfilled. As much as I miss her, I am finding a little gladness she was spared what she would have felt was an undignified exit.

June 14

A friend sent me an article out of *The Chronicle of Higher Education* written by Mark Edmundson, an English professor at University of Virginia. He was writing about how he saw his college students experiencing music and offered a couple of perspectives I found interesting:

> *Music does sometimes kick a door open inside the mind, but it also sometimes insulates the house, secures it from all wayward feelings and thoughts. And when a song does seem to kick a door open, we frequently listen to it over and over again until it loses its power and all of its passion is spent.*[12]

For the past ten months, this has certainly been true for me. Some of the songs that kick doors open can't be defused right away, though. You have to keep those doors nailed shut.

Listening to music has provided me with so much comfort while also uncovering so much pain. A scab on feelings is what music has been.

Edmundson then says:

> *Schopenhauer says that most reading is letting other people think your thoughts for you. I'd add that most music listening is about letting other people feel your feelings for you.*

Now who am I to disagree with Schopenhauer, a man Wikipedia describes as a "German philosopher known for his pessimism and philosophical clarity." I am a huge fan of both pessimism and clarity.

---

[12] Mark Edmundson, "Can Music Save Your Life?," *The Chronicle of Higher Education,* June 3, 2012, http://chronicle.com/article/Can-Music-Save-Your-Life-/132040/.

But I do disagree with Edmundson's extension of the point to music. Ringo Starr sang that you have to pay dues before you can sing the blues, but I suspect most of the musicians I've listened to haven't paid nearly the dues to sing about what they sing about. So I think for the most part they haven't had my feelings—so they can't feel them for me. What they have is an ability to make a connection to people. That's an amazing ability—but what it does is help me feel my feelings.

My birthday is coming up. I have a ticket to go to New Orleans for the day. I asked my psychiatrist about it today. He said there isn't a right answer...I noted that has been true for 10 months now. He asked why I was still seeking one. Okay, one point for him. He said that going is okay because it just means I am still mourning how things are supposed to be. He said not going is okay because it means I am learning how to accept that things are going to be different from now on. He thinks it's fine for me to be either of those people. I figure that I am both of those people, and I'll figure it out as long as he only bills one of us.

June 17

> 10:18 p.m.

Spencer arranged a table at The Spence, his mentor's newest restaurant, for Reid and me. Tremendous meal. Reid and I enjoyed every single bite, and it was great to catch up. He and I have been together here for a couple of weeks, but it was our first chance to have an uninterrupted talk that lasted more than a few minutes. It made for a nice Father's Day celebration.

In the fall of 1988, Shannon and I were living in a little rental house in Lawrenceville, Georgia. We got a deal, as we were renting it from a woman Shannon knew from work. Although I had a great deal of financial support from Tech and faculty research grants while I was in graduate school—and although Shannon was working—money was always tight.

One day that fall Shannon came home from the grocery store. Already the story is weird. She didn't go to the grocery store; that was my job. She drove up and unloaded over $100 in groceries. I am not sure what that translates to in 2012 dollars, but $100 bought a lot of groceries in 1988. As she finished dropping the last of the groceries on the kitchen table, she started to really cry—hard crying.

To say I was confused would be an understatement. I didn't know what I was supposed to do with all those groceries, and I had no idea why my wife was a wreck. Just as I was approaching her to give her a hug and to see what was wrong, she just blurted out, "I am sorry I spent all this money. I know we don't really have it. I don't know what's wrong with me!" I did what I could to comfort her, and I did what I could to help her make the supplies fit in our tiny kitchen.

A couple of nights later, Shannon took me to dinner at a place in the neighborhood—Slocum's. It was a good place—grilled tuna sandwiches were what we always got. She again apologized for the groceries. I told her it was not a big deal. She told me her theory was that she had been acting all crazy because she was pregnant. That's how I found out I was going to be a dad.

In the summer of 1992, Shannon took me to dinner at the short-lived Essen Lane location of Louisiana Pizza Kitchen in Baton Rouge. We were enjoying dinner, and I couldn't figure out why Shannon was insisting on talking about our plans for Christmas. Did I want to go see her parents in Houston? Did I want to go see my parents? Did I want to stay in Baton Rouge? I don't remember just what I said, but it basically was "do we need to decide Christmas in July?" She said that she wanted me to know that we probably should plan on staying in town because she was due on December 25th. That's how I found out about Reid.

Let's just say from that day forward, I was always nervous when she invited me to go out for dinner.

The best part of Father's Day all these years was getting to thank Shannon for everything she went through to make it a day I could rightfully celebrate. Thanks, Shannon. The boys did good.

Summer

June 24

| 10:20 p.m. |

Happy Birthday to me.

Today I am 51. A year ago, I was doing better than I am today. But today I am doing better than I was a few months ago.

It's been a week since I wrote an entry. There are lots of reasons, but the single biggest reason has to do with the time I've been spending in an effort to re-read and edit what I've shared with you. It's been a while since I went back to September. I did that the other night. I made it from my first entry on September 13th to the end of the month. The biggest feeling was odd—it was, "Wow, this all really happened." That's the thought that was in my mind, and I don't even know what to make of it. That it really happened should not be news to me. But it was.

I didn't go to New Orleans for my birthday. There are lots of reasons, but the single biggest reason was that I got a better offer to do something in the present. In thinking about it, I realized that my birthday was a good day to think that way—I decided to make spending a day in the present my present to myself. It was a good day sailing on Lake Lanier followed by a slice and a beer with Reid for my birthday dinner.

June 29

I sat down to write last night and I couldn't come up with anything. I think that's a first. Nothing to write means no relief. Or does nothing to write mean no relief is needed? Last night it felt like the former.

Tonight, some thoughts have come more quickly to my mind. Both are things left over from Father's Day.

I called Shannon's dad on Father's Day. I just wanted him to know that I was thinking about him. He seemed pretty down—his first Father's Day without Shannon—since the one in 1963 when Shannon's arrival had made him a dad. That had to be difficult, and it sounded like it was. That brought me back to Mother's Day and my worry for the boys as they dealt with that "first." Shannon's dad and the boys have each suffered a terrible loss in a way that will never be remedied. In a way, they may have suffered a more permanent loss than I have. He'll never have another daughter; the boys will never have another mother.

That night, I had what I think was the fifth dream starring Shannon. I had gone to bed very late and had to be up very early, so I went off to sleep knowing it might be a bit fitful, and it was. I only had about four hours to sleep, and it felt like the dream took the entire time to unfold.

In the dream, Shannon left me. She went "back home," though it never was really clear where that home was. I found my way to her and saw she was happy there without me. I tried to get her to come back with me, and she wouldn't. She wasn't angry, she had no explanation to offer me, and she resisted every argument I tried. This process—finding her, trying to persuade her, and hearing her tell me to just go back, that I was supposed to go back now—was repeated in slight variations over and over. That was the essence of the dream.

The sleep was fitful, but when I woke up I wasn't restless or upset or angry or disappointed. It's just what it is. I think I know what that one means.

July 1

10:34 a.m.

At GSU, one of the popular teaching tools is a personality test developed by a guy named Hogan. I am getting certified next week to be an official user/interpreter of the test. As a part of the process, I had to take the test and have a session with a coach to discuss my results.

I've done these things before—the process is familiar. You answer a bunch of questions online, you get a report that is carefully written in a way that gets you to think about strengths and weaknesses without turning you off entirely, and then a guy gets paid to read to you over the phone the same report that you are holding in your hands. Great. Would it surprise you to find out that my highest score/strongest characteristic indicates I am skeptical?

So I have this opportunity to learn about myself and to have an expert tell me even more—the nuance I would be unable to distill from the effort of reading the report on my own. Two things happened on the debrief. First, my "reserved" score impressed him. According to the test, I don't divulge anything about who I am, but I am adept at getting others to disclose things to me. I guess Hogan hasn't been reading this blog.

Second, one of the bumps...he told me the results indicate I am stubborn. But, he added with a chuckle, "I am sure your wife tells you that all the time!" Not so much. Why do people assume others are married? A similar thing happened in class a week or so ago—a guy asked how my wife would feel about something I had said in class. I can't remember what my comment was. I deflected the question a bit and called on another student. While I was listening to that second student's question, I could see a neighboring student passing a hurriedly scribbled note to the original guy. I know what the note said.

My psychiatrist says my last dream about Shannon was what's called a "release dream." It's a common thing for someone in my uncommon state. I'm not a big fan of the release dream, although I guess it has to mark some sort of acceptance of where things are.

Yesterday, I read the entire blog in order to try and edit it. I think we have it down to 200,000 words. The project is divided into seasons—fall, winter, spring, and now summer. Each volume is a bit skinnier than the one before. That's a visual that also makes a point.

Reading it was a terrible thing to do—I don't want to do it again. It hurt to remember how much I hurt. That said, I am 1,000 more times thankful that I wrote and that you read. I don't want to forget how much I hurt, no matter how much remembering hurts. And I especially don't want to forget how much I was helped.

Just as I finished yesterday, Reid got home from a getaway to Athens. His timing was perfect to bring me back to the present, and I am glad for that.

Anyway, I prefer the way the Hogan test tries to make me feel not so bad about being stubborn. The nice way to say someone is stubborn is, apparently, that they are "charming, independent, and hard to coach."

So if any of you hear from a spouse/significant other/coworker/kid that you are being stubborn, you just tell them you are being charming, independent, and hard to coach. See how that flies.

July 1

9:09 p.m.

Reid is off to a lake with friends and their families for the Fourth, so I have the house almost to myself. Just me and Andre. The picture is Shannon with a much younger and smaller Andre—probably summer of 2010. He weighs about 75 pounds now. I think it's safe to say Shannon wouldn't be carrying him quite that way. She loved this dog, as you can tell by the grin on her face. She'd be all over this dog-sitting task, even if there was little she could do except complain when Andre tried—and he would repeatedly try—to be her lap dog.

I was having lunch Sunday at a mediocre Mexican place in the neighborhood. I was reading a magazine and came across an interview with the comedian Louis C. K. He had a great quote in there about life after a divorce—it fits my experience, too.

Getting divorced is like stepping out of a time machine...But it's a really shitty time machine. It's the kind of time machine that takes the real amount of time to take you to the future.[13]

---

[13] Rob Sheffield, "Louis C. K., the Jerk-Off Genius," *Rolling Stone*, June 25, 2012, http://www.rollingstone.com/movies/news/louis-c-k-the-jerk-off-genius-20120625.

It was great to have a chance to "Shannon" some people this week. It had been too long. I made great friends with a guy in midtown Atlanta who approached me as I was heading to meet some former students for a beer. I could see him coming—he said, "Hey, I love your Jeep." If I was cynical, I would say that was code for, "Would you like your Jeep to be there in one piece when you get back?" but I am not cynical. He wanted to trade me 5 quarts of motor oil for transmission fluid. I don't think he meant the fluids actually IN the car, but who knows. He explained that his car was parked down the street, and his kids were in it, and the city was about to tow it. If he didn't get transmission fluid, he would lose his kids.

I am thinking that since he looks at least 60, his kids might be able to take care of themselves. I asked him if $5 would help. He thought that was a great idea. I gave him the money, we did fist bumps, he was very excited. He was so excited that he headed off in a direction perpendicular to where his "kids" were supposed to be about to get towed away. Maybe that's where the all-night transmission fluid store is in Midtown.

Almost everything people have told me would come true about how I remember Shannon seems like it is coming true. I get so incredibly sad when I look at pictures or read this blog—but there isn't the same sharpness and hopelessness to it that there was months ago. Trust me, the sadness is plenty shitty enough. But most of the time, when I think of Shannon, my first reaction is a smile. Then I cry. So that's progress.

I spend a lot of time thinking about what really comforted me over the past nearly 10 months. Did it help when people told me how it would one day be? It helped me to realize they wanted to help me—but what they said didn't help. It made me mad. It doesn't matter precisely what they said—I can't really remember exact words now anyway. What I heard in my injured brain was, "Someday Shannon won't matter so much to you." That made me mad. She's always going to matter to me.

I guess that's a lesson—people thought they knew who they were talking to when they tried to comfort me. People thought I would process messages logically. They probably underestimated how damaged my head was. I wasn't me then.

July 4

> 7:14 a.m.

There have been some days when I want to write and can't. Yesterday was one of the days when I can't get to a keyboard quickly enough. And I couldn't get to a keyboard. Instead, I made some voice memos so that I wouldn't lose my thoughts as I went about what was a good, but somewhat crazy day. Any day that starts at the dentist is bound to be a bit like that.

The thought that came to mind that had me wishing for a keyboard had to do with the way Shannon went out. I have written that she would be okay with it—going out suddenly. I'd prefer that, too, I think. The downside is all the unfinished business you leave behind. I realized yesterday that if the book effort is successful, I can use the acknowledgments pages as a way to help Shannon finish her unfinished business. There are people she would want to have been able to say things to. I'll do my best to say them for her then. That's what I had to get to a keyboard to start working through. The whole idea just brought with it some calm. The calm was nice—another last chance to do something to help Shannon.

In an entirely unrelated thought, a New Orleans memory popped into my head yesterday as I was listening to Pandora. When we worked at the Chart House, we found ourselves part of a network of bar and restaurant employees—another sort of fraternity. We took care of one another with free food and drinks at each other's places. It was a lot of fun.

One of the places where Shannon and I had such a friend was Feelings Café in the Marigny neighborhood. It's a great little creole spot—off the beaten path. Small bar with a piano, great little patio. Nice menu. When Shannon and I were dating that was one of the places to go for a special celebration. We had been introduced to a bartender there through a friend at the Chart House. The bartender was in charge of the music system, and he played great stuff from his collection. Shannon just loved the mix of 40s and 50s music. He made Shannon a mix tape of the music he played at the bar—it's a cassette she listened to up into her last year. She kept her high school boom box just so she would have a place to play that one cassette. Anyway, it all came to mind because just before Shannon died I had introduced her to Pandora. She had created just one station—Nat King Cole. She listened to it a lot—but not for a very long time. Cole is a classic representative of the stuff on that mix tape—which the bartender had titled "Way Bitchin' Rad." Every once in a while, I listen to that station for her.

When we moved back to Baton Rouge, we tried to reestablish a habit of going to Feelings. Spencer won't remember, but we used to bring him—he was just a couple of months old. We'd set his car seat on the piano as they played. He loved, we guess, the sounds and vibrations. Spencer and the tip jar would sit up there. Shannon would be drinking a Campari and soda. I think I was in a vodka stage at the time. We'd sit at the bar, have some appetizers, and talk with all the staff. Those were good nights.

July 7

4:15 p.m.

Today it is ten months since Shannon's collapse. The closer it gets to a year, the less the marking of the month matters. I find myself almost eager for it to be a year so that there are no more firsts. In about a month from now it would have been our 27th anniversary, and then about a month after that it will have been one year without her after 28 with her.

It was a difficult trip to go check in on my dad this past week. Progress is so slow and so vague that it truly is hard to tell what is really progress and what is just basically random variation around the way he just is now. Though the surgeon is pleased with the results of the operation, my dad isn't really walking better. He does report less pain. His memory has become much worse—before the surgery it really wasn't an issue at all. He might sometimes need to think a bit before answering a question—and he would get stuck trying to remember a particular word—but he was 100% rational. Now he is confused so much of the time—he suffers from "sundowner's syndrome"—in the late afternoon he really becomes a person I don't know. The last night I was there he explained to the psychologist that he had a job as an editor of a book series, and he needed to get back to work to not let people down.

He has a month to go before they decide it is something more than just what could be considered usual for someone his age getting over surgery. But I anticipate that in a month (or sooner) I will again be needing to make decisions for someone else, like I had to for Shannon. I really am not anxious to be back in that position again so soon.

The decision-making thing brought Shannon to mind. It was pretty typical for me to just ask her what she wanted to do that night. She'd say she didn't care—"just something we can do together." That was her criterion. Easy enough. I'd say that I didn't want to make decisions for her, but she'd insist she trusted me. Then I realized that after all the time together, I really was making decisions with her—even if she didn't say anything more than "let's do something together." I knew her well enough that I really could have a conversation with her in my head—she didn't need to be there talking for me to "know" what she would enjoy doing. I had tons of data on the things that Shannon enjoyed.

The sense that I knew Shannon well enough to make decisions with her even though she wasn't there was a source of both strength and relief as she died. I didn't really think I was making decisions "for" her. And it's been a source of strength for me as I try to find my way forward without her. I am sad that I am not sure I know my dad well enough to have that same feeling now that I will soon have to make decisions for him. I'd rather have been able to feel like I was making them with him. It's too late for me to get there with him, but I've already warned Spencer and Reid that we are going to get there in terms of my wishes.

July 10

9:19 a.m.

Last week, I left my laptop on a plane. I had hoped someone would "Shannon" me, and I'd have it back, but no such luck. Whoever found it feels they need it more than I do.

It's been hard to operate without it. I miss being portable around the house, around Atlanta, and around and around. I am thanking Shannon for helping me remain calm about it. If I hadn't learned what I've learned since I lost her, I would have been manic that entire day, up and angry that night, and still without a laptop. Perspective. Losing a laptop is really not much of a loss.

Last night I was flying back from a day of work in DC. I had all my "i's" charged and ready—my iPad and my iPhone and my iPod...clearly not a lack of technology for entertainment. But none of those devices works for me when it comes to typing. As a result, this is the first blog entry that began entirely as a handwritten note. I am glad you are reading a second draft because the first one was quite a bit more self-pitying than I would want to share.

My flight was on a ground hold in DC due to weather in Atlanta. I had time to kill, and I couldn't find anyone to entertain me with text messages. That made me miss Shannon—she'd have been the one to help me pass that time. Then I thought it was at least a good thing my lateness wasn't going to mess up anyone else's plans. Then I was sad that I had no one's plans to mess up. The arrival of self-pity is easy to see coming.

And that led me to think about the difference between being lonely and being alone. Being lonely is easy to fix. Being alone isn't.

And that led me to an irony I appreciated. Over the past 10 months, technology has been central to how I have coped. Last night, technology was the reason I felt alone.

July 11

7:04 p.m.

As my Facebook friends know, I have been reunited with my laptop. Many thanks to the Delta people who work at RDU. The laptop came back this morning via FedEx and wrapped in a blanket that I suppose no one else had claimed for some time.

My laptop and I are now at a resort called Watercolor in the panhandle of Florida. I have work here tomorrow leading a strategic planning session for a company. The resort is all about families at the beach. I prefer to work in a place that looks like a workplace. I am all by myself—it would be easier to be in work mode if everyone else had a zombie-like disaffected look on their face—like they'd experienced too many planes and too many hotels in too few days. But everyone here is in happy/relaxed/family mode. I don't begrudge them that for a minute. It's just not a place I fit in. There are a lot of shops here, but

I don't really feel like shopping. If Shannon were alive, she'd be here with me and shopping would be fun. If she was waiting for me at home, I'd be excited to go hunt for something cool I could bring her. Seeing families with kids does get me to the bittersweet place—I am glad I don't have kids who are 8 and 4 anymore. But when I see a mom, a dad, and kids that age, I do experience a nice feeling. I don't want to go back, but I am glad I was there, then. The only sad part of the memory is that it makes me own that I'm older than I'd like to be. But that's just something to get over.

When I consider being here as a widower, I don't experience a great feeling. I just feel loss. The family thing—I moved through that the way you are supposed to. I had it, it was great, and now I am on to a different—and age-appropriate stage—like flavor-restricted diets. On the Shannon thing—that's just plain loss. I can't get to "I had it, it was great, and now I am at a different stage." That's not it. I had it. It was great. And now it's gone.

A friend e-mailed me the other day, after my note about the laptop. He shared that he worked with a Vietnam veteran who, in spite of a very dysfunctional workplace, was never rattled. My friend said the guy's view was, "There are only two things that warrant really being upset; one is when you have reason to believe that a loved one may not be able to take their next breath, the other is when you suspect that you may not be able to take your next breath." Otherwise, he said, "You have time and ability to work it out." I guess Vietnam gave people plenty of perspective.

When I try to call Reid at the house, my iPhone pops up a picture of Shannon...the one from Jazz Fest where she is posing by a sign that says "Beware of Ditches"—but a clever Jazz Fester modified it with a Sharpie to say "Beware of Bitches." Always makes me smile. That was a great Jazz Fest, but which one wasn't?

July 14

I was working at GSU yesterday and Reid called me—oddly—from the landline at our house. It is the first time someone has called me from my own house in many months—on my cell phone it tells me that Shannon is calling. If only it were that easy. It'd be nice to talk to her.

That's an example of the sort of thing I need to change. Roots from a relationship are everywhere. I would be fine if my phone just said, "Home calling." But I don't want to commit the act of removing Shannon's name from my contacts.

Yesterday was the psychiatrist. I've been off the antidepressants for a while now, and I think this time it's for good. He asked me how things were going—of course. That's my cue each time we are together. I told him about how I had to read the entire blog as a part of the process of trying to move towards a book. He asked what I thought. I told him that I was not in a very good place last winter. He laughed pretty hard and agreed.

I told him that I was so glad to have written when I did because I don't want to forget how badly I felt. He said I need to forget how badly I felt—that it won't really be possible to move forward otherwise. He said I have to let my brain adjust its memory of losing Shannon so that it isn't incapacitating. Going back and reading was close to incapacitating. I feel like forgetting is being disloyal; he assures me it isn't. He doesn't want me going back and reading much more—as for the book project, he said, "That's what editors are for."

What I haven't been sharing much about is what it's like to try and find someone with whom to share what's left of my life. "What's left of my life…" With a spin like that, who wouldn't sign up?

The doctor said I've clearly worked very hard to be honest on the blog and that it would be shame if I started pulling punches now. He also reminded me that I say I want to help people by what I've written and that it would be a shame if I missed the opportunity to share what it's like to try and see the world in color again.

He's right. He asked why I haven't shared it yet. I explained that I have the boys' explicit permission to do this—and that I think I have Shannon's implicit permission to do this. Not so with anyone new in my life. I said it's because I feel like it isn't fair to drag someone else into this—even confidentially, because truthfully it won't be confidential for long. People are smart enough to put things blogged about together with what they see in the real world.

So last night at the first of two retro-'90s concerts on tap for the weekend (Marcy Playground, Lit, Sugar Ray, Gin Blossoms, and Everclear), I explained my dilemma to my companion. She didn't hesitate for even second—she said, "You write what you need to write." She's great.

So maybe I'll make it to September 7th.

July 17

11:05 p.m.

I've written about feeling as if I am two people—one devastated from loss and another trying to find a way to carry on. I am still at a point where I don't see those two people integrating, although I am told they will. The two people first became apparent to me as I started thinking about how I was going to figure out how to parent Spencer and Reid after they lost their mom. I was crushed—I knew they hurt—but I had to be able to help them make sense of things and to "work the plan" to keep going forward, whatever form the plan ended up taking.

Then, the two people were an issue as I tried to find a way to get back to work. I had to be in the present to be even a little effective; I had to put a fence around the past.

Finally, I can say now that nothing so far has made the two people in my head more apparent to me than dating. And I can share that some women have made me feel like a relationship with them was going to reinforce this two people problem. Other women have created a situation where I sense help in bringing the two people into one. So perhaps that's one way to test whether or not someone might work— I think the right person will make the integration quicker, not reinforce the duality.

It's ironic—many days and many, many words ago, I shared the song "Tunnel of Love" that Shannon and I liked. The lyrics are appropriate again because it's now a new start. Now it's me, someone new, and for that someone new it may be that Shannon's hold on me is the scary thing. The right person won't be scared.

More disjoint tonight. I wrote some time ago about what I think is a better way to understand the stages of grief. Along the way, I wrote about how big a fan I was of shock. Shock was great. The power of shock. Now I am at a different place, and I am learning to appreciate the power of hope. From September 7 on, hope was really not a useful part of my life, but it is starting to be again.

Hope is powerful when it's justified; it's a very dirty and cruel apparition when it isn't. I dated a great woman for a couple of months last winter. I remember the first time we kissed. She said in a whisper—it really sounded like a thought meant for herself that simply slipped out—"This could work." That was a moment so full of hope for both of us. It worked for a while; the hope was a good feeling. But then it stopped working. She wasn't prepared to deal with the three of us.

So now I've been dating someone else for a couple of months. Early in June—which was early in the relationship, she had a trip out of town with her kids—a week at the beach. Coincidentally, I had to be in DC that week for work. We'd already had maybe 3 or 4 dates—enough to get the hope process moving. We both dreaded the week apart as a momentum killer. She liked to think of the fact that we independently were unavailable the same week as good karma—after all, it could just have easily been that I was gone one week and she the next.

Towards the end of the week, we exchanged text messages. I had just returned from DC and wrote, "Back in ATL." She replied, "Yay! I'll be there soon. Missing you today." My response: "This missing stuff sucks." Hers? "No—it's actually wonderful. It's been a long time since I missed someone." That's a great statement of hope.

She hadn't missed anyone in a long time. All I'd done for a long time was miss someone.

July 22

10:01 p.m.

So many things make me think of Shannon. What I am starting to appreciate is how differently they make me think of her. The best and the worst happened in the last few days. Last Saturday was the Crosby, Stills & Nash concert. Near the end of the show, I was just looking around and people-watching. I happened to make eye contact with a woman about my age who was being pushed in a wheelchair by someone—perhaps her husband. We smiled at each other. That's Shannon's nightmare in one picture. I am glad she didn't have to live that life. She would have been miserable living that life.

Today, I had my friend and her kids and grandkids over for brunch. One of the grandkids is two; I went down to the basement to find proper plates, cups, and utensils. It was easy to find. Shannon had it wrapped in bubble wrap and carefully labeled—"Divided dinosaur plate, bowl, spoon, and fork." That was wonderful—she was ready for anything. Of course, it was in a box she labeled "Grandparent stuff." That she didn't get there kills me. She would have loved living that life.

I picked up a copy of *Walden* by Henry David Thoreau. I haven't read it in years, but somehow I wanted to read it again now. To prepare, I spent some time online remembering about his life. I came across some great quotes. First, to help me remember that it isn't a good idea to go back and read this, I have to remember that he said, "Never look back unless you are planning to go that way." I don't want to go back. I just need to remember that.

The other just struck me when I came upon it—he apparently said (I have not found the context), "How vain it is to sit down and write when you have not stood up to live." I just love that quote.

July 25

8:30 a.m.

It's quiet here at the house this morning. I have a lot to get done on the computer, and I have retrieved a stack of records from the basement to listen to while I work.

I re-read some of this story, and I had a realization about why it was upsetting. The reason I was getting so upset was not so much because Shannon was gone. I was getting so upset because I was afraid of feeling like I felt last fall. The fact that Shannon is gone is something I can tell I am learning to take. I am so unhappy about it, but I can take it. What I can't take is to remember just how badly it hurt to lose her. That distinction feels somehow like it should be important to recognize, but I am not sure how.

Last Friday, my friend had a day off from work, so we planned to do something together. It ended up that the best option was to head up to North Georgia and hang out at one of the wineries. It was a good day in every respect except for the wine, unfortunately. I took my better camera along just in case—the mountains are pretty and generally wineries are pretty, too. I hardly ever use that camera because it's bigger to carry—but it does a much better job than the one that fits in a pocket.

When I got home, I brought the camera upstairs to see if anything I'd taken had turned out. The computer pulled up what was on the memory card. Pictures of me and Shannon in Napa in June of 2011; pictures of me and my new friend at Monteluce in July of 2012. That's all that was on the card. My first thought was that the camera sure missed a lot in those 13 months.

July 26

Ten (so far, just six) Modestly Offered Pieces
of Advice for Helping a Widower   11:00 p.m.

1. Don't ask me how I am doing. We both know I am crippled. Tell me you are glad to see me. That is reaffirming without forcing me to acknowledge how miserable I am and without forcing me to lie to you.

2. Don't tell me it will get better. I won't believe you, and it will sound like you are trying to minimize my loss. Just agree with me that this is the most horrific thing. Don't say the next thing you want to say—that it will one day be better. I don't care about one day. I only care about now and now it sucks. One day, I'll care about one day. But not today.

3. Don't worry that you don't have the right words. First, I learned there are no right words. Second, I learned that right after someone

said they didn't have the right words, they then shared perfect words. Just be as open with me as my public disaster has forced me to be with the world. What you say is going to be great.

4. Everyone reminds a widower to eat, but fewer people remind them to move around. Lots of people send food, but no one sends "activity." If you live near me, come over and ask me to go with you on a walk. If I don't feel like walking, offer to sit outside with me a bit. We don't have to talk. Sitting outside is a gateway activity to walking outside.

5. After my loss, mark down three, six, and nine months in the future on your calendar. Find a way sometime during those weeks to say hello, to drop off cookies or a plant, or the like. As the shock wears off, the loneliness starts to really hurt. I didn't get to where I could really understand how lonely I was until most everyone had gone back to their lives.

6. If it's been weeks or even months since my loss—and it's the first time we've been face to face—please don't say you are sorry for my loss. I know you want to show your respects so let's stipulate it. When you say it, you bring me back to a place I don't want to go. Give me a big smile, a hug if you feel like it, and let's stay in the present together.

July 26

> **11:00 p.m.**

On the way home from the Yes concert tonight, a Stevie Nicks song called "Say You Will" came on the radio. I've always felt like it could be about Shannon and me, and the opening lyrics were comforting to me tonight—it's about the way the right person makes you someone better than you are.

I've written before that I know one of Shannon's gifts to me was to help me be a better version of me than I could by myself. I'm trying to let her spirit continue to do that for me because I think the boys still need it and, frankly, I like that me better than the real me. I don't want to lose the someone else she helped me become. But it's hard for me to be moved by a spirit or a memory.

July 27

10:35 p.m.

Today was a visit to the psychiatrist. As is usual, he started with, "How are things going?" I said I would tell him how things were going, but that I wanted to ask him something first. He agreed.

I told him that I needed a suspicion confirmed. He knows I have been dating this woman for a couple of months. I explained that every time I meet a family member or friend of hers, the next day I get a report from her...the family member or friend has called her to share their opinion of me, whether or not I am a dangerous person, etc.

She's met a number of my friends, and no one says anything to me.

I said my suspicion was merely that this was normal. He said it was. He said my decisions about dating won't be on the timetable some people think it should be. So some people will disapprove of the "concept" of me dating; some people will just be uncomfortable entering in to the topic. Some people will still be missing Shannon too much.

It's interesting. I completely understand all the different ways it could be uncomfortable for others. Guess what? There are a few reasons it's uncomfortable for me, too. On the other hand, what a reminder of how alone it is to be a widower.

So then on to his agenda. I told him I was headed to New Orleans to visit Shannon's tree for what would have been our 27th anniversary. He asked what my friend was doing—he wanted to know if I had invited her. I looked at him as if I was a confused dog. He pointed out that what I was going to do was a pretty unpleasant thing and that sometimes people who care about you would like to at least have the chance to be there to help you through an unpleasant thing. I acknowledged that, but added that I thought it was sort of creepy to ask her. He said something to the effect of, "She's a big girl, right? Why not let her make the decision?"

So at tonight's concert I explained all this to my friend. She said I have a smart psychiatrist. I think I have a ridiculously understanding friend.

August 1

9:24 p.m.

When I started this, sitting down to write was very much like opening a dike. I never knew what I would write; sometimes when I thought I didn't have much to say, I couldn't stop. Niagara Falls—somehow the water never runs out.

Sitting down to write is different now. My thinking about Shannon is more like a dripping faucet. I collect thoughts over the day. Sometimes I remember the various thoughts—but I know I have forgotten some things I really wanted to share. Other times I make notes or leave a voice memo on my phone so that I can be reminded.

Here is what is on the list I gathered today.

1. A few weeks ago—maybe months by now—I called Shannon's cell phone to hear her voice. It wasn't there—the phone had just the generic greeting that the person with that number was unavailable. So that's the end of Shannon's voice.

With that gone, it was safe to go today and end her contract at AT&T. So I did. The salesperson explained that the contract had 8 months left on it, so I could cancel it, but I would still owe them for that time. I explained why the phone wasn't being used anymore and asked if that made a difference. She said she was sorry—and that it did. She needed a death certificate and said I could fax it to her later.

She was a sweet girl—before she killed the number, she stepped back in role and said, "I have to tell you that closing the number is something I cannot undo—the number will be permanently gone." I thought, *I'm not going to get to call it again anyway.* I said, "That's fine."

2. I think I wrote months ago that between January and September, Shannon and I went to hear music about 50 times. All those ticket stubs are neatly organized in the souvenir book she gave me for Christmas. All the tickets for the shows since have just been tossed on to a pile that sits center stage on her desk. I counted today. I've been to 63 events—6 hockey games, 2 baseball games, and 55 concerts since Shannon died. She'd be pleased that I didn't stop. She never wanted to keep me from something when she was alive; I know she wouldn't want to keep me from something now.

3. This is around the time of year that I got my iPhone last year. That means I have texts from Shannon on it—all the ones she sent between when I got my new phone and the days before she went in for the surgery. This weekend last year, Shannon, Reid, and I were in NYC to see *Book of Mormon*. All the texts are about the three of us trying to find each other in Times Square. It's a nice memory.

4. One of the nicer things today happened as I headed downtown for a meeting. I passed a neighbor, and she gave a smile. Not remarkable without the context that describes the way I saw it.

For a long time, the minute people saw me in a casual encounter their faces went in to a sort of a pity/sad/panicked because they didn't know what to say face. I understand—I've made the face at other people during other times.

The face today was just a smile—but to me that's just the point. I think it's the first time that in an entirely casual moment I sensed or registered a friend just seeing me as me—not as the me who got destroyed last September.

August 9

3:32 p.m.

Happy Anniversary.

I am in New Orleans at Shannon's tree. Tomorrow would have been our 27th anniversary, but since I will be teaching all day, I am observing today.

New Orleans has provided some classic bad weather for the sojourn, but it brings back memories. I had to drive through some pretty deep water on Carrollton Avenue and St. Charles Avenue to get to the park. I had planned to sit on Annie's bench to write this, but her bench is surrounded by water. As it is, I had to leave my shoes and socks in the car and wade through a mixture of water and mud (I hope it was just mud) up to my ankles to make it to Shannon's tree. And it is still raining.

So now I am in my rental car, with muddy feet, composing this before the battery dies.

As has been the case, I love being at the tree. It is really quiet here— everyone and every critter is hiding from the elements. The only sounds are the occasional streetcar and the bells from Loyola.

Though I love it, as I sit at the tree, I just don't know what to do. I try to talk to Shannon—the same thing over and over—I can't believe you are gone, we miss you, the boys are okay, I am okay, but we miss you...after a few cycles I realize that's dumb, so I stop. It's nice to just be here.

Reid has a ton still to do before heading back to school. Yesterday, he went off to buy sheets. He was asking me what to look for—he asked, "What is the deal with sateen?" I said, "I don't really know, but I know Mom didn't like them because they didn't wear well." I said he could try them if he wanted. He said no, if Mom had an opinion, it was evidence enough for him. He then said, "This would be so much easier if she was here. She would be driving me nuts, but it would still be easier. I miss her."

I miss her, too. And I really hurt for him—it was the first time in a long time that I felt hurt in my gut, not just in my head.

As for the present, I guess it is safe to use Linda's name since she's been outed on Facebook anyway. I tagged her at a concert a while back; usually a Facebook "check-in" from a concert gets a handful of "likes" and comments. That one didn't. I am not making anything out of it, but I could work something up.

All I can say about it is that I know Shannon well, and I truly know Shannon would approve.

> **6:09 p.m.**

Now I am out of the rain and waiting for what has become a long-delayed flight back to Atlanta. Plenty of time for the rest of the story.

On our anniversary, I can't help remembering the event itself 27 years ago. We started on a Thursday with what became known as the "prenuptial tubing trip." Neither Shannon nor I wanted to do separate bachelor/bachelorette parties—we wanted to spend all the time we could with all of our friends all together. That's how she always wanted it. Tubing was a New Orleans tradition—on the Tchefuncta River. So everyone piled into cars; we stopped at Fat Harry's Bar (our second home) and raided their walk-in cooler for many, many cases of beer and off we went. I don't remember it—I do have pictures.

Later that night, Shannon and her maid of honor went out to get rice. They took a taxi. Probably only in New Orleans does a taxi driver not wonder about a 2 a.m. run of two inebriated young women to buy 10 pounds of rice.

On Friday the 9th—today—we had the rehearsal dinner. The wedding party was small—there were maybe 15 of us. We had reserved a private dining room at Arnaud's in the French Quarter. Shannon's folks didn't show up on time. After a while, we got a call where they told us they had a flat tire. Remember this was long before cell phones—it wasn't easy to get messages around. Finally, we had to order their entrees for them—we had waited nearly 3 hours, and the kitchen was going to close. They did eventually arrive. Shannon was convinced that her mom and dad were not dealing with a flat tire— that they were in Houston fighting about whether or not they would even come to the wedding. Her mom had told her she wouldn't come if we got married outside the church; her dad had told her he wouldn't come if we got married in a church.

On Saturday, we got married in the morning—I think at 11. We had a wonderful reception. The restaurant where we both worked—and

395

where really we had met—let us use the building for free. We hired friends to work it and paid them cash. The manager gave us all the oysters and liquor we used at cost. We had a caterer that put on a good spread. It was a blast. We had to get married early so the reception at the restaurant would be cleared in time for their dinner crowd...and because Father Buddy wanted to be back at his church in time to watch the Saints' pre-season game.

Shannon and I stayed at what was then the Hotel Iberville. I think it's a Westin now. It was very nice back in the day...I stole a fork from our room service breakfast with the Iberville imprint as a souvenir. Shannon was not happy about that. Sunday we flew off to the Virgin Islands to honeymoon. I had to smuggle stolen property first out, then back in the country.

Shannon's favorite memory of the trip was the days we spent on St. John. We rented a Jeep and drove all over that island. I had a Jeep at home in New Orleans—but I learned how to drive a manual there where it is flat. Wicked flat. St. John is not flat. As we would drive along, natives would scream at me "Shift!" I never knew if they meant up or down. Shannon just laughed. She loved that.

Then 26 years passed in what feels like a blink of an eye. I think about that a lot—I am thankful for the boys because if they didn't exist, I'd be tempted to believe I had dreamt the whole thing.

When I think about 26 years we had I then think of all the years ahead. That's a long time to miss someone. Nearly one year down, a lot to go.

August 11

9:45 a.m.

Another first has passed. The first non-anniversary. Late last night, the phone rang. It was Spencer's number on the caller ID. Can't be good news, right? Spencer was letting me know that they were at the hospital. Reid had somehow ingested peanuts and was having an allergic reaction. They took a taxi from the music festival to the hospital, and Reid was being well-treated.

Spencer let me know Reid just wanted to send me a picture of him in bed with the oxygen mask on and IV in. Spencer thought he'd save me a heart attack.

We texted back and forth for an hour or so. The hospital released Reid, and they are going to be ready to go back to the festival—but not to that food booth—again today. At least they know where the nearest hospital is.

This picture is Shannon on St. John. Twenty-seven years ago tomorrow would be our anniversary. She still takes my breath away.

August 13

Monday edition of the psychiatrist this week. As is customary, he opened with, "How are you doing?" I told him that two thoughts had struck me recently. First, I told him that I thought my brain injury was clearly healing—I feel pretty "clear" in terms of my head. And I told him that my heart still hurts. Second, I told him that on the way to work this morning, I was struck by a good description of where I think I am.

Imagine that you just got off a carnival or amusement park ride—one that was so rough you thought you were going to puke, crap, and wet yourself all at the same time. You were literally scared to death. Then imagine you are off the ride—you are in no danger from it; you know you aren't going to ride it again. And then you realize a false sense of bravado beginning to swell up in you. You know it's false because it only exists in the mental space created by your promise to yourself never to go on that ride again. That's how I feel now. Sensing a bit of false bravado.

After Shannon died, I had a freedom that I am losing as I get better. I think this is important to understand. I didn't lose everything when I lost her, but I lost a hell of a lot. It is easy to be unguarded when you don't really have anything to guard. I guarded the boys; I tried to guard my job. I didn't try to guard me—I didn't care to because I just couldn't see how I could feel worse.

But people do get better, and as they get better, I am learning they start to have things to guard. But this stops being a true story if it's a guarded story.

Here I go trying to be unguarded.

The doctor asked me if I had any idea how lucky I am. I said I can't believe how lucky I am. You probably wonder what makes me think I qualify as lucky. I am that lucky because somehow or another I have found my way to a tremendous person who gets me, is good for me, and is happy to hang around me. She and I have each tried for three months to come up with a reason to question our good fortune, but the efforts have been to no avail. We have both been paying attention for some "gotcha" moment that makes it clear it's been a dream or a complex gag on some show like *Punk'd*. So far, no such moment.

Linda has a lot of the qualities I admired in Shannon. She is reflexively kind. She is great at taking and giving teases. She is smart and quick. She has an amazing smile. She has a ton of energy. She takes great care of her family. She has been through a number of very hard things in her life, and she is so buoyant and positive anyway. And she gets me. All those things were true about Shannon. But Linda isn't Shannon. The differences are less uncomfortable with each day that we spend together. That requires more explanation...it isn't something about her that is uncomfortable. What is uncomfortable is just getting used to holding a different hand...there is nothing wrong with her hand.

Shannon had two views of her likely future. In one, she lived to be 180 with a sharp mind in a body that couldn't do anything...that didn't even have enough energy to die, she used to say. In the other, she died before me. She was so insistent that when that happened I needed to go find someone to be with. I told the doctor that was yet another gift. I can imagine a man like me—but instead of losing his wife in the manner I lost Shannon, let's say she died suddenly in a car accident. I can see how much guilt that man might feel in trying to find a new partner.

Shannon is part of why I am lucky now. I am just doing what she would want. That doesn't take any of the strangeness away, but it does take away the guilt. And my hope is that would make Linda easier for my friends to take. My psychiatrist assures me that I am of sound mind. And I haven't made a bad decision about who to spend my time with for nearly 30 years...actually, I don't think I've ever blown that decision.

So Linda and I will continue for a bit to keep an eye out for the hidden camera. But at the same time, we are going to enjoy hanging out and taking care of each other.

I think that was sufficiently unguarded...it's all true, anyway. It was harder.

August 18

> ### 1:01 p.m.

A year ago today, Shannon and I were in the midst of dropping Reid at college. I have reposted the picture of Reid with Shannon in his dorm—this is what I saw through my camera a year ago today. This year, Reid is already in Boulder. He went to a concert at Red Rocks last night and will go again tonight. I fly out tomorrow, rent a big car, and we hit Ikea, the mall, and wherever else they take my credit card, I suppose, in an effort to furnish his rental house.

I can tell these next couple of weeks running up to the anniversary are going to be bad. I have toyed with the idea of getting back on the Lexapro for a while, but by the time it kicks in, I will be past a year and probably feeling better. If I'd seen this feeling coming a bit earlier, maybe that would have been a good thing.

Things continue to hit me in small ways. I was getting the Jeep checked out before the trucker came to load it and take it to Boulder and needed a ride to go get it. So I called Shak the cab driver I introduced you to a while back. He was full of chuckles and smiles, as usual. As we drove down my street to head towards the dealer, I noticed the ride was a bit rough and that he was really fighting the steering wheel. I asked about it, and he told me—laughing all the time—about how he was rear-ended a few days ago and was having to tough it out until the insurance companies figured out how to get the car fixed. I couldn't believe his positive attitude. I said it must be tough as a taxi driver to have your car in the shop. He said yes, but it was tougher to be in the hospital for a couple of days. He hadn't mentioned that at all. Still smiles and laughs. How does he do it? When I start a pity party I need to think of Shak. I should just call him to take me around the block and cheer me up.

I skipped Jazz Fest this year. I wouldn't have enjoyed it. But I am thinking about going next year. It is something I love, I always have friends there, and it may be the only thing I can offer the boys that would motivate them to visit me. To get ready, I contacted the woman who we've used as an agent to rent a house the last couple of years. She wrote back, "I was so sad when I heard about Shannon because both of you were such a neat couple, the kind of folks I would like to be friends with. (This is mostly NOT the case with the people I encounter on a daily basis…HA!)"

Her note made me feel good. I like it when someone or something reminds me of how Shannon was and how she struck people. I insist that if we were a neat couple, it's only because she was who she was and because of how well she smoothed whatever wake I left.

One more thing about the past, then something about the present.

I continue to think about the whole survivor guilt concept. I am more impressed by, to paraphrase from former Saints coach Jim Mora, "woulda, coulda, shoulda" guilt. I feel guilty about all the times I could have been a better husband. I think about how I wouldn't agree to replace the washing machine when Shannon was frustrated with it. I think about the times I could have been a better listener. I think about the chances I missed to make her life better. Those are terrible, pointless thoughts. It is so too late for them to do anything but make me miserable. There is a lot I woulda, coulda, shoulda done for her.

As for the present, Linda is very supportive of my writing, but she is not eager to read it. She read some rather by accident—too convoluted to explain—and said that if I needed her to read it, she would, but left to her own she'd pass for now.

I have no problem whether she reads it or not. I told her that if she read it the big takeaway would be that I really loved Shannon and that we both felt ridiculously lucky to be together. And she already knows that.

A few days ago, though, I wrote the post where I "outed" her by name. I cut/pasted that entry into a separate document, and when she came over a day or two later I told her what it was and said if she could, I'd like her to read it. She was glad she did. She quickly composed herself and teased, "I have a name!"

It has to be hard for her to deal with me, to deal with what others might presume about me and caution her about, and all that. But I learned that if I am talking about someone who isn't here almost as if they are—and talking about someone who is here almost as if they are not—that's pretty diminishing to them. Those words are not quite right, but I think you get it.

August 19

> 11:45 p.m.

There are not many occasions that I know just what I was doing at a specific time and date. I know where I was at the moment I got married, the moment Spencer was born, the moment Reid was born, and the moments Shannon collapsed and died. There aren't many others, though I could figure out things like graduations, friends' weddings, first days at work—that sort of thing.

Tonight is one of those few others. One year ago right now I was leaving this hotel to go to a concert. It was an outdoor concert—in the parking lot of the Boulder Whole Foods. Todd Mohr—of Big Head Todd and the Monsters—was playing. It was raining, and Shannon wasn't up to going. She understood I really wanted to go, so off I went. The texts back and forth between us are saved on my phone. She got a kick out of the fact that the concert had no beer tent, but there was a place to get a massage and another place with a bubble machine to entertain the kids.

It was our last night in town after moving Reid in to his dorm. She was packing as I was listening to the concert. She texted me, "This is the worst packing job I have ever done. Everything is just kind of thrown in—no order. It fits fine with room to spare." She had been worried about stuff fitting because earlier that day we had gone on a bit of a spree. She found a boutique on Pearl Street that had great clothes. She bought a bunch of outfits that were going to be easy to get on and off after her shoulder surgery—loose, drapey things. She felt characteristically guilty about the splurge, but they were going to be good. She never got to wear them, obviously. I gave them all away, tags intact.

I got back to the hotel around 10 that night. I sent her a text asking if she was up. She wrote back, "Yes/no—dozed off." I said I was going to have a nightcap in the bar if she wanted to come down. She said no. She said, "Love u."

This year, I spent the day with Reid at his house, Bed, Bath, & Beyond, and the hardware store. I met most of the roommates and parents—everyone seems mostly sane and reasonable. Time will tell. I couldn't help but spend the day thinking what Shannon would make of the place. I can tell you she would have spent the day with rubber gloves on with a bucket of Lysol. She wouldn't have just cleaned Reid's room—she'd have gone room to room wiping down the walls, dusting the sills, etc. All the kids would have a cleaner room than they do right now. The place is a wee bit on the gross side. But Reid and his roommates are beside themselves at the adventure ahead.

August 21

9:51 a.m.

I was riding up the elevator today with a woman my age—obviously the mom of a new UC Boulder freshman. She had a tray and a paper bag from the lobby Starbucks. I said someone was lucky that she was willing to be the runner. She said she had a daughter who was moving into the dorm today; it was her last chance to do something like that for her daughter. I sure hope it wasn't her last chance. I would have been better off observing elevator etiquette and remaining silent. I am now stuck thinking about all the things Shannon didn't get to do for Reid this past year.

Last night, I took Reid to Costco to get more house stuff. I figure he should have a membership card on my account. We go over to the membership desk to ask about it. I should have seen it coming. Just like I should have seen the inevitable path of the elevator conversation coming. The girl said, "With this membership you can only have two members, and you have you and Shannon on the account." So I got to let her know Shannon was gone. She made Reid a card. Awkward. I wish I had thought beforehand to take Shannon off so that Reid didn't have to experience that moment.

It is good I am leaving today—the freshmen and their families are arriving in force. Seeing the moms and dads with their freshmen is just a bit much. I told Reid I am going to visit him this fall, but not on Parents' Weekend. That about killed me last year. He is fine with that. I think that weekend sort of sucks for him, too.

August 22

8:22 p.m.

At the psychiatrist last week, I turned his favorite question, "How are you doing?" back on him. I asked him, "How am I doing?" He said I am getting better as fast as someone could cautiously get better.

I think that sounds like a fine epitaph…"He got better as fast as he cautiously could."

August 27

1:48 p.m.

I am on my way to Vancouver for some work tomorrow. To get to Vancouver, I had to make a connection in Salt Lake and that brought a nice memory to mind.

The last time I was in Salt Lake was a couple of years ago. Shannon, Reid, and I came out so he could snowboard at Park City. We met up with some friends—each family had rented a condo. It was a nice few days. Reid got lessons from a cool guy from Argentina, and Shannon and I lounged around, but that's not the memory that sticks out.

After the last day on the mountain, we decided to head in to Salt Lake. Shannon and I had "done" Park City, the people in the condo above us were incredibly loud—dozens of people marching around in ski boots. I found a nice hotel, booked a couple of rooms, and in we went.

Staying there was a nice change. We had a great dinner in town; we took Reid to see the Mormon Temple. Later that night, though, things changed. Reid—maybe just exhaustion from running so hard on the mountain—became very sick. He didn't want to bother us, so he spent the night alone in his hotel room, throwing up over and over.

When we checked on him the next morning, the situation became clear. Shannon and I both felt terrible that he'd suffered alone, but she felt especially bad—comforting the sick was her strong suit.

Anyway—the memory. The memory was how Shannon just kicked into gear in situations like this. And how well we could work together. My job—call the airline, push back our departure so we could see if Reid could get it together. My next job—the shopping list. I had to get Gatorades, medicine of some sort, and cleaning supplies. Shannon would not leave that for the hotel housekeeper. She stayed with Reid and helped him out; I shopped; Shannon cleaned; Reid rallied, and we made it back to Atlanta on the later flight.

That's an odd memory to keep from a vacation to Park City, but it's such a perfect encapsulation of one of the things that made Shannon Shannon.

August 28

8:48 a.m.

I get a lot done when I am on Pacific Time. So nice to be wide awake at 4:30 a.m....

I have been thinking a lot about my friends in New Orleans and hoping that Isaac turns out to be a dud as a hurricane. I have been thinking about Shannon's gingko in Audubon Park and hoping that it can take whatever wind the storm brings. And I have been thinking about all the sheetrock the MBA students and I have hung in St. Bernard in the 7 years since Katrina and hoping all those families make it through unscathed.

This is another trip that Shannon would have joined me for had things not taken the turn they took. She'd love the view from this room—out on the harbor—sea planes taking off and landing, mountains across the way. She'd be less crazy about the hills and how much harder that made it for her to move around. That's one mind shift that it's odd to be making. I loved to travel with Shannon—and I never felt that I missed anything. But it is true that the planning was around her limitations. It was okay—the boys and I understood, and it never was a problem. The few times I have travelled with Linda, it's about possibilities. I think it may well be that going forward it will be my limitations that are the hindrance to adventure.

Linda and I were going somewhere in the Jeep a week or so ago and an Electric Light Orchestra station came on. She started a bit of a chair dance and said, "This is one of the songs I had to do a routine to for my high school drill team tryout." I had to stifle a laugh. I have told you how many times Shannon sat next to me in a car and did exactly the same thing. I don't think 100% of high school girls were on the drill team. But it seems like 100% of the girls I find myself drawn to were.

Since it is 6 a.m. and I have already done a day's worth of work out here, I was trying to figure out the whole Facebook timeline. It requires a picture, so I was looking around for one. The one I posted here is Shannon, Spencer, and me in Baton Rouge—probably in the early fall of 1989—posing in front of our first house. Shannon struck me in it. We had so much hard work ahead of us. It reminded me of the trip I made to come close on the house. Spencer was born in April—his delivery was really hard on Shannon, and she needed follow-up surgery to take care of damage done. The trip I had to make to close on the house was around the time of that surgery—I don't recall. If it was before, she was physically miserable from the damage;

if it was after, she was physically miserable from the recovery. So she was miserable. And she was having to take care of a brand-new baby.

I remember after the closing, I stopped at a pay phone at a carwash on Perkins Road to tell her it was done. I remember my words—I said, "I want you to know you now own a really great house in Baton Rouge." I was excited. She sounded so tired—and I remember her words—all she could say is, "When will you be home?" I never understood the difference between a house and a home better than I did in that moment. And it never felt like it took that long to get to her to help than it did that day.

August 30

> 11:17 p.m.

Two quick thoughts. First, I thought—and people said—a new job was a great thing because of the fresh start it provides. I have learned already there is no such thing as a fresh start for a widower. During a break in class the other day we were chatting. I mentioned something about Reid and a student asked, "What does your wife think about that?" A harmless and perfectly fine question. So I had to say, "My wife is deceased, but if she were here, I am sure she would find it funny." It's the right thing to say—because it's the truth—but it creates sadness, and I hate that. It happens with colleagues, too. We have lunch or something and they say, "One day we should get together with our wives." Again, it is simply a kind gesture. But it's a gesture that reminds me there are no fresh starts. I think that's important for someone in my shoes to know and admit.

Second thing—I was driving in to work today and thinking about how long a list I could make of the things about me that are a mess. We all could make such a list—we are not perfect and all that.

Anyway, I think I could make a really, really long list. And that made me think about how special it is to feel loved in spite of having such a damn long list. And that made me want to thank Shannon. And it offered another way to measure what is lost when you lose a spouse. Unconditional love is something that exists at a whole different level from companionship, etc. There are not a lot of people in the world who will love you unconditionally. When you lose one…well, it is a big hole left behind.

Thinking about that made me wonder how long my list was when Shannon and I met—I have to think it's gotten longer over time. I have had more time to develop idiosyncrasies, to become set in my ways, to let my appearance go, and all that. In college I could lure Shannon in with a short list of dysfunctions and some sort of vague potential. As faults and failures emerged over the years, Shannon had to overlook more every year to continue to want to be next to me.

And that made me appreciate Linda more. She is having to deal with the long list from day one. It's jumping right in to the deep end of the pool. It's like I am already full-on crazy—not just "a bit different." I haven't hid anything from her, and she isn't scared. It is such a relief to feel accepted again—in spite of—not because of—things. I think it is probably easy to find someone to accept you "because of" something you have. It's harder to find someone who accepts you "in spite of." Shannon wasn't worried about the "in spite of" list and neither is Linda. That makes me lucky.

August 31

6:08 p.m.

Psychiatrist today. He noted tomorrow is the first of September. He's right. He wanted to know how I thought things would go during this last month of firsts.

I remember when Spencer was little—he'd be so excited the night before one of his t-ball or soccer games, or before Pinewood Derby, whatever—he wouldn't be able to sleep. When he was younger, I'd trick him. I'd go in to check on him and he'd say, "I can't sleep because I am too excited about X." So I would spend ten minutes convincing him X was not tomorrow, but in two days. He'd sleep. When he got older, he actually used to call me in before something and say, "I can't sleep—I need you to tell me we are NOT going to Disney tomorrow." I'd laugh, try to sell him on it, and he'd sleep.

I shared this with the doctor and told him I planned to tell myself that the 18th, the day Shannon died, is the date that matters. Then, when the 7th, the day I really lost her, passes, I will tell myself that the 7th was the day that mattered, and I missed it, and so I will just have to carry on. He doesn't think that will work.

So I told him about my other plan—that I am just going to keep reminding myself that it is just another day. After all, is the 365th day after a death really any different than the 364th? He said I'm great with the logic, but sadly logic is not involved.

410

On the 7th, I'll be in the middle of teaching a class at the moment the doctor told me about the success of the procedure, the moment they told me to get the car, the moment they made me come back in, the moment they told me what happened, all the moments they made me wait in that crappy little consultation room alone, the moment they brought me back to see her (the moment I feared she was gone) as they were readying her for the ambulance. Should be an interesting class.

On the 18th, I'll be teaching class for a client in Las Vegas at the anniversary of the moment Shannon died (thanks to the time zone difference). On the 21st, the anniversary of her service, I don't have anything to do. So what I think I am going to do is to go be with her tree in New Orleans—if it is still standing after Hurricane Isaac. I can work really hard to make the 21st the good-bye to this horrible year.

September 1

4:30 p.m.

Many years ago, Shannon and I went to see *Rent*. My first Broadway play—she'd been to many with her parents over the years. No one told us that no one dressed up anymore for plays. We did—it was fun. The play was powerful. The song "Seasons of Love" is great, and it's one I have thought about an awful lot this year. It asks how you measure a year—in minutes, cups of coffee, sunsets, laughs?

So five hundred twenty-five thousand six hundred minutes ago, give or take, Shannon and I went to Sarasota to see my dad and his wife, Lily, for Labor Day weekend. It was our last trip together. I took Lily and Shannon to St. Armand's Circle to shop; Lily bought these ridiculous hats with sequins all over them—bright yellow for her, bright blue for Shannon. Shannon was blown away, but sported it proudly. The last non-hospital picture I have of Shannon is the two of them wearing those hats. Lily has a copy up on the kitchen wall at her house. I promised Shannon I'd not ever share it with anyone. The hats are so outstanding that I am terribly tempted to break that promise, but I am going to be strong. As I said before, the picture here on the landing page is the last nice picture I have.

A lot has changed in all those minutes because this Labor Day I am again going to Sarasota to see my dad and Lily. This time, it's to try and talk with him about the need for him to move to the Boston area to an assisted living facility. My sister was there last week—she says some of the time he seems to know this is the plan; the rest of the time he acknowledges that one day there needs to be a plan.

Linda is going with me. I don't think I mentioned it yet, but those of you who love coincidences will love this; those of you who don't think there are coincidences will also love this. Linda works in assisted living—she is the VP of Marketing for a company that runs a number of adult communities/facilities in the North Georgia area. One of her many duties is to understand what level of care someone needs so they can be properly placed. Basically, her job is to help people in my position. Cue the *Twilight Zone* music, but it's another nice reason to have her in my corner. I am glad she is happy to come meet my dad and to try and help me help him. I think she'll be much more effective communicating with the people at the facility there than I am.

One last other thought...a few years ago when Shannon and I sought professional help to make sure our financial house was in order, we were introduced to a group through which I've bought life insurance. They are a good little company and have taken good care of us, though I have never become comfortable with being worth more dead than alive.

Anyway, since Shannon's death, they've been very thoughtful. Each quarter, they send me the next book in a series called *Journey Through Grief* by Kenneth Haugk. He's a founder of Stephen Ministries, is a chaplain, a psychologist, and a widower. Lots of qualifications to write on the topic.

I don't identify with the religious messages, and some of it is rather obvious in terms of advice, but there is a lot there that is helpful. And it's been a very kind gesture on their part to remember me month after month.

In this book—the last one—there are some great quotes:

Shakespeare (in Othello)—"What wound did ever heal but by degree?"

Helen Keller—"What we have once enjoyed and deeply loved we can never lose, for all that we love deeply becomes a part of us." I cried when I read that, and I am crying now typing it. I hope it's true. I think it's true.

Frederick Buechner (need to Google him)—"Even the saddest things can become, once we have made peace with them, a source of wisdom and strength." I haven't made peace with the saddest thing— I am mostly these days so disappointed that Shannon is going to miss so much. I am not sure how you make peace with the fact that she didn't get the next half of her life. But it's a good quote.

The part that helped me the most this time was the title of the second to last chapter—"Rebuilding is Not Abandoning." The main point— don't let yourself think that you have to choose between living again and remembering your loved one. I don't think someone in my position can hear that enough. I really want to do both of those things as well as I can.

September 4

It was a tremendous comfort to have Linda's help yesterday during my visit with my dad. It's a lot like having a native guide help you manage in a foreign city. I am trying to make progress today on finding a spot for him up in Boston near where my stepmom is moving, but oddly they aren't that interested in returning calls.

Before we headed down, I was looking at flights to go to New Orleans on the 21st and realized I have to teach that day, too. So I managed to schedule work on all three anniversaries. When it was two days booked, I felt okay about it—work is important to me; being back to work is important to me. But when I realized all three days were days I had accepted work, I was upset. No one to blame but me. It will be okay one way or another. Linda was planning to come down with me on the 21st—she immediately set about finding the next day that would work for us to go. Now I just need to verify the tree is still there! After finishing with this morning's list, Andre and I headed out to Spencer's old house—the one Shannon and I bought to rent to him and friends during his time here. I needed to see just how bad a shape it is in and how much work will need to be done before the next tenants arrive. In a word, tons. But truthfully that was money I agreed to spend the minute I let two teenagers with two big dogs move in. On the way there, I realized that Andre is heavy enough to make the "seatbelt" alarm in the car go off. Shannon wasn't.

It was a bit sad walking around the house—the last time I was in it empty was with Shannon as we were deciding whether or not to make an offer on it. She had a vested interest in the house because it was her plan—should I drop dead one day—to move there. She wouldn't want this big house all by herself, so she wanted us to be buying something in a decent neighborhood, with everything on one floor, and with privacy. This house passed those tests, and so we bought it.

There is still some trash inside that needs to be brought out. I rescued a big glass that says "Texas Ice Tea" from among the rubble. It was Shannon's. Spencer had "borrowed" it. I have borrowed it back. I don't think Shannon had any huge sentiment about it, but it is something that will always make me smile and think of her when I see it. Certainly I couldn't leave it to be trash.

The sixth stage of the grieving model is rebuilding. So that's:

Anger
Defeat
Detachment
Confusion
Acceptance
Rebuilding

It all still feels true to me. Rebuilding is, of course, the process of learning how to see the world in color again, of building something great that you'd be afraid to lose, and of opening yourself again to others. I wish it had come sooner, but my sense is it can't be hurried and still be done well. Now that it's here, I just have to try and do it as well as I can.

I have been thinking about stopping. I don't want to say things over and over again—at least not too much. And I certainly don't want to talk a lot but fail to say anything. So my plan continues to be to end soon. I wanted to end on the 21st, but I want to end at Shannon's tree.

So something will have to give.

September 6

There was a mass last night at St. Ann's to remember those who died this past year. I appreciated being invited, and I thought seriously about going. In the end, I just couldn't get comfortable with it. Shannon wouldn't expect me to go. The last time I was at the church was for Shannon's service. Today I feel just a little regret for not sucking it up and going, but even though nothing bad has happened to me at church, it just isn't a place I feel comforted.

Just two other small thoughts have been on my mind today, and they both have to do with trying to process what's taken place this past year. When I was a child—maybe 10—I remember being troubled by the fact that when someone died so little really changed. The same songs played on the radio, the Red Sox game was still on TV, and all that. It just seemed to be the world should be more impacted by a death. I can't remember what made me go down that path of thinking; I don't remember someone dying.

I think about those feelings now and about Shannon. Her death did change a lot—locally, anyway. My life, those of her kids, parents, friends—lots. But somehow it is important for me that her life have an even broader impact, and that is why I am hopeful for this project. I don't expect Major League Baseball to change the schedule, but I'd love for more people to know Shannon. I can't think of anyone who is worse off for having known her.

The second thought is more random—some words simply popped in my head as I was thinking about how fortunate I am to be seeing a bit of the world in color again. I suppose it's the chorus of the next great country song...the words that came to mind were that I thought I knew what it meant to be tired, but then we had a baby and I really knew. I thought I knew what it meant to hurt, but then I lost Shannon and I really knew. I thought I knew what it meant to be lucky, but then I survived this to find out how lucky I really am.

Given the meaning of the next couple of weeks, that's probably the last upbeat sentiment I'll be sharing for a while. Linda has been great—she has made herself available just in case I have a meltdown—"Nate Watch 2012" I suppose.

September 8

6:58 p.m.

Spencer's dog, Andre, and I are sitting in the front porch—unseasonably cool evening in Atlanta with a nice breeze. Definitely a preview of fall. I don't know how aware the boys are of anniversaries specifically, but I've tried to keep in closer touch with them. It isn't easy, but I think they are each okay.

Things yesterday went "as well as could be expected." I had a lot of help from lots of friends. Wednesday night at the Chris Isaak concert, Linda (who is pretty low-maintenance as it is) told me that she wanted me to just think of her as a best friend for the next couple of weeks; she didn't want me to feel like I had to entertain her or maintain any sort of communication the way a girlfriend might expect. Whatever I wanted to talk about or not talk about or do or not do was fine. She'd come around or not come around—whatever. Then the morning of the 7th, she sent a beautiful, cheerful vase full of flowers to the house. I took a picture of the flowers to include with a thank-you text I sent her on my way to the office so she could see how they looked; she forwarded the picture to my e-mail and said it was a way she could also send me flowers to have at work. Sweet.

I carried a pocket full of Xanax to work, but I didn't take them. I was thankful for a day of teaching. I think it would have been a more difficult day without something I enjoy as a distraction. As it was, around 1:30—the time, more or less, that Shannon collapsed, I was struggling on the inside. It's just odd; no reason for 1:30 on September 7 to be worse than 1:30 on any other day, but predictably it is. The time of each step taken that day is stuck in my head, and I expect it will be for some time. I made it, and that's a first that won't be a first ever again.

Last night, Linda and I went to Chastain Park to hear Matt Kearny and Train. Sitting at the concert gave me time to think. While I was sitting there thinking, Linda was making friends—just as Shannon would have—with the people sitting next to us. Comparing picnics, talking about the bands, talking about Atlanta traffic. Surreal for me to sit there and watch that.

What I was thinking about, of course, was about September 7, 2011. I was so overmatched; it was clear from the minute I saw Shannon's face in the recovery room—and the faces of those attending to her—that things were not good and were not likely to get better. I wanted a miracle, but I knew better. I was worried about how to get Reid home. I was worried about what to say to Spencer. It was just so terrible.

Thinking back does still engage my gut in a horrible way, but mostly my feelings continue to be anger with doctors who were not compassionate and sadness that I didn't have chances to give Shannon more smiles. Way back when, there were lots of times when we did things we shouldn't have—we lived a lifestyle with a bit of help from Visa and MasterCard. It took a while to work that debt off, but looking back now it was worth it. I would hate to have given her less than I did.

It was really hot last night at the concert, so tears mingled with sweat, and my secret was safe. I was glad to be out with people and live music.

418

Linda and I met after work to go to the concert in one car. After the show, I brought her to her car and then I headed home. On the ride I felt a sense of relief, but was also pretty down. I found myself hoping for some cheesy '70s Bee Gees song that would help me remember Shannon smiling. Instead, I got Bruce Springsteen's "Jungleland." So I turned that up loud and listened to Clarence Clemons play the saxophone and missed him and missed Shannon.

This process has to be pretty hard for Linda. Even though I am not doing anything crazy myself, the situation has plenty of crazy in it for her. She did have the best line of the week, though, when she told me how she was trying to figure out what it meant that her prayers were answered by God sending her an atheist. That is a riddle I can appreciate.

I was very glad to get a report from my team on the street in New Orleans that Shannon's tree survived Hurricane Isaac. I am looking forward to seeing it on the 23rd. As for the 18th and the 21st, I am going to try hard to stick to my resolution to let the 7th stand as the day that lives in infamy. But I will have a pocket full of Xanax just in case.

September 11

6:24 a.m.

Today is the 11th anniversary of the 9/11 attacks. It's one of those dates that we will always remember what we were doing when we heard the news. I had actually dropped my dad off at the Atlanta airport that morning so he could fly back home to Boston. I drove to work, and by the time I got in, the students were watching the news of the first plane on the TV in the common room. I did the math and knew my dad's flight couldn't have been involved—they would have just taken off from Atlanta when the first plane hit the World Trade

Center. But after news of a second plane proved it wasn't just one nut, no one knew how many other planes were involved. Thankfully, my dad's story ended with two days stranded at a hotel in Richmond, Virginia, and then renting a car to drive (the long way around NYC) back to Boston.

I was in NYC with Linda to go see a play Sunday night, but yesterday we went to the 9/11 Memorial. I think it is a stunning design. If you are in NYC, go.

After we visited, Linda asked if I was okay. The site is beautiful, but it is also just terribly sad, and she was worried I'd become collateral damage. It was a hard question to answer. The best answer is that it was a place—like Sleepy Hollow cemetery in Concord was on our visit last month—where I was reminded that I am far from alone in my sadness. My situation just isn't special; lots of people have stories that are just as tragic, if not more so. Being there does make me sad; it does make me miss Shannon; but it gives me perspective and perspective is important.

As our conversation continued, she asked if it was harder to be places with her that I've been to with Shannon than it is to be in places she and I never went. That was an interesting question. I told her that each is different. When I go to a place that Shannon and I have been, a nice memory emerges and then it's washed away by a wave of sadness. When I go to a new place, there is inevitably a small moment at some point where I hear a small voice in my head says, "This place is great, I can't wait to tell Shannon about it." Then that voice is washed away by a wave of sadness. Widower's equifinality.

September 12

Days with a trip to the psychiatrist are always good days to write. And days at the psychiatrist where I don't have an agenda are always the days I end up needing to do the most work. Today I didn't have an agenda.

We talked a lot about how the month was going. The doctor assures me that Septembers are just always going to be a bit bad from here on out. That makes me sad because September has long been one of my favorite months. The sky in Atlanta is the bluest in September. The heat is starting to back off—which ironically is why Shannon never liked September. It reminded her of what was ahead in terms of winter in a city she called Atlaska. In September I always felt relief that I had survived another summer. I suppose that part will still be true but in a different way.

I told him that the 7th had been a difficult day, but that I had made it. I told him that so far, the month did not have more frequent episodes of distress but that it was true the episodes I had were more powerful. Overall, I think I may one day be able to go on a long drive again. For so much of the past year, anytime my head was not 100% distracted by work, conversation with a friend, or something, my mind went to thinking about Shannon. That is why long drives were dreadful. I can think about other things now—at least I can give my brain a break from thinking about Shannon's end.

That made me ask him, how much better is the second year going to be? Everyone assures me the first year is the worst. Is the second year half as bad? Is it 95% as bad? I'd like to know that, but no one can say.

He asked what was going on with Linda. I told him that I thought the offer she made of being best friend and not girlfriend, while understanding and

421

generous, was not working out very well. I've been somewhat closed during this last month of firsts—I am like a person walking through a haunted house waiting to be scared. Linda is holding back, not wanting to make demands of me. This is creating a gap, and when we each see the gap it's worrisome. He thought I was right. I called Linda later and told her I just wanted her to be my girlfriend, not my best friend. She understood—she said it's funny because usually people get the "let's just be friends and not boyfriend/girlfriend" treatment. I was giving her the opposite.

I am in Boston tonight to make visits tomorrow with the goal of finding an assisted living community for my dad. As I arrived at Logan, I remembered all the times my dad came to pick me up—then to pick me and Shannon up—then to pick me, Shannon, and one or more of the boys up. He is the only person who ever parked a car and came in to meet me. That was really nice of him to do. Everyone else just slowed down as they drove past so I could jump in.

Since I mentioned a Garth Brooks lyric a while back and Father Michael was taken so aback, I've been thinking about the next country song to share. This is one by Brooks & Dunn that always made me think about Shannon. Like many country songs, grammatically challenged, but check out "Ain't Nothin' 'Bout You."

And all those things Shannon had that did something for me are things I've missed for a long time. She was such a good girl.

September 15

9:25 a.m.

Last night was a beautiful one in Atlanta. Linda and I went out to dinner and then to see the Indigo Girls at the Atlanta Botanical

Gardens. I counted the other day—Linda has hung in there for 23 concerts.

At dinner, she shared how much she appreciates that we are able to have fun doing pretty much anything. She suggested we should do an experiment—that we should think of something that really isn't fun, do it together, and see if we have fun anyway. I didn't hesitate. I said, "You can try to make the prep for my colonoscopy fun." After a bit of a laughing fit, she said, "Okay. I can do that." We'll see. Twenty-three concerts and a colonoscopy. She's a gamer.

I have been spending a lot of time thinking about and fiddling with what might become the last blog entry. So far, spontaneity has been the rule with each post, but I don't know that I can spontaneously tie any sort of decent bow on what the last year has been like. So far, a lot of time thinking and fiddling hasn't produced much of a decent bow, either.

The house feels really empty this morning. It's easy to sit on the front porch and remember how many Saturdays like this have passed. For years—dozens of years, it seemed—around this time of morning Shannon and I would be developing the plan for the day. Each kid would need to be somewhere for soccer...east of Atlanta, south of Atlanta, sometimes one place and one sport in the a.m. and something entirely different in the p.m. Divide and conquer. She'd grab one kid and head one direction. I'd grab the other kid and head another. I'd make sure she had cash for lunch. She'd make sure she had her book. We'd reconvene hours later and share stories from the games. Then we'd set out to try and do something, just the two of us. I am tired just remembering it.

That's not what today holds. Andre and I will keep each other company. I have to get my 2011 taxes in order...yes, 2011. I wasn't in much of a file taxes mood last winter. Not that I am in much more of a file taxes mood now. Now I don't have an excuse to procrastinate. Georgia State has a football game later at the Dome. Maybe I will go check that out. And there is a stack of grading. Funny—this list makes me as tired as the "running kids around the metro area" list—but it sure sounds a lot less fun. Anyway, it's a gorgeous day, and I am just going to work on my list.

September 16

10:59 p.m.

Many months ago, I had some help taking care of getting Shannon's clothes out of the house. It took a while; I couldn't do it all in one sitting. Last night, a search in the bathroom for a pair of scissors led to the opening of a drawer I don't think I have ever opened before. Apparently, the last person to open it was Shannon because it was full of her underwear. Surprise. The whole thing really makes me, more than anything else, grin. How appropriate, after all, for this discovery to take place around the one-year mark.

I spent some time tonight thinking about the last blog, and I realized how different my thoughts are when I focus on what happened a year ago versus what has happened over the past year. I am still working on that, but they are very different stories.

September 17

11:01 p.m.

On the road again for work. Watched—at least with one eye—a movie on the flight: *Best Marigold Hotel* or something like that. There was one character who had all the best lines. One of them was, "It will all be alright in the end. If it isn't alright, then it isn't the end." I liked that.

I had a bit of a meltdown today. I was getting ready for the trip but also trying to get ready to bring Andre to the airport Wednesday. Reid is so excited to have him. As I was doing this, I realized that when I got back from bringing him to the airport, I was going to again spend time—albeit on a much smaller scale—cleaning up signs of a life that is no longer a part of mine. Somehow that realization, the anniversary I am ignoring, and the discovery of the underwear drawer were enough to bring me down. Around that time, Linda called to wish me a good trip. I told her what I was dreading, and she said she'd go by the house while I was gone and box up all of Andre's stuff to ship off to Reid. That was a relief.

A year ago right now we were all waiting for Shannon to die so she would be free from the prison she fell into. Nothing really more to say than that.

September 18

8:55 p.m.

So now it has been a year. I think it is a good thing that I've pre-planned a bit of the last entry, because yesterday and today I've been at nearly a loss for words. Maybe that is because for the past year I have written primarily about feelings—I have not lacked for those, and those I can describe. On this anniversary I am fixated on an event that is still incomprehensible. What can I possibly say that makes sense out of Shannon's death? I sit, fingers poised above the keyboard, and wait for something to come and nothing does.

I spent the day teaching a group of 30 executives. It was a good day. When I started to feel myself slipping, I just remembered how much support Shannon gave me over the years and how she would want me to do a good job today. And I did manage to do a good job today. I was very glad to have a job I love and a day with a demanding audience that forced me to stay in the present and not slip into the past. It would have been so miserable today to be alone with my head. Of course, now here I am alone with my head...and the red-eye home.

Since I have no good words, I have something I've been saving. The first concert I saw was the Doobie Brothers at the Cape Cod Coliseum in the summer of either 1978 or 1979. I went by myself because the camp I was working at had closed for the summer and everyone had gone home; the owner let me stick around an extra night so I would have a place to sleep after the show. It is creepy to spend the night alone in a camp that the night before was home to 150 friends.

One of my favorites from their repertoire is 1975's "Take Me in Your Arms, Rock Me a Little While"—a remake of an old Motown song. The song has found its way on to my playlist a lot recently.

The song was written by the trio Holland-Dozier-Holland; they wrote lots of songs in the '60s for Marvin Gaye, The Four Tops, The Supremes, etc., but this one didn't get famous until the Doobie Brothers' version in 1975.

Nobody ever likes the way they get to say good-bye—though I wish ours had been different, I know that no matter what it had been, it still would have sucked, and I would still be complaining about it. If I'd had one more chance to hold Shannon or to have her hold me, would it have really made a difference in how I feel today? Nope. Today would still suck.

September 21

For much of the past 10 days, it's been easy to remember what I was doing a year ago. Today is harder, but I have a general sense. People were coming in town for Shannon's service the next day. I was running around with the boys trying to find dress shoes, to get suits altered, that sort of thing. A dear friend hosted a dinner at a nearby restaurant for everyone so that we could all be together. I think it was just the third time my dad met Shannon's parents. I remember feeling some sense of relief for Shannon that she was untrapped. I suppose I was relieved, too, but I hate that word. We use relieved when something is over or a threat is removed—we experience relief when our situation improves. In this case, nothing about the situation was improved. It was just the time to no longer dread the sight of Shannon not getting better and to substitute that with the dread of moving on without her at my side.

And I remember that I felt some sense of "showtime" for me in that I needed to be able to perform and get through the next 36 hours. That was only made possible by the wonder of shock.

It wasn't a particularly good day.

The rental house is rented. It was amazing to be reminded what a coat of paint can do to erase the evidence of two teenage boys with two giant, rowdy dogs. A fresh coat of paint is a new start.

That got me thinking about the hurricane metaphor, my efforts to rebuild, and the opportunities I've had to volunteer with the St. Bernard Project. No matter how many times you've volunteered with SBP, you spend time the first day getting oriented. Part of that orientation is their insistence that you imagine you are working on your grandmother's house. Their experience is that we would be

427

happy to take shortcuts that leave our parents to suffer, but that we wouldn't do that to our grandparents. Later in the day on the job, of course, there comes a time when a piece of sheetrock just won't fit, no matter how much time you spent measuring, cutting, rasping, etc. It is usually a big ceiling piece that takes everyone to hold in place. To help with the frustration, someone invariably says, "Well, I never really liked my grandparents!" We all laugh and then we work to get the piece right.

That made me think about the rebuilding I am doing. I want to rebuild something that is not just good enough for me—It has to be great for my kids and I want it to be something that Shannon would be proud of if she could see it. That's a much higher standard.

When I was in New York on September 10th, we had lunch with friends, one of whom was at work at the World Trade Center in 2001 when the planes hit. He commented on how that day—the 10th of 2012—was a day just like the 11th of 2001: blue sky, crisp air, no clouds. I get the feeling that for people in NYC any day like that brings the memory of those attacks to mind. My psychiatrist tells me September is always going to bring memories to me of what happened to Shannon. I would imagine it will. But I also remember how days like that day in NYC helped me after Shannon's death. It feels like I spent most of September 2011 on the front porch. I was so thankful for sun, blue sky, and for what passes in Atlanta as crisp air. I think every time I see what people here call a "perfect fall day" I will remember how it felt to lose Shannon and to try to find a foothold from which to move forward.

Last September, I didn't have any easy days, any bright days, and I certainly did not have any good reason things were going to get better. Everyone said to be patient. Let me be clear—that advice helps so little. But now I realize that's what I would be forced to tell someone a year behind me on this shitty ride. It has been a shitty ride—bad enough to color every experience I have had since. But now there are easier days, brighter days.

September 21

THE LAST BLOG (?)	9:30 p.m.

I got dressed to go to class today. I put on some suit pants, and in the pocket I found two Xanax. I wonder how long I will be finding them. It made me remember Shannon and her Kleenex. Every pocket had one—that comes with the territory when in order to keep your eyes lubricated you've had surgery to seal your tear ducts and when you can't work your eyelids the way you want to move those tears that can't drain off your eye. Just one of the physical inconveniences Shannon endured without a fuss.

Everything the doctors did to fix one of her maladies came with a cost. Can't open your eyes? We can put in slings to hold the lids up. Done. Now your eyes are dry because you can't close the lids all the way to blink tears around? We can plug your tear ducts so the tears can't drain off your eyes. Done. Now your eyes water all day and night. Kleenex. Done.

I have commented many times, especially this last week, about how it was a day where I could remember too easily what I was doing exactly a year ago. Today is a day like that which a lot of you reading along share with me. We were together to tell Shannon good-bye. Thanks for doing that on that day and for everything you have done since for Spencer, Reid, and me.

I intend for this to be the last blog entry on CaringBridge. My hope is to begin to focus more energy on Shannonsgift.com as a way to do some good in her name for families suffering from mitochondrial disease. I hope you will follow along.

No one is telling me to stop except me. I am stopping because I think I can. The hurt that I used to dissipate through this writing is different;

it's a dull burn now. Writing isn't as useful. I think at some level I need to stop to move forward the way I am supposed to, too.

Last winter, a friend of a friend who works in publishing was kind enough to talk to me about some of what to expect if I was serious about trying to have this published. She asked the question, "When will the book end?" I thought a minute—because at that time I hadn't considered that question. I said that it would end when the boys and I were back on a good path. I think we are on such paths. Of course, that's hard to know for sure without the benefit of hindsight. And I think it is safe to say that our footing on the path is unsure; we may slip.

So with that as prologue, what is there left to say? I haven't had a year without Shannon since 1982. That's really something to think about. 1982 may have felt a lot like this year—it's just a guess, but I can imagine that as a college kid I was lonely and uncertain about the future. That's a lot like this year.

I got a card in the mail from the pastoral care office at Shannon's church to let me know they were thinking of me—that's what the card said, "Thinking of you." That's kind, but to me what mattered is that they were thinking about Shannon.

Thinking about how to end this has had me thinking about how things end. Shannon and I used to like the *Newhart* show—we had kittens at one time named Larry, Darryl, and Darryl. That show had a great ending...Bob Newhart woke up in bed as the character he played in his previous show and shared with his TV wife this horrible dream he had about running an Inn in Vermont. We also liked *St. Elsewhere*. In that last series's last episode, it was revealed that the entire show was a daydream in the imagination of a child.

Unfortunately, the "it was all a dream" ending is not going to work here. This ending is going to be more like the ending of *M*A*S*H*— something that in 1983 Shannon and I—and everyone else in America—watched.

Music has been a big part of my grieving and recovery and so it makes sense that it should be part of the ending I get to pick for Shannon. To the best of my knowledge, her last favorite song (that is so sad to write) was "Funny the Way It Is" by Dave Matthews. The song is all about irony—how one kid walks miles for the chance to go to school while another drops out. And that it's funny that it's the way it is.

She really liked the song because to her it was so true. And it seems in some way true to me about this blog. It's about the end of her life, my nightmare, and our kids' worlds changing in a terrible, irrevocable way. But maybe it will help someone else.

Funny the way it is.

I also get to pick for me. I am going old school. Shannon just loved what seemed like an every-summer act—the Temptations and the Four Tops—"Temps and Tops" is how it was billed. I can't begin to count the number of times we went to see them. It feels like we saw them with original members, then a few original members, then a single original member, and finally just people who knew the original members. The Four Tops were right—our same old songs have such different meanings now that Shannon is gone.

This has turned out to be a bit more random an entry than I had hoped for. I had hoped for some clean finish—some bow-wrapped resolution. That was foolish. I can stop writing, but this isn't over. It isn't ever going to be over. I guess that's why shows like *St. Elsewhere* and *Newhart* end the way they end—with something contrived.

Thankfully, on the drive home today, I realized how this needed to end. It isn't perfect, but I think it is good. And it isn't contrived. There were about 15 minutes left in class this afternoon. It had been a good class and a pretty good day, considering what I was hiding from. We were just beginning to discuss change management practices in organizations. This material always starts with an introduction to Kurt Lewin's "unfreeze-change-refreeze" model. You begin a change effort by unfreezing peoples' positions—you create some dissatisfaction with the status quo. Then when you have softened them up through the seeds of discontent you carefully planted, you introduce a change. People will be ready for your "better" way of doing things. Then freezing is making the new as normal as the old had become.

As I was describing the unfreeze-change part of the model to the class, a memory of how Shannon broke the news of her pregnancies came in to my mind—the dinner at Slocum's for Spencer and the dinner at Louisiana Pizza Kitchen for Reid. She somehow intuited Lewin's framework and softened me up for the news. I took it better because of her effort.

Anyway, that isn't the important point. The important point is that as that realization made its way from the back to the front of my mind, I had the best feeling inside, and I could tell a big grin was forming on my face. I stopped for a few seconds to just enjoy the feeling. I was so struck I almost wanted to explain it to the class—I am sure they wondered what was going on. After those few seconds, the feeling subsided. It was a wonderful chance to be with Shannon for a few seconds. It felt so, so good at the time. It makes me cry now, but it felt good then.

That's what it is going to be like to be with Shannon from now on. I don't like it, but I will learn to take it.

I've taken a year for me. Now it's time to use that energy to try and do something good on Shannon's behalf.

Thanks one more time for sticking with me on this journey.

The
Second Year

October 6

7:21 p.m.

So it's been about two weeks since my "last?" entry. Over that time, two things have happened that brought me back. First, I had a surprising number of e-mails and calls from people who missed hearing what was going on. Second, I realized that I was still learning.

Initially, I was just going to treat the first as kindness. The second I was going to handle by privately journaling. I sat down tonight to do that, and it just wasn't the same. Pretending I am writing "you" isn't the same as actually writing you. Putting all this together makes it seem okay for me to come back here.

So here are some things that have happened these last two weeks that I'd consider important parts of this journey.

My psychiatrist wanted to know if Linda and I talked about the long term. We hadn't. We've been dating a bit over four months now and are still struck by how fortunate we are. He wanted to know when we would. Sounded like homework to me, so I asked Linda when/if she thought we should talk about the future.

I wish I could remember her exact words, but they escape me. Basically, she was referring to what I call my "pronoun problem." It works two ways. I say "we" when I need to say "I"…I say "our" when I need to say "my"…that sort of thing. The house, for example, isn't "our house" anymore. It's my house.

I do it the other way, too. The other day, Linda and I were driving to Charleston for a concert—Edward Sharp and the Magnetic Zeros. On the drive, I had a call…the caller asked what I was doing, and I said, "I am driving to Charleston." Well, I was driving to Charleston—but Linda makes that a "we" thing and not an "I" thing. She thinks it doesn't make sense to talk about the long term until I get my head around the pronoun problem, and I think that's a good idea. I should think of we as a "we" before we worry about anything in the long run.

The Sunday after my last entry, Linda and I went to New Orleans. Our first stop was going to be Café du Monde, but the traffic from folks heading to the Saints game caused an adjustment—so we (got the pronoun right this time) first went to Shannon's tree. You might think that would be awkward—but it wasn't. I refuse to make the tree a sad place. If I wanted a place I'd be sad to go, I could have buried Shannon in a cemetery. In fact, at some point during the trip, Linda turned to me and said, "I haven't seen you quite like this." I wasn't sure what she meant and so I asked her. She said, "You are happy." I think the spot is working.

When we got to the tree, we stood a few minutes, and I told the story about how the spot was picked, how my friends made it possible, and of some of the memories we had about the park from back in the day. After a bit, Linda asked if it was okay with me if I left her alone there— that she had some things she wanted to say to Shannon. So I left her there. I thought that was about the most thoughtful thing she could have done.

After the tree, we made it for beignets, a quick visit to Pat O'Brian's, lunch with friends at a decent place Uptown, and then a quick drop in on Shannon's cousin. Then back to Atlanta. That was a good day.

October 9

October 7 was the 13-month anniversary—I hadn't thought about it until today. I suppose that's a benefit of year two—you don't feel compelled to keep score in months anymore. This year will just be the second year, and I don't have to observe an anniversary until next fall. The reason to write today is that it was a trip to the psychiatrist, and as usual the visit offered me some insight. So while it's fresh on my mind...

I explained that I had considered the "future" conversation with Linda like a homework assignment and had brought it up with her. He was glad I was with it enough to recognize homework when he assigned it. I explained her response in the context of my pronoun problem. I offered that Linda was again being patient in that she was waiting for me to sort things out in my head and to get accustomed to where I am now. He thought that was understanding of her, but asked me to give her a message for him. He said for me to tell Linda to "start pushing."

I said I'd pass it on—it's homework and all—but that I wasn't sure she'd know just what he meant. So he explained. Basically, he said I am well enough now for people to stop treating me like a widower all the time. People should start expecting me to be pretty much in the present; people shouldn't feel like they have to treat me like fragile glass. These weren't his words, but I think he meant that Linda has a right to understand what I thought about what we were doing, what it meant, and what the future might look like. She shouldn't have to wait around forever for me to "get back to her"—so she should push a bit. I think she should, too. People at work push, my students push, my work clients push. Pushing is different in terms of personal life, but I have to get there. I think she should push for me to engage in conversation about the present and the future as a "we" or an "us." Linda and I talked about it a bit today—she always calls to check on

435

me after I come out of a session. She seemed to think, again, that I have a good doctor.

The second thing we talked about had to do with how I remember Shannon. There is a lot about Linda that was true about Shannon—they are similar in many ways. But there are also things about Linda that are different. An easy example I think I've referenced before is her energy. Energy was something—particularly over the last few years—which Shannon had in very limited supply. That lack of energy was a big factor in what we did—or more often in how we did what we did.

When Linda and I do something that Shannon and I couldn't have done—like sailing or standing all night in the crowd at the Allen Stone concert the other night—part of me feels bad. I don't think it's guilt exactly—I am not sure what the feeling is. My mind can't accept that I could be enjoying something new with a new person, I guess. It creates dissonance in that I worry that if I like something now that must mean I missed it or didn't like it as much before. That would imply there was something "missing" or wrong in my relationship with Shannon. But there wasn't anything missing or wrong—not anything that mattered, anyway.

And those thoughts make me feel bad because I have no interest in comparing relationships. This fairly cracked the doctor up. He loves it when I struggle with the fact that I am not Spock and that in spite of my best efforts, I can't build a rational argument to defeat my emotions and resolve my mental struggles. He said people compare stuff all the time—that it's a big part of how we make sense of where we are in life, how we feel about how we are doing, and so on. The comparisons don't need to mean anything derogatory about Shannon; they just will help me understand how I am doing today.

Looking back, Shannon gave me so many amazing memories, and there are so few things about our years together that I'd want to edit. Most of what I'd want to edit has to do with me—not her. She worked so hard and did such a good job of being a wife and mom and friend.

I'm not going to get to make more memories with her, and that's just brutally sad. Luckily, I have someone to make some new memories with. Tomorrow, we are off to Amsterdam and Prague—work and play. It's the first thing that Linda and I will do together that neither one of us has done before. Whatever the future holds, it'll be our first memory like that. And that's hopeful.

October 30

> 8:58 p.m.

It's a nice night for an outdoor fire so that's the plan. I took a quick trip down to Sarasota today to see my dad and to make some progress for his move here to Atlanta early next week. I was able to ship some things for his room, find some important papers that needed to be found, and talk with a realtor about selling the house.

The house is mostly vacant; Lily has moved on to Boston to be near one of her daughters and was able to use most of the furniture. One of the remaining pieces is the dining room table. Less than a year ago, Spencer, Reid, and I joined my dad and Lily, my sister and her husband, and my aunt and uncle for Thanksgiving dinner at that table. That won't ever happen again—nothing really like it will happen again. That was sad, but mostly the trip was not. I was glad to be checking things off a list and making progress towards getting my dad in a good situation. He's a really good guy, and I am glad to be able to do something to help him. I owe him for many, many early morning trips to various hockey rinks around Concord. And for some other stuff he did for me.

On the flight home I was bored. I brought only an iPad, so I couldn't really try to work. I have the CaringBridge app loaded on it. If I go to the journal part of the display for Shannon's page all my entries are there in rows. It's a great game to just let your finger fly across the screen, watch the entries buzz by like the Wheel of Fortune wheel, and then to just read whichever one it lands on. You can spin the entries up or down. It's an odd way to kill time.

October 23

1:59 p.m.

Something nice happened last night. I was dodging the debates and couldn't make myself care about the Bears-Lions football game, so I looked to see what I had on the DVR. One of the shows Shannon and I used to enjoy together was *Treme*. It's set in New Orleans in the immediate aftermath of Hurricane Katrina. The show follows a dozen or so characters as they try to do their own personal rebuilding.

For the most part, the show is "sort of" accurate—at least in my eyes. What the show does really well is drop in references, lines, and locations that locals understand and really get. In fact, there is a website that dissects each episode to make sure everyone can understand every one of the references.

When we were first married, Shannon worked, and I went to school. She worked at the Gallier House Museum in the French Quarter. Just down the street was a classic corner grocery store—the Verti Mart. It was gross, nasty, funky, whatever. But that did not deter customers who wanted a Coke or, believe it or not, food cooked in their kitchen. Everyone at the Gallier House called it "Dirty Mart."

In the episode of *Treme* I watched last night, one of the characters was explaining to a fellow musician that he was writing an opera about New Orleans. The friend was giving him a hard time and asked something like, "What do you mean, 'an opera about New Orleans?'"

438

The character was frustrated and said something like "An opera—you know—like Verdi—opera!" The friend said, "You're writing a song about the Verti Mart—that's great!"

Shannon would have laughed so hard at that exchange. It was the first time I've thought of something she missed and didn't feel crippled that she missed it and that I wouldn't be able to share it with her. I missed her in that moment, but it was okay.

October 30

> ### 9:44 p.m.

Tonight I am in my dad's house in Sarasota. My dad is in the assisted living community outside Atlanta. His wife has made it through Sandy (hurricane or whatever it became) outside Boston. It's hard to come to Sarasota and not remember the first time we visited—my dad having come in to meet us—the whole family. We were all surprised at how even the escalators move at a pace that fits the demographic. That's still true. They are still slow, and I am still surprised.

Tomorrow I need to finish going through my dad's remaining things, and I need to meet with a realtor about selling the house for him. Maybe life has provided me this to do as a way to have a forced break from what I have been doing. Whether it was provided or not really doesn't matter—it's here, and I have to deal with it.

It's been amazing to watch Linda with my dad. She is great with all the residents because she is great at her job. But she is just incredible with my dad. They have already become good friends. She checks on him several times a day and extends the visit whenever she can. I suppose it's an interesting early test for a relationship to move your dad in to the assisted living community where your girlfriend works, but neither

439

one of us hesitated for a minute. It was the obvious thing to do. Similarly, I am renting Spencer's old house to her son and his family. Another possibly interesting test for us, but no hesitation came with the decision. Over the past five months that lack of a need to hesitate characterizes a lot about how we get along. We are both still a bit uncertain how we fell in to what we have, but we are doing great at just going with it.

I am going to Boulder for Thanksgiving. It has been neat to talk to Spencer and Reid about preparing the Thanksgiving meal. It's still obvious who isn't around, but it is a bit easier to be focused on the three of us enjoying the three of us...and Andre. Linda is coming out for a bit, but will be back in Atlanta for work and family Thanksgiving week. She is threatening to break my dad out of assisted living and bring him home to her family for turkey. No hesitation there, either.

October 31

8:36 p.m.

I hadn't intended to write tonight, but I have apparently become some sort of odd neighborhood recluse where the kids don't dare trick or treat. I have had two doorbell rings for a grand total of three kids. Granted, I didn't get home from the airport until 7:30. Still, I tend to overbuy candy to begin with, and this year it's going to be ridiculous. After the trip, I can say it is equally creepy to go through the material possessions of a living loved one as a lost loved one.

Now I have time to kill...saw the psychiatrist earlier this week. He continues to be on my back about owning the present. It's proper harassment to receive. So here is a story about the present—or at least the recent past.

Linda and I had a wonderful trip to Amsterdam and Prague. In Amsterdam, we did a guided bike tour that was a lot of fun. In Prague, we did a long guided walking tour. There are so many beautiful sights in Prague, and the day of the tour was simply perfect—bright blue sky, not too cold, not too hot. We feel like we saw everything in a nearly grueling 5-hour adventure. Our guide wasn't satisfied with telling us things—we were quizzed regularly.

Her: *"Now what material that I told you about was used in this building here?"*
Us: *"Sandstone."*
Her: *"So what century does that mean it came from?"*
Us: *"1400s."*
Her: *"Good!"*

On the walk, one of the spots she showed us was the love lock wall on the canal in the Mala Strana near the Charles Bridge. I suppose it's a European tradition, and the wall in Prague is "known." She explained that couples fix a lock on the fence over the canal as a romantic gesture of their love. Who needs to worry about carving initials in a tree?

The last morning we had a very short time at the hotel before we had to head to the airport. Linda said to me, "Let's find a lock." I thought, *Really? Where? Now?* and one other word, befuddled thoughts. Then again, we were at the Four Seasons...no need goes unmet. So I asked the concierge where we might find a hardware store. Turns out there was one a few blocks away—and more or less in the direction of the bridge. We hustled there and bought a lock. Next need—a Marks a Lot marker. No luck at the hardware store, so we hustled back to the hotel. Surely they had one. When the people at the front desk figured out what we were up to, it became a team project. We had four or five people looking around for a marker. No luck. We had to make due with a regular pen.

Time was passing, and we still had to hustle to the fence to install the lock. So we did. When we got there, we worked hard to find a spot—

it is pretty competitive—and we locked the lock on the fence. I suspect it will be there for quite a while. Then we hustled back to the hotel just a few minutes late but still in time for the trip to the airport.

I am really glad Linda had that idea and that we were able to make it work. It's a great new memory. The picture is us at the bridge during our march through Prague.

November 20

I am sitting on the back porch of my rental house in Boulder, Colorado. The weather is ridiculously good. Not a cloud in the sky; temperature is supposed to be just 58, but I am hot sitting in the sun wearing jeans. Waiting for Reid to wake up so we can begin today's visit.

Linda and I flew out here on Saturday. We arrived early enough to have morning time to explore Pearl Street. After lunch, we went by Reid's place. We were glad that both Andre and Reid recognized us. Andre was cautious at first, and then after about 20 seconds he figured it out and was very excited to see us. The four of us went on a long walk around the CU campus to see the sights. Later that night, we took Reid to dinner at Flagstaff House, a pretty good restaurant up on the mountainside with a great view of Boulder.

After dinner, Linda and I were talking about Reid. She saw a lot of Reid coming and going last summer in Atlanta, but it really was just that— not much conversation. This was the first time they did more than exchange hellos. The meal was good and so was the conversation. In my talks independently with both Linda and Reid afterward it is clearly still a bit awkward for everyone. It's easy for Reid to imagine that Shannon and I would be doing this with him and that she would be the one in that seat at the table. It's easy for Linda to imagine the same. Even though it was surreal for all of us, we all had a good time and enjoyed each other's company. It's a process...

It's been important over the past couple of months for Linda to do things with me that are new experiences for both of us. Prague was an incredible example. She wants us to make memories that are not encroached on by the past. I can understand that entirely, but I am finding that it is also important for me to do things with her that I have done with Shannon—like visiting Reid in Boulder. Over the past year and a bit, I have come to see Reid a few times alone. I spend the time from the moment I get on the plane in Atlanta until the time I return home missing Shannon—because I am remembering what it was like the last time I was here with her. It hasn't been any different in Atlanta—at restaurants, concert venues, and so on. Until I have a memory in a place with Linda, I only have memories of that place with Shannon. Only having Shannon memories in a place hurts and makes me very sad, but somehow those memories are sweet when I have them in the context of a current happy memory in progress. So I am still learning.

Linda is headed back to Atlanta Sunday night to work and enjoy the holiday with her family, and I have been going between working, getting provisions ready for Thanksgiving here, and spending time with Reid. It's fun and lonely and quiet and relaxing all at once. I borrow Andre for an outing each day. Last night, Reid and I went to see Bruce Springsteen—Reid was a good sport. Tonight, I am off to see Steve Winwood. Reid's got plans of his own.

November 21

8:20 p.m.

Spencer and Reid are out together with Andre, as it should be. I took advantage of the empty house to cut all the veggies we'll need for the Thanksgiving feast—onions, peppers, celery, mushrooms, green onions. Spencer makes fun of my lack of proper knife skills so it is less embarrassing for me if I do the prep when he isn't lurking around. The cranberry sauce is simmering on the stove. Maybe I'll do some of the things, like stuffing, that are better the second day.

The boys' plan is to be back to get me and then to go out for dinner. I asked Reid where he was staying tonight—here at the rental house or at his apartment. He thought for a minute and said, "Probably here, it's nicer." I had to stifle a laugh; I am not sure what wouldn't be nicer than his apartment. The other day after Linda and I visited him, Linda turned to me and said, "I know I didn't know Shannon, but she would not be happy with that apartment." She's right.

At the Bruce Springsteen concert the other night, he did a different version of his ode to his long time sideman, Clarence Clemmons. He dedicated the song "My City in Ruin" to anyone in the audience who lost a mother or a father, a sister or a brother, a husband or a wife, and so on. I hope it wasn't too awkward for Reid—he didn't know the lyrics, but I did. He is singing about how can he begin again without her.

I saw Springsteen last February or March. Atlanta was one of the first nights on his 2012 tour—I think the Denver stop was one of his last. Back then, he was introducing Jake Clemmons, Clarence's nephew, as a new member of the band—taking over his uncle's very prominent parts. Jake killed it last winter, but he was so shy. Springsteen had to coax him to the front of the stage several times—it seemed he couldn't get back to his place with the other horns towards the back of the stage fast enough. Not this time—Jake was hamming it up like he had been on the road for years. He killed it again.

So Bruce Springsteen and the E-Street Band are finding their way forward without Clarence. I know they miss him. It isn't right without him, but what they have now is pretty good in its own way.

November 22

10:05 a.m.

Just a few quiet moments before the real work of preparing the Thanksgiving meal begins. Reid wants to eat early enough to be sure he is hungry enough for leftovers before going to bed tonight so the turkey needs to be in the oven in a few minutes.

What a treat to have both kids under the same roof last night. They both allowed as to how they had been looking forward to it, too. That was great to hear because when we are together it is so clear Shannon is missing—it's actually been easier for me to be apart from the boys or in pairs for that reason. I miss Shannon the most when it's so obvious she's gone, and it's most obvious when the three of us are together. The fact they are getting comfortable that we are a smaller family relieves me a bit.

I poked around on Facebook for a while and saw all the posts from folks describing what they are thankful for. I am thankful for a lot, but what comes to mind is exemplified by what happened last night. My dad—back in Atlanta—was running very high blood pressure—200/100—all day. He was disoriented, etc. Linda stayed with him—including driving to the hospital behind the ambulance when he had to go at midnight. She was missing her family time to take care of my dad so I could try to enjoy my time with my family. The last I heard from her last night was around 2 in the morning. She stayed with him until the hospital released him and he was back home at the assisted living. She only headed home herself after he was settled. This morning, she is going up there to have Thanksgiving dinner with him so he isn't alone before driving clear back across town to have another Thanksgiving dinner with her family.

I am thankful she's somehow found her way into my life.

November 23

12:48 a.m.

Thanksgiving is over and the Patriots soundly defeated the Jets. It was a pretty low-key day for us, and that was fine. The meal was delicious both as lunch and leftovers. We took Andre for a walk at Eldorado Canyon State Park in between feasts. And we really didn't do much at all after that except hang out. I will admit it was nice to crash for a bit on the couch and have Andre climb up to join me.

Since I was not quite ready for bed, I was killing time looking around Facebook. I couldn't believe how far back it goes. Apparently, I joined Facebook on July 14, 2007. Spencer was 18, and Reid was 14. My first action was a comment from Spencer that says, "I'm your only friend." A short while later, Reid posted, "Hurry up and get some friends so I can stop being your friend." They had bet me I couldn't get to 30 friends. Reid was sympathetic enough to not want me friendless—but couldn't wait to ditch me.

So now I am some 750 friends later and thankfully the boys have not unfriended me. They have blocked me from aspects of their pages, but I realize that's really for my own protection. Yet another thing to be thankful for is to have them in my life. They are good kids. All of you with kids will get this—they make me crazy; if they'd only listen things would be easier, and so on. But wow—they are growing up just fine. I wouldn't change a thing about either of them, even though— like with me—some adjustments might be in order.

I continue to learn things that lots of people already know. The second Thanksgiving without Shannon sucks just as bad as the first, but it hurts less. I am not sure how much the hurt is less because you can only feel hurt for so long, if it is because you "get right" in your head, or if it is because life offers new reasons to be thankful that offer a buffer. I suppose it's some of all three.

447

What I do know is that tomorrow night I will be alone at home. I'll get up Saturday to go see my dad and will be hoping he is okay. I may not have another night like this with Spencer and Reid under the same roof for some time. That's going to be something I miss.

The picture is today's sunset in Boulder. Remarkable.

November 27

7:29 p.m.

There are lots of times when I miss Shannon, but one that I know isn't going to subside is whenever I am presented with a classic "parenting moment." Whether the moment is precious or precarious, it is better when shared with someone as biologically and/or emotionally responsible for the kid as are you.

I don't talk to the boys very often. It might be two weeks between the times I hear their voices. A quick text exchange might happen a few times a week. It isn't that I can't get them when I need them—or vice versa. It's just how it works out. So it was odd for me when tonight I was on the land line phone with Reid helping him with a situation at the same time Spencer called on my cell phone for help with his situation. Couldn't help but think how nice it would be to do a quick triage on each boy and then hand the phone carrying the problem most suited to Shannon's skills to her (that would have been Spencer tonight) while I dealt with the other. Instead, I had to put Spencer on hold.

I am scared sometimes by these moments. Not that I can't handle them. And that isn't a dare to the boys to come up with something that sends me to an asylum. I am scared because of the way it reminds me that I don't have Shannon anymore and the boys don't have a mom anymore. They have some 30 years to miss something they should have. And there is nothing anyone can do about it.

Tomorrow it's off to Istanbul. Linda is meeting me there on Saturday after she wraps up her work in Nairobi. I am told by all who have been that Istanbul is a fascinating city, so I am looking forward to it. And to Linda's company. I think she is going to be loaded with stories from Africa—but hopefully there is room for some adventure in Istanbul. After Istanbul, I will make a last trip to New Orleans to join Georgia Tech MBAs volunteering in St. Bernard Parish. According to Delta, I will end 2012 having flown 102 times. I will do that and end up in the same place I started the year—at least geographically.

December 16

Shannon got a letter this week from Sister Margarita at the Handmaids of the Sacred Heart of Jesus in Athens, Georgia. When Shannon was active in the church here in Marietta, she was part of the Women's Guild. They did good deeds, raised money, and distributed it to local organizations that were doing important work. Sister Margarita runs an organization from a trailer park outside Athens that helps women who are in need. Shannon just identified with the mission, and it became one of her favorite causes. Sister Margarita was sending holiday wishes to Shannon. I sent her a letter to explain to the Sister what happened to Shannon and a contribution Shannon would have appreciated.

I am in New Orleans for my last trip to volunteer with Georgia Tech MBAs at the St. Bernard Project. I think this is the thirteenth trip, but I am not sure. I am glad the second year students—who I taught last fall before I left for Georgia State—were open to having me along. It will be a good couple of days.

Coming to New Orleans is a mystery to me. Sometimes it feels so wonderful—like coming home. Today it did not. Today it was a lonely experience. Today I wondered whether or not I should keep the city in my rotation. The biggest thing that happened here was Shannon and my beginning—there is no way to be here and not be reminded of that. You can't think about the beginning without being reminded of the ending. But lots of other wonderful things happened here, too: friendships, experiences, education, and just plain growing up. Can't see turning my back on that, either.

I met an old friend and her daughter for drinks before dinner tonight—it is something when you can legally be with the child of a friend for drinks—that means you are old. Anyway, the woman lost her husband eleven years ago this month. He was a good guy. You can still see the loss in her face—even though she is such a strong and accomplished woman. And you can see the loss in her daughter's face—she would have been something like 12 years old at the time her dad died. That is such a long time to be sad—such a long time to miss someone. I think about that and how far I have to go—and the boys have to go—and it is quite something.

Then I had dinner with Father Michael. He has had his own set of medical adventures this fall—it was great to have time with him and to get caught up. He happened to have visited Shannon's tree when the leaves were the stunning yellow gingkoes turn each fall, and he brought me a handful. They are beautiful. I am looking forward to the chance to spend some time at the tree tomorrow. It will be the usual— me trying to talk to Shannon about how the boys and I are doing, me unable to talk, and then me just sitting and thinking. And that will all be fine.

It's been a bit over a week since Linda and I returned from Istanbul. What a wonderful trip. Istanbul is not in my top five European cities, but it is a place worth visiting. Linda met me there after her trip to Africa—we took a boat from the European side of Istanbul to the Asian side so that she could boast that she was on four continents in one week—Africa, Europe, Asia, and North America. That's pretty cool. I had to settle for a mere three continents. Oh well. Linda's been amazing at helping me get the house ready for the boys. If it were up to me I would have skipped Christmas again this year. But instead we have a tree, it's decorated with ornaments made from concert tickets we've used this year and ornaments that are from the places we've visited. As we were finishing, Linda sent me to the basement to get some ornaments the boys liked—and told me to be sure to pick out a couple that were special to Shannon. She's great to offer—but when I was confronted with the box, I realized that Shannon didn't care about an ornament—she just loved Christmas with her boys.

December 17

It was a much better day in New Orleans today. I love spending the day working with the students on a house. It is incredible to spend 8 hours at work—hard, physical hours—with 12 people and not hear a single complaint. Everyone wants to be there, everyone identifies with the mission, and everyone wants to do a good job. Not like many "real" workplaces.

After dinner last night, Michael gave me the yellow leaves from Shannon's tree. I put them in a go cup—that's appropriate—Shannon was a big fan of the go cup. I was worried the housekeeper at the hotel might misunderstand and discard them, so they spent the day today in the hotel's room safe. I went by the tree tonight—the leaves have all fallen; the Park had spread fresh mulch around it. The tree definitely grew this year—it looks a bit more solid. I am excited to see it next spring. The sunset, the birds, and all the joggers made for good company at the tree.

Another day of sheetrock mudding tomorrow and then back home. Before I know it, Spencer and Reid—and Andre—will be home for Christmas. Should be interesting.

December 25

11:54 p.m.

The second Christmas without Shannon has passed. Our holiday looked a little more like a conventional Christmas than it did last year. It was fairly obvious, but still I spent some time night before last going back one year to the posts from our Jekyll Island Christmas. What's different? We have a tree. It's covered with concert tickets, ornaments from the places Linda and I have visited, and ornaments of the boys at various ages. I made an ornament out of one of the beautiful yellow leaves from Shannon's gingko in New Orleans. The boys, Linda, and I drove up to my dad's to have dinner with him at the assisted living center on Christmas Eve.

Other things are the same. I spent Christmas Eve and Christmas night without human company, but with Andre, while Spencer and Reid were out. Spencer has made three extraordinary meals for us—but this year no dressed up Ramen noodles and beanie weenie. It's good to have their company, to see how well they are managing, and to see them get along together. That was true last year, too.

It's now Christmas night. I am sitting in bed with Andre by my side. Spencer and Reid and I dined together, but they are now out with friends. Linda stopped by on her way home from her daughter's house. She has been extraordinary these last few days as she worked to put Christmas on for her two kids and three grandchildren—and as she found time to spend Christmas Eve with me, my boys, and my dad—AND as she found time to be with Spencer and Reid so they could get to know her a bit better. It was fun to stop by her family's celebration today and to remember what the day is like with little kids.

Shortly after Spencer came home last week, I realized he might want to know about some savings bonds he'd received as a kid that were now mature. I thought the money might help him out. We came up to check their dates and amounts—they were in a fireproof box in my office.

As I opened the box I found on top a bunch of cards Shannon had given me at various times. They were saved there rather arbitrarily while I waited for that special day where I would organize everything and all these random piles from around the house would come together in the right place and be put in the right order. On one envelope from a Valentine's Day, Shannon wrote, "You take a bunch of broken sticks (us) and weave us in to a beautiful bouquet." Quite a bit of hyperbole on her part, but what struck me was how much of a rush it was to see her writing and to "hear" her words. I helped Spencer with the bond question, and then after he left I read the rest of the cards to try and get the rush back. No luck—moment had passed.

In short, the whole experience of the past few days perfectly sets up a "Christmas past, present, and future" dream/nightmare. I guess I have been warned.

In about two weeks, Shannon would have turned 50. I wonder what we would have done to celebrate. I had a lot of ideas that were only half-baked—when I last thought about planning something I still had over a year to make it happen. She gave me a great 50th. I miss that I can't return the favor.

January 9

Shannon's 50th Birthday	10:21 a.m.

Happy Birthday, Shannon. I don't know what we would be doing today to celebrate—I had parts of big plans made, but of course they were never finished. It's one of Reid's last days home, so it is entirely possible Shannon would have wanted to hold our big celebration off until he was back at school—she wouldn't have wanted to travel if it meant missing time with him.

It was good to have the boys home. I think we all managed to enjoy Christmas a bit. Spencer was back in San Francisco for New Year's, and Reid was in Nashville with friends for a concert. I continued to be what my psychiatrist calls the luckiest unlucky guy he knows because I had someone so special with whom to ring in the New Year.

After New Year, Reid flew to San Francisco to spend some time with Spencer. After a couple of days, I hadn't heard anything from either boy, so I checked in with a text message. Reid's reply was, "Dad, the hookers are great here, and I had no idea tattoos were so cheap!" Spencer's reply was, "Dad, I haven't seen Reid since his plane landed." What great kids, eh? They will forever remain the best thing Shannon ever did, although I don't hold her responsible for their senses of humor.

I will spend much of today with my dad. I need to get him to a notary to take care of a bunch of documents for the selling of his house next week. He had a TIA last week, so I was in the emergency room with him for a few hours. That's never going to be a place I want to be, but then again, who doesn't feel that way?

January 24

9:45 p.m.

It's been a long time since I wrote. I tried a few times, but just couldn't find words that I thought mattered. Not much new has happened, though a few insights have revealed themselves.

I decided to try writing again tonight when I was back at the not-that-great neighborhood Italian place. I was sitting there with my Kindle reading the Steve Jobs biography. The salad is served family style, and I had a flashback to how Shannon and I would split the salad—no cucumbers, no chickpeas for her. Things like that happen every day. It happened today as I finally found time to try and sort through and store her jewelry. Actions such as this used to hurt so badly. Now they just give me an empty feeling—it doesn't really hurt, it's just so, so sad. There is a giant hole, but the edges around the hole have scabbed over.

The psychiatrist says that I have abandonment issues and that I probably will for a long time. I think he is right. I was very connected to Shannon—emotionally and practically. Her family was her focus— that meant she was nearly always there to get a call or a text or an e-mail, and she'd reply right away. She's gone, so that's gone. And it isn't just that she's gone—it's that I was left behind. I do find it frustrating when I can't get through to people I want to talk to or when calls/e-mails aren't returned as quickly as I'd like. I've got some other issues, too. Maybe for some other time.

I went to Tech for a meeting a week or so ago and had time to walk around the building and visit people. I got a, "How are you doing?" from one former colleague. It was offered with a bit of a knowing grin because they know how I dreaded that question for so long. I was glad I could say I was doing pretty well.

I don't have the hand of cards I was dealt, but I will play these cards as well as I can. And thankfully there are some really good cards in this hand, too.

February 4

11:30 p.m.

I am teaching a night class this semester—just as I was the semester Shannon died. Driving home late at night to an empty house is a stark reminder of how things were but also helps me feel hopeful because of how much different things are now.

When I am bored and alone one of the things I have taken to—just sometimes—is to find the entry I did a year ago and read it. One year ago today I took on the task of emptying Shannon's closet. I remember that very clearly. It was a surreal task, and it remains a surreal memory. Her closet is still empty, but it won't be much longer.

I ended the entry that day with these words:

I can't get over how unprepared Shannon was to die. We left the house that morning with every reason to believe we would be back that afternoon. Things were not supposed to be like this.

If you knew you were walking out of your house for the last time, what would you finish? Shannon would move the wash ahead. I know that.

I have different reactions when I go back to read what I wrote. Sometimes I am embarrassed that I sounded whiny, but other times I am proud because I captured something true. Sometimes it hurts to remember how badly I hurt; sometimes I am relieved to see that I am surviving as well as I have. I am pretty happy with the words I wrote a year ago today.

I wish it was easier to find a way to share Shannon's story. So far, the story—and the manner of its telling—has been considered by experts to be too unconventional. It is too long, it is too disjointed in its telling, etc. To me, the things held against it are the reasons it's different. It's honest. Some smooth, flowing, perfectly told story would be a misrepresentation of what life and death are. Life, love, death, grief— they are all messy. Anyway, enough from that soapbox...

As to the closet—Linda is moving in at the end of the month. It's exciting. We have been working to make the house a place she can be comfortable. She has been very good about being honest about what is hard for her to have around from my time with Shannon—and I have been good about making sure the things that matter to me are still around. Like everything else she and I have taken on during the past eight months, it all just works out—no drama. I've told Spencer the plans, but I haven't found the right moment yet to share it with Reid. It's hard to talk about this with them.

A year ago tomorrow I had a concert twofer—Railroad Earth at the Variety Playhouse and Mike Doughty at Eddie's Attic. I remember it well. I ended that entry with the following words...

> *I think I am always going to be two people from now on. The one who lost Shannon and the one who is trying to figure out what to do next.*

That's been true for a year. I suspect it will be true forever.

February 21

9:44 a.m.

A couple of weeks ago—maybe longer—Linda told me that Facebook recommended that she and Shannon should be friends. That had to freak her out a bit, but she is indeed a good sport. And today Linda is being a good sport by being okay with me spending our first day as what I romantically call cohabitants by visiting New Orleans.

Right now, I am sitting at the levee in uptown New Orleans after a visit to Shannon's tree and a po'boy from Domilise's. I wanted to visit the tree before Linda moved in, but that just wasn't in the cards. Move-in day was yesterday; today was the first day I could get free to come down. It has been a good day. As I arrived, a worker happened to be finishing up putting fresh mulch all around the base of the tree. It was nice to see it getting a little TLC. The tree is just beginning to bud—not as aggressively as the older specimen nearby, but I suspect it will be full of leaves when I come for Jazz Fest at the end of April.

Part of me wanted to visit the tree to somehow let Shannon know what was going on with Linda. Though I had plenty to say, I couldn't really find words to say much of it. Not that it matters, anyway. If some form of Shannon could hear what I would have said out loud at the tree, I am pretty sure that same form of Shannon would be clairvoyant enough to read my mind. So if she knows anything from today she knows that the boys and I miss her terribly, that she is never far from my mind, and that we are finding our ways forward and that our lives are good.

I shared a story from my childhood with Linda the other day. I don't know what triggered my thinking, but I remember being maybe 11 or 12 and fascinated with death. Maybe a grandparent had died—just not sure. My biggest surprise was that after someone died, very little changed in the world. It made me very sad—someone's death should matter more that it seemed to. Same songs on the radio, same homework, same television shows on at night—nothing interrupted, not even a ripple in the cosmos. I remember lying awake many nights thinking about that—and obviously now I still remember trying to wrap my head around that element of death. It should matter more when someone is gone.

I suppose that's one reason I so badly want to give more meaning to Shannon's life. Her life has lots of local meaning—for me, the boys, her friends. But that isn't enough—she wasn't done putting good in the world and I want to see that finished. So I still try to find ways to "Shannon" people—for Valentine's Day I sent a rose to each of the residents and staff at the assisted living center where my dad lives—that's the sort of thing Shannon would have thought to do, and I was glad the idea popped in to my head. Linda handled distribution for me so I could remain anonymous—and she got a kick out of receiving, at least for a moment, 10 dozen roses on Valentine's.

March 13

The last few weeks have been very full. Two moves had to be executed—my dad to an assisted living facility nearer to me, and Linda into our house. My dad's new place is wonderful—Linda did a great job in finding it. After she toured it the first time, she came back to tell me about it and had a great story. On the hallway from the front entrance back to what would become my dad's apartment is the salon. The salon has a large glass wall. Embedded in the glass are dozens of bright yellow gingko leaves. So every time she or I go visit my dad, we are reminded of Shannon.

That same night, Linda had to go by her place to get some last things. We had taken a small ladder over there so we could get curtains down, dust, etc. She went to grab the ladder and noticed how Shannon had made a laminated label of a "family business card" so whenever she lent the ladder out it might have a better chance of finding its way home. Linda did great staying light about the two "reach outs" by Shannon in the same night. Things like this just remind us that Shannon is around and is part of our relationship.

Last weekend, Linda and I took my dad to see the Atlanta Opera do La Traviata. I have tried very diligently to get him out as much as possible—not just to doctors, but to eat at restaurants and now to see a show. He is grateful and I, of course, insist it is not a big deal. I figure all the hockey practices, baseball practices, etc., that he schlepped me to entitle him to have me suffer the occasional opera.

I realized, though, that a part of what I am doing when I take him places and transfer him from the wheelchair to the car to the wheelchair to the real chair (if he will let me) to the wheelchair to the car and to the wheelchair again is proving to myself that Shannon and I wouldn't have slowed down, had she lived long enough that her disease forced her in to a wheelchair. She feared that limitation, and I tried to assure her it wouldn't slow us down. If I can do it for my dad, then I know I would have done it for her. It really isn't something I need to prove to myself—I know better. But it is still reassuring.

Last week at the psychiatrist, Linda came along. It's been valuable to me to have her there, and I think it is helping her know how to deal with me. Mostly, he encourages her to stick up for herself in making sure that I cooperate in making the changes needed around the house for it to feel like her home. She'd be too accommodating of me without his encouragement, I think.

March 27

8:25 a.m.

I have learned that there are four stages I go through whenever I am confronted with some milestone, however large or small, in moving on. Taking care of removing Shannon's things from the house and deciding to begin dating are two prime examples. First I deny I am ever going to do it. It doesn't need to happen, I don't want to do it, etc. Then there is a stage where I know the bridge has to be crossed, and I am very angry about it, yet I can't bring myself to do it. Next, that anger turns to deep sadness about needing to do it—but I still can't. Finally, the time comes when I have to do it—nearly in that same moment that I have that realization.

At the psychiatrist Monday, he nodded knowingly as I described what was to me a real insight. Wasn't so much to him. Turns out research on how people deal with change has previously shed light on my "discovery." In the "pre-contemplation" stage, people have "no intention of changing their behavior for the foreseeable future" says one website. The next stage is "contemplation," where the individual is aware a problem exists and seriously considers action, but hasn't made a commitment to action. Then comes "action," where the individual is ready to exert a great deal of effort to making the change.

Linda came with me again yesterday. She tried reading the blog at least in part because she wanted to see if she felt she could add something useful to the story. It's hard for her to read, she shared, because I sound so sad in the writing compared to how I sound when we are together. It makes her worry which set of my feelings is "real." So I tried to explain that both are. I write now when she isn't around. When I am alone is when I reflect on what's happened in the past, what it might mean, and what I should make of it. It hurts to do that, so I write. When we are together, I am in the present. I don't need to write because I don't hurt.

The doctor pointed out that part of the value in what I've been trying to do should be not just to help others understand despair but also to know that there is recovery. So I should write more about how having Linda in my life is helping me see in color again.

I've been reluctant to say too much about Linda and our relationship for a few reasons. In the beginning, it was that I wanted to not drag her into the drama. I was scolded for that, and so I outed her. She's in the blog, but I suppose in a somewhat neutral way. Since the doctor, I've been thinking about why I hadn't revealed more since outing her. A few reasons come to mind. Months ago, I started writing for catharsis and support, then I got a little bit better and began to write more to try to understand grieving. So a goal was to try to honestly account for that process. Now I am better still, and I am coming to understand more about recovery. In that context, it's easy to talk about Linda.

On the other hand, it's equally true that the blog has been about my love for Shannon. And I think that's how most of you still reading seeing it. In that context, it seems odd to talk too intimately about Linda.

And, I know Linda's daughter reads the blog. That's been interesting—I have taken to providing Linda with an "advance copy" of recent entries so that she isn't blindsided by something in a call from her daughter. I think Linda's daughter is great—but I think she may be the only reader who could be less than 100% on my side, which I understand; she owes much, much more loyalty to her mom than she ever will to me. And I understand that she wants to protect her mom. But I've become so comfortable talking to people I know are in my corner that the thought of someone understandably less so is a little disquieting.

Finally, I sometimes feel embarrassed by my situation. My doctor is right; I am without a doubt the luckiest unlucky guy in the world. So many people never find—as one friend so eloquently put it—the lid that fits their pot. I had the perfect lid, I lost it, but somehow I found another one. Amazing. That makes it a little hard to write about, too.

March 29

8:07 a.m.

Late yesterday, I learned that one of my former students had just died from pancreatic cancer. His wife of 20-ish years is also one of my former students. They have kids—I am not sure how old. My guess would be high school age. Younger than Spencer and Reid were when Shannon died.

From what I can gather, it's been a two-year fight. On some level, maybe that helped her prepare to lose her husband. As I write that I think it's a great example of something we hope is true because we want things to be easier. My guess is that today it's of no help at all and that she just hurts like she's never hurt before. Maybe in a year she'll be thankful for the memories they made in between the diagnosis and the death, but right now it's of no consequence. My bet is that no matter the warning—her life—and her kids' lives—have just been shattered.

So later today I'll go look for a card, and I'll struggle to find the right words to offer her some comfort when comfort isn't possible. I'll try to find some way to welcome her to the club, so to speak. I already marked my calendar for eight months from now. That's when everyone but her will have moved on. And that's when I'll try and do something nice for her and her kids in his honor.

April 2

8:53 a.m.

Last week, Linda and I went to hear Eric Clapton with a group of friends. It was an amazing concert—he is just outstanding and has such a repertoire of great songs. I can't play guitar—I don't really know much about music or technique, but what I do know is that his playing is really perfect. It's never too fussy, never over the edge; it's always grounded and controlled. Fast or slow, loud or soft, every note is exactly how it should be.

Friday morning around 4:30 a.m. the phone rang. I managed to answer and found myself talking to a woman wanting to know if I was Reid Bennett's dad. In my semi-awake state, I did my best to figure out if this was a scam or something serious. The woman was good at her job—she let me wake up, and she calmly explained to me that she was calling from a hospital ER in Cabo San Lucas and that Reid (there on spring break) was their newest patient. Reid had a bad infection in his leg and was there for treatment. She gave me the number to call back to talk to him, so I did.

Long story short—he missed a step running up some stairs and scraped his leg. Later, he washed the leg in the shower—but not with

464

antiseptic. The famous local water gave him cellulitis. A day or two later the leg swelled, etc. The doctors also said the shin was broken.

We talked a bit; Reid was really tired and wanted to sleep. We made plans to talk again in a few hours after he got some rest. I hung up the phone and filled Linda in on what happened. And now I finally get to my point—Linda knows how to help me just like Clapton knows how to play guitar. Her every note is perfect. I am so thankful for that—it would have been so much more terrible to hang up from that call and then be alone in a dark bedroom. And I didn't just have anyone to listen, console, support, and advise—I had someone who did it perfectly. Every note.

All the uncertainty about Reid made for a very unsettling weekend. I looked at flying out, but he'd be on his way back to the US not long after I could get there. We made it so either Spencer or I called him every two hours or so in the hope he wouldn't feel too alone. He made it back to the States Sunday, as scheduled, to find his apartment had been flooded by a burst pipe. So he arrived back from spring break with cellulitis, a broken leg, and homeless with a ruined computer, damaged school books, etc.

I talked to him yesterday morning and asked that he just keep in mind that today was the day it all was going to begin to get better. He went to doctors here and found out the leg isn't broken; he chipped his shin. He went to an infectious disease specialist who reassured him the treatment he got in Mexico was proper—but that there were concerns the Mexican drugs were not always "right"—some irony there, I suppose. Their illegal drugs are supposed to be pretty good. Anyway, that doctor gave Reid 5 more days of the antibiotic made by a good old US company. On Thursday, he goes back and gets checked out—hopefully the infection will be gone, and if it isn't, they'll start more IV treatment. And slowly, the living situation will get sorted out.

April 3

I never was able to muster the will to write to my friend, P, yesterday, so I made sure I did it today. P is my first friend to lose a spouse since I lost Shannon. It's been a struggle to try to find the best message to share with her. I have tried to recall what I was thinking and feeling those first few days after Shannon died, but my mind won't let me stay there long enough to really get it. If I could get it, perhaps I would know the right thing to write. But though I can put myself back there for a moment, my thoughts quickly return to the present—returning isn't a choice I am making; it's automatic. I suppose that's a good thing.

I sensed from nearly the first card or e-mail I received after Shannon's death that people who had been through something similar somehow had a knack for finding the right words. It bothers me that my experience hasn't given me enough insight to "know" how to help her—but I suppose the true insight is that there really isn't much that could go in a card that would help her.

This is what I wrote. I give myself a B-.

P,

It's just terrible you lost K. I think about you and your kids now every day. When I do, I look for some magic words of comfort to share, but I'm not convinced they exist. From the first days you and K began to be a couple all those years ago at LSU, you struck me as a powerful team in so many ways. I hope you will remember that one of the reasons you guys have been such a great team is that you are so powerful yourself.

I realize losing K may not feel to you like losing Shannon did to me, but I want to share that for the longest time after I lost her, I couldn't see the world in color. It feels like so much work and it feels like it takes forever, but now I can. I hope the kindness of friends provides you the lift the journey ahead will take. Never hesitate to reach out if I can help.

I promise I'll be thinking about you and wishing you strength.

It has been a month since I wrote, but here I am alone in a hotel in DC with not much else to do. And Shannon's been in my thoughts a lot lately—what with Spencer's birthday, Jazz Fest, and soon Mother's Day. Tuesday will be 20 months since I lost Shannon. That seems like such a long, long time.

When I was in a more hopeful place about something bigger coming from the blog, I agreed to do an episode of Story Corps. Although I still like the idea as a way to leave some more evidence of Shannon's good heart behind, when it got to be time to do the recording, I couldn't. I feel badly about it because I let some people down. They had prepared a list of questions that I should be ready to answer. I wanted to know what the questions would be—who wouldn't want to know what was going to be on the test? I wanted to be prepared. But I think knowing the questions was part of why I couldn't go through with it.

Here are some of them:

How did you meet Shannon? Was it love at first sight?

How did you know she was "the one"?

Did you have a "best time" with Shannon?

How has Shannon's death changed you?

Shannon and I met first at my fraternity house at Tulane. I was not there much—I had started working at the Chart House and that had become my fraternity. I had a night off the night of a mixer with her sorority and that is where we met the first time. She was not impressed and I was not paying much attention.

A few months later, she appeared at work at the Chart House. I remember coming up the stairs to get ready for work. It must have been a Saturday, and I must have been the closing bartender that night because I was arriving after the restaurant had opened. As I came up the stairs, there she was at the hostess stand. It really could have been something staged for a movie—the hostess stand sat on a catwalk that had been built between two buildings that had been combined to make the restaurant. The catwalk had a huge skylight that ran its length. So the effect was that whoever was the hostess was, at the right time of day, bathed in sunlight at the top of a long flight of stairs. I re-introduced myself. I don't know about love at first sight, but I remember that I did feel at first sight that I had to get to know her and that I wanted her in my life. And I remember how jealous I was when practically every single other guy who worked in the restaurant was taking their best shot. It didn't take long for us to become a couple and that is what we faithfully were for a very long time.

How did I know she was the one? I am living all this again now with Linda. I suppose everyone needs his or her own data to reach that conclusion. For me, I think it is acceptance. And I don't mean that in the sort of "settling" sense of the word. That's not it. It's feeling that who you are is all they need. It's feeling that who they are is all you need. It's realizing that neither of you is perfect, but knowing that they are perfect for you. You are accepted for who you are and what you have to offer. "You" is all you need to be.

Did I have a best time with Shannon? We had millions of precious moments. Most of them are lost in the madness of life's pace, but there are a bunch still around. The best times, though, were whenever she smiled at me.

How has Shannon's death changed you? That's a good one. It destroyed me, but I am still here. One of my favorite bands is the now disbanded New Orleans Radiators. They sold a T-shirt at their shows for years that said "Too stupid to stop." Sometimes it feels like that to me, but I think it's more likely that I'm "too scared to stop." That might have been true, too, for the Radiators.

I sit here and don't know how to seriously answer that question. I do know that however it changed me, it wasn't worth it.

The last time I wrote, Reid was in medical limbo from his entire spring break episode. No need to go into great detail here—it will have to suffice to say that he is healed and ending the semester—he assures me—in good form. Linda and I went to see him early in April and he looked wonderful. What a great kid.

Linda and I had a wonderful time at Jazz Fest. 24 bands in three days, untold plates of amazing food, and pretty good weather made for a great experience. I am so glad that Linda is a convert—she already has her eyes on next year's Fest, and we already rented a house in New Orleans for the first weekend of May.

Mother's Day is next weekend. So far, Shannon's birthday, the kids' birthdays, and Mother's Day are the worst. I think the reason is obvious. On Mother's Day, I hurt for the boys. They don't have someone to bitch about having to celebrate. That sucks.

A year ago today, I was sad to be missing Jazz Fest with my friends, but I knew I had to take a pass. This year, things are so different. A year ago today, I hadn't met Linda. The one year anniversary of our first date is in about three weeks. That doesn't suck.

The new picture is morning dew on a leaf on Shannon's gingko in New Orleans, taken when Linda and I visited the tree last weekend. The tree looks wonderful.

May 15

9:30 p.m.

One of the tasks I have struggled with for years was my desire to convert the pictures of the kids into digital files. I have done some scanning over the years, but it was clearly going to be an endless task. After Shannon died, the pictures became both more important and more impossible to handle. Thankfully, I have help. I found an online service that does the scanning for you—using machines that I trust are a lot faster than the little scanner I got from Office Depot. I hired a friend to disassemble the family albums and pull photos from all the Eckerd's Photo Shop envelopes Shannon had carefully labeled and organized over the years. I e-mailed the company because they need to know how many you are sending in order to charge you properly. I asked if I really had to count all the pictures—there were a lot. I told them I guessed there were maybe 1500.

They said that in the end, the machine would count but that for now I could guesstimate using a rule of thumb—an inch of stacked pictures is about 100. So after my friend stacked up the pictures I went downstairs to measure them—fifty inches, 5,000 pictures. What an odd way to measure life. Shannon and I had fifty inches of memories together.

In the context of how things have been going, the conversation today with the psychiatrist came around to this blog. It's grown complicated because its ending depends on its purpose. He asked me what the blog is about. I reiterated my view that the blog began as a way for me to organize feelings, to achieve some sort of a catharsis, and to be heard and helped by friends—and even some strangers. As time went on, I remained committed to it because I saw in the effort a way to possibly help others faced with pain like the pain I was enduring. I felt an opportunity and even a responsibility to try and document, as honestly as possible, what I thought, felt, and feared after losing Shannon.

I have known for some time that most of the people who have followed along—especially for this long—don't see it that way. They see it first as a story about Shannon or a story about our life together. It's those things to me, too, but that isn't what I sat down to do. I sat down and wrote to grieve. Then I sat down and wrote to try to make something good come from something awful. The former was nearly as important as Lexapro. The latter has become a frustration.

If the point of the blog was to help me grieve, I can stop. I am not well, but I am better. Certainly better enough to be able to get what I need to move on from my work, my friends, my family, and Linda. If the point was to tell a piece of Shannon's story or of our life together, well, plenty enough of that story has been told.

If the point was to tell a truthful story about what it is like to lose, grieve, and try to live again then it's more complicated. Trying to live again requires talking about Linda and what she is going through in trying to be with me. And it requires talking about what it is like for me to be in love again. Linda, like most of you reading, sees the blog as the story of my life with Shannon. Like me, she appreciates that the blog honors Shannon and what Shannon helped me build and helped me become. Even though she knows she is part of my story, she isn't sure she belongs as a part of that story.

471

So when I put all that together I know that it is time to end this. I have talked bravely about ending before—I suppose those were times I wished I were well enough to stop. Now I know I am well enough to stop.

So how does it end? I am going to miss Shannon forever. The way I miss her will probably continue to change—it's different now than the way I missed her in September of 2011. I am going to be sad and angry forever that she didn't get to have the second half of her life. It was going to be great and she earned it. She got screwed. And I am going to worry forever about Spencer and Reid and how they are managing without their biggest fan. Sometimes it's hard to be with the boys because as they grow and start their own lives the one thing we still have in common is Shannon. And that thing we have in common is nearly impossible to talk about.

But I am also going to remember how afraid Shannon was of whether or not her body would hold up, and I am going to remember that the exit she had was likely not that different than the exit she would have designed. She would say that she got out at the top.

As far as recovery goes, I have already admitted the doctor was right and I was wrong. I was so afraid of being alone, but there are women out there, and it is possible to find a perfect partner for the journey ahead. The path from Shannon's death to where I am today began in a horrible place, but every small step forward brought me closer to a beautiful place. It's been over a year and a half to get here, but where I am today is wonderful and the forecast is pretty good. I have a really ugly scar on my heart and still a lot of work to do to heal my injured brain, but I have found a beautiful and amazing partner who isn't afraid of any of that.

I think this is about as neat an ending as any story about life can provide.

Postscript

Linda has proven she can more than keep up with my addiction to live music. More important than keeping up with me, though, she's proven she can put up with me.

In conversation one night late last fall, she revealed that she had never seen Van Morrison. I told her I couldn't imagine how she has managed to cope so well in her life while carrying around such a deficiency. I set out to chase Van Morrison down. He was playing in Ireland on St. Patrick's Day, but we couldn't have organized quickly enough to get there. However, a seed was planted. I spent some time online checking out who was on tour in a great locale and quickly found the show to see—Bruce Springsteen in Rome, Italy in July. It would be our splurge for 2013.

We built a great itinerary around the concert—a few days in Athens, Greece, and then a few days in Rome. The fact that Linda broke her foot in June—just two weeks before we left—didn't cause her to flinch about the plans for even a minute—we were off.

I was so glad she wanted to carry on with the trip because I had decided last winter that I was going to ask her to marry me. Greece was going to be the venue. Some people might point out that Rome would be more romantic, but there was no way I was going to manage a secret and try and keep track of a ring—while keeping it hidden from her—for days on the road. We saw amazing things on the trip; Springsteen was great, but the fact that Linda said yes was greatest.

My psychiatrist had prepared me to be patient as friends got used to the idea of me being with someone else. He said it would be the hardest for Shannon's friends. Well, Shannon's friends have more or less disappeared from my life. I'm not complaining, although I had hoped some of her friends were "our" friends. I think these people did their part to honor Shannon's memory and then just got to a place where they thought it was safe to back away. By backing away, they have saved themselves awkwardness. They might be surprised to know I miss them, but I understand.

My friends have been great in welcoming Linda, but watching them watch me also taught me a lesson. I have written about the tremendous space people give a widower—for a time, you experience a great deal of tolerance regarding the way you look, what you say, and what you do. As you regain your footing over time, people expect you to be more and more normal. Dating is the last place you lose this slack—my friends were kind and supportive about me dating women who they just must have known were not a good fit. It took reflecting on the end of one such relationship for me to realize that. It may be the last place that a widower gets his good judgment back. And I am so glad I did.

The boys have been amazing about Linda's presence in our lives. From the start, they welcomed her as a friend. They weren't just polite, they didn't just tolerate. They have absolutely treated her as an equal part of our family—at least the way our family plays at being family. Of course, she is great with them, too. Over the past year, they have all done a wonderful job of making sure that this relationship that is so important to me is nurtured. They make a great team. I wouldn't wish to change a single thing about the way the three of them get along.

One night towards the end of our trip, Linda and I were winding down from a long day of sightseeing. We are both fans of irony, and we both knew the trip was providing its share. I had long anticipated one day travelling abroad again with Shannon. It was always a possibility that her health would have declined; perhaps she'd need to be in a wheelchair and perhaps there would be places we couldn't go. Instead, I was travelling abroad with Linda who, because of her broken foot, needed to get around on a knee scooter, and there were just a few places we couldn't go. Some people in my position would be deterred or at least frustrated by the way a partner's broken foot changed a trip—especially one who had plans to make a proposal. But nothing about the trip's circumstances was anything I hadn't long ago agreed I could handle.

It's just another way that Shannon prepared me to carry on and live. I am betting I'll find more.

Acknowledgments

Shannon didn't have a chance to say good-bye. Or perhaps she was spared that sorrow. Either way, I want to help her with that.

Shannon's adult life revolved around our sons and me. No one worried better, no one anticipated needs as well, and no one was more constant and unwavering in their love and support than Shannon. For those reasons, I know she would want to say thank you to all the teachers, doctors, coaches, coworkers, and friends who helped her take care of the three of us.

Shannon had a modest number of very close friendships that sustained her. She would want to thank her gang from high school for helping her have a place while she was in a place where I don't think she ever was entirely comfortable. After we began dating in college, Shannon formed the friendships that would carry her for nearly three decades. I hope those people know how special they were to Shannon. They are all still in my life, so I have, I hope, many more years to remind them of how important they were to her.

Shannon had two very important friends during the years the boys were growing up, Victoria Tomaszewski and Teri Jarley. They were such important supports for Shannon during a time I was less available than I would have liked—and when the kids were a bit more challenging than she would have liked.

Acknowledgments

Shannon would want me to thank her "cousin," Dionne Ducote, in New Orleans. Dionne has been her best friend since childhood— we've spent many Mardi Gras celebrations, many Jazz Fests, and even a hurricane drill or two with her and her family. Now, Dionne keeps an eye on Shannon's tree in Audubon Park for me. And Shannon would want me to thank the entire Alello family, but especially Diane, for being such good, kind, and dependable friends during and since our years in Baton Rouge. I know both Dionne, Diane, and their families will continue to be important to Spencer, Reid, and me.

I'll close this way. Shannon would want to encourage the doctors who treated her and all those who treat people with mitochondrial disease to keep working towards treatments and eventually a cure. Let's make it so good people like Shannon can stick around a little bit longer.

Shannon and Mitochondrial Disease

Shannon was diagnosed with mitochondrial disease during her college years and while she and Nate were dating. She was seeing Carlos Garcia, a physician she dearly appreciated, at the LSU Eye Clinic in New Orleans for problems with her eyes—particularly a droopy eyelid. Among the many tests she underwent was a muscle biopsy. That biopsy was sent to Salvatore DiMauro, a neurologist at Columbia University in New York City. Dr. DiMauro was of the opinion that Shannon was afflicted with mitochondrial disease.

Little was known about mitochondrial disease in the early 1980s; there was no cure, and while there were experiments going on with various nutritional supplements, there was no demonstrably effective treatment. Shannon determined it was something she was going to have to live with; she was told her decline could be fast but that it was just as possible that she would live a good life and die from some other cause before the mitochondrial disease became a more serious problem. Her main concern was whether or not she would pass it on to any children she and Nate might have. She was told the greater risk was to her health in carrying a child. She was not deterred.

Shannon's mitochondrial disease was very much in the background during her twenties and early thirties. Her pregnancies were hard work, but she delivered very healthy boys who appear free from mitochondrial symptoms. As she entered her late thirties, it was a more regular occurrence for her to quickly become tired. Many times she could have a very active day, but that would need to be followed with a day of taking it very easy to recover. In her forties, other symptoms that could have been attributed to mitochondrial disease began to appear. In addition to the furthering of easily tiring, she had problems with her vision, difficulty eating, and with digestion.

So what exactly is mitochondrial disease? Mitochondria are entities or organelles that exist inside of almost every cell in our body. They perform a vital role—supplying the energy that our bodies need to function. Everything that we do with our mind and body—seeing, breathing, thinking, moving—requires energy. Mitochondria are "power plants" supplying that energy. They turn raw materials found in the food we eat and in the air we breathe into a substance called ATP (adenosine triphosphate). Our cells use ATP as fuel.

Without enough ATP, children cannot appropriately develop, grow, learn, move, or even sleep. Adults like Shannon are unable to sustain brain, muscle, and other vital organ function. A deficit of ATP can also cause invisible damage in some disease states, leading to early failure or dysfunction of organs, or just a chronic state of inefficiency leading to pain, fatigue, changes or limitations in thinking and learning, and increased susceptibility to acquired diseases.

While Shannon's case may seem unusual, it's very likely that you know more than one person whose life is impacted by a mitochondrial disorder. Mitochondria play a role in autism, Alzheimer's, Parkinson's, Lou Gehrig's disease, Type II diabetes, heart disease, chronic fatigue, and some cancers, including breast cancer. In short, nearly every major disease that affects humans as we age may have part of its genesis in mitochondrial dysfunction.

Even though scientists have known about mitochondria since before 1900, the area of mitochondrial medicine is still relatively new. The discoveries of most mitochondrial diseases have occurred within the last thirty years. Because the field of mitochondrial medicine is relatively new, drug development for mitochondrial disease has really only just begun. The road to successful new drugs and drug therapies is long and expensive.

So what happened to Shannon during that routine procedure that caused her death? As in many cases, it is hard to say without a doubt. Mitochondrial diseases are complex disorders that can have serious effects on many organs. Even minor illnesses and procedures can be a significant cause of morbidity and mortality. Sadly, Shannon's health became increasingly fragile. Like many individuals with mitochondrial diseases, her body could not tolerate even seemingly simple surgeries. Mitochondria are in all of our cells. They take the food we eat and turn it into energy, the energy that every cell needs to survive. Without this energy, cells fail.

Shannon had been living with her mitochondrial disorder for her entire life of forty-eight years. For some mitochondrial disorders, this is a very long time. Organs become weakened and fragile. Although I never met Shannon, I had the honor to meet Mr. Nate Bennett following her death. My hope is that our discussions would help Mr. Bennett understand the disease and understand why we lose our loved ones with mitochondrial disease prematurely. I reviewed the information that Mr. Bennett kindly provided. Shannon certainly had a rare mitochondrial disease called Kearns-Sayre Syndrome. This disease is pernicious, advancing slowly and damaging many organs during a person's life. The eyes stop moving over time, and it becomes impossible to hold the eyelids open. It becomes impossible to even look up, down, or side-to-side. Almost all other organs such as heart, liver, kidney, breathing muscles, hearing, and brain are affected, slowly losing their ability to function. All this happens because the mitochondria are failing and cannot produce enough energy. Her body was unable to handle the stress of a routine outpatient surgery, most importantly the muscles that are important for breathing. What is routine for most people was not routine for Shannon.

Today there is hope for people like Shannon with mitochondrial diseases. Shannon represents what we need for all our patients with mitochondrial diseases, no matter which of the hundreds of types a patient has. Shannon is a force for physician education and awareness, a force for improved understanding in management and care, and a force for treatment. As I have diagnosed and managed patients for almost thirty years, I have worked on discovering gene mutations that cause mitochondrial disease. Our first understanding of these diseases allowed us to diagnose patients, but sadly offer them few treatments. My greatest excitement is that we are now studying new treatments in our laboratory, as are other scientists around the world, which will help children and adults with mitochondrial disease. Shannon will forever be part of the energy of discovery.

With great honor and respect,

John Shoffner, MD
Medical Neurogenetics
Neurology, Biochemical Genetics, Molecular Genetics
Atlanta, Georgia

About the Authors

Nate Bennett is a professor at Georgia State University. He moved from his home state of Massachusetts to New Orleans in 1979 to attend Tulane University. There he met Shannon, and in 1985, they married and began their life together. That life ended in the fall of 2011, when Shannon, who suffered from mitochondrial disease, died from complications of what was to be routine outpatient surgery. Nate now lives in Marietta, Georgia, where he has begun a new life with his second wife, Linda.

Echo Garrett, a thirty-year journalist, is the author of a dozen nonfiction books, including the multi-award-winning *My Orange Duffel Bag: A Journey to Radical Change* (Crown Archetype, June 2012). She and her husband Kevin reside in Marietta, Georgia.